Lines of Activity

Measurements of interior molding taken before the 1963 demolition of the Hull-House Settlement—in anticipation of its "restoration" as the Jane Addams Hull-House Museum.

Lines of Activity

Performance, Historiography,
Hull-House Domesticity

SHANNON JACKSON

Ann Arbor

THE UNIVERSITY OF MICHIGAN PRESS

2003   2002   2001   2000   4   3   2   1

*A CIP catalog record for this book is available
from the British Library.*

Frontispiece *Photo courtesy of University of Illinois at Chicago, the
University Library, Jane Addams Memorial Collection.*

Library of Congress Cataloging-in-Publication Data

Jackson, Shannon, 1967–
    Lines of activity : performance, historiography, Hull-House
domesticity / Shannon Jackson.
        p.   cm.
    Includes bibliographical references and index.
    ISBN 0-472-11112-4 (cloth : alk. paper)
    1. Hull House (Chicago, Ill.)—History.   2. Social settlements—
Illinois—Chicago—History.   3. Addams, Jane, 1860–1935.
I. Title.
HV4196.C4 J33   2000
362.84'009773'11—dc21   99-055252

Preface and Acknowledgments

For some time now, I have found myself trying to integrate performance and scholarship, a combination that took many forms depending upon changing definitions of both of those terms. Sometimes it meant bringing homework to cattle calls; later it meant taking fieldnotes in rehearsal; and later it meant seeing performance in places not conventionally defined as "theatrical." At its best, I found that performance functioned as a vehicle for understanding the big questions. Whether conceiving performance as practice, as paradigm, or as epistemological location, it was to me the most useful place from which to speculate upon the nature of identity, space, temporality, and social interaction. More recently, performance provided a point of entry for thinking about memory, history, absence, and presence. My animating belief is that the skills of the performer—her navigation of sight lines, props, and blocking—can be expanded to understand the intimate mediation of visuality, material culture, and embodiment. Practiced in the co-ordination of words, gestures, image, light, and space, it seems to me that the theatrical artist is particularly well-positioned to speculate on the interdisciplinary event of culture. Combining such proprioceptive intelligences in the day-to-day decisions of rehearsal, performance knowledge further requires attention to the operationality of culture, moving between acts of abstract speculation and the urgent and stubborn pragmatics of getting the production "on its feet."

That someone with such peculiar preoccupations found herself reading Jane Addams's *Twenty Years at Hull-House* is a geographic coincidence for which I am perpetually grateful. Being a student *in* Chicago meant becoming a student *of* Chicago. For the would-be performance scholar, it meant learning of the relation between highly theatrical episodes of social history and the construction of Chicago's civic identity. From the Haymarket Riot of 1886 to the Democratic convention of 1968, such events illustrated the distinctively gritty, grimy, pork-barrelling style in which this City of Big Shoulders performed itself. This civic sensibility also underpinned Chicago theatre where companies and playwrights claimed "Chicago" as an adjective for a theatre that was raw, spontaneous, authentic, wore a crew cut, and suffered no fools. At the same time, the highly gendered, cross-class nostalgia of such theatrical work—what some of my colleagues dubbed Chicago's "sweaty boy theatre"—braced against another of the city's performance genealogies. This one—recorded by Jane Addams—had a differently gendered and differently valenced type of cross-class nostalgia. Initiated by women, if not exclusively composed of them, its trajectory of social performance directed itself outward to the Chicago collective, advancing the city's and indeed the nation's concept of public welfare. Significantly, it created and maintained the festivals, playgrounds, neighborhoods, parks, community centers, museums, sidewalks, and streets in which Chicago could continually re-perform itself. *Lines of Activity* is an attempt to re-stage that second strain of Chicago dramaturgy.

This re-staging would not have been possible without the support of numerous individuals and organizations. The first round of thanks goes to the members of my exceedingly encouraging and patient dissertation committee at Northwestern University—Dwight Conquergood, Tracy Davis, Margaret Thompson Drewal, and Micaela di Leonardo. I will always appreciate this group for the different types of expertise each brought to this project and for their encouragement during the rewriting process. Other colleagues from Harvard and numerous professional sites commented on different parts of this manuscript, and I am grateful for their generous and luminous insights: Lawrence Buell, Marvin Carlson, Dorothy Chansky, Gay Gibson Cima, Natalie Crohn-Schmidt, Elin Diamond, Judith Hamera, Loren Kruger, Jeffrey Masten, Nancy McLean, Ann Pellegrini, Della Pollock, Rebecca Schneider, Marc Shell, Werner Sollors, Lynn Wardley, Stacy Wolf, and especially Joseph Roach. This group joins another list of people whose advice and teaching have strongly influenced this project and/or who affectionately and ironically maintained my professional and emotional equilibrium: Marilyn Arsem, Leo Damrosch, Jill Dolan, Nancy Fraser, Frank Galati, Henry Louis Gates, Jr., Jacquelyn Dowd Hall, Ewa and Martin Lajer-Burchardt, Françoise Lionnet, Gregory Nagy, Alex Owen, Peggy Phelan, Susan Pedersen, Alice Rayner, Janelle Reinelt, Sandra Richards, Bernie Sahlins, Jonah Segel, Alan Shefsky, Kathryn Kish Sklar, Doris Sommer, Edward Wingler, Nancy Yousef—and most especially Marjorie Garber, Barbara Johnson, and Bill Handley.

I want to thank a coterie of Hull-House interlocutors with whom I have cherished those "do-you-know?" and "have-you-seen?" conversations that annoy all but the most devoted Hull-House aficionados: Mary Ann Bamberger, Mary Ann Johnson, Barbara Polikoff, Dorothy Mittelman Sigel, and particuarly Lucy Knight. This project would have been logistically impossible without Pat Bakunas of UIC's Special Collections and without the contributions of my amazing research assistants: Sara Kimberlin patiently sorted through letters and numbers while sharing her own stories of social work. As an emerging comedian and performance scholar in American Studies, Camille Forbes discussed this project's method and managed its mechanics with energy and, quite literally, good humor. Cristin Hodgens critiqued my writing and researched the appendix with incredible diligence (showing that there was a reason why none of my friends believed that she was an undergraduate). Sara Guyer and Domietta Torlasco entered at the end to fulfill the seemingly impossible task of making an index. I also want to thank LeAnn Fields, Alja Kooistra, and the editorial staff of the University of Michigan Press. Portions of chapter 5 and chapter 6 first appeared respectively in "Civic Play-Housekeeping: Gender, Theatre, and American Reform," *Theatre Journal* 48 (October 1996): 337–61, and "Performance at Hull-House: Museum, Microfiche, Historiography," *Exceptional Spaces,* ed. Della Pollock (Chapel Hill: U of North Carolina P, 1998), 261–93.

For necessary financial and research support, I am extremely indebted to the Spencer Foundation, to the Committee to Advance the Status of Women at Harvard, to the Mary Ingram Bunting Institute, to the Radcliffe Junior Partnership program, and to Harvard University's program for junior faculty research support. My "sister-fellows" and the wonderful staff of the Bunting Institute influenced the re-writing of this book more than they realize. I particularly relished my conversations with the Work and Family group and with Ellen Herman, Deborah Levenson, Evelyn Lincoln, Carol Ockman, and Esther Parada. Sitting at the table of the Schlesinger's study group in American women's history—organized by the wonderful Mary Maples Dunn—was appropriately anxiety-producing for an untrained historian and always thrilling. The final phases of manuscript preparation coincided with the first phases of a new job. I am grateful to all of my new Berkeley colleagues and particularly to those most responsible for seeing me through the transition: Janet Adelman, Judith Butler, Mark Griffith, and William Worthen. To the diehards (and members of the Chorus), Joyce Dorado, Gina Schmeling, Adrian Chan, Matt Calvert, Richard Jones, Jennifer Holmes, Jessica Thebus, and Miryam Sas, I thank you for not caring too much about this book—except insofar as its completion made me a less stressed friend.

Finally, here's to my fabulous family for their unending love and patience and to the ever-present memories of Giacomo Oliveri, Pearl Boyden Jackson, and my father, Robert Jackson. John Korcuska and Olga Zouncourides Korcuska have been incredibly tolerant of their curious daughter-in-law. And my mother Jacqueline Jackson has been an integral support during many changes of mind, heart, and geography. Michael Korcuska's "healing domesticity" has been constant, effusive, and essential. Finally, it is my privilege to dedicate this book to my much-loved and much-revered grandmother, Patricia Bailey Oliveri.

Shannon Jackson
Berkeley, CA

Contents

Chapter 1

Theorizing: "The Scaffolding"

The tasks which face the human apparatus of perception at the turning points of history cannot be solved by optical means, that is by contemplation, alone. They are mastered gradually by habit, under the guidance of tactile appropriation.
— Walter Benjamin, *Illuminations*

Occasionally I obscurely felt as if a demand were being made upon us for a ritual which should express and carry forward the hope of the social movement.
— Jane Addams, *Twenty Years at Hull-House*

Daily I sit before a microfiche machine perched on cement-colored formica in a fluorescent-lit room, looking at reels of copied archives in the Special Collections room at the University of Illinois Library. While microfiched urban reports, blueprints, essays, letters, and diaries flit and flash across my screen, my left hand grips a knob that takes the reels backward and forward. My right hand has been pressing upon a number 2 pencil for hours, making the callus on my middle finger sting more than usual. My left index finger is ready to push the COPY button when called upon. The only break from the glare of the screen is the wall of corkboard behind it, which, before long, appears to expand, move forward, and close in on me. I shift in my chair; my body feels slightly stiff. I sink lower in it, extending my legs under the formica. The reel flaps along. My back hurts. I shift forward, back straight. I bend my left leg. I then raise my left knee and place my foot on the chair. My ankle tenses from supporting my knee; I raise the other one. I try to stay balanced. The reel flaps along. Slowly, I extend my right leg and place it onto the top of the formica desk, then the left leg, turning my body slightly sidewise. This feels comfortable. I cross my ankles. Eventually, my legs go numb; I swing them back down again, face forward, back straight.

Sitting, writes Elaine Scarry, is controlled discomfort.

Thinking, I write, involves an awful lot of sitting.

Jane Addams, cofounder of the Hull-House settlement, at her desk.
Addams reportedly wrote with both a pen and scissors, re-ordering
sentences and paragraphs on strips of paper into well-wrought essays.
*(Photo courtesy of University of Illinois at Chicago, the University Library,
Jane Addams Memorial Collection.)*

    The screen of the microfiche machine projects the documents
that I am using to write a book on the women and men who took up
residence at the Hull-House Settlement of Chicago in the late nineteenth century. Calendars, account books, and bulletins appear on
the illuminated surface of a tool that became ubiquitous in what
used to be the age of mechanical reproduction. Sometimes I squint
at a single image for a long time; sometimes I become impatient and
let the reel go, turning the knob forward farther and farther to see
how fast the history will fly. When I get to diaries, notes, and
handwritten letters, I usually stop. Even when I cannot make out the
penmanship, I often linger before foraging ahead to something more
legible. The curls of cursive lettering—even when it crosses out
something typed—can be somewhat therapeutic, as if confirming
that a body was once there: "Mrs. Kelley is toiling away on her
sweaters report," Hull-House cofounder Ellen Gates Starr is writing
a letter to her sister in a somewhat decipherable hand, expressing an
awed regard for new settlement resident and Marxist labor investigator, Florence Kelley.

She has got all her material, fortunately, & doesn't have to tramp about in the heat. She couldn't do it anyway. Her feet have got fearfully sore and swollen, notwithstanding her wearing very large shoes. She sits by the half hour with her feet in the washbowl.[1]

I cannot make out the next sentence. Is that two _r_s or one _m_? Is that how Starr makes her _a_s? I move on.

Contemplating her swollen feet in the washbowl she said reflectively, "I wonder if those are ever coming back to their natural size or if they're going to remain, like everything else in Chicago, the largest of their kind."[2]

My toes tingle. I dare myself to move my left foot. It moves. Then my right. It moves.

Walter Benjamin had words for episodes like this, moments when the historian finds her view to the past interrupted by the sensuous self-recognition of the present. "The true picture of the past flits by. The past can be seized only as an image which flashes up at the instant when it can be recognized and is never seen again," wrote Benjamin, implicitly and surprisingly linking the skills of the historical materialist to those of the surrealist. For him, the liberatory possibilities of historical writing emerged in the capacity to register flashes of resemblance and palpable similarity across temporalities.

For every image of the past that is not recognized by the present as one of its own concerns threatens to disappear irretrievably. . . . To articulate the past historically does not mean to recognize it "the way it really was" (Ranke). It means to seize hold of a memory as it flashes up at a moment of danger. . . . Only that historian will have the gift of fanning the spark of hope in the past who is firmly convinced that _even the dead_ will not be safe from the enemy if he wins.[3]

Callused fingers, numb limbs, and swollen feet are all quite literal reminders of the bodily basis of research. To place them within the same memorial space is not only to evoke Benjamin's strange tactile ironies, however, but also to suggest something of what it means to join performance and the past. For me, the sentient recall of Benjamin's "dialectical image" seems a prerequisite to writing a history of performance; at the same time, its shock to the historical continuum helps me to understand the performance of history. Working amid preserved Hull-House documents, lingering stiffly over peculiar penmanship, such flashes of transhistorical resemblance would at first seem to challenge the Progressive Era sensibility about which I am writing. Such moments admit doubt into the belief that the next era truly has the capacity to transcend a previous one. As a series of dialectical images unfold throughout this book, I nevertheless hope to show a Progressive institution that struggled with similar kinds of doubt and found heuristic potential in its ironies. As such imagery moves from the archive to less benign historical resemblances, I also hope to dramatize the social stakes of not attending to the safety of the dead.

The Hull-House Settlement of Chicago was a symptom, reaction, haven, and self-styled antidote to what many have called one of the most volatile periods in American history. Upon close scrutiny, of course, any period seems volatile, even and perhaps especially those strips of time renowned for the tranquillity, stability, and self-certainty nostalgia grants them. During what is now called the Progressive Era, however—the period beginning at the end of the nineteenth century and continuing through World War I—the suffrage movement, immigration, industrialization, and urbanization continually disrupted anyone's attempt to assure themselves that American society was not changing. Enduring what Jane Addams would call "that between-age mood," the United States was in transition, occupying a liminal zone that struggled to understand itself. Gramsci's statement from the *Prison Notebooks* seems applicable. "The old is dying and the new cannot be born; in this interregnum there arises a great diversity of morbid symptoms."[4] It was within this complex nexus of forces and in what they thought were the most "morbid" locations that settlement workers set up house. Hull-House was one of many self-labeled "settlements" begun in cities, and later rural areas, throughout the nation. In 1889, when Jane Addams and Ellen Gates Starr moved into an immigrant, working-class neighborhood in the Nineteenth Ward of Chicago's West Side, they only vaguely knew of a similar experiment in New York's Lower East Side. Later, they would meet fellow settlers such as Vida Scudder at the Rivington Street Settlement, Stanton Coit of New York's Neighborhood Guild, and Robert Woods of Andover House in Boston. In 1891 there were six settlements in the United States; by 1900, over one hundred, and, by 1910, more than four hundred settlements were located in the nation's "slums" (a word most would come to despise) and outlying rural areas, seeking to ameliorate the social dysfunction of American modernization. For many of these reformers—and for the liberal bourgeoisie who visited—the settlement was an education in morbidity, whether it was an exposure to the disease and garbage of city wards or acquaintance with the neglect, greed, and indifference of the businessmen and government officials who allowed such conditions to persist. Sometimes it occurred by way of introduction to the dehumanization of the factory system, a confrontation that mixed both moral outrage and guilt as settlement workers faced the unequal industrial mechanisms by which their family livelihoods were being maintained. Other times, following a late-nineteenth-century wave of southern European immigrants, "morbidity" manifested itself in encounters with immigrant cultural difference. This dense and unfamiliar diversity of language and behavior, magnified and distorted by deleterious urban and industrial conditions, resulted in differences of hygiene, family practices, and work patterns that fueled the nationalist anxieties of hereditary Americans concerned with the racial purity of the United States.

Some residents stayed at Hull-House for their entire lives; some stayed for two years until marriage or another opportunity came along. By 1907, thirteen buildings surrounded the original Hull mansion in the urban district where Jane Addams "came to live." Eventually, Hull-House became the most famous settlement, and, in a mutually constitutive relationship, Jane Addams became one of the most famous women in the United States. She was awarded the Nobel Peace Prize somewhat belatedly in 1931 and died four years later. During her tenure, she and the other residents who gathered around this institution exercised power and worked for reform in almost every venue and for every cause imaginable—education, labor reform, juvenile protection, immigration protection, welfare, suffrage, housing, and more. Historians have located Hull-House as a vital force in—and sometimes original site of—the programs that have since come under the umbrella term of *social welfare*. As such, Hull-House and its affiliates played a key role in redefining, in the midst of a turn-of-the-century tumult, the definition of the state and its relationship to an ever-changing American polity.[5]

Hull-House's legislative and governmental accomplishments are well known to scholars in American history. In this book, I seek to track an adjacent history. By following the set of affective, aesthetic, rhetorical, and ethical preoccupations that propelled such large-scale transformation, I want particularly to understand the messy and paradoxical nature of reform work. This means conducting a sociological investigation of the cofounders of sociology and a pragmatic historiography of one of the most important sites for the articulation of Chicago pragmatism at the turn of the century.[6]

Such an understanding gives richer insight into a kind of participatory fieldwork practiced, if not always recognized as such, by settlement workers. While the daily life of Hull-House is intimately bound up with activities in larger public spheres, social encounters and artistic practices are usually relegated to the periphery of critical inquiry. In other words, the stuff that I am interested in considering is often referred to *in passim* to color and spice retroactively constructed narratives of legislative successes and failures. Knowledge of how the Hull-House story "ended"—where that ending is defined by the subdisciplinary interest (immigration, labor, child welfare) of the analyst—usually predetermines what she or he selects in order to construct the satisfying story. I would not propose that there is a way out of that conundrum, since I possess implicit and explicit principles of selection myself. Without denying the privilege of hindsight and the contingencies of my partial perspective, however, I hope to retain methodologically something that most settlement workers began with ideologically: a commitment to locality. Locality represented an approach that was more highly principled or more urgently felt to some than to others; it also derived from an array of experiences and intellectual predispositions that differed with gender, region, religion, age, education, occupation, and political persuasion. For bourgeois female settlers in particular, such a proximate epistemology drew from a discourse of domesticity, a nineteenth-century formation that positioned women as sympathetic interpreters of the microperformances of everyday life. How such an orientation could be posited as an origin for the host of centralized, federally administered programs called the welfare state is a mammoth and infinitely complicated question—a "colossus" in the words of Kathryn Kish Sklar, one of the most eminent analysts of the process.[7] Taking the lead from Hannah Arendt's critique of "the social" as a force of state conformism and normalization, contemporary critics might condemn the settlement impulse based on this ultimately unpalatable result.[8] It has become clear to me, however, that the formation of the social cannot be exclusively interpreted as an intended project, gleaned from so many readings of so many writings by people who thought up what they enacted (and presumably anticipated all conditions and consequences). Settlers did have intentions, however, and their own ever-altering understandings of what they were doing. And it is the ambivalences of this local epistemological realm—blind by some standards, deeply nuanced by others—that I want to consider. It is one that could be reflexively spontaneous and reflexively rigid, improvisatory and limited, perceptive and shortsighted. As Clifford Geertz says, local knowledge's "feel for immediacies divides as much as it connects."9 As an emotion, principle, and method of social change, locality had the capacity for both naïveté and genius. In light of larger structural forces, its unwitting blindness could be considered a key factor in system reproduction. At the same time, its bottom-up angle of vision could see heterogeneity, agency, and dynamism where structuralist ways of knowing tended to categorize, flatten, and fix. I will argue that this doubleness has feminist implications for social theorists, particularly for how we reconcile the paradoxical gendering of *both* proximate knowledges *and* large-scale state apparatuses.

The settlement movement, and Hull-House in particular, represents a particular brand of experience whose complexity, risk, and sheer gall seem important to understand as the United States begins a new century, facing another version of "that between-age mood." Hull-House is in part a story of bourgeois women and men working to share their privileges and, with varying degrees of commitment, working to undo the very system that guaranteed them those privileges. This kind of project was made up monthly, daily, hourly of encounters between individuals who did not understand each other. The enthusiasm of the settlement workers could not in itself change the habits inscribed into their bodies and minds. At times, the fulfillment of the social agenda may have been at odds with the "personal fulfillment" a reformer hoped to extract from her participation. And so, perhaps she retreated; perhaps she sacrificed the social agenda. Other times, perhaps, she changed herself. Many privileged settlement workers understood that changing the situation of the marginalized required a reciprocal change in the lives of the dominant. Much of the settlement's efficacy lay in the ability of individual agents to internalize and reinternalize that lesson. As such, it is also the place where many find its limitations. From several points of view— whether that of the vulgar Marxist or the vulgar Foucauldian—the story ended where it began. Whether one's cynicism is that of the academic or activist, this task taken up by this kind of group was doomed from the beginning. From many contemporary analytic perspectives, the viability of their mission was overdetermined by their class status and/or by an evolutionary belief in concepts such as "better" and "progress." Their hopes were misplaced by an idealized notion of human nature and/or by their ignorance of how technologies, bureaucracies, and global economies would reconfigure and diffuse their implicit concepts of democratic governance. And so the arguments categorize, flatten, and fix them—this group of well-to-do, turn-of-the-century reformers who tried to change and to make change. Patronizingly celebrating a limited agency for those marginalized in history, these arguments cannot conceptualize whether and how privileged persons transformed in light of settlement knowledge. Indeed, our undernuanced contemporary discourse on privilege contains much more defensiveness than it does analysis. Framed through a series of self-deflecting moves and abstract confessionals, privilege functions most often as something to be condemned in others and disavowed in oneself. Besides the obvious disingenuousness, I have found such lines of thought to be epistemologically confining for this project. The most thorny philosophical paradox of privilege, it seems to me, is the way that it shields a person from contingency, allowing the subject to marshal the resources of racial, gender, or class superiority under the unregistered guise of normalcy and naturalness. Privilege is a performance whose efficacy relies on the feeling that nothing dramatic is happening. My decision to devote a book to the partial perspectives of Hull-House workers comes from a desire to understand this conundrum and to explore their ongoing, self-displacing attempts to reckon with it.

Reformance

To bring issues of performance into a study of the Hull-House Settlement of Chicago is to provide a framework for analyzing the fundamentals of reform. Hull-House was one incarnation of a larger settlement movement—itself one method of social change during the cultural and industrial tumult of the turn-of-the-century United States.[10] As a mode of inquiry that takes issues of identity, enactment, embodiment, and social process as central points of entry, performance raises ontological questions about the nature of social change—of what it means to re-form individuals, communities, or urban spaces. Sharing an etymological root that means "to bring into being" or "to furnish," *performance* underscores the material acts of construction implicit in the term *reform,* elements that are often obscured when the Reform Period is wholly equated with a series of legislative and policy changes. As I demonstrate below, this obfuscation is especially ironic in light of the profoundly contextual everyday pedagogies of a place such as Hull-House. Intervening in abstracted narratives of the settlement's "results," performance complicates mystified assumptions about how these reform endeavors worked in daily life. Performance analysis incorporates critical theories of social interaction, of the relationship between space and subjectivity, of human behavior as signifying practice, and of the

material and embodied basis of identity formation. While such issues emerge in many histories of the socioscientific imagination of
the Progressive Era where, for instance, scholars analyze "symbolic
interactionism" or "Progressive Environmentalism," I consider such
questions central both theoretically and methodologically to modeling a microhistory of Hull-House.[11] That is, reformers' fundamental
interest in the constructed nature of human realities also drives my
analysis of the social processes they constructed, of the human realities they re-formed. From another direction, to bring the Hull-
House Settlement of Chicago into the multifaceted arena of performance and cultural studies is to offer a complicated case study in
social change—one that self-consciously contested the nature of
society, identity, culture, and art and innovated methodologically in
arenas of space, performance, public welfare, and practical politics.
As such, Hull-House offers an historically and regionally situated
arena in which to test contemporary cultural and performance

Chicago children carrying small Christmas trees in an abandoned lot.
*(Photo courtesy of University of Illinois at Chicago, the University Library,
Jane Addams Memorial Collection.)*

theory even as it situates some of the ahistorical assumptions of such theoretical frameworks.

Both the term *Hull-House* and the term *performance* conjure an array of heterogeneous—sometimes competing—associations. As convenient terms of reference in historical and theoretical scholarship, each has acquired a network of connotations, partly dependent upon disciplinary and subdisciplinary predispositions. Given such debates on Hull-House and performance—where the exchange of keywords often stands in for engaged conversation—the juxtaposition of the two phenomena offers an opportunity to sort through the paradoxes of each. Consider Jane Addams on the relationship between aesthetics and reform.

Participating in a kinetic brand of "reformance," neighborhood children would assemble for dance, rhythm, and other movement classes under the trees of the Hull-House courtyard. *(Photo courtesy of University of Illinois at Chicago, the University Library, Jane Addams Memorial Collection.)*

There was in the earliest undertakings at Hull-House a touch of the artist's enthusiasm when he translates his inner vision through his chosen material into outward form. Keenly conscious of the social confusion all about us and the hard economic struggle, we at times believed that the very struggle itself might become a source of strength.[12]

In linking settlement work with that of "the artist," Addams mingles and enhances the connotations of both. She underscores the creative undercurrent of settling, while suggesting that "creation" is not a decorative or expendable endeavor but a fundamental act of social life. Settlement workers' enthusiasm for their work was partly derived from the shared feeling that they were making something new, bringing into being something that had not been there before. Such acts of creation suggest a poetics of reform, where a settlement "artist" gathered sustenance in the act of making and took pleasure in the form of the thing made. The nature of such acts and such forms seems continually to shift, however. In this first sentence, Addams refers to a reflective creative gesture; a smooth and transparent arc tracks the move from the artist's "inner vision" to "outward form." Anticipating the art of "high modernist" social planning, such an analogy repeats several historical interpretations of Progressive reform, positing it as the "search for order" amid arenas of "social control" and "immigrant assimilation."[13] Within these arguments, capitalists, elitist reformers, and state bureaucrats worked to subordinate the reluctant matter of urban cities—industry, immigrants, poverty, dirt, built environment—into an outward expression of their inner vision, whether that vision was of the ordered industrial society, the ideal city, or the proper American. Although Jane Addams invoked such a model of settlement practice, her next sentence seems to trouble such self-certainty. "Social confusion" and "hard economic struggle" intervene in attempts to re-form their neighborhood. Interestingly, Jane Addams does not perpetuate a neat opposition between such disorder and an ordered inner vision; instead, she shifts the terms of settlement practice onto a different register—that of process. "We at times believed that the very struggle itself might become a source of strength." The emphasis now is not on the product made by the settlement artist as much as on the activity of making, where the significance of that activity cannot be measured in terms of what it completes. Deferring result and finalization, the rest of the passage offers exemplary enactments of this creative struggle on the part of her neighbors, recalling "the devotion of mothers to their children" and "the dread of men lest they fail to provide" for their families. In so doing, Addams removes the struggle from the internal processes of the settlement artist to those of the neighborhood. Seeing the nobility of creation where other Progressive reformers saw disorder, she concluded by arguing that the work of re-form was already happening within the reforming environment. The tensions that I see in these quoted sentences will be repeated in many accounts of the settlement. To the degree that Hull-House practitioners subscribed to a model of reform as result-oriented and derived from the ideals of their own inner visions, they exemplified the authoritarian dispositions many attach to Progressive Era reform. To the extent that such familiar assertions were often followed with qualifications, with reorientations toward process, and with attempts to listen to the experiences and practices of urban inhabitants, settlement workers offered more subtle models of who was doing this work, of what they were re-forming, and of the unfinalized nature of this making.

Jane Addams and her colleagues' routine invocation of the artistic process in application to reform testifies to their sense of the constructed nature of the social world, one that makes the match between Hull-House and contemporary literary, cultural, and performance theory an apt one. Predating such social theory, Hull-House reformers necessarily worked with a model of the world as invented, mediated, and constituted rather than pregiven and preordained. Located only a few miles from the university that figures prominently in the origin narratives of sociology, this fundamental view spawned a range of inquiries into such acts of invention. Later, this sensibility would underwrite the work of a multidisciplinary array of theorists who use dramaturgical models to interpret social constitution. From rhetoricians and speech act theorists such as Kenneth Burke and J. L. Austin, to anthropologists and sociologists such as Victor Turner and Erving Goffman, twentieth-century theorists developed performance paradigms to theorize society, culture, and identity as the products of human enactment.[14] However, like differing views of settlement artistry, performance theories were and are by no means consistent. Take, for instance, one particularly resonant strand of debate—the nature of repetition. With Kierkegaardian enthusiasm, performance theorists argue that the practical and analytic power of performance lies in its structures of repetition— whether in the actor's rehearsal, in the repeatability of Turner's "ritual process," or in the productivity of Richard Schechner's "(re)storation of behavior."[15] As such, their paradigms coalesce with the environmental premise of the settlement movement; human realities are not only invented but also continually reinvented, that is, re-formed. Alighting upon the ambivalence of Addams's description of the artist's enthusiasm, however, a more recent group of theorists suggests that some of these social models presumed a kind of stability between repetitions—between inner vision and outward form, between "original" and copy. Critics argue that concepts of repetition without difference inadvertently reinscribe static notions of culture by positing a uniformity across enactments. They thus repress the losses, improvisations, and unpredictably new inventions that accumulate and disappear with each repetition. Whether extending process-oriented social theory, Derridean citationality, Bakhtinian unfinalizability, or theories of postmodern performance art, recent critics invoke performance and performativity precisely to trouble notions of stability, to evoke that which cannot be fully repeated, to theorize the agency of different kinds of repeating, and to mark citational conventions that exceed the stabilizing will of individual performers.[16] The tension among these orientations (each of which is itself internally disputed) unsettles the consistency in presumed "patterns of culture." As a performance theorist and historian of Hull-House reform, my task will be to keep various orientations in productive conversation: (1) understanding how the repetitious, multisensual, and embodied nature of performance makes it an effective means of social legitimation and, hence, system reproduction, while also (2) suggesting that precisely this temporality and materiality make such "reproductions" vulnerable, that is, subject to a different kind of repeating. Something that often distinguished Hull-House workers from those of other reform institutions was, I would suggest, a competence in navigating a doubleness of a similar kind. While Jane Addams could speak of the need to translate an inner vision into outward form, she could also, in the very next breath, express an ethic of vigilant instability: "The one thing to be dreaded in the Settlement is that it lose its flexibility, its power of quick adaptation, its readiness to change its methods as its environment may demand."[17]

Of course, despite the attempt to distance themselves from the righteousness of religion or the noblesse oblige of charity, settlement reform still meant changing the persons that one encountered. As a journalist would later write, "the ladies fully believe with Tolstoy that 'Enlightenment is not propagated by pictures,' not 'chiefly' by the spoken word, or the medium of print, but by the infectious example of the whole life of men."[18] Settling's principle of "infectious example" was different from other movements more forthright about the goals of social control, but its mimetic logic initially assumed that imitation ideally occurred in one direction more than another. Whether using the language of "education," "reform," "control," or "conversion," all of the words that historians attach to the settlement foreground the fact of, and interest in, human changeability. And depending upon politics and theoretical orientation, one might support or dismiss such change as necessarily (given its social mission) "good" or as inherently (given its presumptive stance) "bad." What both sides of that weightless coin repress is a capacity to formulate a considered, complicated, and pragmatic ethics, for many settlers were expressly interested in finding a register of practice outside or between self-righteous intervention and self-righteous skepticism. Indeed, all instances of social interaction testify to the capacity of human beings reciprocally to transform each other. It is simultaneously true that power inequities place limits on the nature and potential of each person's capaciousness. Rather than assuming the possibility of a pure stance, it is perhaps more helpful to acknowledge the reformist impulse propelling all sociality—not in order to find a mythically pure realm of nonintervention—but in order to change and be changed with more honesty and caution.

The significance of Hull-House mimesis was by no means lost on its settlers, and many spent a great deal of time trying to evoke its ethics, its politics, and its pragmatic register of experience. Several theorists—from the most well known residents to the less famous club leaders—came to value the improvised and encumbered position of the Hull-House practitioner. Implicit in the settlement's attempt to overcome the geographic boundaries separating cultures and classes was an attendant belief in the vicarious power of contact and face-to-face conversation—a reminder of the *social* character of what came to be called social work. Through local interactions and daily conversations, participants would generate more equitable and relational methods of negotiating American diversity. The ideas of philosopher-reformers such as George Herbert Mead and John Dewey at the University of Chicago contributed to this shared project, working in the philosophical field of pragmatism to theorize sociality in light of the felt conundrums of social interaction. While Hull-House's relationship with Chicago School sociologists was significant if occasionally contentious, the philosophical school of pragmatism more intimately reinforced and was reinforced by the spirit of settlement epistemology. I will suggest that Hull-House affiliates' own performance-centered models of the self, of pragmatic interaction, and of democratic pedagogy trouble a purely presentist notion of performance theory and its self-framing as a late-twentieth-century theoretical formation.

With thinkers such as Mead and Dewey constantly visiting the settlement—whether to teach a college extension class or to share in

an evening meal, Chicago pragmatism and Hull-House domesticity
continually fed off of each other. Trying to develop a philosophy that
resisted Cartesian dualisms and its cognitive notions of subjectivity,
resisting at the same time the deterministic implications of Marxism
and Darwinism, Dewey, Mead, and others struggled to understand
aspects of the social environment and human behavior that exceeded
the terms of their inherited philosophical schools. The premise of
pragmatism was that theories of the world were to be derived from
action in the world; thought was to follow from practice rather than
exclusively in reverse.[19] For liberal-minded pragmatists, this also
meant that the ideal intellectual was not to remain sequestered in an
ivory tower but to submit and commit himself to the world of action.
In the course of their mutually supportive exchange, for instance,
Mead developed the ideal method of social reform, paradoxically
stating that it should not resemble Idealism per se. Mead espoused
instead the more mobile conception in the form of a "working hypothesis."[20] Replacing finalizing terminology with this present parti-
ciple, reform might begin with ideas or goals, but they should stay
flexible, "provisional rather than absolute or dogmatic."[21] Echoing
Jane Addams's rhetoric, pragmatic reform required revision and adaptation to meet a variety of circumstances and unanticipated developments. As Charlene Haddock Seigfried has argued, pragmatism's critique of epistemology strongly resonates with feminism's ethical
critique, though this philosophical connection is often omitted from
pragmatism's account of itself.[22] A contemporary feminist preoccupation with "situated knowledges," "contingent foundations," "asymmetrical reciprocities," and the "politics of location" will provide a
useful point of entry into the pragmatics of settling.[23] Lora Romero's
feminist work on the generative arena of domesticity in the nineteenth century also points the way to a historical connection.[24] By
contextualizing pragmatism's co-imbrication with the discourse of
domesticity and the workings of Hull-House, I seek further to unpack
the feminist underpinnings of an exceedingly contextual array of
philosophical paradigms.

Like Mead, Dewey began revising his thinking within the first
year of introduction to Hull-House. Writing to his wife in 1894, he
maintained that the settlement was not really "a thing, but a way of
living—hence it has the same aims as life itself." Participating in a
place where work in the social world was both goal and method,
Dewey began to question the Hegelian tradition that undergirded
his ideas. Dewey and Mead found that their earlier quests for har-
monic synthesis had been unable to understand the "discomforts" of
social action. "I can see that I have always been interpreting the

dialectic wrong end up—the unity as the reconciliation of opposites, instead of the opposites as the unity in its growth, and thus
translated physical tension into a moral thing."[25] A pragmatic
sociality—its constructed notion of a processual self, its recognition
of the contingency of experience, its attention to the diversity of
selves and experiences in a changing American democracy—would
also become the basis for Dewey's pedagogical theory. Indeed, to
consider Dewey's role as one of the most active and widely read
philosophers during the Progressive Era is to reconceptualize the role
of pedagogy and of pedagogical questions in the analysis of social
life.[26] At the University of Chicago, Dewey chaired a Department of
Pedagogy, Psychology, and Philosophy, a sign of how intimately the
fundamental preoccupations of the latter two fields aligned with his
educational concerns. Based partly on his intellectual heritage and
partly on his interactions with Hull-House, John Dewey combined
a developing psychological theory with new methodological approaches to learning. He would argue that education must be "a
continual reconstruction of experience," in which transformation
and growth drew from and added to an individual's store of adapt-
able experiences. Transformative repetition—the adapted restoration of past events into the present—was a central tenet of active
learning, where each repetition adjusted to fit new circumstances
while new circumstances added to a set of repeatable experiences. A
curriculum was most productive and knowledge retained more easily
when it replicated practical activity in the world. Arguing that
knowledge did not always manifest itself as an articulated set of
abstract principles, that individuals learned tacitly through "doing,"
new knowledge became an integrated aspect of identity formation
when it took pragmatic form. Concepts such as the working hypothesis, the continual reconstruction of experience, and learning by
doing constitute the indigenous performance discourse of Hull-
House. Anticipating contemporary performance theory's attention
to repetition, citationality, and the restoration of behavior, such
theorizing took place in a larger historical domain acutely preoccupied with the stuff of performance, one whose innovations and
ambivalences can provide alternate ways of incorporating the theoretical and the historical.

To bring performance into both the history of the settlement
movement and the field of cultural studies is also to bring us back
full circle to the nature and role of art. Riding a general shift in the
associations attached to the term *culture*—from a mark of "high"
cultivation to its prevalent range of anthropological connotations—
cultural theorists have spent a great deal of time arguing for consid-

ered political and economic analysis of the social production of
aesthetics.[27] Historians of Progressive reform have not needed cultural theory to critique artistic practices. Reformers' interest in
sharing something they called art with less privileged members of
society is interpreted at best as a temporary phase before a more
enlightened stage of social action and at worst as a signal of a
reformer's cultural elitism. While a valuable critique, this orientation also can be epistemologically confining. It ignores, for instance,
how aesthetic forms and performances can create alternative spheres
of identification that encourage interactions that other deliberative
spheres constrain or censor.[28] Indeed, their status as fictive, as temporarily suspended from other modes of social reality—precisely
the thing that prompts many to call them expendable—lends the
frame for such intensely critical, personal, and collective engagement. Through the functional liminality of spoken, visual, sonic,
tactile, and embodied media, such forms indulge vicarious and
untested expression.[29] An undernuanced assessment of aesthetics
also risks ahistoricism. Jane Addams and John Dewey would use the
term respectively to convey the poetics of "sociability" or the fullness of experience, not only the measure of cultivated tastse.[30] It is
also in danger of ignoring particular aesthetic movements that,
however ambivalently, have taken the relationship between art and
economic space, between creativity and class, between art and everyday life, as their point of departure.[31]

Consequently, a wider interpretation of aesthetics and performance might challenge the interpretation that many have given to
nineteenth- and turn-of-the-century reform associations—the move
from less significant cultural activities to more important work at
the level of policy and legislation. Most significantly, to ask questions about the role of "artistic practices" in the everyday life of
Hull-House is often to illuminate the settlement's production of
locality. Cultural and social formations such as festivals, exhibits,
theater, music, reading groups, dances, coffeehouses, social clubs,
sports, and recreation classes were the central methods by which
Hull-House reformers worked to create neighborhood locality, an
endeavor that was fundamental rather than peripheral to their model
of social change. To the extent that past historical interpretations of
the move from culture to civic advocacy have reinforced an epistemological break between disciplines in the humanities and in the social
sciences—allowing the latter to construct the former as unimpor-
tant, allowing the former to construct the latter as deterministic—
this approach to Hull-House is also an attempt to bring the methods
and perspectives of each of these orientations into conversation with

each other. It is thus an attempt to create, however improbably, a cultural history of social work.

Space and "Experience"

When Dorothea Moore, a young Hull-House resident, wrote an essay for the *American Journal of Sociology* entitled "A Day at Hull-House," she began with a spatial description rather than a chronology of a day's schedule.

> The Old House is almost submerged. With its hooded top story of fanciful brick, and its large flanking of additions to right and left, there remain but the long windows and wide doorway to hint of the aspect that was its own in the long-gone privacy of the estate. . . . These additions are more intrinsic than external—

The former mansion of Charles Hull set back from Halsted Street, just as the Hull-House settlement began to build its "large flankings of additions to right and left." *(Photo courtesy of University of Illinois at Chicago, the University Library, Jane Addams Memorial Collection.)*

growing out of growing needs—and therefore present in them-selves a kind of rough estimate or history of them.[32]

Moore personified Hull-House throughout her text, investing it with an ability to sense ever-widening needs as well as a capacity to expand physically and figuratively to meet them. Its "long windows" and "wide doorway" suggested the grandeur of a former identity, that of mansion to real estate businessman Charles Hull, before tenements and immigrants became its neighbors. The alternative domestic space now reworked boundaries between inside and outside, instantiating the recursive and competing pulls of various lines of activity. The new intrinsic identity of this public household released claims to "privacy" and welcomed architectural incarnations of new needs—the Children's Building to the right, the Butler Building to the left, the extra floor of resident apartments above it. After 1897, more architectural extensions would follow, a spatial genealogy of submergence and expansion roughly matched in the chapter organization of this book.[33] Moore's statement that such "additions" can provide a "history" reso-nates with one made by Henri Lefebvre: "The historical and diachronic realms and the generative past are forever leaving their inscriptions upon the writing-tablet, so to speak, of space: society in its actuality also deposits its script, the result and product of social activities. Time has more than one writing system."[34] Moore and Lefebvre suggest that an understanding of a place entails an under-standing of its spaces and that a history of those spatial formations is also a history of the practices they entailed—in Moore's view of Hull-House, the needs they fulfilled.

Henri Lefebvre's *The Production of Space* goes on to articulate a theory of daily life that almost gleefully thwarts a researcher's efforts at interpretation. As such, it also anticipates the difficulty of track-ing the tacit rhythms of an incarnate domesticity.

> Architecture produces living bodies, each with its own distinctive traits. The animating principle of such a body, its presence, is neither visible nor legible as such, nor is it the object of any discourse, for it reproduces itself within those who use the space in question, within their lived experience. Of that experience the tourist, the passive spectator, can grasp but a pale shadow.[35]

If this imaginary spectator-researcher can expect to glean so very little, what can the historian of social space attempt to grasp? Locked in a world of microfiche and dusty files, assailed by the smell of ink toxin and number 2 pencils, sensitivity to spatial and bodily experience

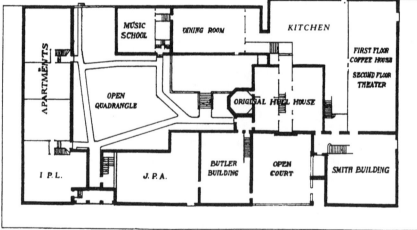

SCALE OF FEET

ALLEY

ALLEY

GILPIN PLACE

POLK STREET

NURSERY PLAYGROUND

MARY CRANE BUILDING

BOYS CLUB

BOWEN HALL

GYMNASIUM BUILDING

JANE CLUB

APARTMENTS

MUSIC SCHOOL

DINING ROOM

KITCHEN

FIRST FLOOR COFFEE HOUSE

SECOND FLOOR THEATER

OPEN QUADRANGLE

ORIGINAL HULL HOUSE

I P. L.

J. P. A.

BUTLER BUILDING

OPEN COURT

SMITH BUILDING

HALSTED STREET

A map of the Hull-House settlement complex at its largest in 1963, though most infrastructural expansion was put in place in the early-twentieth century. *(Photo courtesy of University of Illinois at Chicago, the University Library, Jane Addams Memorial Collection.)*

certainly reminds her of her own corporeality—her endurance capacity, her steadily blurring eyesight—and its location within a larger institutional space—its fluorescent lights, its time schedule, its policy against removing important historical objects. But of the spatial and bodily performance of dead individuals, she can only hope to sense the shadow of that pale shadow. Her location as researcher is, it would seem, thrice removed.

Before capitulating to Neoplatonic longing in the face of Moore's and Lefebvre's historiographical challenges, it might be helpful to situate such perceptions of loss. From a poststructuralist perspective, my longings and graspings sound unhelpfully nostalgic and epistemologically naive. They reflect a lingering, if thwarted, commitment to a history of "the way it really was" and to the possibility of the historian's access to the actual. Such commitments look particularly skewed in an intellectual era that has revisited the relationship between "theory" and "history." Consider, for instance, how the deconstructionist notion that *il n'y a pas hors du texte* argues against the feasibility of even conceiving an actuality outside of the archive's textual operations. For better or worse, the critique of metaphysics translated into debates about the so-called linguistic turn in historical studies. Scholars reckoned with paradigms in New Historicism and cultural history and with the metahistorical musings of thinkers such as Dominick La Capra, Hayden White, and Michel de Certeau.[36] Joan Wallach Scott's advocacy of "language" as a method of historical analysis in *Gender and the Politics of History* became the subject of particularly heated debate in the journals of feminist and labor history. Asserting that in the chicken-and-the-egg conundrum of language and experience that language comes first, Scott used this posited primacy to dictate the character of a new historiography. "Without meaning, there is no experience; without processes of signification, there is no meaning," and "Experience is a subject's history. Language is the site of history's enactment. Historical explanation cannot, therefore, separate the two." For many, Scott's emphasis on language opened new vistas in the effort to understand the nature of past experience.[37] For others, her arguments sounded strangely syllogistic. Many historians reacted with alarm. John Toews argued that "changing worlds of experience [are not] ultimately irreducible to the linguistic forms in which they appear," while Christine Stansell insisted that scholars should not "reverse the terms of Marxist orthodoxy and see 'language' as an ontologically superior formation for which other dimensions of sensuous experience are simply the medium."[38] Most objected to the analytic pedestal on which Scott placed *language* and *theory,* though there existed ambiguity on both sides of the conversation about what exactly was meant by the terms. "Scott slips into the tendency to identify the theoretical with sentences composed of abstract nouns," noted Linda Gordon, "failing to recognize the theoretical in narrative, statistical, or descriptive sentences, or in the nonwritten."[39] The specter of a vulgar textualism propelled these conversations, though it was not always clear whether such a critique described the work of poststructuralists per se or whether it better characterized their critics' reductive conceptions of what textualism meant in the first place.

In her oft-cited 1991 essay, "The Evidence of Experience," Joan Scott investigated what she took to be these historians' misguided notion of "experience" as incontestable and authentic. Inserting a paranthetical qualifier, she critiqued their "insistence that 'social practices,' in all their 'immediacy and entirety,' constitute a domain of 'sensuous experience' (a prediscursive reality felt, seen, and known) that cannot be subsumed by 'language.' "[40] In lieu of the "irreducibility of experience," she proposed "the irreducibility of the literary" and, with it, the recognition that no realm of social life could somehow bypass the contingencies of representation. At the same time, she and others tried to demystify misunderstandings about the nature of language. "The emphasis of poststructuralist positions on language or signifying practices is often taken to be an emphasis on written documents," wrote Judith Butler and Joan Scott. "How are language, signification, and discourse _misread,_ and what are the political consequences of this misreading? . . . How can this be clarified for feminist purposes?"[41] There are probably many types of possible clarifications, but one might begin by questioning whether references to "immediacy," "entirety," or "sensuous experience" need always to mean that scholars are seeking a prediscursive reality. Perhaps such an orientation could propel instead an investigation into how the discursive operates in nonwritten cultural forms. Indeed, copresence, simultaneity, and affective embodiment are, to the performance theorist, fundamental points of entry into the mediation of reality, albeit a mediation that does not always occur in written exchange.[42] The compelling argument that language is an expansive concept, referring to acts of signification more generally rather than exclusively to the interpretation of words, is not helped when critics confine our analyses to print media rather than to other significatory sites. The deflating equation of language with "words" was also subject to critique in literary studies. In debates around New Historicism, for instance, proponents and detractors both concerned themselves with textuality's relationship to social and cultural operations more generally. To Judith Newton, the degree to which

New Historicism's account of representation also concerned itself with nonprint "material conditions" had feminist implications. "For if we wish to be serious about our assertion that representation 'makes thing happen' we will need to explore the way that discursive meanings circulate through . . . a complex 'cultural grid'. . . . Culture, as feminist historians . . . remind us, is constructed on many levels and not in public written representation alone."[43] And to extend Newton (with Linda Gordon) in an anticipation of my own theoretical concerns, it seems important to consider how the discursive operates in bodies, space, gesture, image, sound, and other arenas of exchange. Literary-derived scholarship tends to return to the dynamics of "written representation" and to "sentences composed of abstract nouns." And it is the inertia of this continual return that keeps me from declaring the literary's "irreducibility." Of course, the impulse to reduce the expansive operations of *langue* to the close reading of *parole* is a substitution that most literary theorists would themselves refute.

For me, spatially centered articulations such as those of Dorothea Moore expose the contours and the limits of a vulgar textualism and as such call, quite literally, for another point of entry. The multipurpose agendas, methods, and effects of Hull-House reform required an understanding of social space and of how to manipulate it. In the process of facilitating new kinds of social performances, the settlement also experimented with alternative styles of living and created various kinds of transformational spaces for middle-class reformers, late-Victorian women, unnaturalized immigrants, adolescent girls and incorrigible boys, factory workers, and "children" (as the concept was being developed). The settlement differed in method from other philanthropic efforts of the time in that its reformers moved into the neighborhoods they sought to help. Mingling two connotations of the word *settlement*—(1) a place or region and (2) an agreement composing differences—the movement employed a spatial method to achieve its social mission. A "place" was materially and metaphorically cleared exclusively committed to facing differences of class and culture. To engage in settlement life as a resident was thus to make a spatial commitment, allowing all aspects of one's living, working, and leisure to be transformed and renegotiated. On the other hand, the neighbors of the Nineteenth Ward produced themselves as agents within spaces unfamiliar to many reformers—an Italian farm, a Jewish "ghetto," an immigration detention center, a saloon, a tenement, a factory. A face-to-face interaction between a Hull-House resident and her neighbor was thus an encounter between two sets of experiences, an unequal accommodation between different spatial legacies. Moreover, these legacies permeated the everyday activity of "settling" in which both were engaged. Settling was a process rife with all of the associations attached to the term— an act implying continuity, permanency, territorialization, sedimentation, agreement, and compromise. Confrontation with these kinds of legacies constituted both Hull-House's method and its goal. Furthermore, while space was its "site of historical enactment," settlers in no way conceived of spatiality as a form of experience that escaped mediation. Quite the opposite. Faced with a number of ethical paradoxes, settlers did come to question whether human spatiality could ever be reconciled with the principled declarations that persons self-assuredly used to describe themselves. That is, the decidedly untransparent relationship between espoused words and obdurate experience became the animating concern of their daily lives.

I think of Hull-House, its buildings, its people, its activities, its rhetoric, its methods, and its goals as "interspatial" in nature. The legacies of various spaces intersected and overlaid themselves on its walls, in the practices its occupants performed, in the writing Hull-House reformers produced, in the curriculum its classes offered, in the physical and environmental reforms Progressives sought, in the ruptures and failures of particular experiments, in the architecture of the new buildings it erected. To theorize the semiotic hybridity of interpreted spaces, the term *interspatiality* gestures to a "space as text" paradigm. Like a complex text that contains allusions, suggestions, parodies, and quotations from other texts, strains of many spaces may permeate selected spaces. Reader response theory extends the parallel, suggesting that users of spaces such as Hull-House interpreted it within and against their experience of other spaces. Implicit in a rendering of interspatiality is also its dynamic character, a dynamism that exemplifies not only spatial multiplicity but also a processual and practice-centered orientation. In lieu of purely synchronic readings that fix spatial experience at a single moment, temporally sensitive interpretations incorporate its diachronic aspect by analyzing the accumulated interactions that alter space over time. Such paradigms try, in the words of Della Pollock, to "make history *go*" even as it seems "to *go away*."[44] This is, for instance, to develop a mode of theorizing that matches the motion, the movement, of human geography as Dorothea Moore represented it. After having finished her description of the location and name of each building, she still suffered the difficulty of defining something whose being, she wrote, was "essentially plastic." "This can be but a suggestion of locality, for under the various roofs are harbored many variations of effort, placing themselves according to a natural convenience, and

adding to themselves in slow accretions, much as the function adds
its tool." New interiors and eventually buildings were the spatial
markers of cross-class and cross-cultural interactions between groups
of individuals who were, as Dorothea Moore suggested, "bringing to
it and taking away, altering it and wearing it into certain forms."[45]
Spatial practices at Hull-House did not necessarily "originate" in the
erection of a new building; rather a new building was one step in a
sequence of knotty, not always systematic, repetitions of practices.
Anticipating the arguments of cultural and feminist geographers as
well as Anthony Giddens's concept of "structuration," built environments relied on practices to activate their intended identity, a recursive processuality that made them vulnerable to resistant enactments
as well.[46] Such everyday performances—improvised, repeated, altered, and routinized—force attention on how reiterated practices
give an institution the semblance of fixity, on how verbs prop up the
perceived stability of the noun. At the same time, social theorists of
space remind us that Chicago's unequal cosmopolitanism placed
constraints on the "plasticity" of Hull-House, power differentials
that influenced *who* brought and *what* they took away. The weight
of political economy, leases, ward zoning rules and other privileges
of class, nationality, race, and gender structured the forms and accretions of "natural convenience."

Beyond this mobile, practiced aspect of spatial experience, interspatiality responds even more pointedly to Henri Lefebvre's warnings about the difficulty of theorizing—and of the limits of an
unqualified "space as text" paradigm.

> Semiology raises difficulty questions precisely because it is an
> incomplete body of knowledge. . . . When codes worked up from
> literary texts are applied to spaces—to urban spaces, say—we
> remain, as may easily be shown, on the purely descriptive level.
> Any attempt to use such codes as a means of deciphering social
> space must surely reduce that space itself to the status of *message*,
> and the inhabiting of it to the status of a *reading*. This is to evade
> both history and practice.[47]

Though Lefebvre retains something of the readerly metaphor in his
use of the word "decipher," the lived experience of space is not
always an act of decoding. It is sometimes about motion, sensual
reaction, physical obstacle, and embodied gesture, often elements
whose meaning is not articulated in a verbal consciousness. In the
suggestion that the practice of space cannot be reduced to an act of
decoding, Lefebvre makes theoretical room for that which is not

always semiotically registered. This mode of embodiment apprehends and uses space without necessarily attributing the kind of meaning or semiotic significance derived from an analyst's seat outside the experiential arena. The lack of perceived significance does not mean that it is not there or that an analyst should not be interested in finding it. It simply means that space is not always registered meaningfully. Social theorist Anthony Giddens suggests as much in his distinction between discursive consciousness— "those forms of recall which the actor is able to express verbally"— and practical consciousness—a form of recall "to which the agent has access in the *durée* of action without being able to express what he or she thereby 'knows.' "[48] Resonating with Michel de Certeau's notion of the "tactic," Pierre Bourdieu's theory of *habitus* also accommodates such spatial practices. Defined as a way of occupying and coping with the world based on a collection of past encounters, habitus structures and is structured by a spatial "field"—elements of the world that an individual confronts, moves in, and modifies. A set of practices collect as a network of strategies and resources an individual can apply to given situations, even (and most importantly) without self-consciously "knowing" that she is doing so. As Bourdieu writes, "[W]hen habitus encounters a social world of which it is the product, it is like a 'fish in water': it does not feel the weight of the water, and it takes the world about itself for granted."[49] Such an unregistered register of spatial and sensuous experience thus expands upon the concept of privilege and its capacity to protect the possessor from the weight of contingency. Elsewhere, Bourdieu amplifies:

> It is an immediate adherence, at the deepest level of the habitus, to the tastes and distastes, sympathies and aversions, fantasies and phobias which, more than declared opinions, forge the unconscious unity of a class. . . . [T]he social relations in familiar objects . . . impress themselves through bodily experiences which may be as profoundly unconscious as the quiet caress of beige carpet or the thin clamminess of tattered, garish linoleum, the harsh smell of bleach or perfumes or as imperceptible as a negative scent.[50]

Habitus and tactical and practical consciousness constitute an interspatial collection of environmental practices, recalled, used, and adapted as an agent moves through familiar spaces. Furthermore, its character becomes manifest to the practitioner during "critical situations" or "times of crisis" when an unfamiliar field is encountered,

that is, when something dramatic seems to be happening. As fish
metaphorically thrown from the water, settlement workers would
often find themselves in such critical situations. In spite of a principled commitment to the Nineteenth Ward and to self-
transformation, the inertia and discomfort of their ingrained spatial
practices continually resurfaced, sometimes informally in anxious diary entries, sometimes directly in model tenement exhibits or anti-
sweatshop legislation. John Dewey, one of Pierre Bourdieu's philosophical predecessors, came to locate "emotions" and "dispositions"
in such ruptures between a consolidated self and an unfamiliar context, as disjunctive moments when the habits of habitus were all too
vulnerably exposed. At such times, Hull-House workers could find
themselves entrenched in that paradox of interspatial rigidity against
which Jane Addams so often warned.

> Our conceptions of morality, as all our other ideas, pass through a
> course of development; the difficulty comes in adjusting our
> conduct, which has become hardened into customs and habits, to
> these changing moral concepts. When this adjustment is not
> made, we suffer from the strain and indecision of believing one
> hypothesis and acting upon another. . . . [W]e are continually
> obliged to act in circles of habit, based upon convictions which
> we no longer hold.[51]

Before Giddens's theory of practical consciousness, before Bourdieu's
theory of habitus, Jane Addams and her colleagues were theorizing
the pivotal role of habitual performance in impeding and facilitating
social change. Understanding that reform needed a geographic commitment as much or more than espoused "conviction" or "declared
opinion," Hull-House affiliates matched righteous rhetoric with adjustments in space and everyday performance, using the practice of
settling as the basis for new theorizing.

As such, the interspatial nature of settling also reflects back on
metahistorical reflections into poststructuralism, textualism, and the
linguistic turn. This means having a healthy respect for the rhetorical power of the nonverbal and for the way that identities may be as
moved by a noise or a smell as they are the tropes of an argument. A
performance paradigm potentially unsettles the axis that polarizes
theory and history, unhinging the conceptual apparatus—language
and experience, text and event—by which the literary and the historical constituted themselves oppositionally. Hence, as historians
examine their relationship to cultural theories of representation, as
literature scholars expand their field of inquiry to include the stuff of

social history, concepts of space and performance help to align rather than to divide the epistemological trajectories of these adjacent intellectual transformations.

I know that I am interested in the nonwritten and nonverbal because I believe it helps me to work through the cautious logic of settlement reform and because lack of attention to these realms will always leave us wondering why verbalized principles seem rarely to provide all the tools needed for effective social action—why, in Jane Addams's earlier words, "we are continually obliged to act in circles of habit, based upon convictions which we no longer hold." Principled rhetoric about the importance of "diversity," for instance, does not always foreground how it feels when diverse people come into the same room for the first time—the feelings of dissonance, the nerves unwittingly bracing as if to face a threat, the reflexive urge to back away, the differences in interactional codes of staring, vocal volume, proximity, and touch. This is _experience_— constructed by social forces of gender, class, culture, religion, sexuality, and more. And it is not exclusively manifested in the verbal nor exclusively registered as a linguistic event. A touch of an arm, a meeting of the eyes, a lowering of the head—these are mediated enactments if not always registered as self-conscious signaling and decoding on the part of participants. Indeed, the coding/decoding model risks reinstantiating a Cartesian conception of the subject, figuring a _cogito_ who moves about in a slightly distanced, slightly delayed consciousness of herself, intentionally engaging in the production and reception of meaning as she opens Hull-House's front door and starts up the stairs. The "open" door, the entry, the engraved banister, the kindergarten children running at her feet— all are symbolic. But does their symbolism fully account for how she registers the weight of the door, the tap of hardwood under her boots, or the reflexive shift in her body as she avoids being tripped by a scampering child? This succession of moments—this experience in the Hull-House entry—is discursively (if not verbally) mediated by differences of gender, class, and age, something easily sized up by a social analyst who looks from outside, from above, and with hindsight. And the door, the hardwood floors, the reformer's body are by no means "irreducible" or more authentic than the meanings I can derive from them. My experience sizing them up, however, is not continuous with her experience negotiating them. At the very least, this is a difference of location. I have "perspective" on her mode of habitation, while she is in the midst and mist of it.

It can be difficult to write a history of the tacit and the habitual—
and hence it can be difficult to write a history of space and performance. This book takes its title from a moment in Jane Addams's
preface to her classic book *Twenty Years at Hull-House* when she had
a similar realization. There, she felt forced "to abandon the chronological in favor of the topical, for during the early years at Hull-
House, time seemed to afford a mere framework for certain lines of
activity, and I have found in writing this book, that after these
activities have been recorded, I can scarcely recall the scaffolding."[52]
The processes that Addams called "lines" were by no means experienced as linearity, though her sense of Hull-House's interspatial
motion echoes Dorothea Moore's depiction of an entity that is
"essentially plastic." Addams isolated the historical conundrum of a
location where space is the "topic" and time is its framework. At
Hull-House, the attempt to "recall" is difficult not simply because
the past goes away but because the detached, bicameral position of
the recaller can be so radically different from the embedded position
of the performer. The intentionality of planned scaffolding did not
fully coincide with the act of settling. Hull-House history is thus
difficult to write, not only because its scaffold has been forgotten,
but because the concept of scaffolding is itself a paradoxically retroactive one, constituted by the effort to recall it. Moved by an awareness of the embeddedness that Bourdieu theorizes, that Addams
evokes, and that performers apprehend, a number of performance
historians have worked to understand this opacity and elasticity. In
Cities of the Dead: Circum-Atlantic Performance, Joseph Roach devel-
ops the concept of a "kinaesthetic imagination," "including pat-
terned movements made and remembered by bodies . . . [I]t operates
in the performances of everyday life, consolidated by deeply ingrained habits and reinforced by paradigmatic systems of behaviorial
memory . . . but is also a means of its imaginative expansion."[53]
Roach builds on the ideas of philosopher-historians such as Paul
Connerton and Pierre Nora. Framing the material methods by
which "societies remember," Connerton argues that "many forms of
habitual skilled remembering illustrate a keeping of the past," a
performance that "re-enacts the past in our present conduct. In
habitual memory the past is, as it were, sedimented in the body."[54]
For Nora, such sedimented skills, corporeal translations, and latent
behaviors compose the fabric of "true memory," a realm of implicit
historical enactment that he associates with the *milieu de mémoire* of

lost peasant culture and that, he argues, the operations of modernity have eroded.[55] Less disposed to distribute inherent truth-value, Roach finds that such historical performances persist even, and most intriguingly, when redirected by the civic politics, psychic repressions, and alternate technologies of modern memorial.

Settling exposed the sentiment and sediment of turn-of-the-century everyday lives even as it cleared the terrain on which new corporeal translations could be imagined. To examine Hull-House, however, is also to be reminded of the gendered work behind such spaces of tacit memorial as well as to consider the gender politics of their persistent latency. The world of embodied tradition has never sprung as spontaneously as the flights of Nora's true memory would have it. Feminist theorists and historians of domesticity remind us that such enactments have depended upon the maintenance of enabling spheres of kinship and community.[56] Here one often finds women cultivating the milieus where human beings learned the skills, habits, and behaviors by which they re-member history. And given that such performers rarely feel the weight of their inhabited water, they often barely notice the gendered work required to refill the pool. Moreover, when social actors do notice their dependency on such work, they may react with hostility, casting the nurturer from her field of indirect influence, blaming her for reminding them of their own contingency. The scene replicates in miniature the story of public welfare. Indeed, Jane Addams and hundreds of female proponents of public welfare before and after her would endure different facets of this paradox. Saddled with the task of manufacturing belonging, they were and are positioned as practitioners in the art of human relationality only to be vilified as threats to human autonomy. Such connections suggest that nostalgia over lost *milieux de mémoire* can simultaneously disavow and reinforce the contradictions in contemporary welfare debate. Reflecting Linda Gordon's insights into the term *welfare* and why "a word that once meant well-being now means ill-being," such nostalgias neither face their gendered underpinnings nor their implications for public politics.[57] They also reproduce the formal contradictions of women's predicament, where women's assigned role as society's "nurturers" can constitute them simultaneously and unironically as its "dependents."

The strangely self-deferential role women play in culture also makes it difficult to remember them. The allegorical contradictions that circulate in debates on women's history and on female memorial offer perpetual illustration. Not only is women's work invisible, as feminist historians have argued, their work is more often sanctioned as appropriate when it is done for someone other than them-

Carved in Imperishable Granite

One of many cartoons—along with articles and ceremonies in a variety of national and international venues—that memorialized Jane Addams's work at the time of her death in 1935. *(Photo courtesy of University of Illinois at Chicago, the University Library, Department of Special Collections, Hull-House Association Records, Chicago Tribune. © Copyrighted Chicago Tribune Company. All rights reserved. Used with permission.)*

selves. Their predicament exposes the gender dynamics of another concept in performance historiography, that of *surrogation.* For Roach, Michael Taussig, and René Girard, the term connotes the performative process by which "culture reproduces and re-creates itself . . . selectively, imaginatively, and perversely," confronting the impossibility of pure self-reproduction and using a "stand-in" to repress the violence and discontinuity of its own historicity. The obverse of the *milieu de mémoire,* surrogation's partial fit shadows all modern memorial performance. Surrogated "[p]erformance, in other words, stands in for an elusive entity that it is not but that it must vainly aspire both to embody and to replace."[58] Hull-House and its memorials likewise exemplify the performance of surrogation in historical memory, but they also show women having a particularly difficult time negotiating their double partiality. Indeed, the notion of female surrogacy has a skewed redundancy next to woman's naturalized role as supporter, as nurturer, and as guardian of someone else's origin narrative. Furthermore, the "ill-fit" and "failure" that theorists see in all surrogation is often depicted in women as a personal lapse rather than as a representational inevitability. Such female figures inadequately satiate the nostalgia for a lost past (of family, kinship, and filial connection) that it is their responsibility to re-create. Certainly, this dilemma also animates the history of public welfare, where stereotypes of failed femininity serve as stand-ins for larger structural inequities.[59] However, these allegorical conundrums also shadow the history of historical writing. Clio was Muse to history, not an historian herself—hence, the formal difficulty of conceptualizing what it would mean to have her "consciousness raised."[60] Similarly, Jacques Derrida's *Archive Fever* trips up upon the thorny discussion of Anna Freud's relationship to her father and the archives to which she has been named custodian. In such meditations, a daughter is accepted as her father's keeper but not as her father's representative, ultimately questioned by "the voices of the arch-patriarchs in history" who are "skeptical about the possibility that a daughter could speak in her own name."[61] Thus, facing the vain aspirations of their appeals to cultural inheritance, daughters often have an attenuated and deferential connection to historical transmission. They more often function as the enablers of history rather than as its storytellers—or as the terrain on which memorial occurs rather than as the subject remembered.

Finally, all of these reflections lead up to the necessity of exploring, not only how to write a history of performance, but also how to enter the performance of history. For me, this has meant enmeshment in the archive's network of deferred memories, what Derrida characterizes as the archive's promise to the future and its urge to forget its own interventions into history.[62] From this perspective, my location amid preserved documents and microfiche coils is perhaps less a status to be disavowed than an uncanniness to be explored. Indeed, living in Chicago while conducting research for this book was like walking among unwitting historiographic images. A building, a bridge, a river, a park, a street—all such entities were luminous with a history that I came to learn even when they only partially referred to it. Like an urban form of pentimento, hidden historical images rose from the canvas of Chicago's civic self-portraiture, jostling me into a kind of hypertemporality or what Elin Diamond calls performance's "shifting time-sense, a receptivity both to the contingency of the present and the mimetic figurations of what we might call historical experience."[63] Linking Bertolt Brecht's social dramaturgy to Walter Benjamin's treatise on history, Diamond reminds us that, for both figures, true historicization meant the estrangement of the present. Benjamin called for the integration of past and present in "dialectical images" where "the past and the now 'come together in a flash as a constellation.' . . . [I]n 'now-time' we are palpably, mimetically immersed in the unrecorded history of our social existence."[64] Chicago's version of Benjamin's dialectical image seemed to extend the old adage that "all history is contemporary history" by working in two directions. Even as its juxtapositions fettered my image of a pure historical past, they also unsettled my stable notions of the contemporary. It thus seemed appropriate to incorporate something of this unsettling into the book.

The ensuing chapters are organized around particular "lines of activity," following several trajectories that emerged and receded at different times and places. Each chapter also begins and ends with the dialectical image of a different type of contemporary historiographic object—a museum, an archive, an oral history, a civic monument— thereby juxtaposing the story of Hull-House with the present-day sites that, explicitly and obliquely, propel its telling. While not resolutely chronological, the scaffolding used to interpret Hull-House's processuality is temporal; I evoke it "to trace the experiences through which various conclusions were forced upon" Jane Addams and her fellow residents.[65] In chapter 2, I use documents that surround the founding of Hull-House to interpret Jane Addams and Ellen Gates Starr's "hazy scheme." Negotiating differences of ethnicity, age, class, and gender, I analyze how they experienced their first months of brilliantly and blindly making history in receptions, kindergartens, nurseries, social clubs, and neighborhood alliances. Next to these local acts of settling, I frame the current Hull-House Association as an implicit historical performance of the settlement's founding ethics. Chapter 3 begins with the 1996 debate over the Jane Addams Memorial Park, the first Chicago monument expressly dedicated to a woman. The gendered paradoxes of civic memorial are brought into high relief as the rest of the chapter investigates the gendered work of civic activism, specifically the expansion of Hull-House into art galleries, a gymnasium, playgrounds, a public kitchen, and all-female public housing.

Using as its point of departure the Smithsonian's life-size exhibit of the Hull-House interior, chapter 4 considers the living habits of settlement residents. Interpreting the frustrations recounted in the letters of new residents, considering the initiatory role of daily rituals such as toting and dining, I suggest that Hull-House's residential patterns disrupted heteronormative divisions of private and public to create an alternative model of domesticity and kinship. Beginning and ending with the oral history of a ninety-five-year-old former Hull-House child, chapter 5 examines one of her favorite settlement spaces, the Hull-House theater. I demonstrate that the rhetorical, embodied, interdisciplinary, and collective nature of theater made it a particularly productive vehicle of reform. Finally, chapter 6 begins with the 1963 demolition of Hull-House to erect the University of Illinois. The campus now houses the Jane Addams Hull-House Museum and the Jane Addams School of Social Work, memorial sites that recall the last of the reform practices I analyze—the Labor Museum and the professionalization of social work symbolized by the Mary Crane Nursery, the Boys Club, and the Juvenile Protective Association. Reflecting on the destruction of the Hull-House environment next to the construction of Hull-House memorials, I end the book with a meditation on the unregistered acts of forgetting that undergird public acts of remembering.

When I did not feel like working in the archives anymore, I usually decided to make copies of microfiche in order to read the letters later. As the shiny paper emerged from the machine the microfiche ink smelled toxic, making me wonder what form of lung disease I had contracted with each inhalation of a mimeticized past. The ink always took a while to dry, and I often smeared it when I pulled it from the machine, smudging, sometimes erasing, a word or corner. The ink left its mark on my hands, turning my fingertips black. When I tried to wipe them off on the cement-colored formica, I always noticed the black fingerprints of past researchers who tried the same thing. Everywhere were impressions of the residual embodiment that plagues those of us who work with our heads.

In *Unmarked,* Peggy Phelan defines performance as a thing that "becomes itself through disappearance."[66] Linking this fundamentally ephemeral ontology to the fundamental not-thereness of the past, both she and Della Pollock have followed with their respective explorations—*Mourning Sex* and *Exceptional Spaces*—to frame all "acts of performance theory and criticism [as] instances of writing history."[67] Moreover, the fact that performance "goes away," that it exceeds and recedes from the purview of positivist historiography, is for Phelan and Pollock its greatest opportunity.[68] "My hunch," writes Phelan, "is that the affective outline of what we've lost might

bring us closer to the bodies we want still to touch than the restored
illustration can. Or at least the hollow of the outline might allow us
to understand more deeply why we long to hold bodies that are
gone."[69] An exploration of such longings will recur throughout this
book, sometimes in the desires of a Hull-House settler, sometimes in
more recent civic, museological, and archival performances. At other
moments, however, I see the writing of this performance history as
the reverse of Phelan's conundrum. The melancholic structures behind words such as *lost* and *still* do not entirely match my relationship to a Hull-House that I never possessed. My sense of its now-
absentness is not constituted by a memory of its once-presentness.
The fact that I have no such memory might have meant that my
relationship to Hull-House would go thoroughly unrecognized to
myself. I could (and still do) proceed unfettered, without the least
twinge of historical relationality and without any desire to understand the obfuscated bodies whose histories permeate my urban,
modern, and functionally oblivious daily life. Indeed, only the in-
flated self-aggrandizement of my therapeutic consciousness could
assume that the past was gone because I thought it was. Consequently, in addition to examining the loss of Hull-House, I sometimes find myself facing another kind of historiographic moment,
one telling me that the past is not lost but actually quite resiliently
and unanticipatedly present. The character of such an overpresent
moment or "now-time" is not exactly akin to remembering or longing since that would imply my once knowing or once having. Instead, I find myself caught red-handed in a dialectical history whose
presence I never imagined, stunned to find myself holding onto a
body without ever having reached for it.

Chapter 2

Settling: "Not Quite Classes and Not Quite Clubs"

Human history is created by intentional activities but is not an intended project; it persistently eludes efforts to bring it under conscious direction. However, such attempts are continually made by human beings, who operate under the threat and the promise of the circumstance that they are the only creatures who make their "history" in cognizance of that fact.
  —Anthony Giddens, *The Constitution of Society*

Dear Mary,
I will take part of the time to begin an account of "the scheme." Jane intends to take a house or flat in some district.
  —Ellen Gates Starr to Mary Blaisdell (Feb. 23, 1889)

Anthony Giddens's statement is both a warning to the historian of Hull-House and an interpretive offer. It is a warning because he reminds historical analysts that past social actors such as Jane Addams and Ellen Gates Starr did not know how their story was to end. It is an interpretive offer because he suggests that some desire to feel the pull of history's narrative may have pulsed through Miss Addams and Miss Starr when they began "the scheme." They did not know that they were "making history," but did they want to feel they were? Could these women have been so bold as "to take a house or flat" in an unknown urban district without sensing the threat and the promise? In February 1889, a twenty-nine-year-old Ellen Gates Starr wrote a letter describing the beginnings of a scheme whose ingenuity she attributed to her dearest friend, Jane Addams. "[A]lthough she resents my putting myself out in anyway . . . I am unwilling to let people suppose that I would ever have worked it out. I believe in it now and can chatter about it." Later into the twentieth century, Chicagoans, national and international observers, a Nobel Peace Prize committee, and the Hull-House Association itself would repeatedly attribute the success and brilliance of this scheme to Jane

Addams, a tendency that would prompt Ellen Gates Starr to revise her own early self-effacement. Preserved in a collection of papers that now bear her name, Starr's letter is illuminating still for how it marks—in streams of consciousness—the conditions and emotions that have become identified with the Progressive Era and for how it anticipates—in breathless asides—the distinctive methods of social change for which Hull-House would be celebrated.

Over one hundred years later, it was no doubt with a sense of both threat and promise that "the most famous woman in Chicago" attempted to bring certain parts of her city "under conscious direction." In 1994, television host Oprah Winfrey told reporters of her plans to fund a $3 million program for residents of Chicago's public housing. It was to be administered through the Hull-House Association, a multibranch social service organization with corporate offices in the Loop. Winfrey's connection to Hull-House had been established earlier that year. She attended several Hull-House benefits and donated to the association funds raised from the much-publicized auction of her old dresses ("size 8 to 22").[1] Strategically using her celebrity in the service of social betterment, Oprah Winfrey now joined her legacy to that of Jane Addams—a transhistorical union of the two most celebrated women Chicago had yet to produce. The gesture also spotlighted a struggling social service institution that stood to benefit enormously from a Harpo–Hull-House union. The description of Winfrey's program—Families for a Better Life—borrowed from a late-twentieth-century discourse of welfare reform, condemning the "culture of poverty" and the "failure of the family" in the reproduction of social ills. It also explicitly declared its intended project, thus exemplifying how often social movements—whether philanthropic, reformist, or revolutionary—skirt Anthony Giddens's paradox and act with the hope of directing the next course of human history. "I want to change the way people think about their lives," said Winfrey. "I want to destroy the welfare mentality."[2] I find it illuminating to juxtapose the founding moments of Hull-House in 1889 with the refounding Oprah Winfrey offered in 1994. The later Hull-House Association guides a spatially diffused branch system of professional social workers. It also interacts with a more recent welfare discourse that prescribes its own ending. Next to this "future," the contours of a past Hull-House's commitment to cohabitation and spatial centrality emerge more distinctly—as do its founders' deferential assertions that they actually did not know what they were doing. The contrast is to be expected, for despite its location as the origin point in many histories of social welfare, the settlement's relationship to contemporary welfare debate is strangely

fraught, redirected, selectively remembered, selectively forgotten.
The largely hagiographic mode that celebrates Jane Addams and her
achievements only obliquely makes its way into current distopic
visions of welfare's achievements, for, as Linda Gordon notes, "in
two generations the meaning of 'welfare' has reversed itself."

> What once meant prosperity, good health, and good spirits now
> implies poverty, bad health, and fatalism. A word that once
> evoked images of pastoral contentment now connotes slums, de-
> pressed single mothers and neglected children, even crime. Today
> "welfare" means grudging aid to the poor, when once it referred
> to a vision of a good life.[3]

Mindful of Oprah and of the Hull-House Association as they work
within and against this set of connotations, this chapter sets the
ground for an alternate type of remembering.

A dramatization of Hull-House's beginnings includes a huge cast
of characters. Addams and Starr encountered various populations
after they moved into the Nineteenth Ward, each of them differently constituted by experiences of ethnicity, age, class, and gender.
The ensuing sections each focus on different groupings—middle-
class female settlers, immigrants, children, working-class laborers,
poorer neighborhood mothers—using their respective social locations to introduce large-scale issues and to track the settlement's
institutional development. Their stories thus serve as a reminder of
the intimate connection between early welfare history and other
types of historiography—immigration, juvenile development, labor,
feminist. By placing each of these historiographical strains inside
Hull-House—sometimes in its living room, sometimes its kitchen,
sometimes a bedroom or porch—my introductions are also anticipations. They will require a constant tacking between temporal registers, vascillating between historical actors' immediate sense of themselves and my retroactive sense of them. Linda Gordon reminds
social critics that, whatever its faults, the current state of welfare
cannot be construed as an intended project. "Welfare policies represent the jerry-built compromises that are the artifacts of political
conflict."[4] I find the "jerry-built" metaphor a helpful one for thinking about this early Hull-House scaffolding and the performative
dynamics of settlement sociality. For me, the everyday performance
of settling turns out to be akin to the paradox of "making history,"
for they both walk the same route of impossible intentionality. Both
lines of activity force the humbling realization that the consequences
of one's actions sometimes exceed one's capacity to conceive of

them. It is still a question whether a contemporary discourse of welfare reform will be able to remember and to tolerate the mundane ethics that were fundamental to its founding.

Cordelia

Presentist filters keep us from looking back on late-Victorian, white American women with anything but homogenizing amusement. Dressed in high-throated blouses, lacy petticoats, and floor-sweeping skirts, their image serves as a foil for everything the twentieth century likes to say about itself. The nonhistorian's vague awareness of the suffrage movement does not dilute the capacity of this image to evoke both rigid domesticity and female acquiescence, the dual habit of thought that manages both to demonize and to naturalize women's lack of social power. Diluting the lessons of Foucault, contemporary critics still seem to believe modernism's retroactive

Ellen Gates Starr, cofounder of Hull-House, in a pensive moment after embarking upon "the scheme." *(Photo courtesy of University of Illinois at Chicago, the University Library, Jane Addams Memorial Collection.)*

invention of Victorian sexual repression, allowing such women to function as easy targets for all conceivable condemnations: erotic sublimation, naïveté, moral severity, irrelevancy.[5] The persistence of such untroubled associations are why many respond to the story of Hull-House with the tempered condescension of presentist surprise: "I didn't know they did that." It is also why it has been so difficult for those outside of the field of American women's history to imagine such women as the repository of a decidedly heterogeneous and multiply-directed array of longings, ambitions, social critiques, and social callings. This period saw a shift in the character and reach of women's voluntary associations, a corollary adjustment in the perception of women's role in public life, and an anxious rethinking about the nature of gender difference. The settlement movement was both a typical and an exceptional illustration of this era's structures of feeling. As Ellen Gates Starr and Jane Addams began to speak in lectures and other gatherings, the former exuberantly reported that "the truth of the thing is in the air," highlighting how many responded to the reiterated qualities of their radically new plan. So thick was the air in fact that other young women in various corners of the United States similarly decided to "take a house or flat" in the marginal neighborhoods of New York, Boston, and Philadelphia, calling themselves a settlement movement with their first national gathering in Chicago in 1895. Why did so many find themselves so moved—literally as well as figuratively—by settlement logic?

Within feminist and reform historiography, the story of Jane Addams's early years of confusion and depression is an oft-told tale. Among the first generation of college-educated women, the period between graduation and the founding of Hull-House was characterized by what a much later generation might have called "twenty-something" ennui. After graduating from Rockford Female Seminary, Jane Addams echoed Leo Tolstoy in naming her late-nineteenth-century version of this condition a "snare of preparation" in which young people—exposed to a world of ideas and ideals—found "no recognized outlet for their active faculties."[6] For Jane Addams, the depression, directionlessness, and inactivity had a significantly gendered dynamic, brewing as it did within the context of American familial and social relations. She analogized the plight of the college-educated woman to the structure in which Shakespeare's Cordelia found herself when asked to pledge love of the paternal in exchange for a princess's luxuries.

[King Lear] looked toward her expectantly, but instead of delight and gratitude there was the first dawn of character. Cordelia made the awkward attempt of an untrained soul to be honest and scrupulously to express her inmost feeling. The king was baffled and distressed by this attempt at self-expression. It was new to him that his daughter should be moved by a principle obtained outside himself, which even his imagination could not follow; that she had caught the notion of an existence in which her relation as a daughter played but a part.[7]

The urges that propelled Jane Addams and Ellen Gates Starr's "scheme" conflicted, to varying degrees, with those that ensured female solicitude before the obligations of the privatized family. "Moved by a principle obtained outside" such structures, their act of settling in a West Side neighborhood of Chicago modified, to say the least, the conventions of daughterly social performance. As time went on and the "scheme" took hold, such altered gendered roles would continually brace against the limits of paternal imaginings.[8]

To use the language of performance to describe this uneven shift in women's increased public role is to highlight two particular aspects. First, it emphasizes how much a social performer must constantly repeat, cite, and restore previous behaviors in her crafting of new ones. As a female settler tried to rationalize her life choices, she often borrowed from the language of Victorian ideals, reworking rather than dismissing the association of femininity with domesticity, morality, and virtue. Such citational performance was part of a historical process, not simply a regressive invocation of the feminine.[9] It is important to remember that the significance of such a would-be Cordelia thus lies, not in a totalized break with convention, but in her capacity to recombine the derivative. In addition to this emphasis on different kinds of repeating—the association most often linked to contemporary theories of the performative—the performance paradigm also foregrounds how much a preoccupation with "doing" animated Hull-House women's modified repetitions. I find that the etymology of *performance*—a doing, a furnishing, a bringing into being—nicely frames these women's relatively literalized fixation on "activity" as the antidote to a host of religious, classed, and gendered frustrations. To "catch the notion of one's existence" in a different kind of relation was for these early New Women very much about being active in the root sense of performance. It was about altering the nature of their involvement with the stuff of the experiential.

When Addams named the "between-age mood" that gave birth to the Progressive Era, she more specifically referred to a religious crisis that nagged young Protestants as they neared the century's turn.

Though Hull-House would ultimately bill itself a secular institution (and receive condemnation for being "irreligious"), Protestant legacies and concerns left their imprint on the consciousness of the young settlement worker. Religious questions created a structure and an imaginative arena in which to formulate ethical action, to weigh moral outcomes, and to debate ideals of service. As feminist theologian Jean Bethke Elshtain notes, even Jane Addams's uneasy rejection of the specific content of Protestantism still left a moral framework, an ethical "prism" that "gave her world its shape."[10] Similarly, Mary Simkovitch of Greenwich House in New York— one of the many settlements begun out of the shared impulse "in the air"—emphasized form over content in assessing religion's impact on settlement work. "Religion in common thought of it means the framework of life—the outline by which we measure events, that which makes proportion possible, our sense of the whole of things."[11] Already made skeptical by Darwin's account of human origins, unfulfilled Protestants encountered the religious diversity and industrial inequalities of the American city, wondering what if any connection existed between the church's creed and the conditions endured outside of its four walls. Movements such as Christian Socialism or the less threateningly popular Social Gospel tried to forge a connection. Indeed, to attach the word *social* to an organization or movement during this era—social justice, social settlement, social Christianity, social philosophy—was to announce an ethical commitment to human interaction and to "real" world issues.[12] When in 1897, Social Gospel leader Charles M. Sheldon published *In His Steps,* he subtitled it *What Would Jesus Do?*—significantly not asking his followers to wonder, as they had in the detached realm of the sequestered church, "what would Jesus *say?*" The visceral nature of the stepping and the doing was paramount in this form of "practical Christianity."[13] Of course, the perceived problem with the Protestant Church was embedded in its belief structure; Protestantism's reification of individual autonomy meant that its followers conceived of contingency as something that one had to go out to find.

Many answered the questions of Protestant ethics by condemning forms of Protestant organization. Addams, Starr, and a host of settlement workers found similar ways of framing their religious disgruntlement. First, their version of the language-versus-experience conundrum fell across the divide between proselytizing and practicing. Many Christians would choose participation in the settlement over the ministry because their "religious educator['s] statements appear to them as magnificent pieces of self-assertion totally unrelated to the world."[14] Mary Simkovitch similarly noted a prevailing antipathy toward religion that was only "skin deep," arguing that at a settlement "where there is real belief in common, it is likely to be not the creed professed, but a kind of *sub rosa* creed, the beliefs wrought out in human experience."[15] A related second concern was with the bureaucratic nature of religious organization itself, in which the maintenance of church mechanisms substituted for the enactment of church ideals. "There is to be nothing of the institution about it," declared Ellen Gates Starr of their scheme. "The world is overstocked with institutions and organizations: and after all a personality is the only thing that ever touches anybody."[16] Charity and relief organizations were prevalent in Chicago, and the two friends occasionally had difficulty articulating the difference between their scheme and these other kinds of endeavors. In a preliminary conversation with Dr. Gunsaulus, a popular Chicago minister with much civic influence, he initially proposed that Starr and Addams start "a little morning school where young ladies would be instructed how to deal with the poor"; they "repudiated it," saying their plan was actually far less complex. When he heard "that Miss Addams and Miss Starr simply intended to live there and get acquainted with the people and ask their friends of both classes to visit them he was 'Licked to death,' He said 'good! the kingdom of heaven isn't an organization or an institution!' "[17] From such concerns came Addams's later celebration of the settlement's improvisatory qualities, "its flexibility, its power of quick adaptation, its readiness to change its methods as its environment may demand."[18] The rhetoric of performance thus historically coincided with the evolutionary rhetoric of adaptation, one that reworked the Christian ideal of service while resisting the church's orthodoxy and its bureaucracy.

Abiding in the belief that "a personality is the only thing that ever touches anybody," Addams and Starr cultivated a sub rosa creed whose content and character ultimately linked them to pragmatist philosophy.[19] Revising also thinkers such as Thomas Carlyle, John Ruskin, William Morris, and Leo Tolstoy, they hoped to create a space for cross-class sociability—a commitment rooted in a modest and local sphere of meeting, engagement, and conversation.[20] Another renowned inspiration for this highly local form of sociality came from the example of the Toynbee Hall settlement in England. Arnold Toynbee had been an educated Englishman with a big heart and a poor constitution. While the former prompted him to renounce the privileges of his birthright to teach and live with the poor of London's "slums," the latter failed him, and he died in 1883 at the age of thirty-two. Inspired by his commitment, his friend Samuel Barnett secured a large Queen Anne–style house in the East

End of London where he and young Oxford-educated men moved in "to bridge the gulf that industrialism had created between rich and poor . . . and to do something more than give charity."[21] In addition to reproducing a college atmosphere with lectures, clubs, picture exhibits, and university extension classes, Toynbee residents worked to promote labor issues and other kinds of civic reform, distinguishing their structural and ideological differences from those of Christian missions: "A Mission has for its object conversion," wrote Barnett. "A Settlement has for its object mutual knowledge. A Mission creates organizations, institutions, and machinery. A Settlement uses personal influence and tends to human contact."[22] On a trip to England in the mid-1880s, Addams and Starr visited this Oxford experiment and, as Hull-House developed, borrowed and extended this mix of local interaction and public intervention.[23]

Along with the reform goals of the neighborhood, Barnett explicitly stated that the settlement came to the psychological aid of restless Oxford graduates themselves. Starr and Addams responded to this logic enthusiastically. "The Toynbee men you know, quite repudiate the idea that they are making any sacrifice. They go in with their different occupations and simply live there, they get elected on the school boards and improve the conditions of things as citizens." By performing work that was worthwhile and socially responsible, Toynbee men put "knowledge into practice" and were released from the pangs of uselessness that befell young, well-to-do Englishmen upon graduation. Such feelings of inauthenticity also plagued a privileged class of Gilded Age Americans.[24] Often diagnosed with neurasthenia, this sense of "unreality," "inauthenticity," and feeling that one was "living life at a remove" circulated in the nerves and sensibilities of upper-class Americans who paradoxically felt stifled by the "artificiality" of privileged existence. Responding to the notion that "relief work" was relief not only for the marginalized but also the privileged, Addams adapted the Toynbee impulse to the predicament of young, educated, white women, illustrating that the gender dynamics of class magnified the intensity of this pervasive structure of feeling. While higher education opened to women, American society had yet to make reciprocal changes in sanctioning women's civic and professional participation.[25] Thus, the inequities of gender—restricted access to public opportunities—combined with the paradoxes of class—its anxious feelings of unreality—compounded a sense of futility in upper-class "invalid girls." Starr amplified from her perspective as an art teacher in girls schools, moved to an excessive verbiage by the identificatory force of this religious, gendered, and classed sense of unease.

I pity girls who have nothing in the world to do. People get up in church and in missionary meetings and tell them about the suffering in the world and the need of relieving it, all of which they knew and it ends in them giving some money which isn't theirs as they never earned it and all their emotion over it and their restlessness to do something has to end in that. . . . [N]o body ever shows them a place and says "There _do this._" I _know_ that girls _want_ to do. I have talked with enough of them poor little things![26]

While this motivation may be interpreted as an incarnation of classist selfishness—using the lives of the marginalized for one's own fulfillment—the rhetoric was in a sense more honest than the language of traditional philanthropy that reveled in the benevolence of the wealthy. This alternative argument against class-stratification managed to speak to young white women who needed to be convinced that work toward a more equitable society and the path out of ennui were one in the same.

To advocate such new kinds of "doing" for white women, and thereby lay the basis for the figure of the New Woman, was simultaneously to contest and to rework prevailing theories of gender difference.[27] "Nervous people do not crave rest, but activity of a certain kind."[28] Starr's personal theory countered leading medical discourses on the nature of women's bodily constitution. Doctors such as Edward H. Clarke attributed the high degree of neurasthenic affliction in privileged women to overstimulation that disrupted their volatile hormonal balance.[29] The theory was adapted to intellectual and physical arenas, creating one of the most resilient arguments against women's entry into higher education, athletics, and civic life. Indeed, postcollege depression in women was often interpreted as an argument against coeducation rather than as a sign of women's thwarted potential. Jane Addams was one of many young women (and eventual settlement workers) who was prescribed a "rest cure" to counteract the symptoms of nervous depression after college graduation. Starr too suffered from inexplicable sicknesses during this time, as did Vassar graduate Julia Lathrop, who left a secretarial position in her father's law practice to join Hull-House. Charlotte Perkins Gilman, later a resident at Hull-House for two years, immortalized the well-to-do woman's feelings of uselessness in "The Yellow Wallpaper." Finding the urge toward settlement activity more compelling than any hormonal arguments against their fitness for it, Starr, Addams, Lathrop, Gilman, and many more had to resist biological as well as social arguments on the limits of female enactment.

At the same time, female settlers could be found borrowing from

the language of proper womanhood as often as they opposed it.
Many invoked the Victorian ideal of female self-sacrifice; however,
they used it to argue for women's service beyond the limited circum-
ference of the private family. Similarly, others upheld the belief in
women's innate impulse toward sympathetic relationality, finding
that through such associations they could position themselves as best
suited to the social work of practical Christianity.[30] That such feminine impulses should be publicized, directed outward to ever larger
domains of civic life, lay at the heart of what Jane Addams would
later define as "civic housekeeping." The concept would become one
of the most omnipresent, efficacious, and malleable of discourses to
emerge in American women's history of the Progressive Era.[31] The
language of domesticity also initially provided a framework within
which Starr and Addams interpreted their own early acts of settling.
" 'We' take a house i.e. Jane takes it—furnishes it prettily. She has a
good deal of furniture and she intends to spend several hundred
dollars on some more and of course we put all our pictures and
'stuff' into it. Then we shall both live there *naturellement*."[32] Starr
recorded the excitement of an alternative household, one that Addams would later famously analogize to a heteronormative one.
"Probably no young matron ever placed her own things in her own
house with more pleasure than that with which we first furnished
Hull-House."[33] Acting upon an alternative notion of one's existence
required a different kind of relationality, however, a larger domesticity that would brace against the requirements of a private domesticity. Increasingly aware of the reciprocity between so-called private
and public spheres, settlers' longing to intervene in the macrospheres
of the latter simultaneously would require a reorganization in the
microperformances of the former. Finally, incorporating the deed-
centeredness of a newly secularized practice and the "really doing"
that was antidote to class inauthenticity, Hull-House women ventured into a pragmatically derived form of public sociability.

"Of course our great advantage lies in not being obliged to begin
by asking for money."[34] And there lies, for some, the limits of the
settlement's "social impulse." The viability, even conceivability of
their scheme depended upon the fact that Addams had received a
substantial family inheritance. It is a reminder that financial resources were also a part of privileged boredom and that Cordelia,
however misunderstood, was also lucky enough to be a princess.
"Jane can afford after furnishing the house to spend $100 a month
and we think by economy we can run the house on that."[35] Starr
herself was not quite as well off and continued employment as a
teacher. Still, Addams's wealth indirectly subsidized her. "I shall

make an offer to Miss K to teach. . . . I shall try to get $500 for it and if I can only get $450 it will still be as much as I have after paying board and of course I should have no board to pay."[36] They also moved in with Addams's family servant, Mary Keyser, a third cofounder who "relieved Miss Addams of all household care."[37] Though Addams claimed that this housekeeper "quickly developed into a very important factor in the life of the vicinity as well as that of the household, and [her] death five years later was most sincerely mourned," the presence of Mary Keyser and others who would follow qualifies the image of Hull-House's class equality. The initial ad hoc economics anticipated the shifting financial arrangements of residency. Most settlers had to pay for their room and board while also performing unpaid settlement work, thus making Hull-House accessible only to individuals who had an extra source of income. Some were supported by family trust funds, some by selling family heirlooms, and others found paid employment as teachers, secretaries, researchers, and writers outside the settlement.[38] Later, Addams and other well-to-do settlers arranged loans and fellowships for others to try to minimize the degree to which finances inhibited participation.[39] Finally, the costs of maintaining the mansion and its expanding list of activities proved to be an omnipresent drag on Hull-House's social impulse. While a growing list of benefactors provided some relief from mounting debt, the affiliation of two very wealthy women—Louise deKoven Bowen and Mary Rozet Smith—ultimately proved to be the most fiscally welcome development.[40] The availability of such finances provided the economic base on which the settlement could maintain its "quick power of adaptation," and settlers soon realized that the capacity to improvise did not emerge in a fiscal vacuum. They knew what Oprah Winfrey came to know; social change needed money.

A Cosmopolitan Standard

"We shall need a large room in which to have classes, lectures, or what ever we may wish and to receive people," wrote Ellen Gates Starr, hoping that "our friends from civilization [travel] . . . the distance to see us and our friends from the surrounding neighborhood." In February 1889, an abandoned mansion stood on the corner of Halsted and Polk Streets in Chicago's Nineteenth Ward. Having been the center of an estate outside city limits in the mid–nineteenth century, Charles Hull's family home was gradually surrounded by the city's expanding urban geography in the late nine-

The Hull-House parlor, whose assortment of chairs could be re-arranged at any moment; the "large room" accommodated a flexible spatial dramaturgy. *(Photo courtesy of University of Illinois at Chicago, the University Library, Jane Addams Memorial Collection.)*

teenth century.[41] This spatial extension marked both the impact of unregulated industrialization and the increase in southern and eastern European immigration. When wood-framed structures housing saloons, stables, stores, and tenement dwellers began to surround the house, the wealthy Hull family moved out, participating in a wave of urban flight that would become a routine phenomenon for American cities. That year, while Hull's niece Helen Culver quietly lived outside Chicago's new city limits, a furniture factory leased her former family home for storage, stacking formerly well-appointed rooms with manufactured desks and chairs until a pile of furniture reached the ceiling's hand-carved moldings.

When Starr and Addams discovered the Hull mansion on Halsted and Polk, they arranged with Helen Culver to remove the furniture from one of its downstairs drawing rooms. Even when they had their "large room," actualizing the modest scheme of shared sociability still proved to be a difficult endeavor. The two women experimented with a number of publicizing strategies, attending the meetings of different political, religious, and labor groups, writing and distributing informative invitations to Nineteenth Ward neighbors. Meanwhile, they called on their own friends and contacts from Chicago's civic and social life.[42] As Starr anticipated, they occasionally drew on people's curiosity to ensure attendance—"even the novelty will attract them, I think, and I don't mind banking on that a little; anything to get them and their interests." While they succeeded in getting many of their "friends from civilization" to travel the distance to their Nineteenth Ward drawing room, often their hopes for "a successful evening" were dashed when neighborhood attendance did not match expectation. "The previous evening was characterized by the prevalence of the elite and conspicuous for the absence of invited neighbors."[43] An evening of "elite" guests was not the image of cross-class engagement that Addams and Starr had in mind.

"The house? We had a little frame house," recalled Mary Argenzio, the daughter of West Side Italian immigrants. "The entrance was in the alley. It was behind a great big apartment building. And our little house was a cottage in the alley. And we had to go through the alley to come to our house."[44] Argenzio remembered the spatial mixture of large and small buildings—some old and some new, some boldly public and some darkly sequestered—of a transforming urban neighborhood. The West Side of Chicago was one of several destination points for Chicago's immigrant population. The homes of Chicago's elite and the buildings of the city's rising corporatism clustered along the rim of Lake Michigan. Meanwhile, the factories and sweatshops that fueled the city's economy were located on its outskirts, mostly to the south and west. Housing workers in surrounding tenements and boarding houses, this expanded manufacture depended for its labor force on turn-of-the-century immigration. Thousands of Europeans and later southern blacks left homes, families, counties, and countries to find a better life by crossing the Atlantic or the Mason-Dixon Line. Many types of employment could be found on the West Side— framemaking, dry goods, cigar making—but leather and textile manufacture such as shoemaking, millinery, upholstery, tailoring, and the ready-to-wear clothing of mass production predominated. While the meatpacking industry that Upton Sinclair made famous mostly occupied the South Side, the Hull mansion was closer to the section of Chicago that Theodore Dreiser's Sister Carrie entered.[45] The Nineteenth Ward was not only west of Michigan Avenue, it was also west of the Chicago River. While known for its international diversity and its poverty, the neighborhood was less associated in the Chicago imaginary with the crime and vice of areas such as the Levee District—the "cesspool of immorality" just east of the river that William Stead and Lincoln Steffens exposed in *If Christ Came to Chicago* and *The Shame of the Cities*.[46]

Immigrant experience—the largest obstacle to meaningful neighborhood relations—was both the most anticipated and least understood aspect of the settlement scheme. Though Addams and Starr hoped to "learn to know the people and understand them and their way of life," such cross-cultural sociality between settler and neighbor occurred from within the former's perception of the latter's deficiencies. The hierarchy embedded in Starr's distinction between friends from the neighborhood and "friends from civilization" casually cited a Darwinist evolutionary paradigm. A central structuring metaphor for Progressive discourse, evolutionary theory proposed different stages in the progressive narrative of the human race. Filling in the blanks of this developmental structure with the ethnic groups they encountered, hereditary Americans preoccupied themselves with the placement of different societies on various rungs of the evolutionary ladder. It went unquestioned that white, Anglo-Protestant descendants were on the top. When such a system of human classification received structural reinforcement from other American social ladders—particularly those of civic politics and the industrial division of labor—such categories and hierarchies had the spontaneous, taken-for-granted character of common sense.[47] It also became, not only a way for hereditary Americans to distinguish themselves from immigrants, but also a mode of legitimation that immigrants used to distinguish among themselves. The result was a constant crisis of category. In the postfamine immigration of midcentury, the Irish inhabited the streets surrounding Halsted and Polk. Enduring different versions of the racial and religious prejudice they left in England, they gradually made their way into more powerful civic spheres. Eventually, the largest percentage of Chicago's police force was Irish, backed by a significant number of local politicians—including the Nineteenth Ward's alderman Johnny Powers.[48] While the Irish experienced the dubious privilege of deracialization with their rise in class status and political power, Italians were an immigrant group that had yet to "become white" in turn-of-the-century Chicago.[49] Joining this period's huge wave of southern and eastern European immigration, these reputed members of the "darker race" moved from an array of provinces—Naples, Calabria, Palermo, Sicily, and more. Teresa deFalco recalled that Italian kids "had problems" when they attended public school "with the Irish kids and

Polish kids, you know. And I understand they had trouble. Well, like mothers were told, were telling the kids not to associate with the Italian kids because they're all bad."[50] While Italian Catholicism theoretically rationalized a religious affiliation with the Irish, the latter more often condemned the former's ornate festivals and highly iconic worship of the Virgin Mary as primitive paganism. Meanwhile, various émigrés from the Italian provinces argued against the cumbersome and conflating notion of the "Italian" category. While Chicago Irish proudly embraced their nationalism (indeed, their impulse to do so was the reason they emigrated), so-called Italians more often identified with their provincial identities. Descendents of the northern provinces were particularly keen on making this clear, importing the evolutionary ladder to distinguish between themselves and the presumably less civilized, agrarian peasants of southern Italy.[51] "For that matter, even my own mother would forbid me to ever have anything to do with Sicilian kids," deFalco remembered, noting the apparent flexibility of the language of prejudice.[52]

Similar kinds of disaffiliations and hierarchizations occurred among other immigrant populations of the Nineteenth Ward. When Greek immigrants moved onto Halsted Street, they often resented their confusion with Italians and emphasized instead their connection to the revered ancient culture of Greece. Using a foil and a connection to antiquity to support their own project of self-legitimation, Greeks argued for differences among the descendants of the Mediterranean by laying the metaphors of the evolutionary ladder over the historic narrative of Western culture.[53] German immigrants—Jewish and non-Jewish—were some of the first West Side inhabitants and were often feared for being proponents of socialism and anarchism. In what later socialists would call German "bourgeoisification," their radical image dissipated when Germans moved to more elite parts of the city at a speed that kept pace with their burgeoning economic success. Immigrants with the doubly displaced identity of "Russian Jew" composed one of the largest neighborhood groups. Controversy repeatedly erupted about their relationship to German Jews, specifically around issues of intra-religious benevolence amid the imputed degradation of the former and the perceived assimilation of the latter.[54] Other groups of "Bohemians" and smaller representations of Poland, Sweden, and Norway also lived in the area. The anti-Semitism of an encroaching Russian empire prompted the family of a Polish Jewish girl named Hilda Satt to migrate to the United States—"I have a dim recollection of Father saying that he could no longer live under the Russian yoke. . . . There was only one escape: going to America"—and to a

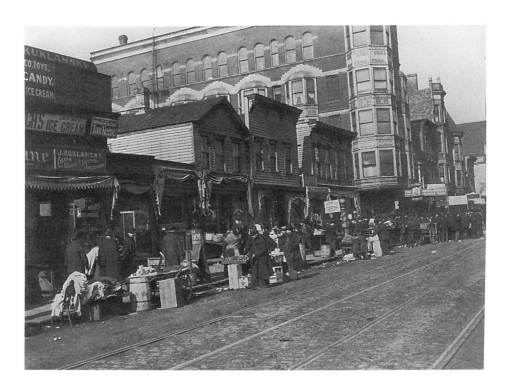

The renowned Maxwell Street Market was one of many immigrant-populated thoroughfares in Chicago and one of many perceived to be unsanitary by moral reformers. *(Photo courtesy of the University of Illinois at Chicago, University Library, Jane Addams Memorial Collection.)*

tenement four blocks from the Hull mansion.[55] For the most part, however, black migrants from the South could rarely be found in the Nineteenth Ward, and then not until after World War I. Their early migration patterns most often constellated in the South Side.[56] On a ladder that emphasized bodily classification and that evacuated the history of slavery, "Negroes" or "Coloreds" most often faced relegation to the lowest evolutionary rung. As such, they became the foil for nearly every other immigrant ethnicity that needed an inferior to legitimate itself. This made habitation among "white ethnic" immigrants (as they would come to be called) thoroughly inhospitable. Such, at least, was the argument made by Louise deKoven Bowen when she later tried to explain Hull-House's less than intimate relationship with "the Colored People of Chicago."[57]

The logic of settlement mimesis presumed that a so-called civilized way of life should be imitated and reproduced. Sometimes, however, these same oppositions paradoxically flipped into a nostalgic fascination with difference, particularly for well-to-do young people disenchanted with the trappings of civilization. The result was highly ambivalent social interactions in which "elite" members of society could refer to both the charm and the degradation of immigrant neighbors without a note of felt contradiction. In their initial scheme, Addams and Starr expected and fervently welcomed new encounters with difference, though they may have had a misguided notion of what they would find.

> We should like to have in it in a neighborhood where there are a good many Germans and French immigrants so as to utilize the French and German which girls learn in school and have little or no opportunity to practice. . . . There are thousands of Italians in the city who have no . . . [one] . . . to raise them out of their degradation and Jane leans decidedly to them! And she seems to think that Chicago is swimming in girls who speak Italian fluently, which I happen to know is not the case. Whereas there are a great many girls who speak French and German.[58]

The perceived primitivity of the Italians was simultaneously the reason Addams leaned "decidedly to them." To an "overcultivated" young woman, such differences of language, habit, and culture were all the more fascinating for being that much more different. Additionally, Starr's hesitation toward Italians anticipated an oft-encountered conundrum—the impulse to select a reform project based on the talents possessed by the reformer (e.g., French and German) rather than on the requirements of the neighbor. The proximity of Italian, Russian Jewish, Bohemian, and Greek immigrants would mean that settlers could not always choose their immigrant friends based on which language they felt like practicing.

Addams and Starr further found that they could not enact their social ideals solely within the four walls of the mansion. Gendered homosocial and familial accommodations would not convince everyone of the desirability of entering a home that looked so much different than their own. "Neighborhood visiting" thus became one frequently used interspatial accommodation. On the one hand, such calls were an important symbolic attempt to elicit mutual trust in lieu of mutual suspicion. Starr and Addams released spatial power by engaging neighbors in their own space, demonstrating that they were willing to inconvenience themselves in order to "get acquainted." On the other hand, unsolicited entry into another person's home was also a violation of privacy. "Friendly visiting" was a fairly common practice of charity distribution by this time in Chicago, one that often

proceeded from the assumption that a less privileged home was open
access to a more privileged caller and that protocols of invitation did
not inhere.[59] Upon witnessing the insensitivity with which friendly
visitors "performed generosity" in Chicago's neighborhoods, Jane
Addams would later critique "the subtle problems of charity" and the
myopic assumptions of the well-to-do caller. Ellen Gates Starr's early
letters, however, suggest that they initially fell into this classed and
gendered mode of interaction themselves.

> Mr. Ryerson, a new young man, is coming down tomorrow night
> to make calls. We find that evening is the best time to call. "He" is
> at home and they are all sitting about, rather bored with each
> other, and glad to be amused. In the day time "he" and all the
> men . . . of the family who work for bread are away, and "she" is
> doing her housework and in some cases doesn't like to be inter-
> rupted. Besides, we think if some men call "he" will be more apt to
> respond. Jane and I have made some very successful evening calls.[60]

After having been an unappreciated afternoon interruption in the
lives of married women, Starr and Addams made another temporal
accommodation to work schedule and family life. Within two
months of moving in to the neighborhood, they also began to recruit
male affiliates. In order to fulfill the mimetic potential of "actual
contact" and "infectious example," neighbors had to see themselves
reflected in the reformer, to feel some sense of identification in the
midst of manifest differences of class and culture. Homosocial alliances between men thus needed to be cultivated.

The pragmatic effort to engage Italians was given a boost when
Addams and Starr formed a friendship with an Italian man and his
wife and arranged language lessons. Senor Mastro-Valerio was a
highly educated Italian immigrant and eventually a temporary resident of Hull-House. The beginnings of their friendship exemplify a
brand of cross-cultural exchange that would become constant in the
daily life of the settlement. One night's Italian lesson in the autumn
of 1889 seemed to go on extremely long to Starr, who, hungry for
dinner, began to wonder when Senor Valerio would leave. "To our
great surprise he said 'I will stay if you wish.' " They went to the
"kitchen and found that we had an especially scant supper—three
'measly' little chops, not quite enough for us, corn, which he would
never eat, and a sticky sort of pudding that he would abhor." Anxious to smooth over this socially discomforting situation, the Misses
Addams and Starr invited Valerio to come again the following Saturday when they would have an Italian dinner prepared. They asked a

neighborhood woman named Mrs. deGuido to "come over to cook the macaroni, and the most absurd time we had!" The evening exemplified how food—its preparation and consumption—can occasion vivid and conflicted types of cross-cultural interaction.

> We offered to buy the stuff for us—cheese, meat, tomatoes, etc. of which we learned that the gravy was made. We thought, from the description . . . that all this stuff . . . is . . . lumped into one dish. She examined our [pots] for cooking and pronounced everything too small. At length her eye fell on [a] dish . . . a huge one and she said "This!" with a smile of content. . . . They cook the macaroni in enormous quantities of boiling water and then take it out and pour the gravy over it. The gravy is the important thing. I thought it would never be done. She boiled the meat till it was as hard as a rock, together with onions. She was much disgusted that we hadn't garlic.[61]

Reacting in habitus to different dietary habits, Starr selected and verbally recorded that which was unfamiliar, documenting also the disjunctures in her effort to "understand" and the tendency to interpret within a culturally specific filter. Moved linguistically to articulate neighborhood practices and habits that violated her own, Starr found certain elements—food that was "lumped into one dish," the "enormous quantities of boiling water," meat that "was as hard as a rock"—noteworthy precisely because they were not *naturelle* to her. Furthermore, Mrs. deGuido encountered successive violations of her own commonsense assumptions about the appropriate size of pots and the necessity of garlic. Starr worked to make sense within her own set of experiences and dispositions, collapsing Italian *bolognese* into "gravy." She continued by moving into a generalizing ethnographic present—"they cook . . . take . . . and pour"—synecdochically substituting the motions of one woman for the cultural habits of an entire society. Finally, having secured ethnographic authority in her downstairs kitchen, Starr felt knowledgeable enough to make a generalization about Italian value systems via indirect discourse: "The gravy is the important thing." In the same letter, she went on to write of the felt dispositions that inhibited spatial proximity between neighbors and "friends from civilization," noting that active gestures of inclusion were still required even when all were in the same room.

> Dr. J was delightful. I don't think there is among gentlemen a country where the caste system prevails who would . . . act as if it

were the expected and everyday thing for a peasant woman to sit at table with him. She wouldn't have sat down if he hadn't insisted.[62]

"She wouldn't have sat down if he hadn't insisted." Mrs. deGuido and her counterpart initially held back from shared bodily proximity. Gendered, classed, and perhaps problematically more comfortable in the space of the kitchen, willing to reproduce a habit of retreat in the face of impending cross-cultural exchange, it was incumbent upon the dominant "Dr. J" to insist that she stay. In so doing, he received the congratulations of a beaming Ellen Gates Starr. On other occasions and in different framing venues, of course, Mrs. deGuido would have retreated. And it would have been perfectly acceptable for Dr. J—mired in the reflexes of habit, propelled by the patterns that *were* in actuality "the everyday thing"—not to have noticed.

After six months of such attempted social gatherings, Starr and Addams hosted one of the first large-scale "successful" evenings between elite friends and Italian neighbors in May 1890. "Mio Carissimo Amico," began the invitation to neighbors such as Senor Agathno, a fruit store owner on East Polk. The rhetoric of the event differed from previous ones in that Valerio himself served as the central organizer of this "concerto musicale." "He opened the door of 335 South Halsted Street himself" as guests entered, thus spatially articulating his role as transnational mediator between settler and neighbor.[63] "The sight was very interesting," recounted Starr. "There were a great many children, babies even & some of the women wore bright kerchiefs on their heads. The rich & vulgar Italians are taking to coming, sporting diamond crosses."[64] Noting the intergenerational mix of people that were to her unusual, Starr also commented on styles of self-adornment, filtering practices of headwear and jewelry through her own religious sensibilities and marking class differences between the wealthy Italians and kerchiefed "peasants." Nora Marks, a visiting journalist from the *Chicago Tribune* that same night, remarked on the drawing room's decor, particularly its "ivory and gold walls, delicate etchings of old statues, and heads of madonnas."[65] Some guests stood "gazing" at the gold and ivory ornamentation in one corner of the room while others moved their hands devoutly between their lips and the image of the Holy Virgin in another part. Thus, different iconic elements of the space provoked varying shifts in bodily composure, gaze, vocal volume, gesture, silence. In honor of the occasion, Starr and Addams also placed a "photograph of Humbert and Marguerite on the mantel," then king

and queen of Italy. "Him no great man," Marks overheard a "grin-
ning Italian" assert.[66] While images of the king and queen were no
doubt intended to create a culturally safe semiotic space, they were
somewhat unremarkable to those less concerned with an aristocrati-
cally defined sense of Italian nationalism. Nora Marks, making fun
of the number of babies named "Rosina," suggested that the novelty
of children actually eased tensions among strangers who—when
they found themselves unable to converse—could always play with
a baby together. She watched as one of the "Rosinas . . . was passed
over heads to the upper end of the room, where some society people
were sitting." Immediately, another voice chimed in. " 'Society people! We are all society people,' interrupted Miss Starr, who had two
Rosinas on her lap and was chattering something that sounded
much like the American baby talk."[67] Addams and Starr's "friends
from civilization" had congregated together in the back of the
room, and Starr's exclamation worked to undo this unbalanced
social geography.

The evening continued with a planned program of "singing in
Italian" and "a violin solo with piano accompaniment,"[68] a performance whose audience layout reproduced class divisions by putting
"rich and vulgar Italians . . . in the back seats & the peasants to the
front."[69] Then, after more *"conversazione,"* the evening ended. "I
never saw anything like it. Here was a simple emigrant people invited to spend a social evening with cultivated Americans and enjoy-
ing it. What does it mean?"[70] However, the evening was not quite
over for some of the remaining guests. "One of the ladies of the
diamond cross recited a patriotic poem with great spirit. I missed it,
being engaged in struggle with Nora Marks, on the other side of the
house, but Jane says it was very spirited and some of the people were
quite moved."[71] Having been absent from this unplanned performance, Marks wrote nothing of it, and Starr recorded it in the
unremarkable language of a secondhand report. The latter thereby
(and fortuitously) left linguistic traces ("spirited," "quite moved") of
the emotional undercurrent engendered by a woman who fleetingly
and spontaneously secured her own performance frame. The evening
had endured all the fundamentals of an interaction among
strangers—each of whom came perhaps despite the fear of making a
mistake. It encountered the reluctant matter of social geography and
the predisposition of some "society people" to be with those "like
themselves." The blank stares some gave and the blank stares others
unwittingly returned also gave over to moments of felt success that
buoyed diverse participants through the inevitable strain, silences,
and discomforts that would follow. There were the sudden impulses

of babble and effusiveness that tried to close gaps of economics and culture, to undo forces of migration and industrialization through willful speech in a face-to-face interaction. And then, the performance—spontaneous or planned—when someone risked the vulnerability of self-display to perform something emotionally binding to an audience who in an act both generous and selfish, allowed themselves to be moved by it.

Immigrant activities continued where the gestural and imagistic aspects of the environment accommodated different patterns of leisure, taste, and cultural identification. Generally, such gatherings moved from parties of single to mixed ethnicity, a transformation that would be both celebrated for being cosmopolitan and condemned for being assimilationist.[72] Sometimes settlers worked in coordination with other immigrant community centers—for instance, the Greek Orthodox Holy Trinity Church.[73] A new nearby venue such as the Hebrew Institute, devoted to the maintenance of Jewish cultural identity, would form an attenuated relationship, while other sites—such as the Catholic Holy Guardian Angel—criticized Hull-House for being irreligious.[74] Such criticisms underscore the politics of settlement mimesis and the condition of its commitment to nonsecular and intercultural inclusion. Settlers would ultimately participate in many turn-of-the-century debates about American ethnicity, often anticipating the exchanges among the likes of Israel Zangwill, Randolph Bourne, or Horace Kallen. While comparing theories of the "melting pot," of "trans-national America," or of a federated "pluralism," Jane Addams, John Dewey, and other settlers would decide that a new American nationalism should be based "not upon a consciousness of homogeneity but upon a respect for variation."[75] As often as they debated their "international nationalism" among liberal reformers, they would also castigate the prejudices of hereditary Americans who suffered from the "lack of a more cosmopolitan standard."[76] As the critiques of assimilation reemerge throughout this story, it is important to remember that individual neighbors most often developed mobile ways of performing their ethnicity—neither wholly autonomous nor wholly assimilated. Indeed they incarnated the impossibility of either of those conditions by adjusting self-presentation to varying neighborhood spaces, modifying bodily comportment and indulging in different identifications depending upon the economic constraints and cultural codes of a settlement, a tenement home, a local parish, a factory, or a city street. "The place bristled with hyphens," recalled one Irish immigrant of the Hull-House neighborhood. "The Americanism was of a kind that opened to the least pressure from without."[77] While such indulgences varied, their practice will reveal the tacit hybridity of cultural identity even in places where it conventionally appears to be singular.

To Live with Children

Addams wrote that she was struck early on by "the generosity of the poor to each other," the willingness of struggling people to share what little they had with neighbors who were struggling more. In many quarters of the Nineteenth Ward, economic necessity was also the basis of neighborly sociality. By giving what they had in times of relative stability, neighbors formed attachments of mutual support and concern. Moved by this brand of utilitarian sociability, settlers too began to form friendships within a material exchange. Starr proudly reported these rhythms of give and take, announcing that she gave one woman a "bag of flour," that another woman "presented us with a bottle of catsup, & another has requested to leave her baby while she moved her household effects."[78] Rather than providing receptions and concerts that assumed guests had leisure time to spare, utilitarian sociability worked within the economically constrained life-paths of their neighbors.

In their willingness to watch the babies, Starr and Addams struck upon a form of utilitarian sociability with enormous staying power. The early gesture also anticipated the centrality of children to the settlement's emerging identity. As person, object, metaphor, and visceral presence, the figure of "the child" would activate nearly all aspects of Hull-House spatial and linguistic life. On the one hand, children populated the settlement as a result of new time-space requirements of the industrial workday. Far removed from the rhythms of an agrarian economy and working for wages too small to maintain a household on a single income, Hull-House neighbors struggled to reconcile the new industrialism with the vicissitudes of child care. Responding to this practical need, Starr and Addams "early learned to know the children of hard-driven mothers who went out to work all day, sometimes leaving the little things in the casual care of a neighbor, but often locking them into their tenement rooms."[79] Of course, the impulse to remove such children from their locked tenement rooms emerged during an anxious time when the child served as the one of the most galvanizing tropes of Progressive Era discourse. In such circumstances, assumptions about what constituted practicality and utility were by no means self-evident to all involved. Reformers often responded from within their own dismayed network of nostalgic longing and righteous outrage when coming up with a definition. Thus, children—as both fact and figure in all senses of both words— offer a rich and thorny object of analysis.[80] Furthermore, as Carolyn Steedman suggests, the analysis of the child provides a reference point with which to consider the limits and opportunities of a textual analysis of culture. "[T]he historical dilemma—what makes the topic worthy of historical inquiry—is that children were *both* the repositories of adults' desires (or a text, to be 'written' and 'rewritten' to use a newer language), *and* social beings, who lived in social worlds and networks of social and economic relationships."[81] Many illuminating structures emerge when the "linguistic turn" is brought to the field of child studies. In many ways, children form the clearest point of intersection between Hull-House's emerging linguistic rhetoric and its emerging spatial rhetoric. Furthermore, the issues at stake in child discourse often revolved around the kinds of oppositions—textual versus social, symbolic versus reflex, psychic versus physical—that animate historiographic debates on the role of language.

The woman who left her baby the first time left it again. And then another woman made the same request, and so did another. Soon Addams and Starr had seven babies routinely in their care, requiring them to solicit help from a growing list of their visiting friends and patrons' daughters. Illustrating the recursive role of repeat performance in the constitution of an institution, they all continued to watch babies, reiterating the gesture again and again until it became a "method" and later the Hull-House Nursery. Over fifteen babies remained in their daily care within the first year. By 1891, the numbers of children exceeded the capacity of the Hull mansion, and, undergoing one of the first settlement expansions, they rented another building a few doors down at 326 South Halsted. By 1892, they moved to a larger structure at 221 Ewing, the cross street just south of the mansion, with a volunteer—Wilfreda Brockway—as its designated director. Twenty-four children on average attended with "a cost of five cents for each child."[82] The adjustments in space, administration, and directorial responsibility coincided with an increase in the number of residents and volunteers. The nursery's move also made more space in the mansion's drawing room for a new volunteer, Jenny Dow, to conduct her morning kindergarten. A nonresident who visited from nine to noon, Jenny Dow could be found playing with twenty or more children under the age of five each day. The routinized gathering made for many a madcap morning as Hull-House workers coordinated breakfasts, meetings, and correspondence amid the mayhem of scurrying children. Florence Kelley recalled her first arrival at Hull-House on a snowy morning in 1891, only to be greeted by Miss Addams, who was somewhat "hindered in her movements by a super-energetic kindergarten child" who was in danger of "charging into the snow."[83]

The antecedents of the Progressive focus on children sprung in part from the kindergarten movement. In the early nineteenth century, Friedrich Froebel—a German philosopher and child educator—challenged prevailing notions of human development and experimented with alternative pedagogies. Most fundamentally, he argued that the child was not "a little adult" and should be understood instead as a being far different in psychic, moral, and intellectual capacity. Froebel embraced the contradictory dynamics of childhood impulses while retaining a Hegelian idealism, proposing the ultimate human being as a "unity of opposites." Ideal development thus required the cultivation in the child of imaginative

Jenny Dow, a settlement volunteer, indulged in the affect of littleness every weekday morning in the Hull-House kindergarten. *(Photo courtesy of the University of Illinois at Chicago, University Library, Jane Addams Memorial Collection.)*

structures and appropriate habits from whence, over time, healthy adults emerged. His paradigm of childhood performance advocated sustained interactions around selected objects and activities that he called "Gifts" and "Occupations."[84] Derived from the shapes, proportions, and colors of the natural world, children manipulated idealized objects in ever more complex and productive tasks. Widely published in the United States in the second half of the century, Froebel found sympathizers who rejected the disciplinary practices of repression and punishment advocated by other child educators such as Amos Bronson Alcott. Instead, they channeled child "interest" and advocated the healthful "principle of self-activity" in human psychology. Additionally, American women found in the kindergarten movement a means of securing a modicum of public authority. They could participate in the theory and practice of a larger agenda that—because its object was children—did not violate their maternal role.[85]

The popularity of such concepts persisted with some modification when, late in the nineteenth-century, reformers placed them next to the bewitching paradigms of Lamarckian and Darwinian evolutionary theory. While Darwin's ideas provided a hierarchical model for the arrangement of human societies, they also mapped a developmental model for the individual human being. Furthermore, as proponents used infantalizing language to describe the imputed primitivity of certain immigrant societies, they also used racializing language to characterize the primitivity of children. The same year that Addams and Starr moved into the Nineteenth Ward, the most famous American popularizer of evolutionary childhood caused quite a scandal in his lecture to a group of Chicago kindergarten teachers. G. Stanley Hall—founder of Clark University and the author of seminal essays on "the child's mind in the classroom"—reportedly told his assembled audience that "the instinct of the savage survives in the child."[86] There and elsewhere he told teachers, parents, and reformers to allow children to conduct themselves like "little savages" lest their connection to the natural order of evolutionary development be compromised. The *Chicago Evening Post* reported shocked confusion since Hall was "advis[ing] us to teach our sons to do what we have been endeavoring to teach the savages to avoid."[87] The shock would subside over the turn of the century, for Hall worked from an increasingly popular theory of "recapitulation" and its belief—to quote its most memorable of phrases—that "ontogeny recapitulates phylogeny." The synecdochically satisfying paradigm held that each child instinctively reproduced the evolutionary path of his predecessors until he matched and eventually extended the civilizing process of the race as a whole. For Hall, the child's primitive location in this natural narrative must be embraced rather than stunted; his aggressive instincts for competition and survival must be given free reign rather than curtailed by excessive discipline or the effeminizing force of overcultivation. As Gail Bederman has demonstrated, Hall worked out his ideas from the midst of his own bouts with neurasthenia and while facing the crisis in masculinity that plagued many late-nineteenth-century men grappling with women's larger public presence. Hall's statement that "the child is the father of the man" demonstrated the gendered preoccupations behind his concepts of childhood, and the strenuous childhood performances he advocated often used the concept of natural man as an antidote to a classed and gendered inauthenticity. For Hall, the restored behaviors that children performed were loaded with re-capitulatory significance, carrying as they did vaguely Lamarckian hopes for inherited racial progress. Moreover, the child's mode of "remembering" his ancestors took place through behavioral enact-ment itself, bodily recalling an ever more complex series of material-ized acts through which the child eventually fathered himself.

Settlers were surrounded by miniature humans, and the discursive and social fact of their presence structured everyday life at Hull-House. Receiving rooms were often a flurry of diminutive activity, filled with incessant motion, punctuated with periodic crying. The lowest planes of the rooms often saw the most action, and settlers constantly found themselves crouching to the floor to keep track of its goings-on. Residents composed their thoughts about child wel-fare while simultaneously attending to children's demands, a confla-tion of the figural and literal that occurred every time a child peered over a desk to see what a settler was doing. The environment thus percolated with the affect of *littleness*. Later, Jane Addams looked back on Jenny Dow's kindergarten.

> [For] three years we saw her almost daily with the little children of humble people. Her varied gifts, her willingness and her ability to become as a little child among them, her abandon to their interests, her merriment over the discovery made one day that the children thought she was a little girl in a white apron and had never dreamed that she was a "grown lady" all combined to produce the most successful following I have ever known of Froebel's command "to live with the children."[88]

While Addams's more self-conscious discourse on Froebel developed later in works such as *The Spirit of Youth and the City Streets,* her picture illustrates the ideal kindergarten classroom and its attempts to elicit the "self-activity" of children. It also shows the lure of adult identification within this play structure. As Jenny Dow "abandoned" herself to "become as child," she created a healthful child environment but also indulged in the regenerative contact that children were reputed to provide for adults. Exercising the child-centered etymology of the word *rejuvenation,* carrying "the very aroma of the *Spirit of Youth*" and a "mirth and buoyancy [that] were irresistible," Jenny Dow's example suggests how privileged white women galvanized their own self-activity by promoting the self-activity of children.[89]

The nursery and kindergarten attracted new groups of people to Hull-House—siblings, parents, and friends—a form of multiplication by familial and filial extension that spurred new gatherings, clubs, and reform experiments. By tending to these children, settlers "made contact" with a group of mothers whose economic burdens might normally have precluded involvement with the settlement. Additionally, older brothers and sisters came by to linger at the place where younger siblings spent most of the day. Sometimes, the oldest children in the family brought along another youngster whom he or she was baby-sitting for the day. Thus, the child who served as a figural linchpin in an evolutionary discourse on the interrelatedness of humanity thus also functioned as a pragmatic linchpin in the expansion of the Hull-House population. Soon a host of young people ranging in age from one to eighteen began to frequent the settlement with some consistency. Gradually, children and their perceived malleability became a recognized means of access to the rest of the family and thus a vehicle for an extended social reformation.

This multiplication further tested Addams and Starr's method of spontaneous sociality, for the sheer number of persons and activities became unwieldy and exceeded their limited space. Within the first year, they moved the furniture storage out of the remaining rooms of the mansion, and, much impressed by their activities, Helen Culver decided to give them the run of the house rent-free "amounting to $2880." Ellen Gates Starr wrote her sister with news of the money and of a new name, "[W]e decided to call the house Hull-House. . . . [C]onnect these two facts in any way your refined imagination suggests."[90] The expanded environment and the heterogenous array of activities required new spatial innovations. The Hull mansion's rooms were originally designed to reflect and enact the habitus of nineteenth-century well-to-do Americans. The social geography embedded in its spaces maintained a set of proper behaviors. Up and past a sizable exterior porch, an impressive entry hall opened on the right to two parlors—the first one larger than the second—and on the left to a library, a small octagon-shaped room surrounded by windows, and finally to a well-ornamented dining room.[91] Stairs with an elaborately carved banister led to bedrooms and a bathroom; the mansion's kitchen was built at the back of the house. At one time, larger groups of guests might have congregated in the drawing room while more intimate friends and family (or well-acquainted "society people") comfortably ensconced themselves in the upper recesses of the first-floor parlor. The house designated certain spaces—the library, dining room, and Octagon—to perform certain kinds of activities such as reading, eating, and correspondence. The messier activities of the hired help in the kitchen as well as the more private matters of family life were sequestered behind and above these more public spaces. The influx of Hull-House residents, volunteers, and neighbors drastically reorganized the mansion's neat spatial dramaturgy. No longer could "receiving" be confined solely to first-floor parlors, for the kindergarten was often using it. Sometimes a clamoring club of visiting children forced a resident to open her bedroom to public intrusion. Far more than dining would be performed in the Hull-House dining room, for it was also the site of settlement drawing classes. A resident would have been unwise to leave her correspondence in the Octagon as it was in danger of being overturned by Starr's class in English literature.[92]

To the extent that Hull-House affiliates welcomed rather than resisted this interspatial heterogeneity, the settlement remained structurally flexible and thus able to maintain its "quick power of adaptation." By resisting the impulse to reinforce a shared bourgeois spatiality, the group performed instead new synchronic and diachronic methods of an increasingly public domesticity.[93] One guest in May 1890 was notably impressed by their synchronic organization of space.

> When I visited No 335 South Halsted street Friday afternoon . . . five rooms were occupied by school girls who were sewing and listening to a young lady read from "Christmas Carols" or "Twice-Told Tales." A cooking class was turning out eggs in every style in the kitchen; the bathroom was occupied, and a heap of sand kept half a dozen diligent pie-makers busy. The long porch was filled with children who were arranging violets and buttercups into bouquets.[94]

Working within the built environment of the mansion, different activities clustered in different rooms. Children performed "occupations" that were both domestic and Froebellian, cooking in one room and playing in the modified "sand gardens" advocated by so many kindergarten theorists. Meanwhile, the arrangement of violets and buttercups—the "gifts" of the natural world—gave children the healthy symbology of an integrated human personality (presumably differing from the arrangement of artificial flowers—one of the most condemned forms of child labor). Often the practices performed in each region troubled even these boundaries, however. Participants in a scheduled civic meeting could not help but overhear children's storytelling. Meanwhile, the storyteller's young audience might be distracted by the smell of cooking eggs while a bored kindergartner dropped her bouquet to run throughout the house. Settlers thus needed to develop the ability both to moderate precariously designated regionalizations as well as to tolerate their violation. Interspatial leaks happened diachronically as well, for practices varied within a single region during the course of a day or week.

> From 9 to 12 a kindergarten under the direction of Miss Dow is held in the long drawing room. In the afternoon the kindergarten furniture is removed and the hall is devoted to the use of various clubs and classes. With its beautiful walls and pictures it is easily turned into a drawing room with the addition of a rug and a chair.[95]

Pragmatically adjusted to the larger time-space requirements of urban life, the diachrony performed an ad hoc developmental structure—one that was spatially derived if not always intentionally espoused. As residents reflexively altered rooms for ever more complex activities, Hull-House offered a spatiotemporal incarnation of recapitulation theory, enacting the evolution from baby to child to adolescent to adult throughout the course of the day. This kind of heterogeneity across time often brought its own difficulties as participants in one line of activity crowded into a room before participants in the previous one had left. Residents rushed to finish their dinner, stepping on a hat left by a Boys Club member while students in Miss Price's class waited to enter for their evening drawing lesson.

To maintain any diachronic efficiency, residents often found themselves and these rooms in a constant state of motion, perpetually assembling and disassembling the configuration of each room. Settling in a place devoted to the play of children required such mobile performances of everyday life. During the Christmas season, Ellen Gates Starr made sure that each club had a chance to decorate the Hull-House Christmas tree, reporting that "this week is mostly to be filled with dressings & undressing & redressing of the festive Christmas tree. Tomorrow we have it three times; first the kindergarten . . . then for the Italian girls . . . & in the evening for the shop girls."[96] Early on Jane Addams and fellow residents developed this mobile spatial habit until it became nearly reflexive. Dressing and undressing Christmas trees, exchanging paper dolls for urban reports, children's stools for folding chairs, settlers constantly worked to deactivate a space's previous identity and reactivate a new one. George Twose, a male resident who arrived in 1897, would write a humorous song about Hull-House life that had "I move a chair" as is repeated refrain. Constantly in motion, Jane Addams reportedly adjusted pictures and moved chairs while she spoke during resident meetings and informal gatherings.[97] Upon her visit in 1898, "the restless movements of the residents" unnerved Beatrice Webb, who found herself disoriented by the mobile spatial practices to which Hull-House performers became habituated. When he began repeatedly to visit the settlement in the mid-1890s, it was this quality that most impressed John Dewey when he called Hull-House not really "a thing, but a way of living." Indeed, this famous pragmatic philosopher and theorist of child education derived many of his observations on human development from settling as an alternative everyday living pattern. His self-critique at having interpreted "the dialectic wrong end up" was, in this context, also a revision and reversal of Froebel—"the unity as the reconciliation of opposites, instead of the opposites as the unity in its growth."[98] Commenting himself on female settlers' raucous environment and unceasing activity, Dewey saw in Hull-House a tolerance for simultaneous opposites, the coexistence of moral mission with physical discomfort. The messiness and the non-Idealist nature of such a spatial life would activate Dewey's antiformalist revisions of psychology and pragmatic interventions in philosophy. It also informed his quest for a child-centered pedagogy that understood the contours of psychic and physical coordination. Hull-House thus set the stage for a discursive interaction between pragmatism and domesticity, a gendered connection performed in the adjustments and mobilities of settlement geography.

Nevertheless, the expansion in attendance soon meant that Hull-House's spatiotemporal organization could no longer remain purely improvisatory. In 1891, therefore, Jane Addams and Ellen Gates Starr began efforts to minimize confusion and to secure an even wider outreach through their first published schedule. Calling it "Hull-House Clubs, Classes, Etc." the decision built a temporal scaffolding beneath settling's lines of activity.[99] When the same people found

themselves in the same space at the same time over the span of
several months, participants felt themselves part of a scheme with
solidity and staying power, even as that solidity recursively relied on
their repetitions to sustain itself. In addition to the nursery and
kindergarten, young people below the age of thirteen came to club
meetings between 3:30 and 5:30, while older teenagers attended
evening programming from 7:30 to 9 P.M. An analysis of the role of
the schedule also suggests some of the ways the Hull-House locale
divided regions and groupings—not only by age—but along differences of ethnicity, gender, and class. For instance, their early
version of the "after school" program in the afternoon assumed that
children were in school rather than working as newspaper boys or
sweatshop laborers during the day. The older young people's club
assumed that adolescents had jobs that began and ended at predict-
able times at a point when Illinois had yet to pass legislation for the
eight-hour day. Thus, with the interspatial structuration device of
the schedule, Hull-House's microperformances inclusively reproduced and exclusively neglected the larger time-space patterns of
unregulated industrialization.

Differentiation by gender also structured early club scheduling
for pre- and post-"adolescence"—a concept that was itself a decade
from full articulation. As a social performance that, according Jane
Addams, "were not quite classes and not quite clubs," these groupings began around a loosely defined practice such as reading and
discussing. Young women routinely gathered in the Hull-House
drawing room on Monday evenings, a practice that began with Ellen
Gates Starr's *Romola* reading group in 1890, repeated itself in 1891 as
Miss Addams's "Girls Club," and continued with the solidifying
power of a new name, "Hull-House Social Club," in 1892 under the
guidance of Mary McDowell.[100] A year later, a visiting male volunteer named Mr. Noyes began a "Reading Party for young men" that
also congregated on Monday evenings in Hull-House's upper hall.
Maintaining a regular attendance of thirty since their inception,
both of these clubs began as reading parties, though fuller descriptions show gendered variations in their respective activities. "The
primary object" of the young women's club was characterized as
"profitable social intercourse" in which "the first hour of each evening is devoted to reading and discussion." In contrast, the young
men's reading group more specifically "devote[d] the first hour of
each evening to debates, largely on topics on national and municipal
interest." Ideologically reinforcing which sex concerned itself with
politics as well as the character of that engagement—a more vigorous "debate" in lieu of less structured "social intercourse"—the

difference in discursive practice solidified in 1892 when the young men took to calling themselves the "Hull-House Debating Club." The two clubs turned into a mixed-sex exchange in their second hour when the Hull-House Debating Club "joined" the Hull-House Social Club (or, as it was put another way, when the Hull-House Social Club "was joined by" the debating club).[101] By integrating a mixed-sex gathering as a programmed activity, the Hull-House space allowed heterosocial exchange within a supervised environment, a brand of amusement that differed considerably in reformers' minds from neighborhood recreational sites such as dance halls and popular theaters.[102] By structuring who joined whom in this interaction, the second hour also enacted a gendered performance of decorum. Young men assumed the active, mobile subject position of gentlemen by calling upon a stationary group of young women who waited to receive them.

The scant material documenting these early days makes it difficult to know what mixture of ethnicities populated the children and young people's clubs. Whatever the representation within these groups, the formation of a network of classes entirely for Italian girls was one noteworthy development. Friday's "girls" clubs did not include Monday's "Italian girls"; the latter were marked with a separate identity distinct from the unmarked generic category. Initially begun in 1890 through a collaboration with Signor Mastro-Valerio, the group reportedly "sewed, played games, and danced," a curriculum that was reduced to sewing and calisthenics in 1891 and finally only to sewing in 1892. Descriptions of the Italian girls reflect the mix of stereotypes with which hereditary Americans perceived "the darker race."[103] At times they perpetuated the image of the low intelligence and uncleanliness supposedly endemic to the peoples of southern Europe. "Sometimes they take a bath when they can be convinced of the beauty of the porcelain tubs, and clean clothes are talked about as a desideratum."[104] On evolutionary chains that placed both children and Italians at the lowest points on respective hierarchies of individual and society, the figure of the Italian child was a near redundancy. Other times, perceptions could flip into the romantic language of one mesmerized by the exotic appeal of an alien people.

> [A local Italian girl] is the most bewitching thing you ever saw. Sr. V. says you could light a match at her eyes and her hair is jet black and curls so tightly that it sticks straight out. I am going to have Jenny Dow try to get a photograph of her. She wears long gold

drops in her ears, like this >I< they glitter through her hair. She is
four years old. We never can get a picture of those eyes—never.[105]

Preprofessional training as seamstresses can only partially account
for the difference in the range of activities offered the "girls" versus
the "Italian girls." Financial hardship prompted Hull-House teachers to change their focus, for the "Italian girls in the sewing classes
would count that day lost when they could not carry home a garment."[106] Dancing or bouquet making might have seemed frivolous
activities to those who could afford little leisure time. Thus, the
domestic and Froebellian principles of "occupation" braced against
the economic location of those who had different notions of utilitarian activity.[107]

At the same time, close contact with Italian children—and
friction-ridden confrontations with the stereotypes placed upon
them—allowed settlers to gain a new vantage point on the racist and
economic impediments to cosmopolitan exchange. Often non-
Italian neighbors harbored their own prejudices against sending their
children to mix with Italians. "A German parent came one morning,
& demanded the removal of *all* the 'Italienische Kinder' on account
of they're being so dirty, & having bugs. She explained this to us, &
said that, if she were in our place, she wouldn't let any of them stay;
that they were *all* that way."[108] Starr told her sister Mary of another
"desperate season" involving a wealthy woman named Mrs. Hoswell
who tried to arrange a cross-class encounter for her children and
those of the Hull-House neighborhood. She "wanted 25 children for
Christmas *day*, & seemed to incline to Italians." When the Italian
parents refused to allow their children to leave on Christmas, and
when Mrs. Hoswell refused to alter the terms of invitation, Starr was
frustrated.

> I felt like saying, "Diavolo!?" several times. People will have to
> learn the poor sometimes have the same parental feelings that
> they have. Our remarkable "methods" that they are fond of com-
> plimenting consist chiefly in conforming to the dictates of these
> common sentiments of the race. The truth of the whole matter is
> that Mrs. Hoswell is doing all this for the development & im-
> provement of her own children.[109]

But the Italians "wouldn't do it," concluded Starr's chronicle of this
effort in antiutilitarian antisociability, "& for my part—I rather
respect 'em."[110] Succinctly summing up the myopia of benevolence,

Starr worked to placate a wealthy woman (and potential donor) convinced of her own generosity. In trying to convey the feelings of the Italian poor—"these common sentiments of the race"—she argued for the importance of human relationality, using the same evolutionary language that hierarchized racial groups here instead to argue for their commonality. Thus, experiential contact with neighbors who endured the prejudice of charity could in turn reform the settlers themselves, eventually stalling their own impulses to indulge class and cultural stereotypes of people they came to "rather respect."

The logistical and curricular fundamentals of Hull-House's social clubs underwent considerable change. As young people from the neighborhood increased, they formed themselves into an everexpanding list of groupings, named after historical, mythological, and settlement figures such as Lincoln, Ariadne, and Henry Learned. Meanwhile, residents worried that this proliferation caused not only a problem of space but also one of discipline and pedagogical im-

A coed field trip with one of Hull-House's later young people's clubs; a younger sibling or two was often brought along for the ride. (*Photo courtesy of University of Illinois at Chicago, University Library, Jane Addams Memorial Collection, Wallace Kirkland Papers.*)

pact. Accordingly, in 1895, they "decided to urge all clubs to take up some work in addition to social entertainment."[111] In 1897, they instituted a set of rules that prescribed the character of their activities and required "at least one lecture a month."[112] Within the liminal continuum of "not quite classes not quite clubs," the 1897 decision thus emphasized the former, making explicit the pedagogical undercurrent behind the rhetoric of neighborhood sociality. Finally, early practices spurred various lines of activity where children were the animating motivation, focus, and reason for being. Moving from the idealized miniature of the Victorian era to the racial recapitulator of the Progressive Era, child development rationalized everything from public school to labor reform, from street cleaning to public housing. At Hull-House, their demands initiated the 1895 erection of the Children's Building—a three-floor structure that relieved the mansion's drawing room of the kindergarten. Later, more complex and scientifically inflected paradigms would lie behind larger structures such as the 1906 Boys Club and the 1908 Mary Crane Nursery. Julia Lathrop would eventually work from her harried settlement room to help found the first juvenile court in Chicago, later extending the settlement's field of activity by moving to Washington, D.C., as the first head of a federally administered Children's Bureau.[113] The affect of littleness—first performed amid mud-pies, white aprons, violets, and buttercups—would galvanize social movements of tremendous largesse.

Words/Deeds

When college extension courses in English history, bookkeeping, and drawing met on Wednesday evenings in the library, Octagon, and dining room, participants overheard the rustle and voices of a different kind of routinized meeting in the drawing room—the Working People's Social Science Club (WPSSC). This gathering represented one of Hull-House's first attempts to interrogate the sphere of industrial labor. As time went on and the economic hardship of the neighborhood became more dire, the issues confronted in the WPSSC forced settlers to reevaluate their methods and to extend the bounds of their local commitment. Consisting largely of working-class men, this club created a counterpublic sphere in which participants worked toward democratic solutions through deliberation, that is, "through the medium of talk."[114] Akin to Signor Valerio's intermediary function, a neighboring Englishman named Alfred Hicks took it upon himself to coordinate the grouping. His invitation informed fellow workingmen of a proposal for a "discussion" where "questions can be debated more fully than is possible in the Trades Union," adding at the end that "Miss Addams has kindly offered the use of the large room at her house, 335 South Halsted St. for the use of such a club."[115] Though Addams and other female reformers became full participants of the club, the language of the invitation rationalized the presence of middle-class females within a male homosocial sphere by casting women as retreating hostesses. The formation of the Working People's Social Science Club exemplified another spatial adaptation practiced to overcome the difficulties of attracting diverse populations—nonaffiliated spatial use. Increasingly, Hull-House came to present itself, not as a centralized organization of reform, but as an available meeting space. Later, labor and civic groups from around the city would use various settlement rooms for their meetings without calling themselves a "Hull-House" organization.[116] The invitation thus matched the deferential language of the Hull-House mission to a deferential spatial rhetoric.

The idea of creating a special sphere for public discourse on labor issues emerged in the years following the Haymarket Riot of 1886. This incident, and the subsequent trial's indictment of anarchists, provoked anxious reflection on the part of many a Chicagoan—indeed many an American city dweller—where the problems of labor now threatened to bubble uncontrollably. Haymarket left its mark on the bourgeois imaginary like no other episode in Chicago before 1886, prompting many to take awkward repressive, ameliorative, or preventive actions of all kinds. Carl Smith writes of the crisis that such disorders caused in Chicago's transforming self-identity. "The passion that characterized the discussion of the meaning of urban life in this period reveals how important the establishing of imaginative control over the city was thought to be."[117] Such passion percolated in the instituted meetings of the new Auditorium Theatre, where citizens of all classes congregated to air grievances and points of view. Following a vaguely organic theory of social control, this civic ritual ideally released mounting frustrations, expending them before another uncontrollable eruption occurred. Nevertheless, the institution of this kind of public sphere was novel for Chicago, and it made cross-class communication a conceivable phenomenon in the minds of many citizens. Implicit in such a forum was a faith in the power of deliberation itself to produce social change and, furthermore, a sense that the practice of lived democracy consisted in the public airing of multiple perspectives. It is thus no coincidence that Julia Lathrop, herself moved to social service by the memory of Haymarket, used a similar oratorical metaphor to

characterize the nature of Hull-House. "The settlement stands for a
free platform. It offers its best hospitality to every man's honest
thought."[118] Believing that there "was a further need for smaller clubs
where men who differed widely in their social theories might meet,"
the Working People's Social Science Club replicated the Auditorium
sphere in miniature.

The formation of the WPSSC also reflected Florence Kelley's
impact on the settlement. A committed socialist and colleague of
Fredrich Engels, many credited Kelley's arrival with the radicaliza-
tion of Hull-House. Known for her vast knowledge of labor history
and her intolerance of naive do-gooders, Kelley promoted participation in forums of "enlightened persons" to analyze the broad
economic dynamics of social inequity. Early attracting around
twenty-five people a night, the WPSSC moved to Tuesdays to accommodate a membership that, by 1893, ranged anywhere from
forty to one hundred. The course of the evening was prescribed.
Lecturers spoke for the first forty-five minutes to an hour, "followed
by an hour of open discussion in which all are free to join." The club
appointed a new chair each evening to call on individual audience
members who were allowed six minutes to respond or to pose a
question.[119] Lecturers came from various parts of Chicago's reform,
labor, and civil society.[120]

In 1893, Jane Addams secured a slew of international speakers
participating in Chicago's renowned World Colombian Exposition.
That year, a Frenchwoman and author named Marie-Thérèse Blanc
ventured behind the scenes of the White City to investigate the
West Side neighborhoods it uncoincidently ignored. She recorded
that "my most interesting visit to Hull House was on an evening
when the Workingmen's Club met," offering a window, not only
into WPSSC interaction, but also of Hull-House on the cusp of the
worst economic crisis the neighborhood had yet to face.[121] For while
the World Colombian Exposition brought in an onslaught of visitors in 1893, it left in its wake enormous unemployment and citywide depression.[122] Blanc attended an evening when University of
Chicago professor and settlement proponent Charles Henderson
came to speak. The evening's delegated president reportedly introduced Henderson "in a jocose tone."

> "We are told that we have with us to-night a person of great
> learning, a famous professor. No doubt he will instruct and at the
> same time amuse us." The satire is appreciated by many. Bitter
> and ominous smiles cross more than one face, then profound
> silence ensues.[123]

Noting the satire as well as the unspoken discourse with which
Henderson's interlocutors received him, Blanc continued with an
indirect report of Henderson's one-hour lecture, sensitive to a dis-
gruntled undercurrent in his audience.

> The death-like silence lasts, without the shadow of an interrup-
> tion. . . . Mr. H discusses the social problems which are univer-
> sally thrust upon the attention of the world. . . . He declares
> himself to be moved with pity for the errors of anarchy, which he
> understands and excuses, but which society cannot tolerate; he
> asks of the laborer patience, steady effort, the economy so seldom
> practiced in America, just as he asks of the rich, in order some-
> what to equalize matters, generous sacrifices which can only be
> voluntary. All that he says is very wise; but we feel, he himself
> must feel, that there is no current of sympathy between his audi-
> ence and himself. Some of the men scribble on bits of paper.[124]

After finishing, the club president mischievously acknowledged that
"you have certainly amused us" and opened the floor to responses.
Blanc recorded that a "Bohemian"—who "certainly must have read
Schopenhauer"—immediately stood to give his own six-minute discourse on the culpability of higher classes. "It may be apparently no
one is guilty, therefore we bear no grudge to any one; but what are
we to do? When you see a drunkard reeling across the street, you
know that it will not last long. . . . Well! when I see a useless man
roll by in his carriage, I feel that the same holds good for him and his
like."[125] Another furious German rose to declare "It is all very well
for professors and ministers, it is all very well for loafers to instruct
those who are killing themselves with work. . . . They know very
well that society is ill organized, and that in justice everything ought
to be changed . . . but they will not admit it for fear they should lose
their places."[126]

The Working People's Social Science Club was a separate space in
which disagreement was a sanctioned social practice. Reportedly,
only once did the entire group applaud the same speaker.[127]
Bounded temporarily within the Hull-House drawing room, the
club meetings provided an alternative setting for interactions that
may have carried more weight and consequence if enacted outside of
these four walls. As Blanc recalled, several members "offered their
hands" to Mr. Henderson after the meeting ended. "I am astonished
to see the fiery German among them. He stands for some time in a
door-way talking and arguing with the victim of his insolent out-
burst, who, like a good Christian, seems to have forgotten all the

An unnamed West-Side inhabitant, one of many working and non-working neighbors whose interests the WPSSC sought to represent. *(Photo courtesy of University of Illinois at Chicago, University Library, Jane Addams Memorial Collection.)*

names bestowed upon him."[128] Commitment to the intensity and to the provisionality of that intensity were both consistent protocol. Indeed, Addams noted how interconnected such oratorical performances were to many members' conception of political practice. "Radicals are accustomed to hot discussion and sharp differences of opinion and take it all in the day's work."[129] Only rarely did a lecturer misunderstand the social convention, and then it was a "college professor who 'wasn't accustomed to being talked back to.' "[130] Jane Addams's reference introduces the ubiquity with which members of certain political groups practiced theoretical conversation. Discursive interaction of this type was a common ritual in the culture of socialist and anarchist political groups for whom the practice of politics was coextensive with the wider theorizing of society. At the same time, such interactional codes replicated a kind of oratorical performance that was familiar to well-educated reformers. A propensity for deliberation—while derived from different political locations—thus provided a performed means of cross-class connection. A performance form whose study spread to women's colleges, oratory was also a mode available to educated Hull-House women. Indeed, women's colleges touted oratorical skill

as a necessary tool to actualize women's dreams of democratic participation.[131] Oratory thus reproduced competencies in impromptu
speech and "logical presentation" that bridged the world of the
laborer and the world of the elite. At Hull-House, it also provided an
interactional code that mediated the gender disproportions of the
space, creating a plane on which a few college-educated women and
many labor-identified men could have a conversation. Even if visitors such as Blanc recorded cross-class disagreement ("amazed that
Miss Addams allows her guests to be so ill-treated" by members of a
lower class), the forum shared an educated elite's faith and comfort
in the practice of verbal exchange.[132]

The caution of this faith, however, is exemplified in the kind of
responses the WPSSC audience crafted, responses that often critiqued speakers who substituted reformist talk for reformist action.
Even as they indulged in the six-minute pleasure and provisional
power of "talk" themselves, club members invoked words-deeds oppositions when targeting a speaker's hypocrisy. One evening, a
cabdriver took Ellen Gates Starr aside to say that he was reluctant to
listen to the pontifications of an invited speaker—William Salter—
since the same man who now spoke of universal brotherhood had
abused him a few days earlier.[133] In some cases, it was exactly the
provisionality of this public sphere that frustrated some audience
members. Speaking and responding in this forum did not in itself
change the social circumstances of a struggling shoemaker or an
unemployed cigar-maker. Nor did it always seem to change the
habitual behavior of liberal-talking reformers toward their laboring
brothers. Subscribing to a palliative belief in the "conviction that all
this rage and rancor require a safety valve," WPSSC speech too
could follow an unhelpfully organic model of social control in which
workingmen expelled their troubles linguistically only to return to
them materially.[134] Through the first decade, more kinds of economic discussion occurred in a variety of forums and with different
participants throughout Chicago. Notable conferences took place at
the 1893 World Colombian Exposition when settlement workers
gathered together for one of their first exchanges. Later, they would
organize arenas such as the National Federation of Settlements in
1895 and the 1896 "Social Economic Conference" sponsored by
Hull-House and Chicago Commons. Increasingly, affiliates left
these conferences with a hollow feeling.

> Miss Addams at the end voiced a feeling shared by many that
> there always seemed to be something lacking in mere general
> discussions of this sort; and the suggestion in the minds of many

as they departed was that this method of conferences might well
be applied next to some of the concrete problems of our city
life.[135]

Thus, Jane Addams and other educated reformers gradually came to
qualify their own belief in the power of deliberation, wondering if it
replicated the form, if not the content, of the "proselytizing" over
"practice" dilemma that they had tried to avoid. Reorienting toward
settlement pragmatism, many began to cultivate an ethics of the
"concrete," refusing to confine their effort to the arena of verbal
exchange.

As she described the final moments of the 1893 meeting of the
Working People's Social Science Club, Marie-Thérèse Blanc looked
over to the other side of the room to record an episode that negotiated this conundrum of settlement pragmatism, fortuitously marking its concretized ethics-in-the-making.

> But Miss Addams is surrounded by a group to whom she explains
> that a great stock of coal having been laid in for Hull-House, they
> can come there and buy it cheaper than at retail. The news is
> welcome at the beginning of winter.[136]

In late 1893, residents and affiliates of Hull-House had begun a coal
cooperative, one of their first concerted efforts to tackle a social
problem by "uncovering the situation and providing the legal measures and the civic organization through which new social hopes
might make themselves felt."[137] Earlier in September, Mr. Coman—
a settlement affiliate—had proposed a cooperative plan whereby
Hull-House would gather funds to purchase coal for neighbors who
could in turn buy it for below the retail price.[138] Meanwhile, the
committee overcame the costly problem of space by locating the
"coal business in the playground."[139] Thus, on that particular evening in the approaching winter of 1893, Addams could inform
WPSSC members that—in addition to providing an alternative
forum to air their ideas—the settlement also provided an alternative
method for securing heating fuel. The men responded enthusiastically; in the first week of December, "Mr. Barnes reported that the
Cooperative Coal Association had taken in $115 in about ten days
without advertising; and that handlets had now been printed for
advertising purposes."[140] As the winter wore on into 1894, Chicago
would also endure rampant unemployment and starvation.

In the midst of such circumstances, Hull-House residents had to
develop a range of spoken and material practices, sometimes directed

personally and sometimes targeted municipally. Indeed, the first half of 1894 would see laborers increasingly unwilling to adhere to the patience and thrift called for by the likes of Charles Henderson. As settlers sided more often with laborers in such disputes, this period would also see Hull-House condemned for its radicalism. The Pullman strike of 1894 succeeded the Haymarket Riot in its impression on the Chicago imaginary, an event in which Florence Kelley and Jane Addams played respective roles as socialist agitator and designated mediator. The wealthy George Pullman had reigned over a very lucrative railway industry devoted to the construction and operation of the Pullman sleeping car. In a social experiment early advertised for backhanded generosity, Pullman also built a "model town" for his employees with stringent rules that maintained Pullman's financial, administrative, and moral authority.[141] When a drop in corporate earnings prompted Pullman to reduce wages, demoralized boxcar workers were ready to strike. Led by Eugene Debs, then head of the American Railway Union and later founder of the American Socialist Party in 1901, the strike had national impact. Eventually, the federal government went over the head of Illinois governor J. Peter Altgeld, charging the strikers with violation of the Sherman Anti-Trust Act and sending federal troops to neutralize the upheaval. With Eugene Debs jailed, liberal reformers outraged, laborers unemployed, and American corporatism vindicated, the event still shortened the reign of George Pullman, who, damaged by this public refusal of his paternal benevolence, died soon after.

Throughout the strike, settlers became involved as protesters, relief workers, and arbiters. One of her most trenchantly eloquent of essays, presented at the Chicago Women's Club, Jane Addams's "A Modern Lear" adapted a familiar Shakespearian scenario to the situation. Struck by the "similarity of ingratitude suffered by an indulgent employer and an indulgent parent," Addams analogized the position of Cordelia to that of the strikers, similarly moved by a "social consciousness" obtained outside the vision of their paternalist figure. "The president of this company desired that his employees should possess the individual and family virtues, but did nothing to cherish in them those social virtues which his own age demanded. He rather substituted for the sense of responsibility to the community, a feeling of gratitude to himself."[142] Delicately noting that "the shock of disaster upon egotism is apt to produce self-pity," the Pullman-Lear story exposed the narcissistic dangers of social reform.[143] Additionally, Addams's reuse of the Lear metaphor made a telling rhetorical link between the lives of workers and the lives of white, middle-class daughters, suggesting that such kinds of cross-class and cross-gender identifications could occur in spaces like the WPSSC by virtue of a shared experience under paternalism. While gender, education, economics, and everyday sensibility polarized these two groups in so many other ways, the rhetorical alliance of Cordelia amid the spatialized alliance afforded by the WPSSC tentatively incarnated Florence Kelley's oft-touted belief that "thinking women of generation" must "cast our lot with the workers."[144]

As the Hull-House groups embarked upon their first economically formulated ventures into political activism and civic organization, they were just beginning to realize how drastically they needed to expand such measures. The same week that Mr. Coman announced the progress of the coal cooperative, a new male resident named Robert Waldo began Hull-House's own relief bureau.[145] The new agency embroiled them in yet another level of civic machination, precipitating an encounter with a man who, from their perspective, was responsible for many of the neighborhood's social and economic hardships—Alderman Johnny Powers. "Miss Addams announced that she had been honored with a visit from Alderman Powers, who proposed giving some thousands of pounds of turkey and beef to the poor of the ward at Christmas, and desired Hull-House to make the distribution."[146] The wry tone of the business meeting minutes came from Hull-House residents' evolving perception of how the corruption of civic government disabled their attempts to produce locality in the Nineteenth Ward. In subsequent settlement efforts—around sanitation or street-cleaning or community recreation—residents continually braced against ward politicians reluctant to support reform. As much and sometimes more than that of any city, Chicago politics conducted itself through the decentralized structure of "Bossism."[147] From residents' point of view, the Chicago machine behind aldermanic elections—offering city jobs and supporting deregulatory legislation in exchange for votes and money—created disastrous urban conditions in the first place. While Powers perpetuated such "boodling" structures in the hidden spaces of machine politics, he compensated with very visible palliative displays of generosity. The tone of the business meeting grew increasingly exasperated. "Moved by Miss Starr, supported by Mr. Barnes and Miss Lathrop that Hull House have nothing to do with Powers and his charities."[148] The motion certainly had emotional support from frustrated settlers; however, it denied some of their friends and neighbors immediate much-needed food. They decided to adopt a modified stance, agreeing to "furnish Mr. Powers the lists" of neighborhood names but that "the Chief" would also write "to the effect that Hull House had so much [to do] at

Christmas time that it would be well for him to distribute his
turkeys through other agencies."[149] Learning to work within and
against the mechanisms of ward politics became increasingly essential in the ensuing years. Settlers realized that their commitment to
locality could only go so far when the conditions of that locality
derived from a space outside of it. Meanwhile, as Hull-House maintained a cautious relationship with Powers in 1893, they also were
formulating their own "agencies" for the distribution of resources.
While the relief bureau went under way in early 1894, the coal
cooperative expanded to become the Nineteenth Ward Improvement Club, a body that not only secured fuel but also worked within
city and legislative structures—such as the Civic Federation and the
Municipal Order League—designed to enlarge the movement for
urban change. These groups of disenfranchised women and civic-
minded men also represented an extended cross-gender alliance that
allowed Hull-House women to participate, however indirectly, in
the exclusive arenas of male civic power.[150]

Finally, participation in civic cooperation required competencies
in arenas other than the oratorically deliberative, a reminder that the
contemporary theorizing of "cultural politics" might also require a
systemic understanding of ward politics. The Working People's Social Science Club was itself a useful, deed-centered practice—unique
for its diversity, the styles of cross-class conflict it sanctioned, its
safety as a discursive frame, and its commitment to gaining perspective on larger social inequities. The sanctioning of such views
brought condemnation from outside, prompting a Catholic newspaper to accuse Hull-House of harboring "frowsy anarchists, fierce-
eyed socialists, professed anticlericals and a coterie of long-haired
sociologists intent upon probing the moonshine with palefingers."[151]
At the same time, residents and neighbors developed other practices
and interspatial linkages to wider civic spheres—shifting in discursive medium and readjusting compentencies and targets. At their
best, all realms interacted; affiliates targeted the personal and the
structural through theorizing and organizing. The process was neither a clean turn from theory to practice nor a neat unification of
two sides of a words-deeds dichotomy. Rather all efforts—spoken
and unspoken—were practices and symbols, communicative activities whose targets, efficacy, and content shifted depending upon
differences in intention, style, arena, power, and what side of the
room a club member was on. These were also repeated lessons in
humility, as residents learned to resist a classed impulse to "stand
aside" condescendingly from the "perplexity of political machin-

ery."[152] It also meant that a settler had to endure the "sickening sense
of compromising his best convictions" in order to work collectively,
unlike Lear and Pullman, "toward a goal that neither he nor they see
very clearly till they come to it." Through such a pragmatism,
Addams wrote, "progress has been slower perpendicularly, but in-
comparably greater because lateral."[153]

Civic Housekeeping

The combination of local engagement and civic politics developed
along alternate lines of gender, class, and age with the affiliation of
the Hull-House Woman's Club. The same week that Mr. Waldo
arrived and the coal cooperative made its first report, another event
took place in the Hull-House drawing room on a Thursday
afternoon—the birthday celebration of Woman's Club president
Mary McDowell. Mrs. Alpha Fuller, a member who often threw
herself into coordinating events, wrote a song to the tune of "Mary
Had a Little Lamb" that was performed that special afternoon.

> Mary had a little Club,
> And oh! how it did grow, . . .
> Everywhere that Mary went,
> Must this Club also go.

Mary McDowell became entrenched in many aspects of settlement
life upon her arrival in 1891, taking over Jenny Dow's kindergarten
and Jane Addams's Girls Club while educating herself about the
operation of ward politics and urban reform. Elected the first president of the Hull-House Woman's Club in 1893, McDowell gained
experiences and assumed responsibilities that would ultimately pre-
pare her to begin a new settlement near the South Side's stockyards
in the late 1890's.[154] After paying tribute to McDowell's charismatic
leadership, Alpha Fuller's ditty ended with a recognition of this
club's sense of its potential.

> Ere long they'll think they own the world,
> Like many a club before it.
> Hull-House to hold its meeting in,
> Hull lots of women joint it.
> With lots of tea, and lots of cake,
> Clear is the way before it.[155]

Mary McDowell's work with this group gave her invaluable insight into the potential of women's organizing. Less than three years before this auspicious birthday celebration, what eventually became known as the Hull-House Woman's Club started, like many settlement activities, by a shared practice. The weekly time on Thursday afternoons was set aside in 1891 as "Afternoon Teas for Women," amplified only by an occasional reference to the "Discussions on Domestic Economy" that took place there. Within a year, this practice was repeated with the regularity of time, space, and people until it solidified into a more self-conscious group. In so doing, the members of the Hull-House Woman's Club also joined the burgeoning ranks of women's voluntary associations formed across the country in the nineteenth century.[156] More specifically, they became another entry on an expanding list of associated women's clubs representing nearly every major city and rural area in the country. These clubs formed into the Greater Federation of Women's Clubs in 1890 at their first national conference in Chicago, a development that no doubt influenced the course of Hull-House's neighborhood women's self-organization. Mrs. Leila Bedell, past president of the Chicago Women's Club, also came to discuss physical hygiene with the Hull-House group early in 1890.[157] The Chicago Women's Club began an active civic program in the 1870s, boasting a huge membership by 1890 with notable members such as Ellen Henrotin and Mrs. Potter Palmer. They remembered the awkward, anxious beginnings of such organizing, describing the role that seemingly superfluous practices such "afternoon tea" had in creating a safe space for initial deliberations. Hull-House's neighborhood women also felt the importance of afternoon tea as "a reason for biding a wee. Many of us mute, inglorious Miltons who had not the courage to speak our minds before several hundred in formidable array, expressed our humble opinions freely over tea-cups."[158] Such environments— "wherein one thousand thinking women absorb the knowledge which is power—power in the civic life of Chicago"—were effective too because they replicated familiar contexts and everyday performances.[159] By choosing to spatialize themselves as hospitable tea-gatherings in lieu of "formidable arrays," such clubs cited previous gender performances as a pretext to the crafting of new ones.

Hull-House's tea gatherings gleaned an early membership through extension of initial family contacts. Exemplifying the familial and filial means by which Hull-House clubs multiplied, many of the women who gathered for afternoon tea in 1890 were "mothers whose children attended the kindergarten, the cooking school or some similar enterprise in which mother's cooperation was essential."[160] Club

members' shared identity as wives and mothers stimulated much of
their early programming and discussion topics—focusing primarily
on domestic economy, the care of children, and "Sick-Room Cooking."[161] Thus, women participated in a curriculum that reinforced the
training and ideological assumptions of the kindergarten, the cooking
class, and the sewing class. While children played according to
Froebel's notions of proper child development, mothers performed in
a reciprocally constituted interspace.

The diversity of this club's membership presumably distinguished
it from other women's clubs. The Polish immigrant girl Hilda Satt
rhapsodically recalled the club's incarnation of this ideal.

> Here was a real venture in democracy. Women from England,
> Ireland, Germany, Russia, Poland, Sweden and many other coun-
> tries were members. Women who had reached the highest educa-
> tional levels and women who could not read or write sat side by
> side at the meetings. Women of wealth and women who barely
> had enough to eat participated in the discussion of the club on an
> equal basis. Each had one vote.[162]

In an earlier 1896 poem written to celebrate the club's fourth anniversary, Alpha Fuller had also exercised her literary skills to celebrate this
diversity. Her assertion, "We've Scotch and Irish, German and
French, / There's even a Judge to sit on the bench,"[163] dramatized the
club's sense of its own inclusivity even as it implicitly delineated the
boundaries of its exclusivity. The absence of Italians and Russian
Jews in the song—given the predominance of Italians and Russian
Jews at this point in the migratory history of the Nineteenth Ward
locality—meant that the club could not claim to being fully representative of local women.[164] While Satt's later account suggests the
steady incorporation of Russian and Polish Jews, if women from the
provinces of Italy participated in such early forums, they did so—
like their "Italienische kinder"—in a separate club that distinguished
"Italian women" from those women whose cultural backgrounds
allowed them entry into the generic category. Indeed, assimilation
into this unmarked group occurred concurrently with a woman's
"American" cultural assimilation. While such negotiations illustrate
the inequities of sociability within this diverse locality, another exception points to the biases built into the settlement's logic of locality itself. As racial prejudices and local economic opportunities im-
pinged on the migratory patterns of black Americans, Chicago's
West Side began an early form of urban segregation with the Chicago River all too conveniently dividing them from the Hull-House

neighborhood of "white ethnics." As an endeavor that relied on geographic proximity to enact cross-cultural exchange, Hull-House tacitly reproduced these racial inequities and, as earlier suggested, did not immediately see past the West Side's structural patterns of exclusion. As this ward's diversity changed and as early immigrants gained more of an economic foothold, Hull-House expanded the membership of the Woman's Club. However, Addams's later description of these shifts suggests that larger time-space instantiations could also be a barrier to participation.

> A club of colored women obliged to meet in the evening because they were all wage earners by day were so absorbed in the housing situation and so determined to find out why their own housing conditions were so wretched that it was impossible for the first year to interest them in anything else.[165]

Thus, the Hull-House Woman's Club Thursday afternoon schedule precluded the participation of wage-earning women, a status that—to the degree that race, ethnicity, and economic privilege intertwined—deterred women of subordinate race and ethnicities. The routinization of Woman's Club gatherings thus participated in larger classed and raced structures of temporal and urban spatialization—enabling access to those whose employment schedules allowed it, producing locality for those whose racial identity allowed their proximity in the first place.

In general, historians argue that the women's club movement followed a trajectory of increased civic efficacy, beginning with an emphasis on promoting "culture" and gradually shifting their concerns to more "scientific" and politicized efforts at reform. Others also place women's clubs' twin goals of "self-improvement" and "civic improvement" along this development.[166] Extant material suggests that the Woman's Club at Hull-House differed slightly from the model. While Roman art, Milton, and Shakespeare could be found in the college extension classes, few such themes comprised the Woman's Club discussion series. The strongest evidence of neighborhood women's participation in the cultural phenomena of "high" taste and distinction was the fact that Hull-House often scheduled weekly program of lectures and concerts on Thursday evenings. Thus, neighborhood women could stay or return to Hull-House later in the evenings for a program on birds or a concert of Beethoven, an interspatial coincidence that was perhaps strategic. For the most part, however, this group of women embarked upon a different path much earlier in its history. Mrs. Abel Hinman came to speak in

October 1891 on nutrition and kitchen efficiency. In 1892, the same year that the Hull-House tea-takers adopted their club name, the interest in domestic economy and child care expressed itself in a slightly more ambitious mission, advertising the "hope to collect statistics in regard to the comparative costs of food, fuel, et cetera." That same year they expanded into issues of public health by sponsoring a lecture on the prevention of cholera. Mixing the language of science with that of social purity, they promoted pure air, clean water, and recipes for whitewash for a sulfuric-acid-based "cure" while also warning against intemperance since "beer and whiskey drinkers become the plague's first victims." The discourse of municipal sanitation reflected the anxieties about cleanliness and disease resurgent in the late nineteenth century as Nineteenth Ward women were encouraged to "clean out the dark and damp, hidden places, burn garbage, clean cesspools, and report [bad things] to City Health department."[167] A visiting-nurses program was also one of the first neighborhood endeavors they sponsored. There were concrete, material reasons for this early emphasis. Jane Addams suggests that an epistemology of proximity made such civic-minded activities more urgent when "members were nearer to untoward city conditions than were the women who lived in more prosperous parts of the city."[168] Living on Harrison rather than Prairie Avenue, on Halsted rather than Walton Place, the effects of indifferent garbage-collection, poor plumbing, and contagious disease were a more immediate element of their daily lives, a felt contingency that spurred intervention beyond their own homes.

As women who came to understand the impact of public corruption on their domestic lives, these club members acted as West Side "civic housekeepers." A concept that facilitated women's participation in public life, this turn-of-the-century term used the language of domesticity to rationalize women's increased knowledge of municipal regulation. It would also become one of the most famous arguments Jane Addams contributed to Moral Motherhood ideology of that era. The Chicago Woman's Club—along with female-initiated organizations such as the YWCA or the Woman's Christian Temperance Union—also used the metaphor, vowing "to consider the conditions in city and state as an extension of their concern—constituting as they do the larger home."[169] In the words of Frances Willard, they sought "to make the world homelike." As a mitigator of women's fears and men's chauvinism—and as prescient response to presentist critiques of its essentialism—club women acknowledged the expediency of this discourse, "thinking that timid souls who feared that woman might get outside her sphere could

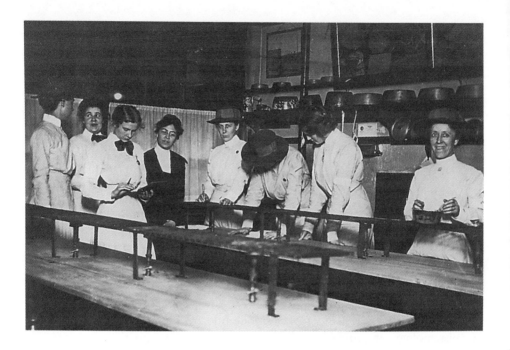

A domestic science class at Hull-House in which women learned the latest skills in sanitation and proper nutrition. *(Photo courtesy of the University of Illinois at Chicago, the University Library, Jane Addams Memorial Collection.)*

surely not object to serving in the interests of home."[170] The orientation and impetus of the Hull-House Woman's Club toward civic housekeeping differed from well-to-do Moral Mothers, however, for their move from "private" to "public" illuminates the predicament of a different class of housekeepers. Rather than using domestic arguments only to extend their moral and maternal authority over the figurative "homes" and "children" of the city, Hull-House club members increased their knowledge of the city's mechanisms in order to maintain the well-being of their own homes and children. While later suffrage activists and historians dropped some of the class-based implications of Addams's theory of civic housekeeping, many of her own reflections reinforced the connection.

> A woman's simplest duty, one would say, is to keep her house clean and wholesome and to feed her children properly. Yet if she lives in a tenement house, as so many of my neighbors do, she cannot fulfill these simple obligations by her own efforts because

she is utterly dependent upon the city administration for the
conditions which render decent living possible. Her basement will
not be dry, her stairways will not be fireproof, her house will not
be provided with sufficient windows to give light and air, nor will
it be equipped with sanitary plumbing, unless the Public Works
Department sends inspectors who constantly insist that these
elementary decencies be provided.[171]

Many aspects of Addams's famous concept can be interpreted as
a process of conversation and translation with the Hull-House
Woman's Club.[172] While some middle- and upper-class women
worked to overcome the separation between "private" and "public"
spheres, Addams reported the experience of neighborhood women
who did not have the option of seeing these spheres as separate in the
first place. Women who did not have to worry about city sewers or
the health of the milk supply had the privilege of remaining blind to
the relation between municipal affairs and intimate spaces; on the
other hand, women of a different class urgently felt the interdependent construction of public and private. Mary McDowell could not
bring herself to criticize a filthy tenement apartment when she knew
that smoke and soot were pouring into it from unregulated factories
nearby. "When I try to apply some of that 'moral force,' " she added
ironically, "somehow I don't know how."[173] Derived from the epistemology of proximity, residents found that they could not honestly
teach proper housekeeping or motherhood skills when they knew
that larger structural conditions prevailed upon apparently local,
superficially private phenomena. Indeed, civic housekeeping was a
humbling lesson in interspatiality, forcing a new perspective on the
recursive and reciprocal structuration of familial and civic spheres.

Cast within the "culture" versus "civic" opposition proposed
above, activities such as the performance of plays, music recitals, or
songs such as "Mary Had a Little Club" would be assigned to the
former, a habit of mind that relegates such phenomenon to the expendable and dilettantish aspects of American women's clubs. What
such a perspective neutralizes is the function of such rituals on the
staying power of the group and hence its civic viability. The celebration of birthdays, anniversaries, and holidays became a routine part of
how the Hull-House Woman's Club performed itself.[174] For the
club's fourth-anniversary celebration in 1896, the ever-productive
Alpha Fuller wrote and performed a poem entitled "Our Club
Names," a poem written with the intention of eliciting the group
response and identification and, as such, a telling index of the club's
self-perception. The opening lines, for instance. "Well, Here we are,

and did you ever see, / A happier band of women than we," recursively
reflected and constituted the feeling of being a "happy band." As the
piece continued, Fuller acknowledged the less privileged backgrounds
of its members, perhaps consciously distinguishing it from the Chicago Women's Club.

> One thing will strike you as rather funny
> There's few of us that have very much money . . .
> But we have resources you've never thought about,
> I'm sure the world can hardly get along without.
> Just listen while I tell you some things
> And you'll begin to wonder why we don't grow wings.[175]

Fuller played with the double entendre of members' last names,
using other meanings and associations to construct a narrative
around this happy band.

> We've plenty of sky but only one Starr,
> And that never fails us so nothing can mar . . .
> A Birch and a Plant we did lately receive,
> If our Shauer comes often they'll thrive I believe . . .

The technique had performative efficiency, for it documented each
person's participation in a larger collective as she waited to hear her
name and to hear it incorporated into their shared story.

Despite internal club performances that reflect the affective bonds
created for club members themselves, Hull-House civic housekeepers
more often deemphasized this "self-expressive" component. The language of self-improvement rang hollow in a context that positioned
women as the vehicle for, not necessarily the recipient of, social
betterment. Consequently, the Hull-House Woman's Club and the
discourse of civic housekeeping more often embraced women's deferential relationship to the figuration of a city collective. Their spatialization within Hull-House further materialized this role as public
nurturers and specialists in the operations of relationality. By 1898, the
Woman's Club membership had increased, its activities and diverse
methods formalized by a constitution. By 1902, the Woman's Club
formed six subcommittees and by 1909, eleven. In between this expansion and self-division, the Hull-House Woman's Club became geographically diffuse. The breadth of their interests meant that its members' influence could be found in every arena of the settlement,
whether administering its library, teaching in its domestic science
classes, raising funds for a public bath, or volunteering their time in

the settlement's nursery and kindergarten. By 1896, they performed many of these maternal services in the Children's Building, a building funded by Mary Rozet Smith's family to house children's recreational activities. After moving from the drawing room to the 1899 Auditorium, the club relocated again in 1905 when then president Bowen donated funds to construct a separate Woman's Club Building (most often referred to as Bowen Hall). The practice that began with afternoon teas, moved to talk of home life, expanded into discussions of municipal politics, and later diversified into a host of civic practices thus finally received its own architectural symbol. True to its heterogeneous membership and mulitasked pursuits, the building—one of the last buildings constructed on the Hull-House block—would house a variety of activities besides Woman's Club meetings.[176] As lectures, protests, and children's theatricals flooded into the building, civic housekeepers continued to "move a chair or two," enabling the many diverse functions and affiliations that the settlement maintained. The tacit genealogy of such Woman's Club practices will emerge and recede throughout many portions of this book. I find further that the self-deflecting diffusion of such gendered tasks matches their categorical diffusion in the Hull-House archives, for their efforts and achievements constantly exceed the file marked "Woman's Club." That the records of these women's work appear sequestered in so many other files testifies to the difficulty of archiving a support system. The bounded conventions of the historiographical object brace against the latency and elasticity of public housekeeping.

Such lines of activity, later redirected, formalized, or abandoned, ultimately led to the Hull-House Association that Oprah Winfrey supported over one hundred years later. The daily history of early Hull-House mixed plans, emotions, money, hopes, habits, frustrations, and amusement, evolving out of robust and unequal interactions between residents and neighbors. Out of these sub rosa creeds and vexed socialities, schemes emerged. Often each responded to the perceived hardships of particular targeted groups—especially immigrants, children, industrial workers, and women. In different rooms and on different nights of the week, residents and neighbors enacted complex negotiations of ethnicity, age, class, and gender through weekly social formations that ultimately anticipated the formations we now associate with public welfare. They also increasingly faced resistance to this alternative social vision. "What people like to call 'charity,'" quipped Ellen Gates Starr, "is far more popular than the cardinal virtue of justice."[177]

The present-day Hull-House Association is not located in the former Hull-House neighborhood. Instead, the "location" of the association is diffused, with one headquarters in the financial district and an administrative site farther north on Broadway. Other branches appear in different neighborhoods such as Albany Park or Rockwell Gardens and interact with different "targeted" populations. Such places implicitly (if alternatively) re-member the history of Hull-House. Without replicating the form of self-conscious modern memorial, the HHA's teen clubs, after-school programs, and day-care facilities function as partial *milieux de mémoire* of the settlement's connection to juvenile development. While such organizing and socializing often happens quietly and without remark, it can sometimes find itself embroiled in abstract debates about the nature of public welfare, about the role of volunteerism, or about the difference between Hillary Rodham Clinton's "village" and George Bush's "thousand points of light." The HHA newsletter displays photos of teen mothers, of community gardens, and of the surrogate grandmothers of Grandma, Please, an interspatially reciprocal program that pairs homebound senior citizens with "latchkey children" for after-school conversation.[178] The newsletter also announces a number of fund-raising efforts adapted to the lifestyles of potential Chicago donors—an annual HHA golf outing or the Friends of Jane Addams for young professionals.[179]

Other legacies are more selectively restored. The HHA espouses the principle of "neighbors helping neighbors," despite a coterie of volunteers and professional social workers who have not "settled" as inhabitants in the neighborhoods served. Any HHA involvement with the labor movement—that is, an affiliation such as the Working People's Social Science Club—is not advertised. As such, it reflects the developing separation between labor and American welfare movements over the course of the twentieth century.[180] Finally, two years after Winfrey's much-publicized announcement, the Harpo–Hull-House union had disintegrated, with five of ten families dropping from the program and Winfrey withdrawing remaining funds. There was much speculation about what went awry; some attributed the failure to "the lives of the poor [that] are so chaotic and infused with a 'mind frame of entitlement' that they defy even programs specifically designed to overcome these obstacles."[181] The language of entitlement—used one hundred years earlier to describe the detached and neurasthenic mentalities of overprivileged young people—was redirected to a new object, exclusively used to psychologize the problems of the poor. Some blamed administrative overload, reporting that enormous amounts of money had been spent on the screening process and "in-home visits" (friendly visit-

ing) before the program began. Others questioned the philosophy of
the program itself, which had replaced methods derived from "the
world of social welfare" with those of Stephen Covey's *Seven Habits*
of Highly Effective People.[182] The discourse on habit—so central to
Chicago pragmatism and to Addams's sense of the intercorporeal
dimensions of social change—had transmuted into something
quite different within the highly privatized, therapeutic context of
self-help. The *Chicago Tribune* suggested that "whether that sort of
corporate program can be translated widely for such dramatically
different clients is open to question."[183] Open to question, indeed.

Chapter 3

Building: "In Bricks and Mortar"

Lately, I've been wondering about the relationship between private
and public grief and trying to figure out if there is any political
agency in public grief for women.
—Peggy Phelan, *Mourning Sex*

A goal was to create a monument that is purposefully nonmonumental, a literal representation would interfere with the act of
revealing the broader meaning of Jane Addams.
—Miriam Gusevitch, conversation with author

The Jane Addams Memorial Park was Chicago's first memorial expressly dedicated to a woman. Its creation resulted from nearly
a decade of campaigning on the part of several female civic leaders,
and its 1996 inauguration—timed to coincide with the Democratic
Convention in Chicago—would have as its mistress of ceremonies
the most public of public women, Hillary Rodham Clinton. While
other female statues populated the cityscape, these women were all
anonymous allegorical figures, stand-ins for such noble concepts as
the Spirit of Music in Grant Park or the Republic in Jackson Park.
As many Chicago newspapers reported, such "buxom, seminude"
surrogates contrasted sharply with the city statues of Abraham Lincoln or Ulysses S. Grant, who received "realistic" or "literal" representation. Walking the edge of Peggy Phelan's concern, the gendering
of Chicago's civic memory illustrated how much easier women slide
into representation as the vehicle for public memorial rather than as
its subject. When Louise Bourgeois—a sculptor with an interest in
"woman as nurturer of child and humanity" since early projects such
as *Femme Maison*—accepted the commission for the park's sculpture, she found in Addams an incarnation of her ideas and decided
that anything like a "realistic" statue or bust of Jane Addams would
be thoroughly inappropriate. She chose instead the image of the
hand, indeed several hands of varying sizes, to convey Jane Addams's
"broader meaning." Working from a passage on hands written by
Addams (one that recounts her vision of a sea of hands when visiting

The Jane Addams Memorial Park, an arrangement of midwestern greenery and sculpted stone hands located in a site off of Chicago's Navy Pier. *(Photography courtesy of Richard Stromberg, Director of Photography, Jane Addams Center—Hull-House, Chicago.)*

London's East End), this *Waltz of Hands* synecdochically represented the bodies, desires, and struggles of persons at different stages
in the life span. For Bourgeois and park designer Miriam Gusevitch,
"their variety promotes inclusion, allowing a diversity of viewers to
feel a greater sense of personal identification than is possible with the
traditional representation of a solitary hero."[1] As an allegory, the
nonmonumental monument also highlighted rather than denied its
status as a substitute, illustrating Barbara Johnson's comments on
the relationship between gender, allegory, and the public sphere.
Instead of reproducing the fiction of "immediate readability," writes
Johnson, "allegory is speech that is other than open, public, direct. It
is hidden, deviant, indirect, but also, I want to emphasize, public. It
holds the public unto itself. It names the conflictuality of the public
sphere and the necessity of negotiating these conflicts rhetorically."[2]
By choosing not to give Jane Addams a literal embodiment, the
indirection of allegorical representation thus also matched the gendered indirection of civic housekeeping, avowing the rhetorical and
partial—not simply literal and natural—construction of human
collectivity.

Upon visiting the park, I found myself lingering upon those
hands perched atop large stones in a sea of hearty midwestern greenery. In one corner, four hands locked in unity; over in another, a
single hand rested in isolation. Everywhere, detached hands of various sizes extended themselves, though it was functionally unclear
whether they were giving or receiving, offering or withdrawing.
"The final impression was not of ragged, tawdry clothing nor of
pinched and sallow faces but of myriads of hands, empty, pathetic,
nerveless, and workworn, showing white in the uncertain light of the
street."[3] Jane Addams's description of her visit among the London
poor anticipated the anxieties of a modern feminist political culture,
the other-directedness of female sentiment amid the fracturing
world of modernist subjectivity.[4] I wondered what it was like for
Louise Bourgeois to mold these sculptures, to make a hand as an
artist who works with her hands. I imagined a visceral vibration as
she shaped a finger with her own, following the curve of one hand
against the back of another as palm slid across palm and knuckle
touched knuckle. I imagined an uncanny feeling of corporeal self-
simulation as the shapes emerged, wondering which hand was animate, which more lifelike. Which hand was giving to the other?
Two little boys startled me as they ran through the park. I looked up
and out over the curving border of Lake Michigan and moved to the
side as a bicycle rode by. It occurred to me that the park and its self-
deflecting, nonliteral memorial also resisted some of the conventions

of Pierre Nora's much-maligned, modern *lieu de mémoire*. Deferring the spectator's gaze from a detached and solitary individual, it invited involvement not only as a self-conscious rememberer but also as a civic performer who could roam in the environment of pathways, grasses, and beaches in which park designer Miriam Gusevitch nestled the sculptures. The irony of this modified *milieu de mémoire*—and its use of a reversed form of allegory—is that by materially incarnating Jane Addams's philosophy it deflected attention from Addams "herself." As such, it also replicated the paradox of civic housekeeping, that the tacit conditions of its efficacy simultaneously prevent direct recognition of its influence. Concepts of allegory and *milieu de mémoire* face a similar conundrum in that both are indirect modes of remembering, the former by foregrounding the surrogated status of representation, the latter by providing the stabilizing context—if not the content—of social identity. Like civic housekeeping, both allegorical representations and *milieux de mémoire* act as vehicles for sustaining the public sphere without receiving literal recognition for doing so and without representing the "self-interests" of women who are often responsible for its maintenance.

One hundred years earlier, settlers moved in the "modern city" of Chicago to face a deleterious architectural landscape. Whether recalling a rural America or an immigrant agrarian life, many lamented the loss of rural spaces—what Jane Addams called "the immemorial village green"—where societies gathered in traditional performances of a collective identity. Their nostalgic language anticipated that of Pierre Nora, lamenting a lost *milieu de mémoire* and its stalled ritual practices. Rather than entirely capitulating, settlers tried to cultivate different types of restored behaviors and memorial performances, working to create spaces for their healthful, if altered, expression within the new architectural environments of the city. This chapter explores several of those attempts, considering how settlers reconciled the built environments of urban modernity with their hopes for human collectivity. In 1891, settlers secured money for the Butler Art Building located in the space just southeast of the Hull mansion. In 1893, they built a gymnasium and coffeehouse across a western alley directly behind the house; in 1894, they cleared neighborhood space for a local park and playground. And after the 1896 Children's House, they built a residence for single working women in 1898 called the Jane Club. Constructed to serve an array of functions, the relation between such settlement spaces and settlement social life was both interactive and intimate. New buildings provided contexts for social interactions while such socialities in turn structured the experience of these spaces. Neighbors often found their own ways of

moving, sometimes reproducing and sometimes disrupting founding
intentions. These buildings and the lines of activity performed inside
offer a window into pedagogical negotiations over culture, art, literacy, health, recreation, nutrition, home, and taste. Finally, they
continue the story of Hull-House's pragmatic acts of settling, riding
the contradictory pulls of modernist anomie and feminine altruism,
illustrating the economic, gendered, architectural, and relational
work necessary to create an urban *milieu de mémoire*.

Art and Labor

The concept of public art, one that later justified a commission such
as that of Louise Bourgeois, emerged inside different discursive and
spatial frameworks at Hull-House. While social experiments evolved,
the settlement's architectural reach expanded. Classes, clubs, lectures,
and meetings had already exceeded the capacity of the mansion's
interior, forcing the residents to rent space in the surrounding neighborhood. A Diet Kitchen inhabited a cottage on Ewing Street just
south; a small group of male settlers took flats together on Polk. They
outfitted a makeshift gymnasium from a dilapidated saloon behind
the mansion facing Polk. Later, when the constant daily activity of
young children and babies disrupted their own pursuits, residents
rented another nearby building to house the nursery. Meanwhile,
more young people clamored to join clubs than could be accommodated. "Life pressed hard in many directions," wrote Addams of her
neighborhood, "and yet it has always seemed to me rather interesting
that when we were so distressed over its stern aspects and so impressed
with the lack of municipal regulations, the first building erected for
Hull-House should have been designed for an art gallery."[5] Indeed,
Starr—the more versed in the arts of the two—also admitted that
"the question must arise whether it be at all worth the cost to try to
perpetuate art under conditions so hopeless."[6] As a young woman
extremely well educated in European and American art history who
had traveled for overseas tours and taught art to young women, Starr
wanted to make effective use of her skills and passions. Committed
from the beginning to give of "their culture and leisure and over-
indulgence," settlers' work in aesthetic appreciation began gradually.
Enacting the logic of settlement mimesis, Addams and Starr decorated
all parts of their new home with "beautiful" images, hoping that
neighbors would admire and replicate the "precept and example" of
"the message of its walls."[7] Not only did the walls of the mansion have
semiotic import, but residents displayed artistic excellence in corollary

reform spaces, even on the lowest planes of the Hull-House nursery. "The Madonnas of Raphael, in the best and largest photographs, are hung low, that the children may see them, as well as casts from Donatello and Della Robbia. The children talk in a familiar way to the babies on the wall and sometimes climb upon the chairs to kiss them." The identificatory behavior of the youngsters could be variously interpreted, of course, perhaps reflecting an impulse to imaginary play or their awe before the holiness of the chosen images. Saying instead that it simply exemplified the power of making "a truly beautiful thing truly beloved," the generalization elided religious and aesthetic responses.[8] The easy alignment reflected a lingering Victorian idealism in which art and religion each functioned as the other's means of moral uplift and access to the beautiful. The nursery also fueled the fixation on the figure of the child as a unique object of moral and aesthetic reform.

Edward Butler was one of the many Chicago businessmen and philanthropists Jane Addams contacted in the early years. He was enthusiastic about the idea of backing an art gallery, being "fond of

The first "addition," the entrance to the Butler art building allowed access both to the street and to the courtyard it formed with the original Hull mansion. *(Photo courtesy of the University of Illinois at Chicago, the University Library, Jane Addams Memorial Collection.)*

pictures himself."[9] In 1891 (and despite its symbolic name), the
longevity of Hull-House was still uncertain; Helen Culver had
agreed to only a four-year lease of the property. Nevertheless, Butler
agreed to pay the four thousand dollars necessary to transform a
nearby livery stable into a permanent building, "calling the gift a
donation of $1000 a year" from 1891 until 1895.[10] The decision also
marked the beginning of a long-term relationship between Hull-
House and architects Irving and Allen Pond.[11] Supporters of Addams
and Starr's initial scheme in 1889, these two brothers had moved to
Chicago a few years earlier to begin an architectural practice, seeking
to unite their classical design training with their reform-minded
social values. In an interspatial echo of Toynbee Hall, they borrowed
the style of its Queen Anne architecture, designing brick buildings
like the Butler with large, wrought-iron windows and restrained
wood ornamentation in its interiors. While social theories espoused
the form of the quadrangle as the ideal materialization of equitable
democracy, settlers resisted its feeling of enclosure, choosing to ori-
ent the buildings outward toward the neighborhood rather than
facing inward upon each other. Though the gallery's placement
directly on Halsted in front of the mansion left less room for a
mediating space between the settlement and street, its doorway faced
the Hull mansion's courtyard rather than the thoroughfare, a spatial
compromise between the enclosure of the quadrangle and the openness of the public street. Hull-House affiliates could see and converse
with each other across the mansion and Butler entrances, creating a
provisionally intimate social dramaturgy between the two buildings.

In many ways, the addition of the Butler Gallery enacted the
overdetermined problematics of cultural philanthropy; a more elite
class gave based on their own notions of what the less privileged
needed. Within the context of Chicago's developing cultural institutions, that argument is somewhat reductive. East of the Nineteenth
Ward and along the lakeshore, Chicago was rapidly undergoing a
transformation in its cultural life. Set on redefining Chicago's identity, the prosperous elite of this midwestern city financed new
sites—such as the Art Institute and the Auditorium Theatre—to
counter its association of cultural backwardness and industrial proliferation. Charles Hutchinson—board president of the Art Institute—was one of the most powerful ideological and financial proponents of this move. Arguing from a position of moneyed privilege,
Hutchinson believed that the arts—"the harmonious expression of
human emotion"—had a role to play in quelling the spiritually dis-
abling by-products of materialism and capitalist greed.[12] It seemed,
however, that Hutchinson's statements on the ennobling impact of

art did not extend beyond the confines of a certain class.[13] As an antidote to overaccumulating materialism, it was administered mainly to those who could afford to be so spiritually and emotionally disabled. Confounded by the absence of comparable cultural spaces in their neighborhood, feeling that immigrants, the poor, and working-class laborers had as much right to a cultural life as anyone, residents perceived the formation of an art gallery inside the Nineteenth Ward as rectifying an urban inequity.

Settlers could appeal to an increasing body of social and aesthetic theory to justify their endeavor, and the writings of John Ruskin and William Morris provided ample grist. Reacting against the ravages of industrialization and urbanization, Morris and Ruskin theorized the importance of the arts to the life of "common" men.[14] Though the former emphasized a concern for industrial laborers more than the latter, they both promoted the ideal of the craftsman as a means of returning a lost sense of wholeness and of promoting a universal fellowship of shared creativity and production. When Samuel Barnett—the warden of Toynbee Hall—came to speak on "Popular Arts Exhibits" at the opening of the Butler Building, he expounded upon the integral role of Arts and Crafts philosophy in propelling the Toynbee experiment. Over the years, settlers came to realize that the nature of the relationship between the common man and the arts could be cast several ways. Did it mean that the arts should be brought to the life of common people? Or did it mean that the arts should arise from common life? Perhaps only half-consciously, the initiators of the Butler Gallery followed the first model. Starr and Hull-House affiliates organized exhibits of works already designated beautiful and artistically valuable by elite harbingers of taste. The schedule boasted oil paintings by "Corot, Cazin, Watts, Davis, etc." and "a valuable collection of etchings and engravings." All of these pieces were donated by prominent men in Chicago's cultural institutions—Charles Hamill, Charles Hutchinson of the Art Institute, Reverend Frank Bristol, and Edward Butler himself.[15] The exhibit room, housed on the second floor of the building, also replicated the display techniques found in the museums of Michigan Avenue. The lighting and layout of the room ensured that each work received its own site and focus with one or more feet of space between each piece, set off to elicit the reverent gaze and quiet contemplation of a classed museum protocol. The exhibit room's location on the second floor and an initial absence of chairs—the former delaying its accessibility, the latter discouraging visitors to linger and talk—further structured a more restrained manner of social interaction.

Cultural historian Neil Harris has written that "[t]he relationship between the museum and that elusive phenomenon labeled public taste has always been problematic . . . [and] exists in an unspecified limbo."[16] The issue proved most precarious for settlers promoting a museum for a marginalized public on the city's West Side, and the conflicted rhetoric surrounding the Butler matched these contradictions. Sometimes Starr, like so many other supporters of the arts, would revert to the tautological statements and goals that so often justify aesthetic education—referring to the importance of developing an aesthetic appreciation by describing it, measuring the impact of aesthetic education by recounting instances of aesthetic appreciation. One ambivalence vacillated between the characterization of aesthetic appreciation as "natural" or as "cultivated." Starr's attribution of naturalness justified the Butler Building in the first place.

> [W]hen one sees how almost miraculously the young mind often responds to what is beautiful in its environment, and rejects what is ugly, it renews courage to set the leaven of the beautiful in the midst of the ugly, instead of waiting for the ugly to be first cleared away.[17]

Certainly, her own interpretation of the interaction between nursery children and Della Robbia casts aligned with this view. When it came to fulfilling the desire for beauty at the Butler Building, however, Addams and Starr often turned to a different set of assumptions. Their exhibitions advanced the simultaneous belief that one needed to cultivate this natural desire, to learn how to be artistically fulfilled. Discussing the "limited space" in the Butler exhibition room, an "effort has been made to show only pictures which combine, to a considerable degree, an elevated tone with technical excellence."[18]

> There is an advantage on the side of a small exhibition carefully selected, especially to an untrained public. The confusion and fatigue of mind which a person of no trained powers of selection suffers in passing his eyes wearily over the assortment of good, bad, and indifferent which the average picture exhibit presents, leave him nothing with which to assimilate the good when he finds it, and his chances of finding it are small.[19]

The image of an untrained spectator with little chance of "finding the good" in the midst of the "bad and indifferent" differed from Starr's previous model of the city child spontaneously responding to the beautiful and rejecting the ugly.

Such contradictions illustrate the ease with which dissimilar positions about the nature of art could be held simultaneously. The arguments occasionally repressed the biases of class and culture that influenced varying definitions of beauty, relegating a variety of cultural production to the periphery and attaching a moral judgment to instances of uncultivated taste. Addams and Starr's references to the "training" and "powers of selection" of the neighborhood public also represent their investment in what Pierre Bourdieu has called "aesthetic distinction" where the reception of art is governed not by its content but by the manner of its execution. Thus, they considered attention to decisions of line, color, orientation, and depth a more valuable strategy of reception, one opposed to a "naive" reading of what a painting represented. Constituting a field of cultural capital by focusing on the *how* rather than the *what* of the cultural world, such powers of distinction value indirect discernment over "immediate readability," an emphasis that Bourdieu links to class privilege. In actuality, residents' stance on the value of figurative and literal reading had a functional, if unself-conscious, flexibility. While linking formal analysis to moral reform in certain instances, they also celebrated nursery children's literal and "familiar" responses to Madonnas and Donatello casts. Later, when advocating for picture hanging in Chicago public schools, their suggestions employed a principle of literality. "There should be pictures of birds, flowers, trees, and animals. Older children should have, in addition, pictures of men and women truly great and lovable."[20] Thus, the concern with technique, form, and figuration—the *how* of representation—shifted depending upon the nature of the *what* represented; when the aesthetic object represented the natural world or "truly great" men and women, immediate readability was just fine.

The 1894 Pullman strike erupted three years after the opening of the Butler Gallery. Provoked into a new class consciousness, Ellen Gates Starr began to revise her ideas in an essay entitled "Art and Labor" in 1895. Her treatise drew from values instilled by her own background in art history, from labor politics, and from her insights as a six-year veteran of settlement life. In pockets throughout the essay, she turned to evolutionary categories to support a partially class-based presumption, arguing that art in education "is a decision as to whether the mass of the people shall be barbarian or civilized."[21] At other points, she took a new approach to Ruskin and Morris, for debates with the Working People's Social Science Club disposed her to hear differently the critiques of these two thinkers. "If [great art] has reached higher than the common life, it has done so only by rising through it, never by springing up outside it and apart from it."[22] While the early curatorial decisions enacted a different model, Starr now espoused a more participatory paradigm, one where art became less an exercise in uplift than a vehicle for creative agency. The Marxist-derived term in Starr's essay title—"labor"—prompted a differently valenced identification with William Morris's interest in working conditions. The concept of unalienated labor spurred her theoretical reorientation from the artistic spectator to the position of the artistic laborer. Now Starr maintained that the function of artistic practice was to provide an outlet for a healthy, connected work process.

> It is only when a man is doing work which he wishes done, and delights in doing, and which he is free to do as he likes, that his work becomes a language to him. As soon as it does so it becomes artistic. Every man working in the joy of his heart is, in some measure, an artist.[23]

Redefining art as the product of unalienated labor, maintaining "that no man can execute artistically what another man plans," she posited the creative process as an alternative to industrial work habits.[24] The argument also indirectly politicized the discourse of Froebellian "occupations," linking the necessity of children's "self-activity" to that of the working-class laborer, adapting a child-centered reflection on psychic and physical integration to a general theory of mankind. The tragedy of contemporary society, she wrote, was that it did not provide the material or social conditions that allowed such ideal creativity to flourish. Instead, the "pain, ugliness, gloom, sorrow, and slavery" of adults and children living in the midst of tremendous hardship precluded any efforts at imaginative work and development. Furthermore, bourgeois consumption patterns maintained these conditions; "we have believed that we could force men to live without beauty in their own lives, and still compel them to make for us the beautiful things in which we have denied them any part."[25] Newly radicalized by her involvement in the Pullman strike, attuned to the interdependence of production and consumption via her conversations with Florence Kelley (eventual secretary of the Consumers' League), Starr brought an analysis of systemic inequity into the realm of aesthetics.

Starr's new discourse on the nature of art also interacted with pragmatism's emerging frameworks on the nature of labor and the nature of the child. As colleagues of William James, Hull-House affiliates John Dewey and George Herbert Mead were already preoccupied with the physical underpinnings of cognition, specifically the "tactile sensations of ideas" informing works such as James's *Principles of Psychology*. Mead sought to construct a physiological psychology that would reintegrate the material and the intellectual, arguing against rigid Cartesianism to say instead that "thinking represents the activities of the body."[26] Dewey, similarly preoccupied, tried to incorporate such values into a theory of child pedagogy and called for the integration of art and labor into a kind of *delighted doing*. Discussing these ideas over the Hull-House dinner table while Dewey's children literalized them in the Hull-House kindergarten and art studio, Mead and Dewey found themselves at a site where issues of labor, child development, and artistic practice converged. They joined William James and other settlers in avidly supporting the industrial-arts and manual-education movements, arguing that the "unity of head and hand" created a "keenness of intelligence" unavailable in the detached and divisive realms of traditional classrooms and occupational spheres. Indeed, the trope of the "hand"— noble, multiply significant, secretly intelligent—appeared in their statements both philosophical and polemical on the epistemological necessity of healthful human embodiment (a trope that gives Louise Bourgeois's 1996 sculpture another layer of resonance).[27] Initially, practical arts and manual education were an antidote to a rising middle-class anxiety, often redemptively integrated while sequestered from the urgency of economic hardship.[28] The uprisings of the labor movement called the bluff of such philosophical questions, however, provoking pragmatists to align the political with their critiques of the metaphysical. Within a philosophical discourse that tried to link the struggle over labor and education to a revision of the human subject, the restorative tactility of artistic participation was both the means and the end of its achievement.

Hull-House had already advertised drawing classes several evenings a week during its first two years. Led in different seasons by an array of settlers and volunteer teachers, the class usually met in the dining room of the mansion, a scheduling decision that made for a backlog of eager students in the doorway as residents hurried through their evening meal.[29] Members of the kindergarten and children's clubs also performed such creative activities in the parlors, porches, and courtyards every afternoon. The new Butler Building allowed these and other classes—painting, sculpture, watercolor— to continue in a separate space with fewer disruptions. By 1892, the fine arts program was primarily under the direction of another settler, Enella Benedict, a woman who another resident described "in her effacing dress, like a Holbein print, her hands busy, her tongue silent."[30] The delegation of art management to a single person facili-

A later Hull-House drawing class conducted outside in a nearby alley. *(Photo courtesy of University of Illinois at Chicago, the University Library, Jane Addams Memorial Collection, Wallace Kirkland Papers.)*

tated the integration of art with the larger ideals of the social settlement. Later, Benedict would change the function of the Butler's yearly exhibits, organizing them to display the artistic work produced by her neighbors rather than to import aesthetic "harmony and reasonableness" from outside. Like many other civic housekeepers who contributed so intensely to the settlement's operations of relationality, Benedict spent more of her time working and teaching in studios than she did writing and publicizing.[31] As a lifetime resident, however, she was a symbol of continuity to many a neighbor. It was she, for example, who set up the easels so that John Dewey's children could incarnate the healthful integration of art and labor.

With the arrival of Enella Benedict combined with changes in her conception of neighborhood efficacy, Starr took on new aesthetic projects. Having learned her early lessons in neighborhood visiting, Starr knew that there were limits to the influence Hull-House could have from within its four walls. She thus began another interspatial innovation by founding the Chicago Public School Art Society in the 1890s. Upon visiting the public schools in her neighborhood where children (ideally) spent most of their day, Starr found the classrooms in these structures "barren and repellent." She decided to raise funds to decorate the school walls in the same way that she and other residents had decorated the walls of the Hull-House nursery. While securing donations of "beautiful and suggestive" paintings and casts, she acquired knowledge of the civic rules of the school system.[32] Here, two forums—educational and aesthetic—unified to mutual benefit; each became the solution to the other's problem. The former needed a "suggestive" means of achieving its pedagogical mission, while the latter need a systemic means of dissemination. By 1895 "good sets of pictures and casts for several schools" had been provided for "the schools nearest Hull-House, and one or more into five public kindergartens."[33] Such pictures and casts were mounted in well-traveled hallways following the codes of display found in the Butler art exhibit.

Just as artistic practice at Hull-House exceeded the Butler, so the practices of the Butler exceeded the category of artistic practice. Changing the analytic orientation on the Butler from a question of art ideology to a consideration of daily practices opens the door to the more interspatial flexibility. While the second floors of the Butler housed the exhibit and drawing room, its first floor was fitted up as a public reading room, a formalization of a practice begun in the receiving rooms of the Hull mansion. Just as Addams and Starr deliberately hung pictures on the walls of their home for public perusal, so they also opened their book collections and magazine subscriptions, making accessible a variety of reading materials throughout the house. Cultivating reading as another form of settlement mimesis, Hull-House began lending books in 1889, eventually delegating the responsibility of tracking the loans to Anna Farnsworth, who combined this responsibility with her greeting duties.[34] Meanwhile, several civic-minded people in the center of Chicago were beginning to coordinate a public library system. While centralized in a downtown building near other noteworthy cultural institutions, the library gave organizers a mechanism for distributing books to various branch stations throughout the city. In so doing, the library compensated for the relative inaccessibility of the central building by dispersing its resources.[35] The "library" was thus not only an isolated space but a dispersed practice. By incarnating a concept of the "public" with such spatial rhetorics, the organizational structure dovetailed effectively with

Hull-House's local literacy efforts on the city's West Side. Joining forces in 1891, Hull-House became a branch station of the city public library that supplied the first floor of the Butler with four hundred books, sixty periodicals, and the services of two librarians.[36] The selection in the reading room varied, offering not only classic texts in English but also immigrant newspapers of various nationalities. Its location on the first rather than second floor of the Butler Building created a feeling of accessibility, allowing neighbors to walk directly into the space from the entry rather than solemnly to mount the stairs. Eventually, the size of the collection combined with Hull-House's increased spatial needs prompted the Nineteenth Ward branch to move from Hull-House to a neighboring block. Not only did the move allow the settlement a more variegated use of the first-floor space, it also marked one of many times that an endeavor initiated at the settlement would shift responsibility to municipal organization.[37]

While some neighbors frequented the Butler Building for art exhibitions, others for drawing classes, and others for library privileges, the site had still a variety of other associations for neighbors depending upon their work schedule, gender, age, or ethnicity. For the forty-eight weeks out of the year when there was not an art exhibit, the Butler exhibit room housed a variety of college extension courses in the evenings—including American history, Amalie Hannig's needlework class, and Florence Kelley's course in elementary German. Meanwhile, on Monday nights after 1891, the Hull-House Debating Club came to occupy the exhibit room, situating them even farther from the female Social Club. The expanded gendered segregation thus forced the young men to perform a larger anticipatory walk when they "joined" the young women waiting in the Hull mansion. And while drawing classes were held in the studio some evenings, other nights it was the location of Starr's Shakespeare class, Miss Stone's chemistry class, or Mr. Comstock's electricity class. Meanwhile, children's social clubs burst from the cramped accommodations of the mansion, taking over all corners of the Butler Building each weekday afternoon.[38] Thus, Hull-House's interspatiality persisted. The nomination of the Butler Art Building did not determine practices enacted within it anymore than did the names of the drawing room, dining room, or library in the mansion.

In some ways, the Hull-House stance on aesthetics neatly sets up Bourdieu's critique of the relationship between art and class.

> The aesthetic disposition, a generalized capacity to neutralize
> ordinary urgencies and to bracket off practical ends, a durable

inclination and aptitude for practice without a practical function, can only be constituted within an experience of the world freed from urgency and through the practice of activities which are an end in themselves.[39]

What settlers did not accept, however, was that artistic activities inevitably fell into the category of nonutility or impracticality. Rather they posited creative activities as a human right—central rather than peripheral to healthful development and collective expression—and used that belief to argue for changes in social conditions that would allow them to flourish. Settlers and fellow pragmatists came to locate the benefits of aesthetics in the labor of participatory production, not only that of readerly evaluation. While such a position could lead to its own conundrums, the ideals of Arts and Crafts, practical arts, manual education, and philosophical pragmatism qualify ahistorical critiques of aesthetics, notions that remain curiously blind to movements that have taken the limits of critical detachment as their point of departure. Hull-House's artistic practice would always come into contact with what Dewey termed "life itself," sometimes by encouraging children to make a sculpture, sometimes by allowing a science class to meet among the Butler's paint cans and soaking brushes. Finally, such a milieu also acutely depended upon the unpublicized work of people competent in maintaining it. It depended upon the operational intelligence of women such as Enella Benedict, who— "hands busy, tongue silent"—remembered to warm the clay, arrange the brushes, and buy the paint.[40]

(Re)creation

As a space of public recreation, the Jane Addams Memorial Park of 1996 extends, not only a genealogy of public art, but also that of play and recreation. "The boys came in great numbers to our provisional gymnasium fitted up in a former saloon, and it seemed to us quite as natural that a Chicago man, fond of athletics, should erect a building for them, as that the boys should clamor for more room."[41] So began Jane Addams's account of the lines of activity intersecting in the 1893 gymnasium. Containing a "Public Kitchen" (later the coffeehouse) on the first floor and a large gymnasium, public baths, and rooms for a men's club on the second, the building created spaces for recreation, hygiene, and alimentation for populations whose habits differed with ethnicity, class, and gender. Such differences were manifest in embodied registers—in taste (in both senses of the

word), in physical gesture and self-presentation, in standards of
personal cleanliness. Appealing to discourses of play, health, nutrition, and temperance that fused prevalent social theory and bourgeois anxiety, the gymnasium activities illustrate John and Jean
Camoroff's insights into "the implications of actual bodily experience for imagining and acting upon the forces of history. It is in this
respect that projects of physical reform become especially revealing,
for they represent efforts to rework the physical grounding of conventional realities, efforts to intervene in the dialectic of the person and
the world."[42] Unlike other social or pedagogical club endeavors,
athletic and recreational activities required more space for motion,
bodily extension, and team interaction. Gradually, as more and
more young people flooded such gatherings, residents saw fit to
refurbish an abandoned saloon and developed a modified type of
indoor baseball. Several children's clubs had also incorporated similar activities into their programming, dispersing and multiplying
recreational activities in the sandboxes of the mansion's porch or in
the kindergarten games played in its drawing room. With each
weekly repetition of each recreation class, the practice of Hull-
House gymnastics acquired the feeling of continuity even before the
building of the Hull-House gymnasium solidified it.

The athletics performed in the building both replicated and
deviated from those of larger recreational projects in the late nineteenth century. Movements such as the YMCA, the Ethical Culture
Society, and the play movement were parallel "efforts to intervene
in the dialectic of person and world." Recognizing that an increasingly dense urban environment left little opportunity for the exercise, sports, and other physical games conveniently performed in
rural areas, such reformers worked to create new urban spaces and
activities. Spurred by research into the health of routine exercise,
such efforts also coincided with child development, promoting
physical activity as a valuable outlet for childhood emotion. Ex-
pounding upon the intimate relation between the physical and
the mental, theorists of athletics and physical culture argued that
the key to reforming the latter lay partly in the manipulation of the
former. Public recreation meant, quite literally, human re-creation.
The concept of calisthenics had emerged earlier in the nineteenth
century expressly to develop a form of physical exercise that could
be performed in the smaller spaces of the city—"a park, hall, or
schoolroom"—and derived from the Greek meaning "beautiful
strength."[43] The mid-nineteenth-century physical culture movement
advocated a philosophical and practical approach to moral development by unifying the lessons of elocution (the physical apparatus

that allowed mental expression) with active exercise. Proponents such as F. G. Welch and J. Madison Watson published *Moral, Intellectual, and Physical Culture* and *Elocution, Calisthenics and Gymnastics* respectively, each discoursing with equal verve on the benefit of parallel bars and hanging rings, on "rules of conversation," on the necessity of "producing a friction of skin and circulation of blood after every bath," and on subjects as diverse as ventilation, fashion, manners, and food."[44] Later adaptations of these ideas went in several directions, sometimes by resisting the ideological homogeneity that drove earlier texts, sometimes by dividing these lessons into different specialties.

In a "commercial civilization such as ours, there is always a danger of laying too little stress upon the more virile virtues . . . which are fostered by vigorous, manly out-of-door sports."[45] The concern was voiced by a rising politician named Theodore Roosevelt in 1893, anticipating his lifelong pursuit of a naturalist, racially fit masculinity through active physicality or what he would later term "the strenuous life."[46] Writing alongside G. Stanley Hall, Roosevelt worried too about the debilitating effects of overcivilization, a preoccupation with bodily repression that he retroactively characterized as an effeminate aspect of Victorian culture and a dangerous precursor to racial decrepitude. Paralleling Hall's advocacy of mankind's reconnection to a primitive state, Roosevelt advocated compensatory participation in heightened bodily activities, vigorous recreation that incarnated the potential of recapitulation theory. New Progressive Era theorists of physical education took the hint. Prophesying a feeble future for middle- and upper-class men who were alienated from physical labor, athletic proponent George Eliot Flint's ideas were saturated with the same evolutionary metaphors.

> Now man's struggle for existence lies much more in mental than in physical competition. The result . . . man . . . is becoming metamorphosed into a mental giant and a physical dwarf. The principle of inheritance has an important bearing in physical culture. . . . It is a duty we owe to posterity.[47]

Rather than solving the classed problem of alienated "mental" labor with a shift in the means of production, Flint advocated strenuous exercise for privileged men (an athletic analogue to Arts and Crafts and manual education's quest for a displaced bodily authenticity). Moreover, the Larmarckian notion of acquired inheritance allowed him to attach racial progress to this physicality, one that stressed strength and competition over beauty and control. Gender as much as race and class anxiety drove this strain of Progressive physical culture; the increasingly public role of women spurred men to develop novel ways of performing gender difference.[48] When adapted to the urban environment, theories about the importance of "vigorous play" targeted the realm of enactment as solution to juvenile delinquency, a discourse that often exclusively equated juveniles with boys. They also positioned recreation as an embodied means of imputing and hierarchizing the primitivity of different immigrant groups. Some reformers focused less on evolutionary hierarchies, however, and more on sports and play as a mitigator of the urban inhabitant's psychological alienation. Of course, because such theories stemmed from reformers' own (much differently derived) experience of alienation, recreational theorists risked locating material reform only in the individuated physicality of the performer rather than in the economic structures that created a deleterious material environment in the first place.[49]

Hull-House's multiple uses of gymnastics and athletics reproduced and resisted such movements, sometimes by following different trajectories in the profession of physical education. Early gymnastic classes in the refurbished saloon were offered both for "boys between fourteen and eighteen years of age" and girls "between fourteen and sixteen." The age boundaries of these two clubs suggest their intermediary position between children's clubs and the "older" young people's clubs, a performed incarnation of "adolescence" just as G. Stanley Hall was giving the term conceptual ballast.[50] Both sex-segregated clubs mixed "gymnastics" and "discussion," emphasizing their transitional function between children's activities and the mixed-sex gatherings of young adults. The inclusion of a pianist only in the teen-age girls' athletic club suggests a dance-based form of recreation different from what the boys performed on other nights of the week.[51]

The creation of the 1893 Gymnasium Building coincided with the appointment of a new resident, Rose M. Gyles, as its new director. With a degree from the Hemenway Gymnasium at Harvard University, Gyles was well acquainted with theories and techniques of healthful athletics and gymnastics. Despite the anxiously masculinist rhetoric of athletics, Rose Gyles was one of a rising group of young women who trained in physical education and advocated for its restoration in city neighborhoods and public schools.[52] In the same decade, Jessie Bancroft, the director of physical education in New York's public schools, published books and lengthy articles extolling its importance in physiological stimulation, posture, and psychological power. "If the instinct for activity be unduly suppressed, it in time yields to an enforced habit, and the result is not only a motor mechanism weakened in its power, but, what is even worse, a will crippled at the very time when it is taking on its habits for life."[53] While women's involvement with physical education violated codes of proper femininity, such educators appeared somewhat less threatening when they positioned themselves as the facilitators of athletic performance rather than as its enactors. By casting gymnastics as a form of human development and reminding people of women's sanctioned role as altruistic guardians of civic virtue, women could rationalize their expertise in this field. Physical education was thus made palatable by self-allegorization. After all, the female physical educator created the conditions of healthy performance for others rather than for "herself."

Rose Gyles promptly organized an array of classes for all ages and charged fees to cover the expense of maintaining the facilities, uni-

Bloomer-wearing women during recreation classes at the Hull-House gymnasium. *(Photo courtesy of University of Illinois at Chicago, the University Library, Jane Addams Memorial Collection.)*

forms, and equipment.[54] Meanwhile, the gendering of the gymnasium followed an uneven discursive and behaviorial path. Indeed, a measure of that unevenness resides in the disconnection between verbal and bodily representation. Consider Hilda Satt's recall of her participation in these classes as an immigrant girl.

> My sister and I next joined the gymnasium. We managed to scrape together enough money to buy the regulation gymnasium suit—wide bloomers and blouse, though if anyone could not afford the suit, she could attend anyway. Miss Rose Gyles was the teacher, and she put us through the paces once a week. The gymnasium was like an oasis in a desert on Halsted Street. Hundreds of boys, who had not other means of recreation, could go to the gymnasium and play basketball till they were so worn out that they could only go home and go to bed.[55]

Indeed, young men's basketball was a very popular form of early recreation at Hull-House, spawning a team that played those of other recreational institutions and elicited a spirit of collectivity among neighbors and spectators. On April 18, 1894, for instance, residents advertised "A Match Game Between the Hull-House Team and the West Side YMCA Team," using the fifteen-cent admission to raise money for gymnasium equipment.[56] Interestingly, Satt's memoir followed a description of her participation with an abstraction that stressed the significance of athletics for boys. Echoing prevalent theories of play, she characterized basketball as an outlet for young male energy that, if sufficiently expended, left them "so worn out that they could only go home and go to bed" and thus too tired to commit delinquent activity. Despite the presence of female recreation, this kind of gendered rhetoric permeated descriptions of the gymnasium, including Addams's own earlier origin tale of "boys clamor[ing] for more room." Despite the constant participation of girls and young women, their verbal eclipse testifies to the ambivalence with which its practitioners reconciled athletics with prescriptions for appropriate female behavior. It may also illustrate Hull-House affiliates' reuse of an available boyhood rhetoric as a means of deflecting attention from the transgression performed inside.

Physical educators cultivated a heightened awareness of the interaction of person and world and, with it, an understanding of "biopower's" intimacies.[57] At Hemenway, Rose Gyles received instruction in several kinds of gymnastic techniques, some derived from the aesthetic movements of the Delsartian corpus, some adapted from the drills of military instructional technique. She also learned the complicated command sequence of Swedish systems and the method of repetition promoted in Germany's gymnasiums. Hemenway graduates developed acute insight into the vagaries of bodily habitation. Such educators knew of the "class consciousness" and "solidarity" that could be achieved when a group of youngsters enacted the same bodily movements in "rhythmic concord."[58] They possessed an awareness of how a momentary pause could elicit psychological receptivity and of how attention to rhythm solidified new gestures in developing bodies.[59] Many cultivated a highly nuanced understanding of the relationship between metaphor and embodiment, knowing how much easier it was for a child to elevate his head if he pretended to be pulled from above by a magical string or for her to inhale fully if she imagined herself to be smelling flowers. Their techniques worked to reconcile the ocular-centrist image of child performance with the child's own proprioceptive awareness of bodied space. "There must be intimately associated with the memories of sound, sign, and volition the memory of how it *felt* to do the exercise. . . . They can only feel their good posture whereas others can only see it."[60] The kinesthetic acumen of physical education thus extended the epistemology of civic housekeeping, reforming the microperformance of corporeal styles within a ludic space of public domesticity.

Exercise and play mediated also Hull-House's immigrant cosmopolitanism. Sometimes such lessons recreated self-presentational styles antithetical to those of immigrant national cultures, providing a physical means of assimilation. Other times, reformist activities could simultaneously be used as an expression of cultural identification.[61] The wrestling promoted by Hull-House gymnasium instructors for sound boyhood was simultaneously a way for Greek immigrants to perform a nationalist affiliation. In fact, the confluence between the gymnasium movement and the athletics of classical Greece could serve many ends. When Teddy Roosevelt visited Hull-House, he would make use of this connection, too, appropriating the image of Greek boys wrestling at Hull-House to his own evolutionary discourse on the origins and importance of manly, strenuous activity. Meanwhile, though someone like George Flint promoted baseball as a well-structured source of manly vigor and racial competition, Addams used a very different set of metaphors to interpret baseball's social function.

> [Players and spectators] are lifted out of their individual affairs and so fused together that a man cannot tell whether it is his own shout or another's that fills his ears; whether it is his own coat or

another's that he is wildly waving to celebrate a victory. Does not
this contain a suggestion of the undoubted powers of public
recreation to bring together all classes of a community in the
modern city unhappily so full of devices for keeping men apart?[62]

Addams's description theorized ideal play as a complex process of
mimesis, identification, and substitution. Such performances thus
laid the basis for an alternative sociality. Not coincidentally, many of
Addams's elaborations on the nature of urban cosmopolitanism appeared in her essays on public recreation. As a sphere detached from
the traditional "village green" of immigrant and rural cultures, she
argued that the modern city should provide substitute forums that
loosened the boundaries between self and other. The affiliative codes
of play and sport produced an emotional expansiveness that "fused"
the varied members of an international nation. If cosmopolitan
enactment was the goal, Addams contended, recreational performance was its form.

Despite the preference for masculine imagery in descriptions of
athletics, Hull-House does not seem to have enforced strict gender
divisions. In addition to dancing, young women participated in sports
that pushed the bounds of feminine performance, a development that
occurred despite (or perhaps because of) the fact that Hull-House did
not produce a widely publicized theory of female sports.[63] Basketball
was a popular mode of recreation for more than just Hull-House
males, for Rose Gyles also organized her group of Tuesday evening
regulars into a female basketball team. With a skilled coach and skilled
athletes, the Hull-House woman's basketball team emerged as one of
the most formidable in the city. The women were undefeated during
the 1897 season, beating the "Olivet girls team" 23 to 5 and responding to "a challenge" from the Armour Institute girls team by shutting
them out 27 to 0.[64] While their pattern of success after 1900 followed
an ideological trajectory that increasingly supported the importance
of female exercise—a discourse that became more prevalent as a signal
of the New Woman's independence later in the century—such displays of athletic competence in women were received ambivalently at
the time. The discourse of play cautiously met the discourse of gender
in a *Chicago Chronicle* article, for instance, when its author framed the
character-building role of athletics within the codes of female character. He supplemented recreational assumptions about the significance of basketball—that it "affords good exercise and plenty of
excellent sport"—with additional comments saying, "[B]ut what is
much more in the eyes of its followers, [it] conduces to beauty of form
and gracefulness of carriage." Reconciling the oxymoronic status of

the female play-er, basketball was thus a recreational activity that reinforced rather than disrupted proper female bodily comportment. The writer went further, interpreting basketball as a sport that did not overly challenge the limited aptitude of the female.

> And then it is a game girls can play. Football is too rough, baseball is an impossibility, for women never will learn to throw straight enough to become proficient in the national game. But basketball is different; it is not so rough as football, yet affords as much exercise; is not so exacting a game as baseball and still gives keenness to the intellect and develops presence of mind and self control.[65]

The final phrases invoked a materialist argument on the role of play, that certain physical enactments promoted particular kinds of mental development important for good Americans. It was preceded, however, by assumptions about women's limitations in fully achieving the keenness and precision of such ideal character. The cerebral stereotype fell easily into a generalization about women's bodily capacity; obviously, they "never will learn to throw straight." He did refer to the physical reprieve of "[c]ostumes [that] . . . are easy and comfortable, affording free play to the body and limbs." The next statement neutralized the significance of dress reform, however, saying that "[n]avy blue flannel seems to be the favorite color and material" and thus casting the uniforms within the language of fashion and gendered consumption. The gender recuperation continued.

> [A]nd when a bevy of girls clad in this picturesque garb is running, jumping, and scrambling over a long waxed floor, or upon a springy sward, the poses exhibited and the movements attained are graceful, beautiful, and beneficial to the mind and body.[66]

In these closing sentences, the writer shifted between statements about the benefits of basketball to female players and indirect assertions about the "benefits" of female basketball players to the eye of a spectator. The phrases "picturesque garb" and "poses exhibited" assumed the position of outside observer for whom such picturesqueness is displayed. The confusion in referents made it less clear whose "mind and body" found such poses "beneficial." Finally, as a loaded term in a masculinist rhetoric of racial fitness, the "competition" factor was entirely absent from the review. Thus, spectators sanctioned neighborhood women's participation in sports when they could find ways to interpret the practice through traditional prescriptions of gender.

The practices of play and athletics traveled beyond the circumscribed arena of the Hull-House gymnasium, multiplying in other spaces and mixing with the styles, codes, and gestures of other recreational forms. They also fueled another endeavor outdoors—a neighborhood playground. By 1894, Chicago was one of many cities throughout the nation that participated in the public-park movement. In response to transformations in the urban landscape brought by population increase and industrial expansion, well-to-do city-dwellers and urban architects such as Frederick Law Olmsted worried that the natural environment was being overrun by the buildings, railways, and paved streets of rising cities. Like the gymnastics movement, "[T]he initial rhetoric in favor of establishing parks within cities was built on boyhood images: The country boy had advantages that city youth also needed," while the adult male needed environments in which to reconnect with a natural past.[67] To counter this increased alienation from nature, movements sprung to construct pockets of organic matter—trees, flowers, man-made lakes, lawns, and arbors—in selected sites throughout the city. Like the move to create new cultural institutions, this impulse coincided with the construction of Chicago's civic identity. And again, like the move to create cultural institutions, the public-park movement most often confined itself to more privileged city neighborhoods, offering well-manicured strolling paths to the families of wealthy businessmen just outside of their Gold Coast and Prairie Avenue homes. Settlers of the Nineteenth Ward's high urban density recognized this inequity and joined a submovement for the creation of small civic parks in all areas of the city.[68]

While debates over the location and size of public parks carried on in the late nineteenth century, a dispute over appropriate behavior in such spaces sparked an intense controversy. For many, city parks were to be a place for quiet contemplation, casual strolls, and thoughtful viewing of publicly funded flora and fauna. The position of the park's ideal guest, therefore, was one of spectator, watching nature from designated pathways, stepping on the grass only if absolutely necessary. From such a perspective, a visitor would no more climb a tree or play a game of tag than would a museum visitor paint a picture. Indeed, the protocol proposed for both the museum and the public park resembled each other. A well-do-to couple could roam from the museum's indoor cityspace to a park's outdoor one—quietly stepping arm-in-arm, moving their heads from left to right—with barely an adjustment in pace, focus, and

Children playing around a May Pole at the newly razed Hull-House playground. *(Photo courtesy of University of Illinois at Chicago, the University Library, Jane Addams Memorial Collection.)*

bodily comportment. Meanwhile, other proponents drew from prevailing discourses on the role of play to argue for more vigorous forms of embodied participation in the city's recreational spaces. Such recreation meant that maintenance of a well-manicured vista was a near impossibility. Playing children and active sports teams would trample flowers and scare away swimming swans. Consequently, arguments between these two ideals translated into a division between proposals for "parks" and proposals for "playgrounds," each promoting geographic methods and codes of conduct to facilitate or deter one or the other.[69]

Unsurprisingly, Hull-House residents wanted their neighborhood space to be a playground. Charles Zeublin—an early affiliate and eventual founder of the Northwestern University Settlement—became one of the playground's most vocal proponents. Codes that disallowed participants to raise their voices, to engage strangers in conversation, or to transgress classed prescriptions for embodied behavior also discouraged neighborhood interaction. Not only did playground logic shun such park rules, it also promoted new forms of play technology. Like other playgrounds in Chicago, Hull-House residents planned to fill the space with "swings and other enticing apparatus" such as sandpiles, shovels, buckets, a Maypole, and a baseball diamond.[70] Ideally, the social space of the playground was also flexible enough to allow neighbors to formulate their own ways of using it, adapting preexisting forms of enactment and performance. Once installed, settlers were delighted to find that, after work "[t]hrough the summer evenings, many parents came with their children." Addams's prose later twinkled with pride when she noted, "The music furnished by an organ-grinder every afternoon often brought forth an Italian tarantella or an Irish jig with curious spontaneity."[71] Such moments of spontaneity were exactly the indigenous forms of unplanned sociality that Hull-House sought to accommodate. Pierre Nora might have been equally delighted with such moments, incarnating as they did the bodily habits and "living memory" of an urban *milieu de mémoire*.

"We are bound to sustain said committee in its negligence of clear duty." The business-meeting secretary was referring to the House Committee, the group of settlers saddled with the task of installing the "enticing apparatus" and managing the schedule of this place of memorial spontaneity. The group proved to be remiss in meeting its obligation, receiving an impatient rebuke during a February meeting that condemned "its nefarious action in neglecting to carry out the imperative communicated in writing to said committee . . . that the swings should be placed in the playground and that the playground should be opened."[72] The mechanics of creating this playground were not nearly as idyllic as the rhetoric of play itself. Civic bodies would not donate the funds necessary for a West Side space. Even after a space was cleared and the swings were installed, the matter of maintaining this public space under the ambiguities of Hull-House's private regulation became an even greater burden.[73] For an initial period, playground duty was a required settlement duty; each resident— including Addams, Lathrop, Zeublin, and others—received a weekly responsibility of monitoring the playground from six to nine in the evening.[74] Residents bristled under this added obligation, proposing in subsequent meetings to close the playground on Sundays and to close earlier on weeknights.[75] Within six months, they decided to install a local policeman, Officer Murray, as the official playground manager, trying to overcome the limits of his authoritarian status by listing him in their residents directory. Officer Murray later planted willow trees in the playground, repainted the swings, and coached a baseball team that competed against Mr. Barnes's team every weekend.[76] Thus, amid settlement headaches and valued ideals, Officer Murray symbolized another connection between the settlement and municipal administration, using the former to acquire local knowledge and indigenous support while the latter brought the playground into the sphere of civic responsibility.

Other aspects of the building continued a project of bodily reform, proceeding again from the presumed relation between the material and the mental. Such a thrust continued with more urgency in the installation of baths for public use. Few tenements in the neighborhood provided facilities for inhabitants to bathe. Most inhabitants had to heat water on the stove and fill a laundry tub or some other container with water.[77] For new settlement residents, the difference in cleanliness between the neighborhood and their previous habitats was one of the hardest elements to overcome. Differences in personal hygiene, wrote Starr, could likewise be one of the greatest inhibitors to cross-class sociality.

> I don't love my fellow man with an over-flowing fervor at this temperature, especially if he doesn't smell good, & he mostly doesn't; especially my unfortunately and hard bested fellow creature, the Russian Jew. It isn't altogether his fault poor dog. That he wants to wash & be clean is proved by the increasing numbers of him who stand waiting their turn (sit on our fence waiting it) for a bath.[78]

Appropriating an animal metaphor and stereotypical language, Addams, Starr, and their colleagues still differed from the individuating and condemnatory rhetoric of other reform movements by emphasizing instead the social conditions of urban uncleanliness. Presumably, everyone would want to be clean if they had the choice, they rationalized; it was lack of access to adequate showers, not cultural backwardness, that was the problem. For unmarried bourgeois women to open their home to prospective bathers was no small domestic adjustment indeed.[79] Besides the constant risk of impropriety, the logistical contingencies of public hygiene strained a house whose pipes were not ready for this form of civic housekeeping. "The tremendous increase in the use of water during this heat makes the pressure low, & when people are using the tubs below we can't get a stream upstairs."[80] While it did not solve all of these headaches, the opening of the first municipal bath just blocks from Hull-House late in 1893

was a welcome relief to settlement workers who—with the Hull-
House Woman's Club and the Nineteenth Ward Improvement
Club—lobbied the city council for the twelve thousand dollars
necessary for its construction.[81] Like the library and the playground,
they once again released a settlement endeavor to municipal administration, a process that increased civic interest in public welfare while
also unburdening settlers of a cumbersome responsibility. It only
happened, however, after they engaged in a personally inconvenient
and cross-culturally presumptuous form of inverted civic housekeeping. Not only did they extend domestic concerns outward but they
also reworked the functionings of domesticity inward, casting a
neighborhood playground as a task for their House Committee,
rerouting their water pipes for someone else's shower.

Despite all of these machinations over the bodily realities of
"gymnastics," they still did not encompass the range of activities
performed in the second-floor gymnasium. This space was not only
an arena for sports and exercise classes, it was also "the largest room
in the possession of the settlement."[82] As such, it became one of the
central venues in which Hull-House residents, affiliates, neighbors,
and children developed and restored their collective identity. Rather
than separating and diversifying clubs in different regions throughout the mansion and the Butler Building, the gymnasium allowed all
to fit in one room, thereby spatially solidifying a potentially decentralized membership. Whether for dances, theatricals, sports events,
Christmas entertainments, WPSSC speakers, or college extension
lectures, the gymnasium room was constantly in demand for occasions that required large-scale attendance. As a result, it was also
subject to the same diachronic interspatiality as were other spaces,
alternately housing clubs and events that activated and deactivated
its identity with shifts in people, seating arrangements, and intentional frame. There were also temporal leaks between these boundaries that confused the gymnasium's schedule, a particular source of
frustration to Rose Gyles, who threatened to leave due to the interruptions.[83] Gyles stayed, but such interspatial motion persisted. As a
compromise, residents "[m]oved . . . that the gymnasium committee
be empowered to decide absolutely all matters pertaining to the
gymnasium."[84] Gyles received a double title as both gymnasium and
space manager for all nonathletic uses of the gym. Eventually, settlers learned to welcome leaks in diachronic interspatiality. On the
night of a Christmas entertainment, a jubilant "victory of the
Hull-House basket ball team over the University of Chicago team"
seemed "to have lingered in the gymnasium through the holidays."[85]

Recreational performances thus left marks of affect and emotion, lingering histories that accumulated in a *milieu de mémoire* of strewn chairs, basketballs, and Christmas ornaments.

Oekology

As biological necessity and social construct, food is one of the most illustrative of cultural indexes. Feminist historians of domestic science place food at the center of reform, showing how issues of cross-cultural engagement, health, community, and women's attenuated relationship to society intersect around alimentation. Food literalizes Louise Bourgeois's fixation on "woman as nurturer of children and humanity," an operation that elevates woman's necessary function in the perpetuation of culture even as it can short-circuit her direct claim to its fruits. Alimentary traditions, rituals, and discourses recursively illustrate and constitute deeply held values. As a behavior that involves the incorporation of the external into the internal, eating monitors the boundaries of self and society. It can spur the most intense exclusions as some find themselves nauseous upon encountering that which others find nourishing. Food can also snap the social actor into the connective comforts of the familiar. Of course, like parallel *milieux de mémoire,* a meal's preparation often instantiates different gendered performances and divisions of labor. Moreover, a woman's ideal embodiment of a literalized nurturer can become difficult if she has other work to do—whether as a full-time settler or as a factory employee. And the role can be even harder to fulfill if her tenement flat does not have a kitchen.

Such sensibilities and concerns propelled the settlers' decision to construct a public kitchen on the first floor of the Hull-House Gymnasium Building. First and foremost, settlers hoped that a centralized means of food distribution could solve a number of perceived problems. It would lift the wasteful burdens of private domesticity from the shoulders of women, provide healthy food to a low-income population, and function as a social center for a cosmopolitan neighborhood. At the same time, the Hull-House public kitchen symbolizes another type of spatial conundrum, for to move from the top of the Gymnasium Building down to peek into the first-floor public kitchen in 1893 is also to find Hull-House reformers moving top-down in another way. Unlike the "boys" of gymnasium folklore, settlers' stories of the public kitchen (later the coffeehouse) did not begin with a description of neighbors "clamoring" for such a space. Rather what most distinguished this "undertaking" was that it was

"preceded by carefully ascertained facts."[86] An honorable appeal cer- 125
tainly, but it did not match Hull-House's rhetoric of sociability nor
settling's method of tacitly derived reform. This slightly different *Building*
generative impulse would thus begin an alternative reform story, one
more memorable for the lessons it taught the residents than for the
influence it had on Nineteenth Ward neighbors. In general, this was a
story of failed social control.

In actuality, the ascertaining of careful facts about neighborhood
cuisine came a few years after the erection of the public kitchen, a
commitment to built environment that reversed Dorothea Moore's
depiction of a settlement "growing out of growing needs." What did
precede the public kitchen, however, was settlers' general dismay at
the eating habits of the poor. The same working parents (read
working mothers) who kept their children locked in tenement apartments also relied on candy and canned goods to feed their families.
More inclined to interpret this behavior as a structural condition of
poverty rather than as a lapse in proper motherhood, settlers believed
that providing access to healthier, less expensive food was unques-
tioningly utilitarian. Alarm over nutrition focused, not only on the
poor, but also on the new wave of southern and eastern European
immigrants. Following the trajectory of many turn-of-the-century
investigations and bodily reform projects, hereditary Americans were
baffled by newcomers' styles of cooking, eating, and drinking. Starr's
reaction to Mrs. deGuido's "gravy" was far more tolerant than some
who interpreted immigrant alimentation as a sign of a lower-order
civilization. The unfamiliarity nevertheless violated reformers' commonsense assumptions of appropriate bodily habituation, and the
Italian propensity for "garlic, onions, peppers, and other spices"
disrupted the gastronomic equilibrium of settlers to such a degree
that they reflexively associated it with ill health. Not all immigrant
populations were equally suspect. In a partial invocation of model
minority discourse, Hull-House food investigator Carolyn Hunt
suggested that the Italian "might well take a lesson from his neighbor, the Russian Jew, who by long, slow cooking makes a most
palatable, nutritious dish of his chuck beef."[87] On the other hand, in
the polyglot neighborhood of American cities, reformers more often
worried that immigrants were learning poor nutritional habits from
each other.

> I recall an Italian who, coming into Hull-House one day as we
> were sitting at the dinner table, expressed great surprise that
> Americans ate a variety of food, because he believed that they
> partook only of potatoes and beer. A little inquiry showed that

this conclusion was drawn from the facts that he lived next to an Irish saloon and had never seen anything but potatoes going in and beer coming out.[88]

Concerned over the proliferation of certain forms of cross-cultural mimesis—and their ostensibly misrecognized performances of "American"—Hull-House residents hoped to share their own dining practices with misguided neighbors.

The story of the Italian equating the goings-on of an Irish saloon with the goings-on of being American presses on another public kitchen issue. Behind the concern over improper eating habits lay an attendant alarm over the drinking patterns of urban inhabitants. In the last decade of the nineteenth century, saloons were particularly prevalent in the single square mile surrounding Hull-House. The phenomenon unnerved many settlers who perceived such social spaces as unwholesome and their multiplication as an impetus to undignified, corrupt, and sometimes violent behavior—especially in men. In the national reform imaginary, excessive drinking encouraged everything from unemployment to criminality, from ungodliness to domestic abuse; saloons themselves housed prostitution and served as organizational sites for the political machines of boodling politicians. Prohibitions against drinking supported a general discourse against perceived excess, and often the language of temperance was used to reflect back on the evils of other "vices" and suspect consumption. Carolyn Hunt suggested that the Italians were addicted to spicy and garlicky food much as an "inebriate" required "strong drink."[89] Couched in a sexualized language, alimentary excess often became equated with certain national identities too easily seduced by the lure of "overstimulation." The barometer of excess of course proceeded from reformers' graduated reactions to immigrant difference, one that imputed high drama onto all that appeared unfamiliar and that characterized certain digestive habits as an index of a susceptible and addictive moral character. Since the saloon was seen nationally as an enabler of almost every social problem, its evils figured prominently in many reform movements, while projects exclusively devoted to temperance gained a strong national foothold.[90] Not surprisingly, urban saloons were actually complicated sites, differing depending upon location, owner, and clientele. Within the exclusive patterns of a male homosocial sphere, saloons enacted their own version of practical sociability, providing cheap, relatively well cooked meals and sometimes offering a loan when a trusted client was down on his luck.[91] While fluctuating in their capacity to recognize these aspects, Hull-House settlers of the early

1890s hoped to substitute the saloon with the public kitchen, seeking both to replicate its function as a food distribution center and to displace its revered status as a social space.[92] Moving squarely within the paradox of reform, this Hull-House sphere aspired to be like the thing it mimicked, but always to be like differently.

Meanwhile, the field of domestic science rapidly developed in the early 1890s. Part of the same legitimating push that justified the merging of private and public in civic housekeeping, proponents of this field sought to combine the expertise of two seemingly divergent spheres—that of the home and that of the scientific laboratory. As Dolores Hayden has argued, these Progressive descendants of Catharine Beecher espoused a nascent materialist feminism, one that understood that the reevaluation of women's subordinate social role depended upon the restructuring of the private household. From there came a host of innovations in cooperative housekeeping and shared cooking, eventually transmuting into expanded experiments for the larger urban milieu of working-class and immigrant society.[93] Ellen Swallow Richards—the inventor of the public kitchen—was one of the most famous innovators, working with academic scientists and reformers in Boston on technology for efficient food preparation. Coining the name *oekology* to represent "the science which teaches the principles with which to found healthy and happy homes," she and her colleagues experimented with steam heating, pressure cooking, and alternative baking mechanisms. Together her domestic scientific laboratory sought to extract the maximum amount of nutrition from food using the most fuel-efficient technology available. While a student at Vassar, Hull-House settler Julia Lathrop had heard of Richards and returned to Massachusetts for a few months in the early 1890s to learn techniques in more detail. Meanwhile, Richards's assistant—Mrs. Hinman Abel—visited the Hull-House Woman's Club in 1891 to educate further the settlement's own budding oekologists. Abel lectured on "the comparative nutritional values of various foods" and demonstrated the latest technological innovation—the Atkinson oven.[94] By 1893, the ideas of Ellen Swallow Richards came to a high point of sophistication and fame when she displayed her "Rumford Kitchen" at Chicago's World Colombian Exposition. Here, the skills of domesticity, the logic of science, and the ideals of feminist reform combined in a kitchen that produced large quantities of food at reduced cost. Richards hoped "that cheaper cuts of meat and simpler vegetables, if they were subjected to slow and thorough process of cooking, might be made attractive and their nutritive value secured for the people who so sadly needed more nutritious food."[95] Impressed with the exhibit both for its vision of cooperative domesticity and for its capacity to feed a large neighborhood, Addams and her colleagues promptly purchased the equipment for their own public kitchen.

Everything was carefully planned. And yet, at nearly every level, the project's feminist and scientific ideals braced against the politics of cross-cultural engagement. With architectural plans in the works, settlers began interviewing candidates for the cooking staff, electing to pass over a Bohemian woman with much experience as a cook in favor of a woman with less experience but who had taken courses in domestic science.[96] After the space, equipment, and cooking staff had been arranged, the settlers opened the doors to the first public kitchen on Chicago's West Side. Inside, visitors found a restaurant whose decor drew from the Arts and Crafts movement. Its shelves were filled with its distinctive blue pottery, and the setting's "low

A group assembled before the camera and under the beamed ceilings of the Hull-House coffee house and public kitchen. *(Photo courtesy of University of Illinois at Chicago, the University Library, Jane Addams Memorial Collection.)*

dark rafters, diamond windows, and large fireplace" were "built in
imitation of an English inn."[97] Evoking for the residents and the
Pond architects the nostalgia for nature and the life of the peasant
craftsman, settlers felt that this rustic Ruskinian ornamentation
would be more appealing to transplanted immigrant craftsmen than
the formal decor of the mansion's dining room.[98]

> The Hull-House Public Kitchen has been carefully fitted up with
> double-jacket steam kettles and Aladdin ovens. Food is cooked
> after scientifically prepared recipes and is on sale in quantities for
> home consumption. Customers are invited to visit the Kitchen.[99]

Thus spoke a circular distributed in the ward to announce the
opening. Similar prose also appeared on the kitchen's menus and in
the Hull-House schedule. Its rhetoric assumed that prospective
guests shared settlers' own enthusiasm for advanced technology, that
the "double-jacket steam kettles" and "scientifically prepared recipes" would be an attraction in and of themselves. Neighbors were
further "invited to visit the Kitchen," thus positioning a "whole way
of life" as an object of imitation. The menu read like an inventory of
Anglo-American gastronomy: codfish balls, mutton stew, welsh rare-
bit, and corned beef hash. The "gravy" bore no resemblance to Mrs.
deGuido's *bolognese.* Indeed, the fact that many similar experiments
around the country called themselves "New England Public Kitchens" more explicitly acknowledged the "Americanizing" impulse behind the construction of "scientific recipes."

Within months after opening, residents realized that the public
kitchen was not attracting its public. An initial problem stemmed
from its interior decor. While its visual and environmental elements
signaled "rustic" to settlers holding nostalgic images of "the peasant," the immigrants and laborers themselves responded to the Arts
and Crafts aesthetic quite differently.

> When the coffee house was opened, with its stained rafters, its
> fine photographs, and its rows of blue china mugs, it had a
> reflective visit from one of its neighbors. He looked it over thor-
> oughly and without prejudice, and said decisively: "yez kin hev de
> shovel gang or yez kin hev de office gang, but yez can't hev' em
> both in the same room at the same toime."[100]

This moment of alternative reception by a nonresident guest—his
accented speech recorded to mark class difference—suggested that
such imagery of the peasant life was alternatively a signal of class

status. While blue china mugs were a material form of class effacement for some, they were a sign of class privilege to others. Consequently, the "substitute for a cheerful saloon," commented the
ironic Julia Lathrop, "turned into a crypt . . . inducing reflections
so somber as to inhibit indulgence in our proffered ginger-ale and
grape juice."[101] Lathrop's reference to "ginger-ale and grape juice" of
course illustrated another enormous deterrent to male attendance—
the absence of alcohol. While a settlement committee was given
the substantial sum of twenty-five dollars to "experiment on soft
drinks" and while the House Committee elected to purchase "an
expensive soda water fountain [and fancy] slender glasses of grape
juice," such adjustments had very limited impact in rivaling the
saloon.[102] "Nor indeed did anyone imagine that we were trying to
do so," Addams wrote later of a guest for whom the interior decor
was not the actual problem. "I remember one man who looked
about the cozy little room and said, 'This would be a nice place to
sit in all day if one could only have beer.' "[103] Other social and
spatial elements inhibited its success as an alternative venue for
the drinking clientele. Unlike neighborhood saloons, its entrance
opened onto an alley behind the mansion rather than directly onto
Polk Street.[104] Furthermore, the public kitchen positioned itself as
both a heterosocial and intergenerational space, including a mix of
women and children whose presence did not reproduce the male
homosocial environment of most nearby drinking spaces. As a space
organized under the settlement umbrella, it incorporated Hull-
House's routine of interspatial motion. Afternoon visitors could
find themselves interrupting one of the cooking or domestic science
classes while evening visitors endured the influx of dancing young
people passing to the gymnasium on the second floor. As Hull-
House sociologist Ernest Moore would later come to understand,
the saloon's identity depended upon a continuous spatial dramaturgy that did not require planned participation. Its patrons relished "the absolute freedom to come and go and do as one pleases,"
counting on the stability of the space to remain in place even as
they left and departed.[105] Marking the outlines of a pragmatic and
tactical deterrent, the Hull-House substitute violated the saloon's
pattern of time-space continuity. Settlers later came to a more
complicated understanding of how their efforts did not restore the
saloon's indigenous forms of social behavior. Such "organizations
created for the purpose of ministering to this social need . . . have
come from the outside," wrote Moore, "splendid schemes to im-
press men, but alas! not to express them."[106]

The impression versus expression paradox similarly held for the public kitchen's nutritious New England food, exposing the biased notion of utility in its effort at utilitarian sociability. To many neighbors, Hull-House's healthy dining did not make for tasty eating. Despite Addams evolutionary-inflected apology that "we did not reckon with the wide diversity in nationality and inherited tastes," all of their food experiences—such as the one over Mrs. deGuido's garlic—anticipated such diversity. What they had not "reckoned with" was how difficult it would be to change these tastes. One woman reportedly exclaimed that though the food was certainly nutritious, she liked to eat "what she'd ruther" while another explicitly targeted the assimilationist impulse behind the endeavor saying, "You needn't try to make a Yankee out of me by making me eat that."[107] In fact, as the decade wore on, public kitchens throughout the nation faced similar resistance. Immigrants, Ellen Swallow Richards also realized with dismay, "have very decided preferences for the looks and flavor of food to which they have become accustomed. They will not try new things and are exceedingly suspicious of any attempt to help them."[108] She of course made no mention of Anglo-Americans' "decided preferences" and of whether they were willing "to try new things." The public kitchen adapted domestic epistemologies to reform alimentary patterns, advancing the logic that such material adjustments could transform the character of an immigrant American. Anticipating Pierre Bourdieu and John and Jean Camoroff, both neighborhood resistance and reformist presumptuousness demonstrated the role of such habits in entrenched personal and cultural conceptions of self.

Later, after the venue changed its name to the Coffeehouse, Hilda Satt—a Jewish immigrant and self-nominated Hull-House girl quite enthusiastic about transforming herself into an "American"—still had difficulty participating in this space of bodily reform. Invited to eat in a nonkosher coffeehouse, her vivid memory of these moments testifies to the bodily impact of the cultural transgression.

> Miss Hill was the first person who invited me to dinner. I had never eaten outside of my home. I hesitated to accept her invitation; she wanted to know why I did not want to come.
>
> "Oh, I want to come," I said, "but I have never eaten any place else and maybe I would not know how to act."
>
> "You don't have to act," she said kindly. "Just eat the way you eat at home."
>
> So I agreed to come. On the appointed evening I arrived wearing a clean cotton dress and my hair in perfect order. Miss Hill took me to the coffeehouse and we sat down at a small, black

square table that had no table cloth. Strange, how this insignifi-
cant detail comes back to me. The thought ran through my head
that my mother always used a tablecloth when we had company.

Miss Hill asked me if I would like a lamb chop. I was terrified
at the thought of eating meat that was not kosher. So I asked her
if I could have eggs. She said, yes, of course, in fact there was a
very nice mushroom omelet on the bill of fare and we could both
have it. I ate the omelet, which was very good, but I was tortured
with the question of whether the mushrooms were kosher. I had
eaten mushrooms many times in soup that Mother prepared, but
I had not yet learned that English word "mushroom."[109]

Satt's reaction to an absent tablecloth complicates monolithic statements about how neighbors received the space. Part of a family who
emigrated to the United States with a chest of middle-class home
decorations (if only to face unanticipated poverty), Satt filtered the
rustic elements of the Craftsman's ideal through yet another set of
dispositions and tastes. Satt's case also illustrates, however, the degree to which differences in taste—liberalized in the form of food—
were in danger of violating fundamental differences of religion and
culture. Miss Hill's kindly assertion that Hilda Satt should "just eat
the way you eat at home" rang hollow in the ears of a girl "terrified"
by the threat of transgressive ingestion.

"The Coffee House Question was well ventilated and several
changes suggested."[110] The minutes of the business meeting reflect
how demoralizing and draining the difficulties of the public kitchen/
coffeehouse proved to be. The dashed hopes also troubled another
idealism, for it had also been an experiment in alternative domesticity
for the residents themselves. Increasingly aware of how their own
"inherited" living styles reified female subordination in the home and
privatized class distinctions between mistress and servant, settlers
hoped to create a modified version of cooperative cooking by allocat-
ing their own meal preparation to the public kitchen. "The family of
twenty-four are placed in direct social and economic relations with
the common kitchen, and the . . . domestic economy is all under one
skilled management."[111] Both an inverted form of civic housekeeping
and a gesture of class effacement, the interspatial ideal further blurred
distinctions between the private domestic realm and public reform.
Because success in the latter was far from forthcoming, a great deal of
organizational and financial distress was placed on the House Committee and on the resources of residents' personal treasury. A Resident
Meeting recorded the anxiety about the coffeehouse's financial picture: "Mr. Bruce from the coffeehouse committee, requested the

residents to see that meals not paid for in cash were properly charged
in the book."[112] After the expenses of the equipment, the cooking staff,
and the day-to-day food bills and upkeep, the kitchen rapidly went
into debt, for residents' own contribution out of their room and board
could only partially cover expenses. After late 1893, barely a resident
meeting went by without discussion over whether or not the coffeehouse was "actively losing money" that week.[113] Additionally, the
residents joined their neighbors in their distaste for the food prepared. "Miss Benedict asked for numerous bits of fare that our
palates may be tickled with more varied substances and concoc-
tions."[114] At times, laments over the food were so extreme that one
coffeehouse chairman requested "that complaints regarding food
be made to Miss Addams."[115] Finally, tension-filled minutes where
"the coffeehouse was once more brought up and mildly reproved by
the error of its ways" left a written marker of their frustrations.[116]
Later the head resident would write of how "the experience . . .
taught us not to hold preconceived ideas of what the neighborhood
ought to have, but to keep ourselves in readiness to modify and
adapt our undertaking as we discovered those things which the
neighborhood was ready to accept."[117]

The first floor of the gymnasium/public kitchen building followed an interspatial trajectory different from Hull-House's more
effective schemes. By committing "brick and mortar" to this untested and underpracticed enterprise, they hoped that the space
would activate a new set of practices. Instead, they were left with a
"crypt" filled only with expensive equipment, blue china, and
dashed hopes. Upon facing their new situation, the residents soon
began fashioning a new pragmatism from their unused resources.[118]
Working within the life-paths of the Nineteenth Ward neighbors,
they started a pickup and delivery service. The clientele increased
under this interspatial adaptation (and with a few menu changes),
for neighbors could buy food on their way to work without having
to endure the discomfort of being "social" in a less than sociable
space.[119] Addams and other settlers also organized the distribution of
coffeehouse food at alternative sites.[120] "Noon Factory Delivery"
grew in popularity, eventually requiring Addams to delegate some of
the responsibility to "the Kirkland club [who] had undertaken to
deliver soups from the Coffeehouse to the Western Electric Co."[121]
During the 1893–94 winter depression, the Hull-House kitchen
joined with the Chicago Woman's Club to supply "hot lunches at
ten cents each to the two hundred women employed in the sewing
room established by [the latter's] Emergency Committee."[122] Hull-
House residents also offered the services of the kitchen in order to

cook "dinners at .05 a piece to children attending public school," thus subsidizing an effort to feed poor children in an early incarnation of contemporary school lunch programs.[123] Finally, the coffeehouse's location underneath the gymnasium—the largest room in the settlement—meant that the space gradually gathered utility from the flow of people who mounted and descended the gymnasium stairs. While some groups hosted dances in the gymnasium, others theatrical plays, and others a well-known lecturer, the downstairs coffeehouse served as a spillover reception area for a host of social occasions.[124] Thus, the coffeehouse gained its own functional identity, settling into sets of spatial practices that Hull-House agents developed from "the ground up," albeit from a ground other than the one that they initially imagined.

Along with these new uses for the kitchen equipment, residents also had to find new uses for the restaurant space itself. Subsequently, the Hull-House Men's Club carved their own homosocial space while still making use of the coffeehouse refreshments. As a male counterpart to the Hull-House's Woman's Club composed of "the abler citizens and more enterprising young men of the vicinity," this group's relationship to a largely female-headed settlement shifted from year to year, and few extant primary documents remain in the official Hull-House archives.[125] While often called upon to exert an influence in ward and civic politics, at other times female residents had to work to make the group behave like "active members."[126] Meanwhile, male residents served as liaisons between the Men's Club and the settlement administration.[127] The Men's Club performed a gendered pattern of measured distance when they requested not to hold their meetings in the heterosocial coffeehouse but in another smaller room in the same building. While they did not drink alcohol, they did fill this space with other accoutrements of a saloon substitute—especially billiards and card tables—and established its identity as a separate male space. Unlike the diachronic transformations of the gymnasium, Butler exhibit hall, or drawing room, no other group or set of individuals occupied the space at other times of the day.[128] Furthermore, within the first year of the new building, "Mr. Barnes [moved] that a speaking tube be put in from the Men's Club to the Coffee House, and that all kinds of tempting drinks, not intoxicating, be kept on hand and served in the Men's Club from the Coffeehouse."[129] Thus, the Men's Club maintained a qualified type of interspatial connection to the Hull-House coffeehouse, one that simultaneously indulged the gendered privilege of being conveniently served and the gendered privilege of remaining separately sequestered. As such, the space reinforced the

tacit connection between the privilege of spatial continuity and the
performance of male homosocial identity, one that secured a singular and self-reproductive geography as opposed to the protean undoings and redoings of the rest of the public household.

Janes

In 1904, a heroine of adventurous naïveté entered the realm of
Chicago fiction. By the time Sister Carrie stepped off the railroad
car and into the "maze, uproar, and novelty" of a modernizing city,
many similarly unattached females had already populated the Chicago imaginary.[130] Like so many of the other groups to which Hull-
House attended—immigrants, children, factory workers—single
women provoked much social concern. And like the stereotypes
attached to so many identities, the image of Sister Carrie obscured
the heterogeneous realities of such women's lives. In the no-nonsense
style of her unpublished autobiography, an Irish tradeswoman,
union organizer, and former single working woman named Mary
Kenney (later O'Sullivan) recalled a generative conversation.

> One day Miss Addams said, "Mary, if you get the members for a
> cooperative boarding club, I will pay the first month's rent, and
> supply the furnishings. There's a vacant apartment on Ewing
> Street. I knew what it would mean for working women to have a
> home near Hull-House. "I'll get the members," I said.[131]

The six members whom Mary Kenney found were employed single
women like herself. The group moved into the nearby flat, an initial
spatial commitment that eventually spawned a larger all-female
living experiment and, by 1896, a new building on the Hull-House
block. In a self-nominating moment of deep settlement mimesis,
the group of young working women elected to call themselves "the
Jane Club."

What did it mean for single working women to have a home near
Hull-House? In the turn-of-the-century city, the unmarried woman
occupied a zone of suspect liminality. Single women did not fit morally stable categories. No longer conceived as children, they were also
past the stage of "adolescence," whose emergent definition only occasionally referred to young females. They were more often defined by
negation—"unmarried." Thus labeled by what she was not, an anticipatory narrative structured a single woman's perceived identity, deferring its stability until marriage and motherhood reconnected her to

appropriate femininity. In the meantime, as Joanne Meyerowitz demonstrates, a "woman adrift" lived with her imputed in-betweenness.[132] Furthermore, to digress from an anticipated marital progression was to risk moral condemnation, and hence the specter of the unattached female often evoked images of uncontrolled sexuality. Social purists, muckraking journalists, and evangelical reformers searched the city for evidence of its delapidation, metonymically equating the walking figure of a lone woman with the onslaught of urban "vice." Reflecting the recursive sexual politics of identity and geography, an unchaperoned woman's entry into particular public spaces (whether a saloon or a city street) could automatically impugn her moral character. Unfortunately, labor movements often did little toward complicating the image of the single working woman. From the perspective of the standard factory worker—a person conceived as male by default—working women presented a threat to male jobs and jeopardized their pay scales. The initial exclusions of working-class women from the Working People's Social Science Club replicated the labor movement's masculinist focus. Furthermore, both moderate and some socialist wings based their platforms on the need, not simply for a living wage, but for a "family wage" that could support male workers' dependents. The issue of working women's rights thus threatened to derail the rhetorical ground of such an argument, for why would women need such rights if their object was to be supported by working men? Indeed, privileged female settlers who became involved with the labor movement found their allegiances torn. While assumptions about the roles of husband and wife were radically at odds with the reality of everyday lives, family ideals were entrenched with such discursive intensity that support for both working men and working women was conceived as an internal contradiction.[133]

As a trade union organizer and representative of the American Federation of Labor, Mary Kenney was an unusual figure, and her early contact with Hull-House proved invaluable. Like those first meetings with Signor Mastro-Valerio, Alfred Hicks, or Edward Butler, it transformed the course of Hull-House history. Like every history-making act, it almost did not happen.

> One day, while I was working at my trade, I received a letter from Miss Jane Addams. She invited me to Hull-House for dinner. She said she wanted me to meet some people from England who were interested in the labor movement. I had never heard of Miss Addams or Hull-House. I had no idea who she was.[134]

Kenney's mother convinced her that there was no harm in accepting the invitation, even if she left early. When Kenney entered Hull-

House's drawing room for the first time, she was immediately struck by the size and decor of this formal space. "I saw furnishings and large rooms different from anything I had ever seen before. With one look at the reception room my first thought was, 'if the Union could only meet here.' " For some time, the problem of a meeting space for an all-female union of bookbinders had pressed on Kenney's mind. Since gender codes inhibited their use of the free spaces in the backrooms of saloons, they had been forced to pay for a room above a saloon—a "dirty and noisy place." Still, Kenney was dubious about forming any affiliation with members so obviously removed in social status. "My first impression was that they were all rich and not friends of the workers."

> By my manner Miss Addams must have known that I wasn't very friendly. She asked me questions about our Trade Union. "Is there anything I can do to help your organization?" she said. I couldn't believe I had heard right. . . . "There are many things we need. We don't have a good meeting place. We are meeting over a saloon on Clark Street . . . but we can't afford anything better." She said, "The Book Binders can meet here." I confided to her that, as I had passed through the large reception room I had thought what a wonderful meeting place it would make.[135]

Addams's modest offer reproduced a tested method of social pragmatism, enacting a labor union's version of practical sociability under the flexible terms of nonaffiliated spatial use. As an official organizer of the American Federation of Labor, Mary Kenney organized several small unions in the next two years, using Hull-House as a meeting space for "the Women's Book Binders Union I, the Shirt Makers Unions, Cab Drivers Union, a gathering of representatives of the Retail Clerk Workers, the strike committees of the Garment Workers and the Clothing Cutters."[136] Like previous attempts, Kenney used circulars to publicize her organizational efforts and, despite her aversion (she sometimes disparaged working women's propensity for "outings"), incorporated "entertainment" with informational and administrative meetings. In an 1892 missive, she wrote, "All Cloakmakers are cordially invited to attend a Musical Entertainment with addresses Saturday evening," and continued, "[N]o one will be urged to join unless they desire, but it is earnestly hoped that there will be a large attendance of Cloakmakers at this first meeting."[137] Her rhetoric placed the social impulse at the heart of collective politics, announcing that the mission of the event was "to inculcate a spirit of fraternal friendship in their relations with each other . . . to make each individual feel that she is not alone in her daily efforts to make a respectable livelihood; to make her look upon herself as a part of that entire body of workers who form an important element in the commercial interests of a great community."[138] During this period, Kenney also lived as a guest in the mansion for several months, marking a period when the spatial split between "residents" and "neighbors" was temporarily blurred.

The conflicted situation of the single working woman reflected the myopias of prevailing discourses, occupational structures, and living arrangements.[139] Until Kenney began her union organizing, Hull-House's own nascent groupings each had assumed a principle of inclusion that placed such a figure on the periphery. Not only was she an ambivalent figure at the WPSSC and the young people's clubs, she also ill-fit membership in the Hull-House Woman's Club. Not a wife, not a mother, and generally unavailable for afternoon meetings, an unmarried employed woman followed different life-paths and required new domestic arrangements. Hull-House thus supported the Jane Club as an alternative interspace to those already in circulation. In fact, single working women's concerns partially replicated those of unmarried female settlers, a coincidence that made the label *Jane* all the more apt. As settlers worked with the new boarders to plan a living quarters, they reportedly "read aloud together Beatrice Potter's little book and 'Cooperation' and discussed all the difficulties and fascinations of such an undertaking."[140] The anecdote's note of condescension notwithstanding, displaced settlers were in a position to discuss cooperative living, having endured many of its "difficulties and fascinations" themselves.

Initially renting only one flat, the membership increased to eighteen occupying three flats. Within a year, Jane Club members lived in all six flats of the Ewing Street building, at one point reaching a cramped membership of fifty. Perhaps after reading Beatrice Potter and after some advice from settlers, the women structured themselves into a cooperative arrangement that interspatially reproduced many settlement practices. With Hull-House supporting their lease, they were able to tax themselves only three dollars for a cook and cleaning service. Like the Hull-House residents, they instituted a weekly meeting "discussing ways and means and management" and formed their own house committee.[141] More stringent than the mansion's living arrangement, the Jane Club was open only to "self-supporting, unmarried women (18–45) or widows without dependent children." Significantly, the constitution mediated a careful relationship with Hull-House. There was an internally elected president but no "matron" in the conventional sense; Mrs. Toomey, mother to a Jane Club member named Maggie, initially lived with the young women and tended the household. Though "[w]e had the great privilege of having Miss Addams and Miss Starr at our meetings," the two women were considered "Honorary Members." As such, they could attend weekly meetings but did not have voting power. The Jane Club structure thus differed from Chicago's other charity houses for single women. In places such as the YWCA or the Eleanor Clubs, boarders were subject to strict rules, etiquette, and curfews set by a well-to-do matron.[142] "There was no curfew," Jane Club member Laura Grose happily recalled. "We were supposed to know when it was time to come in. And we could always receive gentleman guests in the parlors."[143] Though a Jane could be expelled for "conduct inconsistent with the welfare of the Club," it was theoretically the club that decided the terms of that inconsistency. "Any girl who can come into the city and earn an honest living knows enough to run her own evenings."[144] In the secret history of the club, the hands-off attitude actually fluctuated, especially when Maggie Toomey became pregnant out of wedlock, and Addams arranged for the baby's adoption.[145]

In Chicago, the running of young women's evenings would come under increased scrutiny as the century turned, and Hull-House settlers' response to this transformation was more varied than Addams's earlier assertion. When Kenney invoked her fellow women's interest in "outings," she referred to the host of heterosocial amusements on the urban scene. Dance halls, vaudeville, popular theaters, and later ten-cent movie theaters increasingly became favorite gathering sites for unmarried women and men.[146] As Sister Carrie's counterparts roamed new arenas of leisure and consumption, urban reformers and some Hull-House settlers often worried about the moral climate of these spaces and whether young women really did "know enough" to negotiate them appropriately. In the meantime, Kenney differently channeled the impulses to heterosocial recreation. Saying that "the social spirit was just as cooperative as the financial relationship," she and fellow boarders organized many an amusing evening for themselves. As a labor organizer and Jane Club president, Kenney's dual role meant that labor politics and sociality often mixed, and she described herself as a valued link between single wage-earning women and men.

> While I was doing social and organizing work, I had the opportunity of meeting a good many men, and if there was a dance or a ball we wanted to attend, I would tell an acquaintance that about twenty "Janes" would like to attend a certain ball and ask him to bring an escort. . . . Some of us were advocates of the union label,

Prospective Janes—unnamed working women in Chicago's West Side.
*(Photo courtesy of University of Illinois at Chicago, the University Library,
Jane Addams Memorial Collection.)*

and, as the young men entered and we took their hats, we looked
to see if there was a union label inside.[147]

As escorts emerged through union connections, as "Janes" instituted
"label checking" as a collective social activity, the Jane Club performed its link with labor, enacting a prounion politics within the
flirtatious heterosocial performance of a party greeting. These and
other events thus partially reproduced the conventions of popular
amusement, mimicking but mimicking differently according to the
goals of reform. By 1895, the Jane Club regularly hosted dances and
lectures in the gymnasium on the third Thursday of each month, a
weekly time slot that alternated with college extension classes, the
Men's Club social event, and the young people's clubs.[148] In choosing their name and in calling themselves "Janes," the club had
expressed their affiliation with Hull-House. At the same time, the
nomination developed its own particular associations, becoming a
shorthand for desirable single women.

The Jane Club celebrated its anniversary every year, an event that

usually involved a recital, music, dancing, a speech, and visitors from
Hull-House. The year 1897 marked not only its fifth anniversary but
also the announcement of a new Jane Club Building on the Hull-
House block. Fellow Janes celebrated by reciting the history of its
founding and evolution. Veteran club member "Miss Frehl who was
the seventh member to join the club" was given a position of importance, having been privy to most of this club's development.
"Since the incorporation of the club, two members have died, three
have entered sisterhoods in the Roman Catholic Church; as for
marriages, it is impossible to count them, the Secretary reporting
eight during the past year alone."[149] After five years as a pragmatically conceived, indigenous practice, the Hull-House Settlement
made a new commitment of "brick and mortar" to the project.
Through some travail, Addams, Louise deKoven Bowen, and other
residents raised money for the new building, at first being forced to
refuse twenty thousand dollars from "a man who was notorious for
underpaying the girls in his establishment and concerning whom
there were even darker stories."[150] They built the new Jane Club
Building on the southeast portion of the settlement block. Such a
proximate living arrangement ultimately placed the Jane Club more
firmly under the geographic umbrella of Hull-House, releasing the
settlement from the headaches of rental leases and centralizing its
heating bills. The fact that the Jane Club's furnace was "connected
with steam heat and electric plants of the Hull-House building"
greatly minimized costs. The erection of the new building was symbolic, as well as economically expedient. While its placement within
the settlement block announced its Hull-House affiliation, the main
entrance to the building was from Ewing Street rather than from
within the settlement compound. Placing the building's frontage
onto the street thus gave the club a degree of symbolic autonomy.
Jane Club residents were thrilled, saying that they "would be willing
to lay bricks themselves if single rooms and other conveniences
might thus be secured." Hull-House trustees and funders complied,
assuring themselves that "a club which has survived five years of
cooperative life may reasonably be expected to live fifty."[151]

A few extant documents—blueprints and occasional descriptions
in the *Hull-House Bulletin*—remain that give some suggestion of the
Jane Club's daily life. While an architect's plans do not determine
the range of practices performed inside a building, such blueprints
do show separate rooms designated for certain social and household
activities such as dining, reading, cooking, and laundry. Twenty
single and four two-person bedrooms and shared bathrooms were
housed on the top floors. A separate parlor on the second floor

functioned as an intermediary social space between the bedrooms and the first floor's more public receiving rooms.[152] As the fifth-year anniversary description illustrated, there were many, many weddings, and some took place at the Jane Club Building. Though sources do not record how many were "too numerous to count," fleeting references to eight in 1895 or four in the first half of 1902 illustrate how often the membership changed and thus how fundamental patterns of departure and substitution were to the everyday life of this rotational community.[153] President Annie Brown married William Everhart in parlors "charmingly decorated with flowers and ferns and bittersweet, and a wood fire [that] made it look cheery and homelike." As the club president and oldest member "with one exception," this wedding was significant but did not in the least signal an end to the club. Indeed, the casual reference to her age intimated that the group anticipated her departure. The marriage of Lida Evans and Frank Keyser was "doubly interesting," for it marked the union of a Jane Club member with a member of Hull-House engineering and maintenance staff. Brother to the late Mary Keyser, Frank Keyser provided the settlement with all its "heat and light," prompting a bulletin writer to amplify in phrases that (though slightly obtuse) suggest the personal affection with which Hull-House affiliates greeted this match. "If it were not for the fact that the light which Mr. Keyser dispenses comes only at night he might almost be called the sun of the settlement. But neither can we call him the moon, since the moon is never known to dispense heat."[154] Thus, Keyser's nocturnal duties among the "steam heat and electric plants" proved fortuitous for this courtship, coincidentally allowing him to meet Lida Evans among the settlement buildings after she completed her workday. Propelled by an integrated geography and interdependent technology, Hull-House resident George Hooker officiated at the ceremony, one that was followed by "a series of whistles from the engine house" and a Hull-House reception organized by the residents.[155]

The Keyser marriage differed from most Jane Club weddings in that the couple stayed on at Hull-House. Given that most marriages ended in the departure of another Jane, early members had to incorporate this phenomenon into Jane Club identity. By anticipating and celebrating each others' marriages, the group thus constituted this all-female space as a transitional one, building the club's continual undoing into its own self-definition. Bonded not only as working women, these women constructed a shared temporariness, a stage made sensical and palatable by the expectation of heterosexual coupling. In light of heated debates about the rights of working women versus the

movement for the "family wage," this constant celebration of marriage is particularly intriguing. Hull-House labor activists would ultimately throw most of their support into the latter, arguing for an
economic distribution that placed wives at home despite the fact that
Hull-House settlers deviated from such a model themselves. As an
expedient architecture for social relations, labor and welfare activists
became more committed to promoting marriage as a solution to the
liminality of the single working woman, suggesting that her interests
could coincide with those of the workingman if she married him.[156]
The microperformance of Hull-House weddings thus tacitly instantiated this response to large-scale changes in industrial and gender
relations, illustrating too that performance methodologies can reconcile apparently contradictory linguistic discourses. Rather than ending Jane Club identity, marriage confirmed it. Departure solidified
the Jane Club trajectory of an unsupported "Sister Carrie," a temporarily supported "Jane," and a permanently supported "Mrs." into a
single satisfying fiction.

"The first buildings were very precious to us," Addams later wrote;
"they clothed in brick and mortar and made visible to the world that
which we were trying to do."[157] By the end of the nineteenth century
(and after ten years of work), several buildings congregated around
the original Hull mansion, beginning with the Butler Building in
1891, the gymnasium/coffeehouse in 1893, the Children's House (or
Smith Building) in 1896, the Jane Club of 1898, and, as will be
discussed in chapter 5, a new Theatre Auditorium in 1899. Throughout all of these changes, Hull-House affiliates most often maintained
a quick power of adaptation when they allowed the social practices
of the settlement to determine the course of its spatial life—forming
geographic boundaries out of the push and pull of microperformance, being willing to endure boundary violation, and remaining
cognizant of the social inequities that constrained spatial habits. In
trying to sense the experience of this mobility, I find myself most
amused and moved by resident George Twose's depiction of Hull-
House flux.

> Gernon's in the Theatre
> Waltzing mighty slow,
> The Drexels in the Lecture-Hall
> Have a baby show
> Fleur de Lis in Nursery
> Waites in Kindergarten
> Bunch of Lady cracker packers

Want a place to start in.
Miss Addams takes the Drexels
Puts them in the Kitchen,
Then into the Octagon
She the Boys Club pitch in;
Moves the Gernon party
To Mr. Hooker's room,
The English to the Pantry
Miss Landsberg into gloom.[158]

Twose dramatized how dance teachers, lecturers, kindergarten instructors, union organizers, Boys Club leaders, and college extension teachers moved through settlement space, occupying smaller spaces and larger ones, a theater or a pantry, a lecture hall or a bedroom. Occasionally, they endured the "gloom" of having no assigned space at all. In addition to rendering those fluctuations, Twose humorously conveyed the interrelation of several different types of endeavors. "Lady cracker packers" moved amid dancing children, two groups that would typically come under the purview of two very different types of historiography. Simultaneously attending to art and to food distribution, to recreation and to public housing, Hull-House stepped and kicked along the borders that all too conventionally divide the cultural from the social. For contemporary performance scholars, the historical reminder revives the oft-obscured connection between the so-called culture worker and the so-called social worker.

One hundred years later, Louise Bourgeois would attempt to clothe in a cast-iron sculpture what Hull-House had tried to do. Her "waltz of hands" evoked George Twose's choreography, resisting the traditional representation of the solitary hero. Commissioned by Chicago's Department of Cultural Affairs, the sculpture argues for a historical link between itself and Chicago's departments of social services—its soup kitchens, school lunch programs, and public housing. The hands represent aesthetically the operations of giving and taking that justify public and private welfare—and that ensure its continual contestation. The fact that these hands are partial, not connected to a torso much less a torso with a face, makes this eerie representation devastatingly appropriate. As I imagined Louise Bourgeois's hands molding them, I wondered how she decided to stop shaping. When to cut? below the palm? at the wrist? in the middle of the forearm? Navigating the border of the avowedly metaphorical and the perceptually literal, there must have been a moment when she decided to stop adding more clay, ceasing at the pivotal point where the sculpture's audience would still have to decide whether or not these hands stood in for the human.

The partiality of the hands ended up thrusting the Jane Addams Memorial Park into heated controversy. Despite their philosophical resonance, many objected to the nonliteral representation; that is, what made the sculpture interesting formally also made it vulnerable socially. Newspapers asked "why the abstract artwork portrayed a collection of hands instead of its subject," unhappy with this reversed form of allegory from a memorial that was supposed to counter the allegorical use of females. Others wanted "immediate readability": "If we have the one and only park dedicated to a woman, then it should be something people can see and understand what it is," said a representative of SOAR (the Streeterville Organization of Active Residents).[159] Some noted that this allegorical mode still seemed only reserved for women. "Why can't we have some nice heroic sculptures of our own?" wrote one columnist, "at least something approaching the heroic and realistic sculpture accorded Michael Jordan recently."[160] Many newspaper descriptions illustrated the park's successful functioning as an integrated environmental performance, complete with stories of children playing or adults relaxing. However, the fact that a student could be found sitting on a nearby bench, "occasionally lifting her head from her textbooks to admire the way the sailboats seem to glide through a screen of rustling grass," became positively scandalous when she could not say "what lies in that silvery strand of prairie that dips just below her, well, she knows there's *something* in there. She's just never taken a look.[161] Thus, despite the various recreational aspects of this urban *milieu de mémoire,* it did not function properly as a *lieu de mémoire.* It did not replicate the nonspontaneous, officially framed, bicameral structure of modern memorial. The phenomenon of a memorial that one newspaper called "hidden in plain sight" could itself have been another ironic allegory for the gendered work of memory, of relationality, and of civic housekeeping, operations that rely on structures that paradoxically keep them invisible.

That irony was only heightened by the circumstances surrounding the official inauguration of the park with the Democratic Convention in 1996. Hillary Rodham Clinton, her speech prepared on the connection between Jane Addams's ideas and *It Takes a Village,* stepped down as mistress of ceremonies when the organizers learned that Operation Rescue planned to use the First Lady's appearance to stage an antiabortion demonstration. Fearful of having the grass trampled, organizers might also have anticipated a controversy like the one that shadowed the removal of a similar Bourgeois sculpture from proximity to New York City's Holocaust Memorial in Battery Park. These partial hands might have provoked unwelcome associations next to the "fetal imagery" of antichoice rallies. That an antichoice rally interfered with the celebration of, as *Life* called Jane Addams, "the mother of social work" was also uncannily resonant, given how often abortion and welfare debates act as reversed mirrors of each other. Both are preoccupied with separating human "viability" from human "dependency," with deciding whether and when one human being becomes distinct from another, and with pondering the social stakes of arguing for or against their intimate coimbrication. While abortion, welfare, and the Jane Addams Memorial Park continue to swirl in different versions of similar paradoxes around gender, privacy, memory, and publicity, the indirect structures of allegory, *milieu de mémoire,* and civic housekeeping perhaps more accurately reflect the partial and relational nature of all social beings, even those who still pass themselves off—literally—as solitary heroes.

Chapter 4

Living: "Somehow the House Seems All Upset"

The construction of gender operates through *exclusionary* means. . . .
What challenge does that excluded and abjected realm produce to a
symbolic hegemony that might force a radical rearticulation of what
qualifies as bodies that matter, ways of living that count as "life," lives
worth protecting, lives worth saving, lives worth grieving?
  —Judith Butler, *Bodies That Matter*

It may be no coincidence that . . . the vocation of the feminist
thinker and critic has led her to leave home.
  —Seyla Benhabib, "Feminism and Postmodernism"

The National Museum of American History is located on Constitution Avenue in Washington, D.C., where it joins hundreds of
cultural institutions that explicitly and implicitly tell the history of
the United States. It is a performance of history. I visited there to see a
semipermanent exhibit entitled *From Parlor to Politics: Women and
Reform in America, 1890–1925.* It was our national museum's second
exhibit devoted to the display of American women's history—the
other being the exhibit on our nation's First Ladies (and their
ballgowns). After much hard work and many headaches, curators
finally secured a room devoted to the story of a variety of women who
worked for reform during that period retroactively called the Progressive Era. Hull-House and surrounding reform contexts in Chicago are
directly and indirectly represented here. Reformers in juvenile development and juvenile justice, immigration, temperance, education,
public health, and suffrage are pictured, sounded, textualized, and
incarnated in—I looked at my map—room 26 on the back wall of the
second floor. I would have to walk past the exhibit of the First Ladies
(and their ballgowns) to get there.

I was with my mother during this visit—my mother who could
recall the first time she had taken me to The National Museum of

American History. I think I was around ten or eight, or eleven, I don't know, maybe seven.

"You couldn't take your eyes off of those First Ladies," my mom recalled, a little too loudly as we got off the elevator at the second floor. I remember, but don't say so. I remember how much I loved Mary Todd Lincoln's dress because the pattern—its flowers carefully placed between vertical ribbons—had reminded me of my wallpaper in my little-girl bedroom at home. As we walked into the second-floor foyer and down the hall, I flashed on that wallpaper and that little-girl room—"a room for a princess," as my grandmother would say—with its white wrought iron bed and white eyelet bedspread across from a miniature white desk painted with little blue flowers. "Remember how you used to read about the First Ladies?" asked my mom way too loudly, "all of those biographies." I remembered. I had read loads of biographies on famous women while I was growing up. I loved books that told stories of queens, wives, princesses, and women warriors: Mary Queen of Scotts, Joan of Arc, the six wives of Henry VIII, Eleanor of Aquitaine. All of those chopped heads. And then I recalled the biography of Mary Todd Lincoln and her episodes of what I might now locate in the dubious diagnostic history of hysteria but which I then understood as her tendency sometimes to go crazy in the White House. President Lincoln would have to write consoling notes to her, doctors prescribed funny medicines, her women friends never understood why she did not like being a mother to her boys, and the president's staff would work to hide from the public that she was unfit for the most important role available to anyone of the female sex, that of First Lady, that of "mother to the nation." I remembered my fascination as I imagined this First Lady and her looniness sitting in her White House, as if I, then sitting at age seven or eleven in my white eyelet room, had already begun to sympathize.

On this visit, I walked past the First Ladies and the visually sumptuous and mnemonically overpowering display of those dresses—Martha Washington's silk with its flat front bodice, Dolly Madison's embroidered ivory satin, Florence Harding's expanse of pearlized sequins, Mary Todd Lincoln's white silk taffeta woven with those flowers and vertical stripes.

Of course, I was no longer interested. The exhibit that I came to see was titled *From Parlor to Politics* to invoke the utility and ubiquity of domestic metaphors in the discourse of women's reform. The philosophy of civic housekeeping structures almost every aspect of the exhibit, from its first display of four female mannequins holding banners at a simulated protest to its final image of a

1970s march of second-wave feminists. And, since I was with my mother, I amplified on the import of this discourse in various aspects of the exhibit, stopping at displays of social movements to elaborate on how maternal metaphors enabled women's activism in child labor, public health, temperance, nutrition. In addition to offering this history and ideological orientation in didactics, super-titles, and pamphlets throughout room 26, *From Parlor to Politics* uses spatial, sonic, and imagistic techniques to represent the two domestic spaces—a parlor and a tenement—where two kinds of civic housekeepers lived. The parlor section contains information and stories about middle-class reformers along with examples of the badges, ribbons, lace napkins, and tea services that accessorized their club organizations. In the tenement, a mannequin mother and her children make paper flowers inside a poorly ventilated and in-adequately plumbed room. There is also a third, as the museum guide says, "domestic space" represented in the exhibit. Near the end, a museum visitor is invited to enter an architectural incarna-tion of Hull-House, represented inside two rooms doubling as re-ceiving areas and containers for displaying props, photographs, ce-ramic models and "Personal Items of Jane Addams." The rhetorical position of Hull-House in this part of the exhibit spatially and didactically presents it as a place where the inhabitants of the parlor and the tenement met; as the guidebook says, "[M]iddle and working classes found common interests . . . at the settlement—so named because reformers 'settled' in the neighborhoods they served."

I smiled, happy that the curators had noted the significance of "settling" and of the strange, disruptive, and improvised ways with which settlers made this third space. While all of the artistic, pedagogi-cal, and recreational spaces analyzed thus far influenced the daily life of its residents, this chapter is devoted to the strain of Hull-House practices and performances that constituted settlers' patterns of living. Given that co-habitation was both the method and ideal of settlement locality, how did residents inhabit this place? Leaving eyelet bedrooms (some of them a little afraid of becoming loony), settlers learned that civic housekeeping required not simply an externalized maternality but also a socialized internality, not simply an extension *beyond* the domestic interior but a reciprocal undoing *of* the domestic interior. Practices such as dining, bathing, even sleeping faced continual re-structuring in a "home" that simultaneously presented itself as a public kitchen, a public bath, and ad hoc guest quarters. Such every-day acts countered falsely literalized conceptions of the home and private family, substituting avowedly figural performances of house-hold and kinship that un-settled the hold of naturalized modes of belonging. Adapting the insights of queer theorists who locate the self-deconstructing threads of apparently stable sexual and gender categories, this chapter further underscores the skewed referentiality of the term *civic housekeeper,* encountering women who justified themselves with maternal metaphors despite not being biological mothers, encountering less publicized civic housekeepers who were in fact not women. The first section surveys the relationship between familial and social claims, conceiving them less as two sides of a private/public binary and more as a simultaneous field of juggled commitments. In the second section, queer theory also helps to loosen rigid types of speculations into publicity and privacy, especially those that revolve around the performances of Hull-House sexuality and kinship. The final section looks at the relationship between the settlement's queer domesticity and its practices of cooperative living. Along the way, this notion of queer domesticity foregrounds the importance of gender and sexuality not simply as principles of individual identity but as factors in social reorganization, as vehicles for reconceiving public and private, and as keys to expanding the field of possible attachments available to human beings who are trying to decide whom to love.

Public Parlors

On the evening of December 14, 1901, Edith de Nancrede—a four-year Hull-House resident, Boys Club leader, artist, actress, and theater director—celebrated her twenty-fourth birthday. In the days before, three residents—Ella Waite, Jessie Luther, and Rose Gyles—put their heads together, wondering what they could do to mark the occasion and appropriately honor Nancrede's artistic spirit of play. That same month, fellow resident George Twose had been exercising his own literary humor and theatrical creativity for his colleagues, writing and performing a series of songs and monologues for their small late-night drawing room gatherings. He called them "Settlement Reflections or Why he left for Egypt: A Comedietta." Spurred by this contagious burst of creativity, gymnasium director Gyles joined with children's club leader Waite and Labor Museum director Luther to match Twose's productivity, writing and performing a humorous set of twenty limericks for the night of the birthday celebration. By this year, there were twenty residents living in the Hull-House compound—eight men and twelve women, two of whom were household employees occupying Mary Keyser's ambivalent position. Each limerick depicted a different settler, drawing from the collective's shared knowledge to direct a lighthearted tease about his or her personality quirks. Though it was Edith de Nancrede's birthday, the limericks began—as did so much Hull-House folklore and so many Hull-House rituals—with a reference to Jane Addams.

> Miss Addams is happy at last
> For the workmen are leaving so fast—
> And now soon we'll be cooking
> and with all the world looking
> We'll build bridges 'twixt present and past.[1]

"Workmen" of various types were an omnipresent sight around the settlement. Whether they were repairing a roof or walkway, installing a new boiler or bakery oven, erecting a new sign or a new building, Hull-House was almost constantly undergoing some kind of construction. By 1901, the settlement had added several more additions beyond the mansion, Butler Building, gymnasium, and coffeehouse. In 1896, the Children's House filled out the remaining corner of the Hull-House block at Polk Street; that same year, Addams secured funds to create a third-floor addition atop the mansion, thus adding eight more bedrooms for new residents. In the next three years, they constructed the Jane Club and the Hull-House Auditorium. In the years following Nancrede's 1901 birthday celebration, Hull-House would add new buildings that significantly affected its residential life—a Men's Settlement attached to the Butler in 1902, a set of apartments in 1902, and a resident's dining hall in 1905.[2] The erection of the Woman's Club Building (or Bowen Hall) in 1904, the Boys' Club in 1906, and the Mary Crane Nursery in 1907 would conclude the settlement's architectural expansion, rounding it out to ·a thirteen-building complex. The limerick's "bridges 'twixt present and past" literally referred to the passageways that were also being built among these new buildings. Since separate structures were in danger of creating environmental isolation—making gymnasium instructors reluctant to run over to the kindergarten if it meant donning a coat or carrying an umbrella—such interspatial bridges helped to maintain an extended social geography.

For Gyles, Luther, and Waite, the phrase "soon we'll be cooking" played on a double, even triple, entrendre. In 1901, it referred quite literally to the kitchen's new, large, economically efficient technology, a set of ovens and ranges that could accommodate the increasing demands of both the dining room, the domestic science classes, and the coffeehouse. "Cooking" was also a metaphor for civic housekeeping. It referenced the centrality of the seemingly mundane activities of domesticity, the brand of continuous and cooperative household management integral to Hull-House's constitution of a third space. Settlers approached divisions of public and private at another register of experience, one suggested in the phrase "with all the world looking" (and inadvertently re-created in the spectatorial structures of the *From Parlor to Politics* exhibit). The logic of Hull-House mimesis generally meant that the daily living practices of its residents—the so-called private realms of experience—were perpetually on display. To hold oneself up as an object of imitation necessarily meant subjecting oneself to continual speculation, to conduct oneself with the knowledge that a neighbor was looking and theoretically learning. Consequently, residents adapted their daily life to gain some modicum of control over the spectacle they presented. This meant pushing the limits of Hull-House's spatial flexibility by continually reconstituting boundaries of public and private. In the course of a day, a resident might release or bar access to the kitchen, to the stairs, to the back parlor, or to the baths as the temporally shifting clamor for more space fluctuated. Thus, publicity and privacy were not stably located in selected spheres; rather settlement practices processually alternated and activated the private or public identity of these regions. Such moment-to-moment adaptations became an incorporated pattern of settlement living, inscribed into the gestural behaviors of a settler who secured much-cherished "privacy" by turning her back and, after a breath, relinquished it by extending her hand.[3] For some whose previous living patterns were too entrenched in the quiet and ordered logic of a well-to-do homespace, these violations—whether manifested as physical invasion, auditory interruption, or excessive motion—proved intolerably disorienting. Amid the jangled nerves and frustrated tears, new rules were made while others were broken, a different door opened while another door closed. Residents then had several choices: they could leave entirely, retreat temporarily, institute a new code to prevent violation—or they could adapt. In the language of Smithsonian curators, they could settle.

New Homes for Old was the title of second-generation resident Sophonisba Breckinridge's sociological study of immigrant living patterns and tenement housing, but it could well have been the title of a book on settlement life. It also could have been an alternative title for the *From Parlor to Politics* exhibit. Addams recalled,

> In those days we were often asked why we had come to live on Halsted Street when we could afford to live somewhere else. I

remember one man who used to shake his head and say it was "the strangest thing he had met in his experience," but who was finally convinced that it was "not strange but natural."[4]

The easy tone underlying Addams's statement mystifies the tumultuous nature of a settlement worker's life in an urban neighborhood—a tumult experienced in gendered, cultural, emotional, intellectual, and economic registers by those who could always "afford to live somewhere else." This third space, this meeting space for the denizens of the middle-class parlor and the denizens of the tenement flat, could only come to feel "natural" after a process of personal change. On a theoretical plane, such a space is also one where the performance of everyday life meets the discourse of public domesticity, where the likes of Erving Goffman and Pierre Bourdieu can be found treading unwittingly upon the territory of American feminist history and upon the conflictually gendered experience of modernity. To recall Bourdieu, "[W]hen habitus encounters a social world of which it is the product, it is like a fish in water: it does not feel the weight of the water, and it takes the world about itself for granted."[5] To leave home was thus always a process of defamiliarization for bourgeois women, a self-conscious recognition of the heretofore tacit. Enduring Bourdieu's "times of crisis" or Giddens's "critical situations," such women spontaneously sought to restore the field of a past home—its standards of cleanliness, its patterns of alimentation—and continuously faced disjuncture. Not only incarnating the disorientations of white female modernity, such moments most brilliantly illuminate how it *felt* to be a Hull-House reformer and how she reconciled those feelings at the microlevel of individual performance. While evidence of these ruptures lies in the autobiographies of reformers, such tales from the field are told with an amused hindsight that lightens, flattens, and edits. Residents were instead more linguistically productive while in the frenzied middle of these changes, liminal moments more often found in primary documents such as letters, diaries, and the minutes of resident business meetings. In general, it was more often when they felt the "weight of the water" that settlers felt compelled to record it.

The spatial legacy of an upper-class home life structured how newly arrived residents responded to Hull-House and how they initially began to move within it. While searching for a space in which to actualize their "scheme," Addams uncoincidently lingered upon the "fine old house standing well back from the street," noting the "broad piazza" and "wooden pillars of exceptionally pure Corinthian design

The settlement added third floors to the top of the Butler building and
to the mansion (house left, upstage center) to connect to the new Smith
or Children's Building funded by Mary Rozet Smith (house right).
*(Photo courtesy of University of Illinois at Chicago, the University Library,
Jane Addams Memorial Collection.)*

and proportion."[6] Charles Hull's former mansion was a unique
building in the Nineteenth Ward. It maintained a safe distance
between its front door and the street, boasting an architectural
pedigree recognizable to a trained eye. Upon entry, Starr and Addams adapted past environmental performances as they inhabited
the mansion's interiors.[7] Later, when many residents acquired free
reign of the entire house, Alice Hamilton similarly responded to
Hull-House's "long drawing room, carved white marble mantel-
pieces, and lofty ceilings," recalling her grandparents' house in Fort
Wayne.[8] Dorothea Moore also imbued Hull-House's "long windows" and "wide doorways" with semiotic significance, for the "hint
of the aspect that was its own in the long-gone privacy of the estate"
created an interspatial bridge that eased the transition to a new
lifestyle.[9] By the time Francis Hackett arrived in 1906, this prospective resident encountered a huge complex of buildings filling nearly
every corner of the Halsted block.

The building in which we lived on Halsted Street did not fall back from the street. It was plump in the middle of the neighborhood, and yet it had a long semi-cloistral corridor and a grave, deep spacious reception hall which declared you were out of the world.[10]

This kind of public/private duality permeated descriptions of Hull-House, evoking the liminality of a public parlor and the ongoing exchange of "new homes for old." They also symbolized the paradox of its residential mission—the commitment to live "in the world" of the Nineteenth Ward while maintaining a sequestered space "out of the world" of immediate hardship.

Illustrating the integral if often opaque relationship between identity and material reality, such spatial apprehensions probably went unregistered initially. Environmental comfort more often manifests itself in nerves that feel less tight, a sense of balance and ease of breath that releases in the presence of the familiar. When Addams and Ellen Starr first moved into their new environment, they brought with them all the trappings of a former existence, placing Addams's inherited silver on an elegant sideboard and hanging brocade curtains in the grand windows.[11] It was later when witnessing the effect of her furnishings upon her neighbors that Addams returned the drawing room's "handsome curtains" to her sister, saying that "the moral effect of them down here is not good."[12] She also eventually packed away her silver and replaced it with a display of copper pans.[13] Rather than retroactively positing the effects of Addams's initial home decoration as the results of conscious intention, such moments are most intriguing for how they move squarely within the habitual, tacit, and implicit rhythms of domesticity. Such a material and ritual network of performed belonging often goes unnoticed to the subject whose position it secures, registered as meaningful only after it has been withdrawn or after someone from outside notices an exclusion. While Addams reflexively made a home by reproducing the sparkle of silver and the texture of brocade, her mode of habitation subsequently signaled class privilege (and possibly a prime chance for theft) to outside neighbors. A spatial practice was received as a message; an embodied re-creation of material life was read semiotically through the "eyes" of her new world. Living in a home that was also on display, settlers thus learned to understand when habitual performances sent "meanings." "With all the world looking," they cultivated a skill in tacking between the reflexively material and the self-consciously spectatorial.

Most of the people who took up residence at Hull-House had also lived in homes outside an urban space, a fact that influenced not only how they adapted but also what kind of reforms they instituted. Journalists made much of the contrast between the "pastoral calm" of Addams's former life in Cedarville and the "metropolitan sprawl" and "urban jungle" where she set up house later.[14] Florence Kelley later nostalgically recalled childhood life in Germantown, a suburb of Pennsylvania, where she moved about "in an ivy-clad, pebble-dashed, gable-roofed old house, on a slightly terraced hillside, over-looking the lovely little Winghocking Creek, long since, alas! a city sewer."[15] A reformer's embodied response to a new urban field filled with pollution and sewage, crammed with "ramshackle" buildings and large factories, was often one of intense disorientation and dis-comfort. The air was too much for Starr, who periodically left to imbibe the fresh air blowing in the breeze of her family's home. Residents bought bicycles and organized outings to Lake Michigan or to the more rural setting of the North Shore.

> I think I could not live through these days if it were not for the thought of a bicycle ride in the evening. . . . We leave the nine-teenth ward steaming and choking and melting and in fifteen minutes we are on the lakeshore drive spinning along with the air fresh on our faces and the lake before us and the moon just coming up.[16]

Meanwhile, settlers mediated the relation between the urban and the rural by installing parks, playgrounds, and rooftop Fresh Air Soci-eties. The settlement all but ceased its activities during the summer, and many residents left during those two or three months because of their difficulty in adapting bodily to the summer heat. "Retreat" spaces—whether they took the form of a summer house or a well-to-do friend's apartment, a trip to Bar Harbor, Maine, or a bicycle jaunt to the lake—tempered the strain of Hull-House life. On the one hand, these interspatial retreats kept reformers from burning out altogether and enabled certain kinds of reform work that were diffi-cult to do while living in a house with constant interruptions. On the other hand, such privileged retreats distinguished settlers from their neighbors who could not "afford to live somewhere else."

Being part of this living experiment also required certain economic arrangements. Jane Addams's early assurance to vocal detractors that "we would always scrupulously pay our own expenses" indicated that this "we" would always be individuals who could afford to pay those expenses.[17] Some affiliates became involved with the settlement pre-

cisely because they possessed both a tendency to social-mindedness
and a family inheritance that made wage earning unnecessary. Anna
Farnsworth—"an agreeable woman of leisure and means"—acted as
"hostess-on-call to some and all who appeared at the front door" in the
early days. Interpreting the arrangement as a socially fair redistribution of resources, Florence Kelley looked on Farnsworth approvingly,
later berating a "squalid and recent social convention . . . according
to which everyone, however abundant and well-assured her income,
must earn her own living or be censured as a parasite."[18] Similarly, the
wealthy Jenny Dow devoted every morning to the settlement kindergarten for two years because she had no financial constraints. Gradually, Hull-House began developing a system for acquiring funds to
support people with special skills but with less economic stability.[19]
Julia Lathrop meshed employment and social investigation as a Cook
County charity visitor, earning a wage while gaining entry into a
system of social welfare whose corruption she eventually critiqued.
Florence Kelley generated income through employment as slum investigator and later factory inspector. As a mother and primary wage-
earner, however, she still found it hard to make ends meet. "The poor
lady is utterly destitute until she gets her next pay," Starr wrote of
"Sister Kelley." Starr gave her material hand-me-downs, another impromptu method of support.

> She is waring one green silk stocking & one blue one of former
> glory & she has no car fare left. She didn't seem to have any cotton
> drawers, so I gave her some, as I chance to be rich therein. . . . She
> has to pay the board of her three children & their nurse, & the
> nurse's wages & it takes all she can earn, but she is awfully sorry for
> people who have no "chicks."[20]

Many settlers worked outside of the settlement in capacities that
were not, as Francis Hackett said, "social work." He himself was
literary editor of the *Chicago Evening Post* and made a fine living as a
Chicago writer. Starr, Nancrede, Gyles, Twose, and several other
residents taught classes in art, gymnastics, literature, history, and
other subjects in surrounding North Shore, city, and regional
schools.

Despite the privileges of family and education—indeed sometimes because of them—would-be settlers still had enormous difficulty fashioning alternate life-paths for themselves. Exchanging a
new domesticity for an old one became particularly difficult for
young women when members of a previous home disapproved of
their ventures.

Jane Addams. *(Photo courtesy of University of Illinois at Chicago, The University Library, Jane Addams Memorial Collection.)*

> If ever a girl expresses any wish to *do* anything for her less fortunate sisters her mother throws cold water on it and probably says "O, my dear, I don't think it is laid upon you to put the world to rights" and then she shrinks up, and feels that she is of no use whatever and that it was of course very foolish and presuming of her to think she could do anything.[21]

At nearly every level of their lives, settlers renavigated definitions of private and public—from their vision of social reform to their vision of home, family, and habitus. In the heated moments of recalibration, female settlers were forced to address anew what exactly it meant to be a daughter, a wife, a mother, and a sister.

> It is always difficult for the family to regard the daughter otherwise than as family possession. . . . [H]er delicacy and polish are outward symbols of her father's protection and prosperity. . . . She was fitted to grace the fireside and to add lustre to that social circle which her parents selected for her.[22]

Contending with what Addams called "the family claim," settlement women continually juggled their social goals with the values prescribed by a gendered and classed upbringing. Eventually questioning public and private divisions between the state and the family, Addams argued, "[T]here comes periods of reconstruction, during which the task is laid upon a passing generation, to enlarge the function and carry forward the ideal of a long-established institution."[23] The family was one institution in need of enlargement. Unfortunately, this rhetoric of domesticity did not in itself ease the transition from private to civic housekeeping. As much as they tried to reconceive their neighborhood, city, and, later, country as a surrogate family, Starr, Lathrop, Addams, Kelley, Hamilton, and nearly every woman who affiliated with the settlement found themselves facing a crisis with a biological and self-labeled natural family. To many parents, spouses, and siblings, a woman's decision to devote herself to the settlement was a violation rather than an extension of her familial duties. Of course, the perception of violation was in some sense accurate. Familial extension reciprocally undid familial convention, and settlers found that the social enlargement of domesticity did not leave intact the operations and attachments of the private.

The duality of being both a settler and a daughter was particularly difficult for Addams, prompting her to devote much of her writing to "the relation between parents and their grown-up daughters" and to similar Lear-Cordelia encounters. After her father died, Addams's relations with her stepmother proved to be the most trying. Upon refusing a marriage proposal from her stepbrother, curtailing her social activities, and moving into the Nineteenth Ward, Addams received much condemnation from Anna Haldeman Addams.[24] "We constantly see parents very much disconcerted and perplexed in regard to their daughters when these daughters undertake work lying quite outside of traditional family interests," Addams wrote later of the entrenched hold of the family claim. "Any attempt that the individual woman formerly made to subordinate or renounce the family claim was inevitably construed to mean that she was setting up her own will against that of her family's for selfish ends."[25] Rather than framing the daughter's longing as a search for self-expression, Addams was careful to construe "the subjective necessity of settlement work" as another kind of female altruism. Directed outward on behalf of a social community in lieu of the private family, she avoided an argument of women's individual will or self-interests, extending instead the rhetoric of female self-sacrifice. Mrs. Addams did not buy it, criticizing Jane for using her inheritance on the settlement and for neglecting the troubles of her siblings and cousins. Addams compensated for her perceived negligence with frequent letters, gifts, and visits and, at one point, was relieved to report to her sister that "twice I have been here there has been no outbreak which seems to me to indicate that she is better."[26] While tensions with her stepmother persisted, friction with other siblings also mounted. When Addams's sister Mary died in 1894, leaving a husband who suffered from depression, Addams stepped in as guardian and benefactor to their four children—Stanley, Esther, John, and James Weber, who lived on and off at the settlement. The Hull-House founder's surviving sister, Alice, still felt that Jane was not meeting the claims of the biological, scolding, "I fear that the children and finances are cutting you off from your natural sister."[27] "Why are your letters so reproachful?" Jane defended herself. "I have my faults, but I am sure I am not snobbish and it is always hard for me to comprehend why you imagine me sensitive about my relatives."[28] That a woman who would be revered as a "mother to the nation" could receive so much criticism on the fulfillment of her gendered family duties was one of the paradoxes of settlement life and of an emerging female political culture. After a trying visit from Alice, Jane Addams further reflected on the imputed "naturalness" of her connection to her sister and the imputed unnaturalness of her connection to the settlement, saying to Mary Rozet Smith, "I have even been reduced to an elaborate theory in regard to it which I shall add to my 'Family Lecture.' "[29] The continually divided predicament of the female settler meant that Addams's "Family Lecture" was constantly expanded.

Settlement work not only distracted a woman from her family but threatened to question the natural and unnatural divide that determined who could make its claims on her. Like her other female colleagues, Dr. Alice Hamilton's exhausting career as a scientist and settlement worker by no means exempted her from the gendered and classed responsibilities of tending to the Hamilton home. "I have come home to be a domestic character for the next four months," she wrote to a fellow settler, "devoting my mind to my grandmother and Quint and the linen closet and the camphor chest and sweetmeats and a new waitress and other unusual things." Ironizing the domestic and professional duality of her existence, she knew that "in a little while I shall forget that I was ever a scientist or a settler. Already Chicago and everybody seems very far away."[30] For her, furthermore, sistering proved to be as time-consuming as daughtering. In October 1899, her younger sister Norah suffered a severe emotional breakdown while studying art in Europe. While Alice

returned temporarily to her professional life in Chicago, Norah's
health grew worse over the next several months, and Alice was
obliged to return home to relieve her mother of the emotional strain.
"When I look back on this winter," Alice would later write, "it seems
all Norah."[31] Once more, Hamilton voiced the competing claims of
her dual existence as sister and scientist. "Norah had just gone to
bed. I live so much in her these days that it seems the only thing I
have to write about, except 'Cell-Division in the central nervous
system of the Newborn Rat.' "[32] When it came time for Hamilton to
return to Chicago in the fall, she temporarily rented a flat near Hull-
House for herself and her sister until the settlement's flexible living
structure found room for both of them. Eventually, Norah became
a resident as well, one remembered as "shy, sidelong, original, a
Bronte, looking at one like a deer through the brake" but who
gradually occupied a position as a settlement artist and director of
the children's art program in 1921.[33] Through this quiet incorporation, a natural sister became a settlement sister, rerouting and diffus-
ing a privatized attachment into a social world of extended kin.

Florence Kelley's pressures of single motherhood exemplify another gendered version of the family claim. As a mother of three who
simultaneously spent much of her time lobbying on issues such as
child labor or the "family wage," Kelley's life mixed private and
public labor on behalf of children both biologically and socially
connected to her. Her case also illustrates the unevenness of this
mixture and the resilient pulls of naturalized family constructs amid
unnaturalized emotional attachments. While earlier pursuing an advanced degree in Zurich, Kelley met and married a Polish medical
student and fellow socialist named Lazare Wishnewetsky. After giving birth to three children in three years, she returned to New York
with her family in 1886, whereupon she endured expulsion from the
Socialist Labor Party as well as domestic abuse at the hands of a
husband with a failing medical practice. Thus betrayed by gender
inequities at both the level of party and family, she left New York
and Wishnewetsky with three children in tow.[34] As the first mother
who took up long-term residence at the settlement, Kelley's circumstance tested Hull-House's plan of living. Having cultivated partial
affiliations with a huge population of neighborhood children,
Kelley's exclusive affiliation to Margaret, Nicholas, and John called
for different strategies. Quietly challenging bourgeois assumptions of
motherhood and family while simultaneously exercising its class
privileges, Florence Kelley worked out an alternative arrangement
with reformers Henry Demarest Lloyd and his wife, who offered to
care for her children in their Winnetka home. Giving their qualified

socialist ideals a domestic incarnation, Kelley and the Lloyds thus manufactured what Jane Addams would call "an annex to Hull-House," a backstage bridge that interspatially negotiated the mix of motherhood and activism.[35] Meanwhile, Jane Addams scrambled together finances to support Kelley's living expenses and her efforts to start a labor bureau for working women. Eventually, Kelley's writing, speaking, teaching, and appointment as a "slum" investigator under Carroll Wright of the U.S. Department of Labor earned her enough income to pay for a Nineteenth Ward apartment on nearby Harrison Street. The financial and emotional stress would be constant for Kelley as she ventured into the harried life of a turn-of-the-century, wage-earning, reforming single mother.

> I have swarmed off from Hull House into a flat nearby with my mother and my bairns. . . . I am teaching in the Polk Street Night School Monday to Friday evening inclusive. By day I am a "temporary agent" in the employ of the Department of Labor—Carroll D. Wright—and, on Dec. 4 (Sunday) I go to Geneva, Dec 11th to Madison to tout for Hull House under the auspices of Mr. Ely, and Dec. 17th and 18th to Oak Park to speak on Hull House and the Sweating System on Sat and Sunday eves. *Me Voila!* There is only a limited amount of me at best; and, such as it is, it works twelve hours on weekdays for 'grub and debts' and on Sundays it goes out of town to tell the outlying public how life looks in the nineteenth. By way of consoling the small fry for these absences I take one with me. Puss [Margaret] is going to Geneva and Ko [Nicholas] to Madison with me.[36]

Gradually, Kelley's children—like Addams's niece and nephews and the children of a few other settlers—became fixtures at Hull-House and participated in children's activities. Often Hull-House residents would console "the small fry" in their mother's absence by taking them on excursions or bicycle trips. As the Hull-House nursery and after-school programs relieved other neighborhood working women from the responsibilities of child care, so this flexible arrangement—a socialized internality—afforded Kelley the time that she needed to conduct her investigations and craft her speeches and essays. Furthermore, some residents developed long-term affective bonds with these children. Indeed, as Kelley socialized her children's relationship to Hull-House, some settlers felt free to indulge the emotions of fictive kinship and surrogate parenthood. "About Margaret . . . I really believe that she has [become] much gentler to all the world," Addams wrote to Kelley of her energetic daughter. "I love her

so dearly that it is hard for me to discriminate and I find myself
absurdly on the defensive."[37] When Kelley left Chicago for a position
in New York as general secretary of the Consumers' League, she
temporarily left her son under Alice Hamilton's watch.

> Ko says that he has written you about this last expedition and his
> unlucky encounter with Mrs. Vance's dog. Don't worry about
> that at all. His leg was pretty much bruised but the skin was
> broken only in a place the size of a large pin-head, and I squeezed
> out the blood immediately and cauterized with pure carbolic so
> that I am sure no germs escaped. . . . He stood the cauterizing in
> a way that made me feel like crying.[38]

In their limericks, Waite, Luther, and Gyles subtextually expressed
similar feelings toward the Valerios' son Milo.

> Oh what should we do without Milo
> And our valiant Senor [sic] Valerio
> For the wonderful sight
> As he holds Milo tight
> Puts us into a state of delirio.[39]

Preparing to return to Fort Wayne for the summer, Alice Hamilton
lamented her separations from Ko. "He stayed for my last lunch and
risked being late to school, which pleased me immensely, and I think
he really hated to have me go. But children can't be as fond of you as
you are of them, do you think they can?"[40] Thus, single women who
had opted out of traditional marriage performed the practical responsibilities and felt the emotional ties of an alternative kind of child
rearing, one that quietly loosened the conventionally interdependent
performances of heterosexuality and kinship along the way. For
Florence Kelley, such impromptu mechanisms of child care helped
her to juggle her family claims. There is an irony in that fact that so
much of Kelley's activist work in this period lobbied for a "family
wage," that is, male-targeted labor compensation that assumed a
nuclear family along with an unemployed wife. The paradox anticipated many more as settlers entered the field of social welfare, often
arguing for policies that reinforced autonomous family models despite their own reliance and affective connection to a different type
of social organization.[41] "Rethinking intimacy calls out not only for
redescription," writes Lauren Berlant, "but for transformative analyses of the rhetorical and material conditions that enable hegemonic
fantasies to thrive in the minds and on the bodies of subjects while,

at the same time, attachments are developing that might redirect the different routes taken by history and biography."[42] The hegemonic thrived at Hull-House even as its everyday reality worked along redirected routes, tacitly incarnating filial and familial attachments alternative to the privatized modes they often directly espoused.

Queer Domesticity

The fact that so many civic housekeepers were not biological mothers is often touted as "contradictory" or "hypocritical" in the history of social welfare. What business did childless women have telling mothers and policymakers how to raise children?[43] A less offensive response to the question might foreground the liminality of public womanhood in this period and emphasize that this interregnum inevitably produced competing values, longings, and assertions as persons tried to make sense of themselves. Rather than entirely capitulating to the perception of contradiction, furthermore, it might be useful to examine its terms, asking why biological connection always serves as the index of motherhood and whether "childlessness" is experienced as an absolute condition. To reconsider these terms is also to brush up next to another question that vexes historians of turn-of-the-century women and of Hull-House in particular—the nature of settlement sexuality. Most often couched as a question of whether or not "Jane Addams was a lesbian," Lillian Faderman and others have claimed Hull-House in an emerging history of gay and lesbian identity in the United States. I would like to suggest that the anxieties that attend this historiographical move—whether one argues for it or against it—have something to do generally with the paradoxes of unmarried, nonbiological mothers in family politics. In the spring of 1996, when I walked through the exhibit *From Parlor to Politics,* the two issues most prominently aired in Washington, D.C., at the time were characteristically unlinked: same-sex marriage and welfare reform. While the former has transmuted often into a conversation about private property, while the latter has transmuted most often into a lament about the failure of the family, the case of Hull-House is a reminder that there might be a historical connection, one where each emerges as the condition of the other's ongoing resolution. Indeed, the alternative frames of queer theory question both the accusation of settlement hypocrisy and the "did they or didn't they" rigidity of positivist sexuality, unsettling the borders of both issues to allow a conversation between them. While sexuality appears only obliquely in the representation of Addams in the *From Parlor to Politics* exhibit (and is not addressed at all in the representation of Eleanor Roosevelt among her fellow First Ladies), its operation more generally unsettles the foundations of the "natural" to open up an extended kinship, thereby forming a tenuous link between the possibility of same-sex love, the undoing of the private family, and the utopic hope for public welfare.

Being a settler meant that one constantly integrated two present participles, living and working, and with them the spheres of privacy and publicity. Historiographical questions into the nature of intimacy sometimes have a difficult time reconciling such mixtures, searching as they often do for sexual and emotional lives in an ever-deferred interior, an isolated place where the realm of desire remains protected, privatized, and individuated. The frame might prompt focused investigations into particular zones of designated privacy, realms such as the bedroom, the diary, or the personal letter. However, such searches can become frustrated by the mobilities of a "queer world," one that is, in Lauren Berlant and Michael Warner's terms, "a space of entrances, exits, unsystematized lines of acquaintance, projected horizons, typifying examples, alternative routes, blockages, incommensurate geographies."[44] Amid the mayhem of Hull-House life, settlers could sometimes count on their bedrooms to function as a space of retreat. During an unusually stressful period, a frazzled Alice Hamilton "would go upstairs" and "hide myself for fear I would cry if somebody spoke to me."[45] Hull-House children remembered theater director Edith de Nancrede's lying down in her room after all-night technical rehearsals, though the ability to recall such solitary moments simultaneously records their interruption. Indeed, Nancrede's bedroom was reportedly always filled with theatrical props and children's costumes, materially marking the integration of working and living.[46] The settlement constantly housed overnight guests, requiring residents to release their bedroom for an evening and double up with a fellow settler. Whether it was to accommodate a guest, a new resident, or a fluctuating summer schedule, residents' individual living spaces were perpetually mobile, requiring a flexible habitus that could be spatially disorienting.

> Somehow the house seems all upset. Mr. Hill goes away, and the Moores; Mr. Valerio comes in to stay in Miss Gernon's room, Miss Thomas moves down to one of the Moore's [sic] rooms, Miss Gyles to the other, Miss Howe into Miss Gyles' room, and Miss Watson comes back to her room again.[47]

Thus replicating the interspatial motions of the rest of the settlement, even this conventionally private realm was subject to violation. At the same time, its incommensurate geography might serve as metaphor for the elusiveness of stable interiorities, sexual and otherwise, at Hull-House. The nomination of a space did not coincide with a singular inhabitant anymore than the coordinates of any other spatial identity stayed put. Unevenly incarnating a queer domesticity, the settlement's unsystematized lines of activity instead formed the patterns of a habitus decidedly off-kilter.

"It is a picture, first of all, of being a resident grouped with other residents."[48] When Francis Hackett wrote an *Atlantic Monthly* essay entitled "Hull-House—a Souvenir," his collected memories were filled with many pictures of intimate residential groupings, a co-presence of people and space that was for many the appeal of living in the settlement. The Hull-House environment borrowed in part

Settlement "family" members of different generations gathering for tea. *(Photo courtesy of University of Illinois at Chicago, the University Library, Jane Addams Memorial Collection.)*

from the alternative arrangements of the dormitory, a space to which many female settlers were already accustomed from their years in female seminaries and colleges. Besides the lessons of a curriculum, the college experience introduced women to new forms of sociospatial interaction.[49] In most cases, women shared a dormitory's living room, dining area, bathing, and toilet facilities; single or double bedrooms with desks and bureaus secured a modicum of privacy. Even then, however, this privacy was often regulated by strict dormitory rules and alternately violated by a spontaneous social life.[50] To what extent college women relied on the domestic service of other women depended upon the institution. At Rockford Female Seminary, Addams and Starr each had "to tend the stove in her room, furnish her own linen and table service, and she was expected to devote an hour each day to domestic tasks."[51] Even at institutions where women performed fewer domestic chores, female undergraduates always had to do more than young men at brother institutions. While this difference in expectation reproduced traditional conceptions of women's sphere and women's work, it simultaneously better prepared women reformers for settlement activities. Additionally, in an effort to restrict male and female contact and especially women's mobility, often women's classes were held in the dormitory.[52] Once again, these gendered limits predisposed college women to mix home, work, and educational spaces. Remaining inventories of Hull-House from 1901 to 1903 evoke interspatial strains of women's dormitory environments, though the rhetorical position of the inventory presumes timespace unity that rarely lasted from year to year. Reminiscent of the standard furnishings of the dormitory room, each bedroom contained a bed with bedding, bureau, desk, chair, and bookcase. In addition to sleeping, writing—a constant reform activity—was conducted in these provisionally sequestered spaces.[53] The extra furnishings recorded in the inventory of Addams's room—"2 straight chairs, 2 Rocking chairs, Sofa"—suggest that it officially tripled as a writing space, sleeping space, and receiving space.[54] The tripartite function replicated that of Addams's room at Rockford Female Seminary, "an available refuge from all perplexities" where college friends remembered sharing late-night deliberations and confidences.[55] While single women more often lived in the top two floors of the Hull mansion, it was not always a continuous homosocial sphere.[56] Married couples occasionally stayed in separate second-floor rooms.

Hull-House cultivated affective bonds among women that reproduced and altered those initially developed in college. While female education for mostly white women was a step out of the "rigid gender-role differentiation" that Carol Smith-Rosenberg argues led "to the emotional segregation of women and men," the segregation within the university fostered an alternative "female world of love and ritual" adapted to the needs of prospective public womanhood. "Within such a world of emotional richness and complexity, devotion to and love of other women became a plausible and socially accepted form of human interaction."[57] Though Addams often mocked what she called the sentimental "spooning malady" of Rockford undergrads, such an intense eight-year friendship with Starr spurred the settlement scheme.[58] As the relationship between Starr and Addams faltered, Mary Rozet Smith would become Addams's longtime companion as well as one of Hull-House's strongest financial supporters. While Smith-Rosenberg and Faderman both choose to solve the conundrum of female same-sex relations by arguing for the social acceptability of Victorian romantic attachments and Boston marriages, the ("nonsexual") romantic friendship argument does not wholly address why such unions remain so difficult to study.[59] At the very least, the fact that Addams later burned most of the letters she received from Mary Rozet Smith (but did not burn others) suggests her sense of a social prohibition, perhaps one responding to the increasingly stigmatized construction of "the lesbian" through the early twentieth century. On the other hand, the urge to decide that this burning simultaneously destroyed the "real" history of Addams's psychic life is also suspect epistemologically, reifying a secreted conception of self that ignores the implications of Hull-House's undoing of privacy. "I want to argue for the possibilities of the 'not said' and the 'not seen' as conceptual tools for lesbian studies," writes Martha Vicinus of the implications of queer theory for gay and lesbian history. "Recognizing the power of not naming—of the unsaid—is a crucial means for understanding a past that is so dependent upon fragmentary evidence, gossip, and suspicion. . . . A more open definition of women's sexual subjectivity, and of the nature of lesbian desire, will enable us not only to retrieve a richer past, but also to understand the complex threads that bind women's public actions with their private desires."[60] Vicinus argues against a curious literalism in the study of sexuality, maintaining that a specifically sexual vocabulary may not be a necessary precursor to a genealogy of lesbian attachment. Indeed, like many other women who ventured into the territory of public womanhood, desires of several different varieties structured and were structured by Hull-House women's desire for each other.[61] It might be helpful to notice not simply that strong women did not take to men (not simply that women with "careers" did not have husbands) but, more profoundly,

that the intial task of developing the field of public welfare was
coextensive with the undoing of a private, heterosexual family.

"There is reason in the habit of married folks keeping together," Addams wrote Smith from inside a hotel room. "I almost cry for your ministrations at night when my conscience is bad and my spirits low."[62] Her out-of-town lecture had not gone well that evening, and Addams desperately missed the woman whose personal care supported her activist efforts in social care. Cultivating what they called "a healing domesticity," Smith maintained Addams's personal equilibrium, sometimes accompanying her on lectures, serving as her secretary, helping her watch her weight, and buying clothes for her.[63] When Addams later wrote a poem elegizing her first encounter with Smith, she ironized a hectic field of activity in which their unshakable couplehood emerged. "A girl, both tall and fair to see, / (To look at her gives one a thrill). / But all I thought was, would she be / Best fitted to lead club, or drill?"[64] From the mid-1890s onward until their deaths, Addams's exchanges with Smith mixed intimate declarations with accounts of the prosaics of reform, recording the day's concerns over financial records, children's clubs, or resident disgruntlement. Writing hurriedly, at a slant, asking her to "please excuse this ink," Addams's letters to Smith were streams of consciousness, simultaneously reporting the rhythms of their attachment ("Your letter was very dear to me") and the rhythms of Hull-House ("Miss Holbrook goes this week and Gertrude Barnum has come to take her place") in a conflation of private and public domesticities.[65] The needs of Hull-House and the needs of their relationship were often indissociable from each other. "I have made Herculean efforts to bring up the nursery account but as yet no one has subscribed. Mrs. Bowen gave $100.00 dollars which paid up the coal bills."[66] Smith's growing status as an active financial benefactor gave this interdependence an especially material solidity. "My dear friend, your letter with the news of the check came to hand this morning. I cannot tell you how relieved and grateful I am, and what a difference it will make in the running order of things for all the next months."[67] Extending Ann Ferguson's insights into the role of women's rare economic independence in enabling lesbian identity, the Addams-Smith partnership further demonstrates a link between a fiscally endowed homosociality and the viability of female reform.[68] Occasionally subsumed by "that old sinking of the heart," Addams often guiltily lamented the mixing of emotion and money.[69] Smith consoled Addams by framing their love and her financial contributions as a combined antidote to her own guilt as an overprivileged female.

I came home with quite a glow at my heart. . . . I am given to turning sentimental at this season, as you know, and I feel quite a rush of emotion when I think of you. I have been having another bad time with my conscience (my "wealth") and I've been in the depths of gloom until yesterday when the sight and sound of you cheered me. . . . I'll put in the January cheque to lend a practical air to this sentimental missive.[70]

Addams and Smith solidified their material connection by buying a house together in Bar Harbor, Maine, and gradually became enmeshed in the web of each other's familial attachments. "Please give my love to your dear father and mother"; such salutations appeared in many a letter.[71] "I do hope that your mother is better," wrote Addams one day, whose concern over family health quickly transitioned into a report on the settlement's health. "Please give her my love and tell your father that [we] had another $1000 for the campaign by Mr. Robinson of the Railway station."[72]

The reach of their alternative emotional umbrella extended to children—not only to each other's nieces and nephews but to children of the neighborhood as well. When Jane Club resident Maggie Toomey gave birth to a daughter out of wedlock, Addams and Smith discussed the possibility of adopting the child under Smith's guardianship. The exchange surrounding the decision occasioned a poignant recognition of their own commitment to each other— even as their eventual decision to give up the child (also named Jane) to Edward and Dorothea Moore reflected the inertial pull of the conventionally appropriate. Addams tried to placate Smith. "Jane shant go until you come back but I really think it is the best arrangement. My heart quaked when I first had it definitely fixed in my mind but I am getting used to it."[73] Quelling the quakings of the heart would take more effort over the ensuing days as Smith hurried home to bid good-bye to the baby. "Mrs. Moore meant to take Jane next Friday but has postponed it a week or she will wait longer if you don't get back before then," wrote Addams, orchestrating the rhythms of separation. Asking her "Dearest Lady" to think positively of the "creative growing" environment of the Moores' "Ohio farm," she spoke to herself and to Smith once more in the commonsensical, self-iterating voice of the hegemonic: "I don't see how you could possibly take the baby."[74] The adjacent history of Smith's relationship to Addams further unsettles the concept of civic housekeeping. More than simply essentialist feminism, the project of female reform also entailed a kind of queer bonding. Even when the discourse reified the category of the heterosexual wife, the performance of civic housekeeping deviated from it, whether in same-sex attachment between unmarried women or in love between adults and nonbiological children. These nonnormative intimacies developed within and despite larger structures that did not legitimize them. And, while this moment in Smith and Addams's relationship shows a reluctance to formalize a prospective intimacy, it would be equally remiss to characterize as "childless" the ongoing lives of these two Hull-House women.[75]

An exclusive historiographical focus on the homosocial "couple" of Addams and Smith would be in danger of ignoring other aspects of the lived performance of homosociality at Hull-House, particularly its function in constituting collectivity among figurative siblings. Moreover, homosocial relations at Hull-House are not adequately interpreted as a "sphere" but as a set of practices, taken up and put away as necessity and emotion dictated. Homosocial interaction altered and fluctuated within a larger collectivity and depended upon individual desires, relative publicity, the discursive medium of expression, the task at hand, and (as will be discussed later) the copresence of men. Upon arrival, many settlement women used _Miss_ followed by a surname to refer to each other, thus replicating a formal and deferential mode of address practiced in the homes and colleges they had left behind. Later, many developed pet names for each other, with Julia Lathrop and Florence Kelley opting to call Jane Addams "J.A." or "Lady Jane." Gradually, many of the residents substituted "Dearest," "Lady," or "Sister" when addressing each other. An intimate habit that at once symbolized and constituted feelings of affection, it was also a performative utterance that reiterated their shared identity as an alternative "family." Such addressive relations were performed—not only in letters to each other—but within the temporally unfolding rhythms of daily life. While letters between other reformers also suggested intense emotional bonds, affective ties were restored more often in the daily rituals of a shared physical space. Addams, Lathrop, and other residents would often wait for Kelley to return from her studies in the law library before going to bed. When Kelley moved to New York City after seven years as a resident, her absence caused an affective rupture in the spatiotemporal ordering of daily life. "Dear Mrs. Kelley, It is just about the time you used to come home from the library and people are sitting around looking as if they were waiting for you."[76] Novice settler Clara Paige missed Jane Addams and had to console herself by reading her latest book; "if you were here tonight and alone in your study, I'm sure I'd come down for a little while and maybe talk about _Peace and Bread_."[77] Not solely the exclusive attachment of Jane

Addams, Mary Rozet Smith had a profound emotional impact on other settlers. "She left no mark on history but she left a deep mark on all who knew her even slightly, for she had a genius for personal relations. . . . Her large and gracious home on Walton Place was a refuge for Miss Addams—and a place of refreshment for many of the rest of us."[78] So important was her presence to Waite, Luther, and Gyles that they crafted a limerick in honor of this nonresident, recalling her demeanor using similarly classed and gendered metaphors of charm, tranquillity, and beauty.

> Miss Smith is so lovely and stately
> and she carries herself so sedately
> Her words are ne'er tart
> And she has a big heart
> And her charms we can't state accurately.[79]

Such flexible homosocial networks were integral to Hull-House's viability.[80] Female residents turned to each other after a failed lecture to a committee on labor reform or for a suggestion on Girls Club activities. Such partial, nonexclusive homosocial ties undergirded much of these women's reform activity through a wider web of intimate affiliation.

Given their participation in the world of reform, relationships between Hull-House women were also not exclusively sentimental in nature. For many women, participation in the seminar rooms of higher education was an introduction to practices of debate and argumentation.[81] Florence Kelley exclaimed of Cornell University, "My freshman year was one continued joy. An-hungered and a-thirst for learning, and for young companionship, which now abounded on every side."[82] Similarly, Addams, Lathrop, Starr, and other "Rockford women talked, argued, and discussed," debating the philosophy of Carlyle or women's emergent role in society.[83] Beatrice Webb would write later of the settlement's bracing deliberative atmosphere. "One continuous intellectual ferment is the impression left on the visitor to Hull-House."[84] Later, prospective residents worried about whether they possessed this kind of intellectual capital. "I wish I knew as much about sociology," Alice Hamilton worried to her cousin Agnes. Not only could she not talk of sociology intelligently, "but I cannot even listen intelligently. Still it would be loads of fun to listen and I certainly can learn."[85] Later she would recall how a little group of residents used to bribe Kelley with hot chocolate to talk to them. "We had to be careful; foolish questions, half-baked opinions, sentimental attitudes met with no mercy at her

hands."[86] To Starr, Kelley's enthusiasm for intellectual betterment
was contagious; "Sister Kelley is such a vastly good talker," she
exclaimed, vowing to study German with Kelley and "to suck that
orange (to use her expression) to the extent of its juiciness and my
capacity."[87] From the fights over the morning newspaper at the
coffeehouse to heated debates in the resident's dining room, Hull-
House women gained verbal competence by testing theories and
questioning each other. The intense friendships underpinning these
discussions allowed them to engage in committed debate, to become
the "argumentative family" that Edith Abbott said "often dis-
agreed."[88] The strength of affective bonds allowed them to push
beyond the rules of tact and compromise regulating social interaction between new colleagues and genteel women, preparing them for
less sympathetic forums outside of Hull-House.

The crafting of an alternative collective was not wholly harmonious, a reminder that Hull-House's world of love and ritual also
recalled the frictions of family life. Several residents found Kelley
intimindating. Madeleine Wallin, a sometime secretary to Addams,
described Kelley as "a bright, restless, strong-minded woman, very
original, progressive and executive, but not exactly pleasant for
steady companionship. . . . Her incessant activity of mind might
prove a trifle wearing," especially to young women still testing their
own insights and stamina.[89] Though increasingly advocating radical
ideas for social democracy, Starr also found herself physically and
temperamentally shaky when it came to Hull-House's cooperative
life. "I had an outward & visible excuse for the bad temper, which
was convenient, but it knocked me up, fearfully." Starr was self-
critical about her tendencies and made consistent, if unsuccessful,
attempts to change. "All the saintliness which I have been singing to
you took flight . . . and I was of the outward color of pale lemon; &
of about the acidity."[90] Madeleine Wallin admitted that while Starr
had "done much for the art sense of the neighborhood . . . I don't
like her particularly."[91] Later, another settler made gentle fun of
Starr's temper and religious fervor, worrying about whether she
would "act up."[92] As Addams rapidly garnered most of the public
attention and solidified her friendship with Smith, Starr occupied an
insecure role. She was unwilling to perform Smith's function as an
unconditional support system; during a testier period in their relationship, Addams told Ellen, "you respect me and love me but you
don't *like* me."[93] While decades later Starr told Addams that she in
no way resented Smith's or Addams's accomplishments, her earlier
depictions of the thrill of political action suggest that she compared
her reputation to Addams's.

The *whole* procession passed the house, & I was leaning out of my window all the time, recognizing my friends, waving to them, throwing kisses to the girls I know. The men took off their hats to me, & waved them & cheered. It was great. I never had such an experience. They cheered the house three or four times & Jane once rather feebly. She said to me, afterward, "I am glad they cheered the house." And I didn't say, "I suppose you know why."[94]

Minor jealousies and tensions of all sorts occurred among different members of the Hull-House clan, partly due to the stresses of co-operative living, partly due to disagreements about the goals of reform, and partly due to the rhythms of love and attention that never extended themselves as equally or as abundantly as everyone hoped.

"Dearly Beloved: The Lady misses you more than the uninitiated would think she had time for."[95] The writer was Florence Kelley, speaking to the beloved Mary Rozet Smith of a forlorn Lady Jane. The statement performs a relationality not only of love—between Kelley and Smith, between Smith and Addams—but also of mundane exclusion, a fine border between the sphere of these three women and the rest of the newer residents. By 1894, Hull-House residents were already using the word *initiate* to refer to their new housemates, thus informally monitoring the processual development of a settlement worker.[96] As Addams and the Hull-House team increasingly acquired a sense of what they were doing, they also became concomitantly aware of the kind of people and skills they needed. "Miss West is growing in grace and poise day by day. The household is simply enthusiastic over her. We would have made a fatal mistake if we had let her go," wrote Addams privately, revealing how much she assessed the development of group members and sought social equilibrium among them.[97] By the mid-1890s, the Hull-House group had given the initiation process a temporal formalization. Prospective settlers applied for residence—usually after having been a volunteer—whereupon they could be provisionally accepted for a trial period of six months. Referring to this liminal time as being "on probation," several felt uncomfortable being watched, worrying whether they would pass muster.[98] Alice Hamilton felt like a "hypocrite" during a conversation with Florence Kelley. "I don't even know whether I believe in not buying sweater's clothes," she lamented, calling herself "a lonely stranded heathen among many elect who scare her."[99] Since they were openly criticized very rarely, settlement workers usually generated their own panoptic structure of self-surveillance, imagining the disappointed eyes of Addams or another settlement leader watching over an unsuc- cessful reform endeavor.

> You see, of course, I was to work among the Italians. In some way I
> was to try to teach them more sensible and hygenic ways of doing
> things. . . . Well, this year it has just been a fizzle. . . . All winter
> long I kept feeling what a farce it all was and how Miss Addams was
> classing me with the people she is always talking about, who have
> had scientific or literary training but are utterly unable to put their
> knowledge into a form useful to simple people.[100]

By reciting publicly their hopes for ideal settlers without defined individual targets, veteran residents circulated a sense of their standards without enforcing them formally. Instead, the atmosphere induced a self-monitoring on the part of every worker who worried about being "classed" as hypocritical or just plain ineffectual. Occasionally, Addams had to intervene in situations where a resident's zealous self-critique became out of control.[101] Addams also spent much of her time worrying over settlers' propensity for overwork— "G. Barnum is on the verge of nervous prostration"[102]—or trying to avoid their departure—"Miss Losfelt is so worn out that she declares her intention of leaving May 1st."[103] The intervention of the charismatic head resident at such moments often made the difference in a settlers' decision to stay. "The only nice thing about all that time," wrote one frazzled resident, "was that Miss Addams seemed so genuinely distressed at the thought of my going away. . . . Well of course there is no need for me to tell you that I am going back."[104]

Hamilton's characterization of the "many elect who scare her" betrays—even if self-mockingly—her perception of a difference in power between herself and the more experienced reformers. While the most formal enactment of status hierarchies occurred when residents sat at the dinner table according to their seniority, more often such differentials were reiterated within the mundanity of social interaction. Hamilton closed an 1899 letter to Kelley expressing her sense of their unequal obligations to each other. "Don't think you must answer this. I know you have more to do than you have time to do it in and I wrote you just as I do to Miss Addams, trusting you not to feel that I expected any answer."[105] Status differences structured minute performances of everyday life in the hallways and living rooms of their shared residence.

Miss Addams still rattles me, indeed more so all the time, and I am at my very worst with her. I am really quite school-girly in my relations with her; it is a remnant of youth which surprises me. I know when she comes into the room. I have pangs of idiotic jealousy toward the residents whom she is intimate with. She is— well she is quite perfect and I don't in the least mind raving over her to you.[106]

Such surreptitious eye contact, measured physical distance, and solicitous vocal tone permeated the daily conduct of an initiate who reinstituted the status of the elect by deferring to it. Within same-sex interactions, the power differentials could galvanize homosocial attachment more often than inhibit it. Alice Hamilton's self-description as a "raving" "school-girl" imported the vocabulary of the female college, where committed same-sex friendships were called "raves" and where a female student's intense fixation on a charismatic female teacher was conventional.[107] Hamilton recorded the knock-kneed, stammering flush of a young woman in the presence of a female idol. In a house filled with women venturing onto unknown territory, in a house filled with women for whom the conditions of that venturing required something other than heterosexual marriage, the person one aspired to be and the person one hoped to love could often be one and the same. Here, the erotics of projection (the urge to be like) along with the erotics of proximity (the urge to be near) coalesced into an adoration in which the desire for sameness was the principle of attraction.[108] While the hope of one's likeness compounded the thrill of one's nearness to an idealized woman, such attractions and identifications were more often collective and diffuse rather than fully exclusive. At the same time, the instability of this unevenly inclusive relationality could also produce pangs of "idiotic jealousy" as settlers worried whether there was enough likeness and love to go around.

The behaviors of new residents positioned settlers such as Lathrop, Starr, and Kelley as the "elect," and later, nonresident funders such as Mary Rozet Smith and Louise deKoven Bowen along with Grace Abbott, Edith Abbott, and Alice Hamilton herself would enjoy a certain status. However, a survey of accounts demonstrates that Addams was consistently revered. Without capitulating to the habit of historical thought that equates Hull-House with Addams, it is important to understand how thoroughly the perception of her unique greatness saturated settlement life. Illustrating the processual historicity of the legend of Jane Addams, residents continually cooperated in maintaining their head resident's identity, often expressing their awed regard in the most rhapsodic of terms. Calling her "the greatest of mortals," Madeleine Wallin noted Addams's insightful interpersonal skills. "She is really a cosmic individual, and is able to get into relations with every sort of person by instinctively giving him what he wants and can assimilate."[109] Addams's charisma—and its repeatedly shared narrative construction—fundamentally bound this array of settlers into a working ensemble.

> The essential fact of Hull-House, the dominant fact, was the presence of Miss Addams. This is strange because while one was living there Miss Addams was away a good deal of the time, and when she was there one did not have a great deal to do with her; yet Hull House, as one clearly felt at the time, was not an institution over which Miss Addams presided, it was Miss Addams, around whom an institution insisted on clustering. However, she might deprecate it, and no one was more skillful than Miss Addams in deprecation, we often said "without her, it's—nothing."[110]

Though by the second decade Addams's schedule kept her away from the settlement, settlers created bonds of community and a shared work ethic by remembering her. Addams's habit of deprecation was also fundamental to her leadership style, for despite the deferential treatment she enjoyed, one of the qualities residents most espoused was her unwillingness to accept it.[111] "Nobody even ventured to refuse her to visitors, or even to take her telephone calls unless authorized to do so. She was impatient of solicitude, and her attitude brought about a wholesome, rather Spartan atmosphere."[112] Addams did of course authorize residents to answer her mail and field sporadic responsibilities. Privately, a settler complained when she had to play this intermediary role: "I am a stop gap and there are so many things I want to do."[113] However, the perception that Addams did not feel entitled to her subordinates' solicitude made them more solicitous; the anticipation of a refusal made them more willing to offer her privileges. A similarly indirect style of leadership characterized her attitude toward residents' activities more generally, allowing her to extract work from the settlers without appearing to do so.

> [F]ar indeed from domineering anybody . . . The residents are all her willing servitors, and she holds them all by reason of her very admirable qualities of mind and disposition. . . . She never drives anyone to work & indeed is most considerate in that regard. But it is impossible to live with her and not feel to some extent the pressure of work to be done.[114]

Several initiates endured a similar paradoxical feeling—the appreciation of the lack of official responsibilities—of not being "yoked
oxen"—combined with the nagging, self-generated sensation that
they were not quite worthy—that "it g[a]ve back more than it was
receiving from me. . . . I always had the feeling I did not do
enough."[115] By securing help while not seeming to ask for it, Addams
channeled the Victorian woman's skill in the realm of "indirect influence," thereby securing loyalty and long hours. The effacement of her
own ego in the midst of attention and reverence thus mitigated the
occupational hazards of female leadership. Unthreateningly circum-
venting the stigma attached to strong womanhood, justifying her activities as performances on behalf of others rather than herself, Addams both negotiated the gendered dilemmas of settlement leadership
and all the more trenchantly secured her power as a moral authority.

Addams's deferential leadership style further mediated another aspect of Hull-House's social life—the presence of men. As a domestication of politics that required men and women differently to inhabit
the same parlor, settling developed a range of heterosocial dynamics.
While female residents cautiously opened their upstairs living quarters
to an occasional married couple, they were less willing to risk the
improprieties of mixed-sex cohabitation. Consequently, the group of
single men who moved into the Nineteenth Ward initially settled into
a building across from the mansion. Later, the "Men's Settlement"
moved from 245 Polk to new apartments built atop the Bulter Building. Rather than a compromise of feminist separatism, this mixed-sex
arrangement is analytically most useful for how it enabled different
types of coalition and kinship, reciprocally unsettling the performance of masculinity within its walls. Hull-House's woman-led
administration required turn-of-the-century men to rethink a conventional hierarchy between the sexes. Playing upon the presumed
unnaturalness of its "petticoat" government, Johnny Powers mocked
Addams's control of her male colleagues with posters of her pulling
out her hair.[116] Beatrice Webb indulged similar stereotypes when she
described the women and men of Hull-House, suggesting that a
reversal of gender power affected its pace and motion.

> The residents consist, in the main, of strong-minded energetic
> women, bustling about their various enterprises and profes-
> sions, interspersed with earnest-faced self-subordinating and mild-
> mannered men who slide from room to room apologetically.[117]

Whether women bustled and men slid, settlers rarely theorized
Hull-House as a space that self-consciously disrupted gender codes.

Rather, accusations of gender disruption came from outside, especially with the early-twentieth-century success of the suffrage movement and the rise of a modern preoccupation with sexuality. Francis
Hackett peppered his "souvenir" with defensive moves against the
presumption of its "unnatural" residency. Mimicking the voice of
the outside critic, he acknowledged that the women were castigated
as "sexually unemployed" and the men as "mollycoddles."[118] Even as
Hull-House embodied Progressive values, its living plan threatened
the anxious codes of Progressive manhood. Over the course of the
century, a man's subordination to female authority would translate
with more ease into an ambiguity about his sexual object choice.
Furthermore, in living with each other as single men, male settlers
walked a tenuous line of homosocial identification, the border that
Eve Kosofsky Sedgwick notes only very finely separates being "a
man's man" from being "interested in men."[119] Hence, Hull-House
could become for a young writer such as Hackett, if not a space of
homosexual practice, then a "*temporal* space where the young, male
bourgeois literary subject" navigated his way through "homosexual
panic."[120]

References in settlement documents to male bachelorhood, to
cross-generational male contact, to male melancholia, or to behavior
that settlers termed "queer" all seem to invite interpretation about
masculine experience only by reifying a host of sexual stereotypes
and ahistorical projections. Hackett's prose panicked around his
memories of fellow settler Frank Hazen: "almost unbearably aesthetic, dancing pliantly, hard at work in the Hull House Theatre . . . with a nervous giggle to hide his inarticulateness."[121] On
the other hand, he assured his readers of the hearty masculinity of
the Yeomans brothers; Charlie, whose "eyes squeezed up when he
laughed, [was] solid worth" while Ned's "crackling laugh [was] full
of the same Saxon manliness."[122] The instability of masculinity frustrates historiographical speculation and prompts a renewed respect
for the ambivalences of sexuality's unarchivability. At the same time,
Hull-House's domesticity did allow the indulgence of a variety of
gendered sentiments and occasioned a compendium of masculine
performances, even when its practitioners only cautiously represented them. Outside of a naturalized family structure and its roles
of husband and father, a sampling of male settlers exemplifies how
Hull-House's social organization made available a range of masculine positions. Described by Alice Hamilton as "our mournful widower," Frederick Deknatel found a role for himself in running the
Boys Club, later becoming an invaluable financial secretary to Addams and several other Hull-House organizations.[123] Robert Hunter

Hull-House residents—"sisters" and "brothers"—assembling for a photo session in the courtyard. *(Photo courtesy of University of Illinois at Chicago, the University Library, Jane Addams Memorial Collection.)*

lived at Hull-House while running the Chicago Homes Association, thus acting as a paternal civic housekeeper. Describing the comportment of another paternal civic housekeeper, Hackett affectionately recalled George Hooker's "steel-rimmed glasses, hair a little untidy, myopic, crammed with statistics on municipal ownership, unoiled, dry and good."[124] In their limericks, Luther, Waite, and Gyles made sure that neither the hypermasculine Mr. Yeomans's compassion nor his coiffure went without notice.

> Mr. Yeomans has finished with toys
> His playthings just now are his boys
> All on end is his hair

And his face full of care
And the world has lost some of its joys.[125]

Thus paternal civic housekeepers also indulged in the sentiments of children's club leadership and the altruistic erotics of juvenile play. For Francis Hackett, "George Mortimer Randall Plantagenet Twose" warranted the most ebullient and affectionate chronicle: "Him at any rate I shall sacrifice without decency." Hackett characterized Twose "as something of the capricious and something of the romantic" and recalled how he "decorated his wall with great squares of tinfoil or silver paper out of tea chests, the whole side of the wall—it was peculiarly ghastly."[126] Luther, Waite, and Gyles ribbed Twose's tendencies toward despondency.

> This tall man is G. M. R. Twose
> When he's childish enough to have the blues
> Into space he will stare
> And deep gloom and despair
> Envelop him down to his shoes.[127]

A person of magnetic if mercurial temperament, Twose was a key figure at the settlement; the space and the man constituted themselves recursively around each other. "Hull House was the only place in Chicago for a restive man like Twose, and Twose was excellent for Hull House."[128]

Despite the personal lifestyles chosen by its founding single women, Hull-House's mixed-gender associations set the scene for many a romantic heterosexual courtship. Perhaps one of the first expressions of heterosexual attraction came from Starr, who wrote at length to her sister of the married Signor Valerio, demonstrating how easily Starr expressed heterosexual desire while, at this time, maintaining an intense bond of affection with her beloved Jane Addams. "He is as delightfully good & funny as ever;—one of the most entertaining men I ever saw, & certainly the most unselfish." Her words suggest that cultural prejudice impeded her affection more than his marital status. "Dear me! What a deal I am saying about him. I'm not in love with him, *quite,* only about half! If he weren't an Italian I would be."[129] As the number of settlers increased over the years, more long-lasting romantic attachments formed between men and women. As Dorothea Moore expounded, "[M]en have been known to come with motives not severely altruistic; there have actually been engagements, and to an interested friend from the far West who asked breathlessly, 'Do they marry?' one might answer the truth, 'often, alas! often.' "[130] As one of the few married early residents, Moore knew that there was reason to lament since, in the first decade's limited living quarters, marriage usually signaled departure. Meanwhile, the twists and turns of budding romance created a melodramatic atmosphere among the residents. Wilfreda Brockway endured a trying engagement as fiancée to John Linn, Addams's nephew. Alice Hamilton had the dubious distinction of being her confidante.

> Thursday night when I had just got into bed [Miss Brockway] came in and told me that John had come back and it was all right again. Oh how angry and disappointed I was. . . . Meantime she and Mr. Deknatel are getting very near to each other. Really it is striding on with marvelous rapidity. Last night they sat out together on the porch and he told her all about his wife. I know she thinks that she loves only John but what she needs is somebody to love, not any particular person, just somebody.[131]

Later, Brockway's romance with John Linn ceased entirely, and some years later she married her "lonely widower" Frederick Deknatel. They joined many other Hull-House couples; Gerard Swope married Mary Hill, and Maud Gernon committed herself to Edward Yeomans.

Male and female residents also developed other less intimate and romantic heterosocial interaction, indulging in more ironic and amused patterns of interpersonal exchange. Such protocols mediated Hull-House's heterosocial environment while simultaneously promoting a self-consciousness about the settlement paradox. Given settlers' keen attempts to distinguish their mission from the class elitism of charity institutions and given their increasingly complex understanding of the civic "maladjustment," they often faced their own position as emissaries of social change with some amount of ambivalence.[132] In order to mitigate a sense of personal superiority, many actively resisted the temptation to take themselves seriously. Sometimes they engaged in individual and collective rituals of ironic mockery—recounting moments of cross-class misunderstanding or critiquing the illogic of their own conditioned bourgeois habitus. Sometimes they reminded themselves of the larger structural inequities, recalling Upton Sinclair's rendering of settlement workers as "standing upon the brink of the pit of hell and throwing in snowballs to lower the temperature."[133] George Twose, the male resident who embodied the competing psychic pulls of an ambivalently modern reformer, was a particularly enthusiastic practitioner of ironic deprecation. "He wanted above everything to be free, and

at the same time to satisfy a conscience which had the disadvantages
of being fastidious and social." Hackett recalled that Twose's other-
directed energy was simultaneously his shameful secret, and he went
through elaborate rituals to "conceal his conscience as he clothed his
nakedness." Twose regularly "poohed-poohed Shaw," that great theo-
rizer of art and socialism; he regularly "pooh-poohed uplift. . . . At
the least sound of indignation," he could be counted on to exclaim,
"Rats, it'll all be the same in a hundred years."[134] Ironically reinforcing the internal settlement hierarchy, Twose encouraged fellow Hull-
House punsters to distinguish between its "Noble Set" and its "Frivolous Set."[135] Persistently proclaiming himself to be a member of the
latter, he parodied this set's lack of pretension.

> Why shouldn't the spirit of mortals be glad
> The "Frivolous Set" is so human
> The Old Guard should help us to take off the life
> Their sorrows our joys to illumine.[136]

Other times settlement men and women indulged a deprecatory
stance toward other reform efforts, ironizing the contingencies of
social change through external rather than internal self-differentia-
tion. Florence Kelley early began her tendency to berate the self-
righteousness of the well-intentioned bourgeoisie, mocking the philanthropic woman's sense of entitlement as well as her blindness to
unequal structural forces.

> Shall I cast my lot with the oppressors, content to patch and darn,
> to piece and cobble at the worn and rotten fabric of a perishing
> society? . . . Shall I fritter away the days of my youth investigating
> the deservingness of this or that applicant for relief when the
> steady march of industrial development throws a million able-
> bodied workers out of employment to tramp the country?[137]

In "The Subtle Problems of Charity" and subsequent essays, Jane
Addams gently critiqued the myopia of less enlightened reformers:
"As she daily holds up these standards, it often occurs to the mind of
the sensitive visitor, whose conscience has been made tender by
much talk of brotherhood and equality, that she has no right to say
these things."[138] Always to be counted on for a parodic turn of
phrase, Twose constantly crafted poems, monologues, and brief
plays that mocked educational reform. Predominantly intended for a
select audience of Hull-House settlers and sometimes accompanied
by Eleanor Smith on piano, he shared his parodies with fellow male

and female residents at informal evening gatherings. In the unflinching "Song of the Noble Soul," Twose wrote a first-person monologue that, like Kelley, mocked the speech and interiority of a starry-eyed prospective female do-gooder. "Three times I've heard your leader speak / At a philanthropic function," the lyric began, referencing the legendary Jane Addams.

> At Manistique her words sank deep,
> And my girlish heart did fill,
> But when she spoke at Stoney heap
> Her words sank deeper still.
> But my youthful soul with sloth obsessed
> First saw its duty true,
> The afternoon that she addressed
> our club at Baraboo.[139]

The song's humor indulged a gender stereotype of "girlish" sentimentality while also mocking the feelings of inauthenticity endemic to this era's "overcultivated" and "sloth-obsessed" young people. The song's repeated refrain further reinforced its sarcastic dramatization: "Yes, yes, my yearning soul, / That slumbered slothful bonds in, / First saw its true and earthly goal, / at Baraboo, Wisconsin." Even more pointed, however, was the way this song used the construction of a naive, somewhat self-centered, persona to make fun of another reform institution—Graham Taylor's Chicago Commons.

> Her lecture in my breast I stored,
> Where it of joy a source is,
> I loved what poor I could afford,
> Took Graham Taylor's courses.
> For philanthropic neophytes
> His institute provides,
> And talks on sweetness and light
> With stereopticon slides.
> Elementary kindness classes
> Blackboard talks on whose [sic] your brother,
> Love's lever used for raising masses
> Small hands as aids to mother.[140]

Twose mocked Taylor's attempt to formalize settlement ethics as well as the sense of self-righteousness fueling his courses on "sweetness and light," "elementary kindness," and "love's lever." At a settlement that initiated new residents by a more spontaneous and experiential practice of daily contact, Twose's song invited Hull-House settlers to laugh collectively at reformers who, presumably unlike themselves, needed "stereopticon slides." To some—such as Frederick Deknatel—this habit of outward mockery was destructive and disingenuous.

> Mr. Deknatel got very down on the House last Winter, and I am sorry he still feels in the same way. I think it is true that there is a pose in the house, which is copied a little from Mrs. Kelley and perhaps Mr. Twose but it is only a pose. We are desperately afraid of thinking ourselves great reformers . . . and we get into the habit which I think all large, clannish households do, of laughing at outsiders.[141]

As a "pose" that coincided with their "fear" of taking themselves too seriously, many residents were able to negotiate the Hull-House paradox by cultivating settlement irony. As a ritualized narrative construction, the ironic mode deflected some of the settlement's occupational hazards, especially a conditioned sense of noblesse oblige and a naive belief in one's superior progressivism.

Also distinctive about such settlement rituals, however, was the way that they enabled heterosocial interaction. The "pose" have Hull-House settlers a logic of alliance other than gender, one that allowed them to constitute a group identity on new terms. By exchanging their tales from the field, by engaging in sarcastic moments of self-deprecation, and by distinguishing themselves from other reform endeavors, they simultaneously created a unique sphere of mixed-sex interaction while importantly reinforcing their own awareness of the Hull-House paradox. Additionally, ironic exchange required wit and sustained mutuality while at the same time measuring a safe emotional distance. Instead of positioning members of the opposite sex as romantic potential, such performative codes constituted a teasing "family." The exchange of the title *Sister* and later *Brother* thus not only signaled loving reverence but also carved an arena for a bold exchange that mimicked that of siblings. Furthermore, the women of Hull-House took advantage of this sanctioned mode good-naturedly to reprimand their metaphoric brothers. During a resident business meeting, for instance, "Miss Lathrop moved that Mr. Hooker . . . not sit around daily at the Club and let his sisters support him."[142] And throughout their compendium of limericks, Waite, Luther, and Gyles took the opportunity to tease the men of their clan. Robert Hunter's flirting received a blow, as the women wondered aloud whether this man's "intentions were severely altruistic."

Mr. Hunter has such a sweet smile
And he loves the dear girls to beguile
But though gentle and mild
Like a very young child
He has eyes for great coats and much style.[143]

Deknatel, who at this time was "down on the House," was sub-textually urged to adopt a lighter attitude.

Mr. Deknatel shuns our society
And in past, for the sake of variety
He dines in lone state
A few things on one plate
In an atmosphere quite of sobriety.[144]

Thus, the performance of settlement irony allowed settlers to expand their homosocial "family" into a heterosocial one. At the same time, this pervasive irony propelled rather then inhibited residents' commitment to reform. People such as Twose were still "incessantly useful and resourceful" and "counted on by Miss Addams" with the utmost trust.[145] Others less overtly manifested this paradoxical pose but engaged in an amused sarcasm about social change even as they threw every moment of their lives into affecting it. Grace Abbott occasionally characterized herself as "trying to sweep back the tide with a broom."[146] Julia Lathrop developed "an almost roguish sense of the tragi-comedy in American politics," a sensibility that early circulated in her disillusioned critique of Cook County charities. Again, it did not seem to quell her commitment, for "you felt she enjoyed the game, and through the game could bring into being the Children's Bureau or anything else."[147] As Hull-House and its affiliates increasingly endured criticism from all sides and ventured into the unpredictable territory of civic reform, settlement irony reconsolidated their sense of collective identity, mediated their heterosocial relations, and mitigated against a belief in their own superiority.

Finally, this queer domesticity is significant not only because female reformers might "really have been lesbians," but because its performance surreptitiously undid the categories of gender and initiated nonnormative attachments among unmarried adults and between "fictive" parents and children. Under this alternative umbrella, furthermore, men attended as public domesticators, whether by intervening politically on behalf of things heretofore labeled private or, their "faces full of care," concerning themselves with the affective lives of neighbors. Rather than positing an essential sexual identity or assuming the inherently liberatory nature of queer domesticity, this space is also intriguing for being an emotional zone that partially unnoticed itself. Hull-House descendants went on to argue for policies that reified private familial arrangements. It seems important to notice such nonnormative genealogies in the history of social normalization. Rather than asking what business nonbiological parents had in the arena of child development, we might ask instead why their extensive involvement as settlers did not prompt them to promote a model of social organization other than the exclusive, biological family—a unit that currently has the emotionally deadlocked distinction of being called natural.

Doors and Dining

"We have worked out during our years of residence a plan of living which may be called cooperative."[148] Like its ritual and spectatorial representation in the Smithsonian, Hull-House's third space functioned as a place where people lived and watched, entered and read. Residents engaged in various activities throughout the day. They rose at different times. Some worked inside the Hull-House block; some outside. Each managed his or her own spatiotemporal ordering of daily life. Addams's reflection situated the settlement within a history of "cooperative" innovation in household economies. Their "plan of living" not only depended upon social interaction but also upon a willingness to perform day-to-day household tasks such as cleaning, cooking, and receiving. The mundane materialism of housekeeping interacted with the performance of kinship, sometimes unsettling gendered divisions of labor. In the ensuing friction over such practices, however, settlers also reckoned with the classed legacies of bourgeois spatiality. As such, Hull-House's queer domesticity also could reinscribe classed divisions of labor, perpetuating the inequities and dispositions of an old home even as settlers tried to leave it. This section is devoted to the push and pull, expansion and retrenchment, of such household performances. It also tracks their eventual instantiation of, and within, an array of architectural changes—the 1902 creation of a separate building of non–dormitory-style apartments, the 1905 relocation of Hull-House's front door, and the 1905 construction of a separate building called the "Resident Dining Hall."

Calling the private home wasteful architecturally and economically, nineteenth-century theorists such as Owen and Fourier spurred a range of experimentation in group living. Differing in their political commitments to socialism or to a collectively conceived capitalism, utopic cooperatives variously organized living spaces, material wealth, personal relationships, and labor responsibilities. Some redistributed capital while reifying gendered divisions of labor; others maintained class inequities while releasing middle- and upper-class women from domestic drudgery.[149] As a place where public commitments reworked private attachment, cooperative living strategies further materialized Hull-House's socialized internality. Those who took up residence at Hull-House shared a central kitchen, dormitory housing, and laundry facilities. However, settlers shared a cooking and cleaning staff as often as they shared the tasks of cooking and cleaning themselves. The young idealistic Misses Addams and Starr did not move onto Halsted Street alone, but with Mary Keyser, an employee who, for the next five years, "relieved Miss Addams of all household care."[150] Though, as earlier stated, she "quickly developed into a very important factor in the life of the vicinity as well as that of the household, and [her] death five years later was most sincerely mourned," Mary Keyser and the household staff occupied a liminal status both inside and outside the circle of residents.[151] The irony of this predicament—in which public-spirited women (and men) relied on the domestic labor of other women—was by no means lost on Hull-House residents and on Addams, who worked through her own unease in essays that critiqued what she called "a belated industry."[152]

> We can all recall acquaintances of whose integrity of purpose we can have no doubt, but who cause much confusion as they pro-ceed to the accomplishment of that purpose, who indeed are often insensible to their own mistakes and harsh in their judg-ments of other people because they are so confident of their own inner integrity. This tendency . . . is perhaps nowhere so obvious as in the household itself. . . . These [well-to-do] women, rightly confident of their household and family integrity and holding to their own code of morals, fail to see the household in its social aspect. Possibly no relation has been so slow to respond to the social ethics which we are now considering, as that between the household employer and the household employee, or, as it is still sometimes called, that between mistress and servant.[153]

Targeting, as she continually would in much of her writing, the gap between an individual's espoused intention and her habitual action in the world how "we are continually obliged to act in circles of habit based on convictions we no longer hold," Addams zeroed in on the disjuncture between a bourgeois woman's conception of morality and the social inequalities that she upheld in her daily life.

Mary Keyser eventually came to a position of authority as the settlement's domestic manager. She attended resident business meetings with some regularity: "Miss Keyser moved that the dining room floor be oiled. Carried."[154] Meanwhile settlers tried to find more ethically conscious means of maintaining their acquired standards of proper domesticity while also serving the neighborhood. They later voted to give their washing to "a laundry and not to individuals" in order to encourage organized labor.[155] Sometimes they would try to hire neighbors in desperate need of work. On occasion, Mary Keyser found these arrangements inadequate to her standards, vocalizing her discontent at one particular resident meeting: "it was decided to give up Valonie and the scrub women and engage two efficient girls."[156] Furthermore, after Florence Kelley left her small women's labor bureau to serve as Carroll Wright's slum investigator, Keyser managed the service in an impromptu form.[157] Thus, within a constrained sphere that still prescribed certain duties, Keyser found a modified status as a valued resident, a position whose development and whose limitations fueled Addams's (self-)critiques of unequal household economies.

The fundamentals of "their plan of living" was subject to much ad hoc alteration as class-conscious settlers occasionally attempted their own "household adjustment." As residents allowed their rooms to shift identity with the entry of each new club, as residents lifted or barred access to alternately public and private spaces several times a day, so their attempts to clean replicated this improvisatory rhythm. "Every resident did what came to hand in the House as out of it," John Weber Linn remembered settler participation somewhat idealistically, "cooked and cleaned and washed windows and replaced furniture that was constantly shoved here and there and everywhere. It was in those days that Jane Addams acquired the habit, persistent till the end, of moving about while she conversed, shutting drawers, adjusting pictures, even shifting desks."[158] Twose parodied this constant process of cleaning and straightening, using the first-person singular to suggest that settling men engaged in such mobile performance of domesticity.

I put back a chair or two
There is no speck or stain
Along come all the residents
And muss it up again.[159]

Residents additionally tended to the cleanliness of their personal room, a flexible rule that by no means eradicated the friction endemic to cooperative housing arrangements. Sometimes habits of personal domesticity leaked outside the confines of an individual room, or—as Waite, Luther, and Gyles jibed in the case of Edith de Nancrede—outside its windows.

> Miss Nancrede is lovely and sweet
> But ah! can we say she is neat
> When to order she's blind
> And her linen we find
> From the third story front to the street.[160]

Even as they attempted to take cooperative responsibility for the household, its residents still decided that they could not do without a separate household staff. They always employed a full-time cooking staff; despite Linn's description, they never shared the burden of meal preparation with any regularity. As Addams would argue in her critiques of unequal household adjustments, this arrangement did progress beyond the traditional logic of the bourgeois home. The hired cook served a collection of people rather than being the sole property of a single nuclear family. In 1901, they also had a rotating cleaning staff and a full-time maid. That same year, both their cook and maid appeared in Nancrede's birthday limericks.

> We are all just a little afraid
> Of the "lady" who will "be obeyed"
> But from soup to the sweet
> All her food's good to eat
> And no visitor need be dismayed.[161]

> O'Hackett is such a fierce maid
> That of her even I am afraid
> You never would think it
> But when she says "O niv it"
> I'm sure that my last card is played.[162]

The phrasing and positioning of both of these limericks still betrayed the two women's ambivalent status. Including but distinguishing them as household help, the limericks enacted a familiar rhetorical strategy by which dominant members of society mitigate social discomfort. By claiming to be "afraid" of their maid and cook, by suggesting that they would rather "obey" than know their "last card is played," the song safely played at ceding power while actually retaining class status.

"There is the usual scanty service; the front door being answered by the resident who happens, at the time, to be nearest to it."[163] Beatrice Webb recalled her visit to Hull-House in 1898 with a degree of disdain, here noting a lapse in the performance of household reception. In an upper-class home, a butler or other servant might have answered the door followed by an introduction into a front parlor. In a place reluctant to resort to practices that inhibited "genuine relations" between residents and neighbors, and in a place whose front living room was used most of the day as a kindergarten or clubroom, alternative procedures needed to be found. Hull-House residents did not accommodate by leaving their front entrance

Hull-House settlers in the resident dining hall. Jessie Binford, Myrtle French, and Enella Benedict sit from right to left at the first table, facing the camera. Jane Addams sits at the second table with Alice Hamilton, Robert Morris Lovett, Agnes Pilsbury, and George Hooker to her right; Rachel Yarros sits to Addams's left with her back to the camera. *(Photo courtesy of University of Illinois at Chicago, the University Library, Jane Addams Memorial Collection.)*

unlocked and open, however. Their "open-door" policy did not have such a literal incarnation. Consequently, the ringing of the doorbell became a constant auditory component of settlement life. John Dewey interpreted it within the range of unplanned and intrusive responsibilities settlement workers tried to juggle, remarking to his wife, "I sh'd think the irritation of hearing the doorbell ring, & never doing one thing without being interrupted to tend to half a dozen others would drive them crazy."[164] Indeed, when Alice Hamilton's exhausting schedule brought her close to a breakdown, the fractured noise proved too much for her ears and nerves: "The place seemed so crowded and they were all talking and the bell kept ringing all the time."[165] Despite Webb's description, by 1893, settlers had devised a plan to make sure that someone was always near the door to answer it, a system that they affectionately (and sometimes unaffectionately) referred to as "toting."

Each resident was assigned a four- to five-hour-weekly period during which they answered the doorbell and introduced visitors to the settlement. Deciding on this calendar was often very difficult, and the minutes of the Hull-House business meetings illustrate how much the activity of door attending preoccupied them.[166] At almost every meeting, this schedule was "revised" for the next week. Extra words such as "finally" and "*again* revised" as well as the many scribbles and cross-outs have left visible markers of tense negotiation. "The Chair suggests that morning toters *get up*," a secretary emphatically wrote after a few too many morning disturbances.[167] Toting was a practice evolving out of the interspatial intersection between Hull-House's collective living patterns, the spatial legacies of its residents, and the social agenda of the settlement. It was a way that Hull-House residents performed the Progressive social spirit in the form of face-to-face human contact, expressed their commitment to social service, and embodied the ideal of shared responsibility in cooperative living. While Francis Hackett found it "the easiest of all duties, and in some ways the most in contact with the neighborhood," other earlier residents did not feel quite as positively.[168] As the activities of the residents increased, "toting" became a domestic chore from which many residents wished to be released. "It was moved and seconded that Miss Watson be relieved of the door tending in the mornings as the Labor Bureau seemed to be enough to occupy her. Carried. Miss Gernon generously offered to take her place till Miss Holden's afternoon hours and Miss Starr was asked to meet Dr. Moon . . . and Miss Keyser to arrange for door-tending in the mornings."[169] In 1898, "Mrs. Stevens has announced that she really cannot tote anymore if she is to do any outside work."[170] To

meet the temporal and spatial requirements of civic housekeeping,
Alzina Stevens—then Chicago's assistant factory inspector under
Florence Kelley—sought emancipation from this particular task of
settlement housekeeping. Early on, the Misses Starr, Addams, and
Brockway were exempted from door attendance, the first two out of
respect for their busy lives and the latter because she was in charge
of running the nursery in a different neighborhood building. When
a resident forgot his or her assignment or the schedule went awry,
residents often found themselves frantically searching for someone to
step in at a moment's notice. When Ambassador James Bryce arrived
for a visit, a resident tried to convince George Twose to assume the
necessary obligation. Unfortunately, "Twose was making his own
tea, and I could not get him to budge."[171]

The resident was anxious to find a toter for Ambassador Bryce
because this practice also had another function. Toting was a behavior
regulated to maintain a front-stage identity by filtering the access and
interpreting Hull-House in the form of guided tours. For visitors
from the wealthy neighborhoods of Chicago, the North Shore, and
other American regions, the settlement soon became a must-see stop
on many a tour. Its unique mission and method elicited the awed or
troubled fascination of many privileged Americans who wanted to see
how they did "whatever it is they do." As one bemused resident
remarked, "[T]hese visitors ask to be shown through the house in the
same spirit in which they would get permission to visit a menagerie
or a collection of curiosities from the Sandwich Islands."[172] Settlers
found all aspects of their lives uncomfortably exposed.

> One of the visitors caught a glimpse through the window of [Miss
> Addams] sitting at the table. The opportunity was too good to be
> missed, and the young woman promptly rose to it. Without
> waiting for an invitation or asking permission she opened the
> door to the dining room . . . "O, girls," she cried "come here
> quickly. Here's one of them eating!"[173]

Thus, curious visitors violated even the small modicum of provisional privacy a settler worked to extract for herself. James Weber
Linn also used a museological metaphor to describe guests who
"poked their inquisitive noses in everywhere as if the settlement were
a sort of museum." He recalled "an amiable old lady who startled
him . . . by putting her hand on his shoulder and demanding, 'Are
you one of the dear boys who have been saved here?;' his own
resentful reply, 'No, ma'am, I am just visiting my aunt.' "[174] While
toting mitigated these disturbances by controlling where guests put

"their inquisitive noses," it still only minimized rather than eradicated the perpetual feeling of being on display. The knowledge that one could be observed at any moment unnerved the otherwise indefatigable Louise deKoven Bowen when she became president of the Woman's Club.

> My first speeches were made at Hull-House. . . . frequently when I was speaking, the door of the room would be thrown open and some of the residents (who were doing what they called "toting"—that is, showing people around Hull-House) would say, "This is the Hull-House Woman's Club, that is Mrs. Bowen, the president on the platform," and it was very difficult not to listen to the comments of the visitors, as I was trying to put my own thoughts in order.[175]

Some residents worried about the impression Hull-House would make on "important" people. Indeed, Beatrice Webb's disorienting visit was notorious for how "higgledy-piggledy" she declared the settlement to be. The prospect of having a visitor "toted" through their living and working space changed its existential status from a mode of habitation to a spectacle; toting threw open a window onto the private household that residents had informally crafted for themselves. While settlers had grown habituated to their own cooperative and heterosocial residential patterns, the intrusion of a spectator made them self-conscious, prompting them to speculate on what behavioral protocols of gender and class they had become accustomed to violating. Hamilton worried about the visit of her cousin's friend Esther Kelley, who "paralyzes me."

> She makes me feel uncouth and ill-mannered. And I am so afraid of the impression the House will make on her. You never can tell how they will act. Only this very evening Mr. Twose and Mr. Yeomans and Mr. Riddle began to scrap in the reception room and actually got to wrestling, and it would give a stranger a queer impression. . . . Last Sunday morning Miss Addams toted some Gospel Settlement people into the Lecture Hall where Miss Nancrede was folding theatrical costumes and Miss Goodrich was doing cross-stitch and Mr. Yeomans was popping corn. What am I to do if that happens while she is here?[176]

Such worries demonstrated residents' periodic awareness of how much their environment and acquired habitus deviated from the proper households and kinship arrangements that they had left behind. Toting kept them periodically conscious of the "queer impression" that they made on the eyes of the world. The structure thus acted as a hegemonic pivot, delaying or short-circuiting alternate routes of biography and history as settlers halted, looked side-to-side, and saw the eyes of convention looking back in.

Dining was another important ritual in Hull-House's cooperative living experiment. Evening supper was a particularly special time-space, a period from 6 P.M. to 7 P.M. when settlers ceased individual activity to share conversation and food. Dorothea Moore indicated that settlers negotiated their internal hierarchy through the dinner ritual.

> The six o'clock dinner hour brings the household and its guests together in the beautiful dining room. This is the meeting ground of the day. Here the generalizations of the over young are discouraged with kindness and qualifying facts; here are the all-experienced induced to reconsider and admit another fact of the great truth; here is the free play of the individual with enough of friction to stimulate and enough of the juice of humor to sweeten.[177]

Hull-House dinners also became a favorite ritual for many of Chicago's intellectual and cultural elite. They boasted visits from writers such as Upton Sinclair and Theodore Dreiser, who "researched" their novels while staying at Hull-House and other settlements. George Herbert Mead and John Dewey joined other thinkers, politicians and visiting reformers such as Henry Demarest Lloyd, J. Peter Altgeld, and William Stead, who counted on Hull-House to be a place of lively conversation. Given the collection of politicized thinkers attracted to Hull-House during the Progressive Era, however, such dinners served to instatiate Hull-House's status as a "counterpublic sphere," an "extragovernmental" public sphere in Chicago's civil society that "confer[red] an aura of independence, autonomy, and legitimacy on the 'public opinion' generated in it."[178] The dinner hour was a microsociological practice that performed Hull-House's macrosociological identity. It was not only a ritual that made a family of its community but also one that enabled deliberation and a participatory sociality.

"On motion it was resolved that residents should take their turn in waiting on the door during the dinner hour, remaining away from the table at the time."[179] Thus wrote a resident meeting secretary in October 1893, recording a new rule instituted to quell residents' complaints over the blurring of two settlement living practices—door attendance and dinner eating. This was another of the many times when the operations of an alternative household unsettled the environmental equilibrium of its residents. The unfortunate person assigned a "toting" duty around six o'clock found herself in a frustratingly liminal position, moving between the reception hall and the dining room, vacillating between more and less public roles with each ring of the doorbell. Meanwhile, other diners did not appreciate these mobile leaks. Nevertheless, the 1893 motion that assigned toters to "remain away from the table at the time" of the dinner hour did not have even one week of staying power. At the following meeting, it was "resolved that someone be employed to tend door during the dinner hour."[180] Less than a year later, residents saw fit to curtail motion within the dining space even further. "Moved and seconded that it be made a rule that residents do not pass thro' the dining room at meal time. Motion carried."[181] Again, rules governing how to inhabit the dining time-space were instituted when the presence of other spatial practices—the proximity of the front door, the constant activity of reform work, the impulse to use it as a hallway between one space and other—threatened to invade it. On October 8, 1893, the residents elected "to engage a person to serve at the dinner table," deciding to fall back on a more hierarchical form of dinner performance and limiting the amount of movement within the space to one person.[182] The fact that college extension classes met in the dining room at 7 P.M. still meant diners would be subject to diachronic spatial breaches as "the leisurely last moments of the dinner hour are apt to be invaded by the classes, and from [then] on there is a riot of young people."[183] The impulse not only to eat dinner at a certain hour but to impose restraints upon all other kinds of movement within the room reproduced the habitus of settlement workers' former home-life. Such restorations occurred in the realm of material culture as much as spatial motion. "Moved and seconded that Miss Gernon be appointed a committee of one to buy a suitable butter dish. Motion carried."[184] Illustrating the persistent impulse to segment and separate—whether to avoid the mixing of living practices or the mixing of food items—such mundane disruptions could eventuate more blurrings of private and public, but they could also prompt new separations.

While some easily habituated to this mix of bourgeois and co-operative living patterns, certain residents never felt comfortable. Deknatel preferred a more solitary environment for eating, making his dinner hour a kind of personal retreat "in an atmosphere quite of sobriety."[185] And some chose not to partake because of their dislike of the food.

Of Miss E. Smith we often have heard
And we know that she sings like bird
But a bird she's not able
To eat at the table
For a vegetable diet's preferred.[186]

Since selected residents found themelves ill disposed to certain aspects of collective living—its excessive motion, its crowdedness, its modified service, or its food—several enthusiastically welcomed the construction of a new building of apartments in 1902. Substantially funded by Bowen, it contained "twelve apartments varying in size from two to six rooms." An array of people moved in to these apartments—former mansion residents, Hull-House students, some Hull-House employees, ex-members of the Jane Club (including Lida Evans Keyser and Frank Keyser), and two Hull-House trustees. The geographic change worked to rectify some of the strongest informal barriers to long-term settlement participation. It provided space for married couples who could and did have biological children. The new building also rectified some of the internal tensions of the Hull mansion by affording a degree of reprieve from its mayhem. The apartments were also an experiment in progressive housing. The Hull-House building was one of a few experimental investments in poorer quarters of the city. Proudly stating that it had "been successful from the financial and social point of view and quite justified the belief that well-built, attractive apartments in this vicinity prove a good business investment," Hull-House workers hoped that their example would prompt the influx of more capital into the neighborhood.[187]

In 1905, the *Hull-House Bulletin* announced two more architectural transformations—the creation of a separate Resident Dining Hall and the relocation of the settlement's front door. The combined change continued an interspatial trajectory earlier generated with the 1893 impulse to "remain away from the table" while "waiting on the door during the dinner hour."[188] More than a decade after residents first began increasing the distance between this hectic entrance and their dining environment, this architectural adjustment spatially separated private and public realms while more efficiently facilitating other lines of activity. "The new entrance is more commodious and proves a great convenience. It leads directly to the stairs of the Children's House and also to the theater and connects with the bridge which this summer was built across the alley from the hallway of the theater to the hall in the gymnasium building."[189] The bulletin

The Hull-House settlement's new front door allowed access to the rest
of the settlement by bypassing the mansion's parlor. *(Photo courtesy of
University of Illinois at Chicago, the University Library, Jane Addams
Memorial Collection.)*

celebrated the new vestibule along one line of argument. Reforming
spaces designated for different activities—wholesome eating, theater,
recreation, municipal housekeeping—now became more fluid geographically, connected by an interspatial network of doors, passageways, and vestibules. However, the addition also separated such
activities from mixture with settlement living. The vestibule led
"directly to the stairs of the Children's House" rather than to the
stairs of the settlers' second-floor bedrooms; it opened into the coffeehouse rather than into the Hull mansion's living parlors. The
entrance also discouraged the use of the mansion as a hallway to
other settlement spaces, allowing visitors "to pass directly . . . to the
gymnasium, the shops, and the Woman's Club" rather than through
Hull-House's residential sphere.[190] While settling's earlier "third
space" had blurred domesticity and reform, the new location spatially rearticulated precarious dualities. Instantiating a division between inside and outside, between local and civic "families," the
entrance enforced a split between internal and external settlement

housekeeping. Together, the new front door, the separate Resident Dining Hall, and the sequestered set of apartments altered settlers' patterns of residence, placing restraints on the flux of Hull-House interspatiality, routinizing spatial distinctions between living and working, gradually refortifying the walls between private and public.

The last image of the *From Parlor to Politics* exhibit is a picture of contemporary women protesting for equal rights, directly asking second-wave feminists to consider what there is to learn from the stories of early female reformers. The difficulties of answering that question very simply demonstrate how disaggregated the discourses of contemporary feminism and of public welfare have become from each other. The women of second-wave feminism more often claimed the "right" to argue on behalf of themselves, bracing uncomfortably next to the earlier female tendency to argue on behalf of others. On the surface, the public motherhood rhetoric that linked women to the larger claims of social welfare now appears essentialist and reductive to a contemporary generation of ahistorical feminists. However, such essentialism loosens with an intimate knowledge of the daily pragmatics of Hull-House's "third space" and of how rarely its surrogated maternalism could ever pass itself off as natural. As well-to-do women and men trying to build different kinds of "bridges" between a conflicting array of "present and past" experiences, settlers' spatial commitment to social change continually confronted old and new patterns of living. Gender difference fundamentally structured these adjustments in family and kinship. Meanwhile, settlers contended with the legacy of a hierarchical environmental practice that did not always conform to their espoused ideals. Along the way, divisions between privacy and publicity underwent constant revision as long-term settlers navigated and choreographed the twist and turns of a queer domesticity.

It is difficult to represent the incommensurate geographies of this conflicted third space within the ordered, bicameral structure of museum display. I find that the segmented and sequestered location of room 26 also begs the question of its relationality to other Smithsonian rooms. Carefully ensconced away from masculine museology, it is hard to convey how the project of female reform could reciprocally alter the everyday performances of the men who entered the parlor. And, of course, speculation on the relation of this queer domesticity to a display of inaugural ballgowns produces as many imaginative possibilities as it stalls. For me, to walk next to the First Ladies exhibit is to be reminded of the cathecting power of a first visit, to remember how appealingly silk, satin, and sequins joined into an exorbitantly feminized celebration of beauty, hostessing, and national mothering. It is also to sense the shaky border separating the First Ladies exhibit from the _From Parlor to Politics_ exhibit—and to remember how much social condemnation women from the first receive when they dare to walk symbolically among the women of the second. Meanwhile, the display of those ballgowns structures my immediate reception of the mannequined reformers who hold banners in a representation of women's activism. Upon entering, I find myself asking not, What were they protesting? but rather, What were they wearing?

Such an impulse sits uneasily next to my simultaneous desire to see Jane Addams as a fusing metaphor for two of the most controversial recent debates conducted at that White House—same-sex marriage and welfare reform. On the one hand, I lament that the loudest proponents of the latter elevate Jane Addams in the history of welfare but maintain a strategic silence about the issue of her sexuality lest it compromise their image of her national womanhood. On the other, it makes me fantasize about a time when Jane Addams (her relatively plump body monitored in a weight diary, her unsequined dresses furnished by her longtime female companion) could become as thoroughly fascinating a queer image as is a very different hyper-heterosexual symbol of classed national womanhood. I wonder, in other words, what it would take to make Jane as trendy as Jackie. I think about this as I walk through the exhibit with my mother (who does not seem quite as annoyed by those maternal metaphors as her daughter is) when two young girls—around ten, eight, maybe eleven, or seven—come racing along in the rapid gait required to make it through the museum's interconnected rooms and hallways. The girls do not linger very long at any of the didactics; they could care less about movements for juvenile justice, public health, or public school lunch programs; they stop for a brief second at the mannequins of the women reformers and look at what they were wearing and not at what they were protesting. The girls run back down the hall to an exhibit they have already seen but which draws them again. They slow and stop before the glass encasements of recessed-lit dresses—taffeta, silk, embroidered satin.

To the performative historian who fancies that she can see the past leaking, cracking, busting through the present, the girls remind me of a thing I never saw, of children running through a Hull-House space utterly oblivious to its ordered environmental logic. They remind me of earlier attempts made by those objects and those gowns to bind another girl to her white eyelet bedroom and to a glorified female performance as wife, mother, hostess, and housekeeper. But they also

remind me of how the scampering, the swinging hands, the slower
and faster paces are not only the meanings that I attribute to them but
also testaments to the lightness of history. They show how two young
girls—feet scampering, hands swinging—can inadvertently claim the
capacity to render the past weightless and playful and fascinating and
ignorable. It is nearly unbearable to the historian who watches and
wants to say, no, don't look there, no, read here, but who finally
might have to relinquish her antiperformative urge to force history,
historical feminisms, historiographical subjects . . . to stay put.

Chapter 5

Staging: "Act Well Your Part"

Genealogists resist histories that attribute purity of origin to any
performance. They have to take into account the give and take of
joint transmissions, posted in the past, arriving in the present,
delivered by living messengers, speaking in tongues not entirely
their own.
  —Joseph Roach, *Cities of the Dead*

There is such a thing as pleasurable learning.
  —Bertolt Brecht, "Theatre for Pleasure or Theatre for Instruction"

"We went to Hull-House every Saturday for Miss Nancrede's
dance classes." Dorothy Mittelman Sigel's eyes held mine as she
spoke. "And after every class we would line up on our way out the
door . . . and . . . you know . . . as we went out . . . 'Thank you,
Miss Nancrede.' "

During the ellipses in her speech, Mrs. Sigel rose carefully and
spoke in another language, that of the body. Despite a foot that was
still recovering from surgery, this former Hull-House child got up to
demonstrate how she and her fellow Marionette Club members
bowed and curtsied in a ritualized performance for their favorite
Hull-House club leader, Edith de Nancrede.

Dorothy Mittelman, later Dorothy Mittelman Sigel, now the
widow of Louis Sigel, was born in 1900 in an immigrant neighborhood in the Nineteenth Ward of Chicago's West Side soon after her
parents emigrated to the United States. She eventually lived alone in
the Winnetka home she and her husband bought when the success
of Louis Sigel's business allowed them to move to Chicago's wealth-
ier North Shore. And it was to this home that I used to go to hear
Mrs. Sigel's stories of her life in turn-of-the-century Chicago and of
the impact that one particular institution, the Hull-House Settlement, made on the course and character of that life.

Mrs. Sigel raised and lowered her body, extending her hand in a
gesture that was at once graceful after years of cultivation and un-
steady after ninety-five years of living. "Thank you, Miss Nancrede,"

she said again, now lifting her head to hold the eyes of an imaginary teacher whose eyes had once held hers.

Since my first meeting with Mrs. Sigel, she has performed that memory for me several times, restoring again and again the learned behaviors that she cultivated at Hull-House and that Hull-House cultivated in her. No doubt she has offered this historiographical enactment to others as well, for Mrs. Sigel is something of a living archive to Hull-House historians. Her name can be found in the footnotes of several scholarly essays, books, and dissertations, including my own. What the standard citation procedure does not document, of course, are the nonwritten elements of the "Personal Interview with the Author," the moments when the individual recitation of the interviewee exceeded the fact-seeking questions of the interviewer. Coincident with the tangential and fallible speech of the interviewee, however, are also the performative aspects of its articulation, the nonverbal elements of intonation, focus, gesture, pace, volume, and comportment that make sense of the story transcribed. Sometimes the pace amplifies a narrative; sometimes a focused gaze tells an alternative story; sometimes a gesture reconstitutes a remembered self. Usually, however, such techniques of memory sink unmarked amid the nonsense, ellipses, or tangents recorded in the fixity of transcription. Consequently, amid archival folders and microfiche reels of my historical research, I find enacted memories such as those of Dorothy Mittelman Sigel quite satisfying, almost therapeutic. On the one hand, the immediacy of Mrs. Sigel's presence seems to authenticate the past she represents. "I was there," she subtextually repeats to me with every story, laugh, and movement. "And I wasn't," I implicitly repeat to her with every question and searching gaze. Pathetically waving the documents from which I have manufactured chronologies and interpretations, I envy her fullness, the vigor with which her presence stakes its claim on the bounties of the past.

More significant than its appeal to a presential metaphysics, however, the subjective component of Mrs. Sigel's narration attests to the fundamental importance of memory in the constitution of social subjects. Whatever its strategies of selection, whatever its capacity for something like accuracy, the act of remembering is the key method by which individuals make sense of themselves. The oral history interview is perhaps less about accessing the past than it is about bearing witness to its robust utility in the ongoing formation of individual identity. The embodied and temporal medium of Mrs. Sigel's memorial enactment is another reminder that Time has more than one writing system. The transmission and interpretation of history occurs in embodied, spatial, imagistic, and sonic media as much as in linguistic markings on paper. These other media are not necessarily more authentic, but they do testify to the multiple ways that the past (sometimes quite literally) *takes shape*. It leaves its markings in Mrs. Sigel's extended arm, forms inside aging muscles that can still manage a graceful curtsy. Mrs. Sigel in turn appropriates such tracings and such shapings, adapting the performance of a once-thereness to a now-hereness as the pull of memory requires.

Dorothy Mittelman was one of hundreds of Hull-House children who frequented the settlement's social and dramatic clubs at the beginning of the twentieth-century. This chapter seeks to theorize the relationship between highly local and intimate moments such as those recounted by Mrs. Sigel and the larger network of discourses on nationalism, industrialization, immigration, and pragmatism charted in Progressive Era historiography. Along the way, I want to suggest further that the arena of the theater provides a means of reconciling various kinds of interpretive dilemmas in American studies and New Historicism. Theater's scripts, actors, and props often elude conventional epistemological frames, continually skirting the question of where the "text" under question ends and its supplementary "context" begins. As a form where the "art" walks hand in hand with its "apparatus," theater's hypercontextuality can confound analytic constructs. When theater is seen in this light, I find that something like Stephen Greenblatt's 1989 articulation of the stakes of New Historicism has an intriguing ring. "The work of art is not itself a pure flame that lies at the source of our speculations. . . . It is the product of a negotiation between a creator or class of creators, equipped with a complex, communally shared repertoire of conventions."[1] In the historicist quest to argue against the idea of a pure aesthetic object unfettered by context, theater's ensemble-based processes of "negotiation" make such ideas particularly explicit. Perhaps more than other aesthetic forms, theater's cumbersome materiality and embedded sociality have never been easy to disavow. Theater both challenges and incarnates the presumed "instability of the text," vacillating as it does between stubborn quiescence and the bold-faced refusal ever to sit still. Using such mediations and the figure of Edith de Nancrede as points of departure, the first section introduces the relationship between theatrical practice and the Progressive conventions of urban writing, ethnographic research, and social change. The next three sections linger on selected theatrical lines of activity, focusing on their role in community formation, in the negotiation of immigrant difference, and in the corporeal reformation of personal identity. As this book has argued thus far, the history of reform cannot be adequately conceived as a series of legislative and policy changes; nor can the role of theater in the mission of Hull-House fully be understood by analyzing the literary content of its repertoire. I suggest that the gaps in both of these lines of inquiry converge and that the point of convergence depends upon a willingness to understand collective formations such as Edith de Nancrede's Marionette Club and embodied performances such as Dorothy Mittelman Sigel's graceful curtsy.

Lady Dancing

When Edith de Nancrede's application for residency was accepted at Hull-House in 1898, she moved into one of the new third-floor rooms built atop the original mansion. Like many settling Cordelias, this daughter of a University of Michigan medical professor had spent a few years traveling in Europe and taking painting classes. Her soon-to-be brother-in-law, Irving Pond, probably encouraged Nancrede to take up residence, perhaps speculating that she too was "dying from restlessness and inaction." Nancrede threw herself into a number of activities, devoting much of her time in early years to supervising Boys Club activities for 120 members. She earned money for her room and board by teaching art at several North Shore private schools and later the University School for Girls, maintaining a balance of paid employment and volunteer settlement work until the last year of her life in 1936.[2] Though trained as a visual artist, Nancrede soon learned that she preferred to "make pictures for the stage." Eventually, she and neighborhood youth formed a network of social clubs that used dramatics as their unifying theme. "To us, she *was* Hull-House," one of Nancrede's club members recalled. Ranging in age from four and eventually to thirty years old and totalling 240 members, they gathered routinely under names like the Migonettes, the Ballarinos, the Merry-Go-Rounds, and Dorothy Mittelman Sigel's Marionettes.[3] Nancrede was nearly always in rehearsal, leaving costumes and props strewn throughout the mansion much to the amusement, and sometimes to the chagrin, of fellow residents. When she died of pneumonia after nearly four decades as a settler, her despondent young people took over the dramaturgy of her funeral. Alex Elson's eulogy recalled opening nights when Miss Nancrede stood "in the wings, her face expressing every detail of emotion displayed on the stage."[4] Miriam Almond (later Elson) wrote a poem that, in familiar imagery, lamented the loss of their "lady dancing. . . . No more among our upturned faces your head / Silvered, beckons and nods us when to bow."[5]

During Edith de Nancrede's tenure, she and other performance directors—such as Laura Dainty Pelham, Eleanor Smith in music, Mary Wood Hinman in dance—guided the rehearsals of an organization that would receive a prominent place in the history of the Little Theatre movement. During the same period, Hull-House would also become one of the most nationally recognized sites for the study of urban reform. Working alongside—and sometimes at a measured distance from—the University of Chicago's coterie of new sociologists, rising with Jane Addams's increasing stature as a luminous interpreter of American urbanity, many Hull-House affiliates produced a huge body of research and writing on the complex nature of the modern city. Nancrede shared dormitory floors with Alice Hamilton, whose factory inspections advanced the field of industrial medicine, and with Grace Abbott, who researched the affective life of migration to supplement her cofounding of the Immigrant's Protective League. Respectively writing books such as *Exploring the Dangerous Trades* and *The Immigrant and the Community,* settlers such as Hamilton and Abbott engaged in textual acts of ethnographic translation, always with the intent to transform that

Saturday dance classes in Bowen Hall *(Photo courtesy of University of Illinois at Chicago, the University Library, Jane Addams Memorial Collection, Wallace Kirkland Papers.)*

which they represented. It is this body of reform literature, and its relationship to the nascent field of social work, for which Hull-House is best known. After the 1895 *Hull-House Maps and Papers,* more studies followed. Books such as second-generation settlers Edith Abbott and Sophonisba Breckinridge's *New Homes for Old, The Delinquent Child and the Home,* and *Women in Industry* broke new ground in the fields of applied sociology and social work. Meanwhile, Jane Addams's ethnographic writing in *Democracy and Social Ethics, Twenty Years at Hull-House, The Spirit of Youth and the City Streets, The Long Road of Woman's Memory,* and many more books innovated in the qualitative rhetorics of urban interpretation. While borrowing the language of the day, settlers argued self-reflexively for a distinction between the "laboratory" models of detached sociology and their interpretive paradigms.[6] Though subsequent disciplinary splits between the social sciences and the humanities sometimes obscure the connection, a second look shows how theatrical performance intersected and overlapped with this sociological project. Theatrical practices particularly engaged with the tenets and conventions of settlement literature's proximate epistemology. In this world, the practices of a "lady dancing" or a "lady singing" were often continuous of those of a "lady writing" or a "lady fact-collecting."

Discoursing on the importance of "adaptability," Isabel Eaton, one of Hull-House's early ethnographic writers and assistant to Florence Kelley, characterized the emotional savviness of the settler-researcher. "One must have quick intuition, and real sympathy—in order to avoid flabby sentimentality, as well as narrowness, inflexibility, even harshness."[7] Her statement echoed those that Jane Addams would make throughout her career. To contemporary scholars of ethnography, Addams's account of settling resonates with the fieldwork methods of participant observation. "[The settlement] should demand from its residents a scientific patience in the accumulation of facts and the steady holding of their sympathies as one of the best instruments for that accumulation."[8] Factual organization and sympathetic understanding could thus be interactive rather than mutually exclusive. The settlement ethnographer would ideally submit herself to the affective relations of the participant while in turn producing a set of utilitarian facts from a position of observation. Her method, to invoke James Clifford, was "a continuous tacking between the 'inside' and 'outside' of events: on the one hand grasping the sense of specific occurrences and gestures empathetically, on the other stepping back to situate these meanings in wider contexts."[9] Throughout her own published work, Addams employed the rhetorical techniques of ethnographic writing, managing focus, indirect discourse, and narrative plotting to

figure this continuous tacking. In *The Spirit of Youth,* for instance,
Addams used indirect discourse to convey her understanding of
young women's self-adornment.

> As these overworked girls stream along the street, the rest of us see
> only the self-conscious walk, the giggling speech, the preposterous
> clothing. And yet through the huge hat, with its wilderness of
> bedraggled feathers, the girl announces to the world that she is
> here. She demands attention to the fact of her existence, she states
> that she is ready to live, to take her place in the world.[10]

The thoughts of this overworked girl spoke loudly and clearly as
Addams reported them from the field. The rhetorical choice conveyed the inner life of an urban other and solidified Addams's own
expertise as a sympathetic ethnographer. Practicing what Chicago
sociologist and Hull-House affiliate W. I. Thomas would call
"sympathetic introspection," Addams demonstrated the power of
"reading the implicit" of social life, accessing an emotional experience that was invisible to the "rest of us." The practice of this
"theological exercise" occurred throughout the texts of America's
rising sage. Addams further figured such interpretation as a gendered skill, implying the unique capacity of a civic housekeeper
who understood the emotional as well as material problems of the
city she tended.[11] The positions of both insider and outsider were
analytically sound, but the former implied a nearness, an emotional
competence, and an intuitive capacity aligned with the feminine.
The parallel exposes a gendered intellectual history behind the
model of participant observation. For my purposes, it also provides
a framework for investigating the participatory fieldwork of theater
making. If gender underwrote the competencies of the civic housekeeping, they also propelled those of the civic play-housekeeper,
where women found agency in generating a theatrical sphere of
intersubjective engagement. As a theater director, a civic play-
housekeeper too navigated a continuous tacking between inside and
outside. In rehearsal, she cultivated the domestic ability to read the
implicit consciousness of performers onstage. Other times, she
grasped their gestures "empathetically," allowing "every detail of
emotion displayed on the stage" to run across her face.

Pragmatists and sympathetic Hull-House settlers maintained a
faith in the power of cross-class and cross-cultural sociality to effect
lasting and relevant social reform, understanding that the course and
character of this lived democracy could not always be foreseen and,
akin to Mead's "working hypothesis," would be subject to constant

revision.[12] To understand the Pragmatic dynamics of the "social self" and the "continual reconstruction of experience" was thus an appropriation of domesticity's epistemology. Additionally, such reconstructions worked on the lives of _both_ privileged and marginalized neighbors who acquired cosmopolitan capacities through "actual contact" and vicarious, "infectious" interaction with each other.[13] In Hull-House ethnography and its theater, some moments of "sympathetic introspection" thus highlighted—not only the dispositions of marginalized shopgirls or displaced immigrants—but also the longing and anxious interiority of the privileged settlers who dared to play. In renderings of what she called "the subjective necessity of settlement work," Addams gave such impulses full elaboration.

> You may remember the forlorn feeling which occasionally seizes you when you arrive early in the morning a stranger in a great city: the stream of laboring people flows past you as you gaze through the plate-glass window of your hotel; you see hard workingmen lifting great burdens; you hear the driving and jostling of huge carts and your heart sinks with a sudden sense of futility. The door opens behind you and you turn to the man who brings you in your breakfast with a quick sense of human fellowship. . . . You turn helplessly to the waiter and feel that it would be almost grotesque to claim from him the sympathy you crave because civilization has placed you apart.[14]

Appropriating the efficient positioning of the second-person pronoun, such textual moments dramatized the interior narrative of inauthenticity percolating in the heads of so many of her class. Positing the thoughts of her readers through the standpoint of a gazing hotel guest, Addams encouraged an investigation of dominant psychologies and the quest for intersubjective enagement. Such introspection took on a more ironic cast in other essays when Jane Addams rendered the interior monologue of a well-intentioned charity visitor, a young woman acting upon her craving for "human fellowship" within a constrained domain that righteously deflated its fulfillment.

> The daintily clad charitable visitor who steps into the little house made untidy by the vigorous efforts of her hostess, the washerwoman, is no longer sure of her superiority to the latter; she recognizes that her hostess after all represents social value and industrial use, as over against her own parasitic cleanliness and a social standing attained only through status.[15]

In cautionary prose, Addams suggested that "friendly visiting" could not produce an emotional field of a reciprocal engagement. With the proddings of Addams's third-person narration, the privileged female turned the evaluative gaze on herself, condemning her own parasitic tendencies and superficial values. Many of Addams's strategically indirect tales simultaneously sympathized and self-differentiated in such rhetorical moves. In the long, complicated, and unending process of personal transformation—from overcultivated daughter to longing hotel guest to well-intentioned charity visitor to self-reflexive settler—such moments followed a would-be Cordelia with certain and unceasing consistency. When she entered the Hull-House theater (as she will in this chapter), the rhetorics of the performance event extended such second-person, third-person, and indirectly first-person positionalities—albeit in the form of a spectator's gaze, an actor's dialogue, or a director's nod. To be a "social self" within Hull-House's displaced domesticity meant undergoing a process of personal un-settling while attending to the re-settling of others. For a civic play-housekeeper, this sometimes meant watching herself being watched by an "upturned face," feeling both the thrill and destabilization of a trust that she accepted more and less securely as she wondered whether the production was going to succeed.

If interactive socialities were to be evolutionarily sound, pragmatically responsive, affectively intelligent, and flexibly cosmopolitan, then performance carried the hope of giving form to such goals. In the midst of large-scale reform endeavors, some performance teachers compared themselves to their sister sociologists and doubted their own efficacy. At one point, music school teacher Eleanor Smith announced that she was leaving, convinced that her contribution was inadequate. In one of the many instances when Jane Addams mollified resident self-doubt, she successfully convinced Smith to stay and firmly recited the many instances when Smith's performance skills proved vital.[16] While troubleshooting around settler residency, Addams drew from a discursive stream of evolutionary, gendered, and pragmatic preoccupations, a mixture that she increasingly used to theorize the role of performance in effecting the socialities of lived democracy. Her compact arguments on "public recreation" joined the evolutionary language of recapitulation with the pragmatic language of experiential reconstruction to mediate on the role of *play*, a word whose "interchangeable" connotations of games and theater she intended. "The two leading qualities upon which play may be successfully founded are anticipation and reminiscence and in point of fact almost all plays exhibit a combination of both. . . . [She advocated] the possibility of making reminiscence a foundation for that public recreation which modern cities must provide if they would intelligently foster social morality."[17] Moreover, "theatre in its ability to bring men together into a common mood and to unite them through a mutual interest in elemental experiences" provided an environmental medium for cross-class and cross-cultural expansion. This complicated network of shared spaces, mimetic interactions, power inequities, gendered hopes, and latent biographies formed the context of settlement reformance. At Hull-House, to be a "lady dancing" was to transmit evolutionary behavior but also to be pragmatically social, to be unthreateningly feminine but also to be alternatively public. Demonstrating the productive power of "the social" amid an embedded sphere of the cultural, theatrical settlers practiced their ethic of neighborliness while, at the same time, communities and bodies were subject to constant recreation.

A Wobbly Organization

When Dorothy Mittelman Sigel remembered how "we came to Hull-House every Saturday," she invoked the simultaneous sense of collectivity and routine that characterized her relationship to the settlement. The "we" referred to a particular social formation—the Marionette Club—that existed within a larger network of social clubs and classes. "Every Saturday" illustrated the degree to which Hull-House sociality became an incorporated part of everyday life and acted as a symbol of continuity within the neighborhood. Stories of the development of theater at Hull-House often begin with references to Ellen Gates Starr and her avid interest in the arts. Thus "drama" along with painting, literature, and music was an organized activity at Hull-House "from the beginning." Starr's Shakespeare Club generated one theatrical beginning, where neighbors were invited to read and discuss plays of England's master dramatist under the supervision of herself and fellow settlement workers. This club's orientation reflected a particular philosophy of reform that was to be revised as Hull-House grew and its residents changed. Its few remaining "syllabi" from 1895 and 1896 show outlines of designated plays, papers, and discussion topics. Weekly discussions of *Henry the Fourth* focused on the characterization of Hotspur, noted differences between "a Historical play and a comedy or tragedy," and debated whether "Shakespeare's idea of the proper education for a Prince is false."[18] Like the Butler exhibits and the Chicago School Public Art Society, the Shakespeare Club sought to expose Hull-House neighbors to this great artist-playwright and to offer the skills in "distinc-

tion" by which its attributes, manner, and execution were best appreciated. Looked at from a broader interpretive framework, however,
the placement of the Shakespeare Club as the origin of Hull-House
dramatics is somewhat circumspect. By more expansively defining
performance through its modes of embodiment, orality, and its
status as a public event, activities in the playground, the gymnasium's social dances, or Valerio's receptions could also be positioned
in alternative theatrical genealogies. Furthermore, the ideological
and pragmatic commitment of the kindergarten and young people's
clubs to the development of the "whole child" sanctioned exercises,
storytellings, and masquerades, ubiquitous practices that leaked outside both the traditional theater space and the purview of the traditional genre category.

By the time the century turned, Hull-House membership had
grown tremendously, all participating in social clubs as an "instrument of companionship" or to open "new and interesting vistas of
life to those who are ambitious."[19] Along the way, Hull-House's
many civic housekeepers paved the way. "It is but natural, perhaps,
that the members of the Hull-House Woman's Club . . . should have
offered their assistance in our attempt to provide recreation for these
restless young people."[20] Trying to create socialities that would
"broaden out in one's mind to an instrument of companionship"
and witnessing years of such interactions in the parlor, gymnasium,
and playground, Addams touted the social value of nonverbal forms
of interaction, recognizing the power of modes other than "the medium of talk" for creating vital public spheres.[21] Her performance-
centered vocabulary furthered the Meadian hope of creating "conditions which favor" the "essentially social nature of human action."[22]

> These public games would also perform a social function in reveal-
> ing men to each other, for it is in moments of pleasure, of
> emotional expansion that men do this most readily. Play, beyond
> any other human activity fulfills this function of revelation of
> character and is therefore most useful in modern cities which are
> full of devices for keeping men apart and holding them ignorant
> of each other.[23]

Predating John Huizinga's concept of *homo ludens* and Victor Turner's well-circulated theories of *communitas,* such a theory of play
underwrote an argument for theatrical practices in pragmatic social
reform, albeit within a modified vision of "art." In the following
passage, for instance, Addams questioned the logic behind some art-
based reform practices.

If we agree with a recent definition of Art, as that which causes the spectator to lose his sense of isolation, there is no doubt that the popular theatre, with all its faults, more nearly fulfills the function of art for the multitude of working people than all the "free galleries" and picture exhibits combined.[24]

While retaining a prejudice against the "faults" of the popular theater, Addams emphasized a different function for the aesthetic object. Focusing on its communicative power and on the kind of felt collectivity it engendered, she connected the medium of theater to the social function of play and to the hope that the singular individual could "lose his sense of isolation." Addams adapted a sense of theater as a "communally shared repertoire of conventions" for the larger democratic effort of "revealing men to each other."

Consequently, dramatics was one of many activities along with

Built in 1899 above the new coffeehouse, the Hull-House auditorium provided a proscenium-arched space for theatrical reformance. *(Photo courtesy of University of Illinois at Chicago, the University Library, Jane Addams Memorial Collection.)*

lectures, dances, classes, and other social events organized by members of individual clubs. Before the 1893 gymnasium, small performances initially took place in the drawing and reception rooms of the Hull mansion, competing for time slots with other scheduled meetings and events.[25] Theatrical productions and rehearsals added to the multiple functions that spaces like the mansion's parlors already served. In a single day, the same room now not only accommodated a kindergarten, a mother's club, and a college extension class but also a rehearsal for *Tom Cobb*. The institution of time schedules went far to managing these limited spatial resources. Evening rehearsal slots responded both to the settlement's need for such rooms during the day as well as to the occupational schedules of the settlers and young people who participated in Hull-House theatrics. Such interspatial negotiations did not always erase conflict, however. In the morning, a Hull-House resident might descend to find the furniture rearranged or entirely removed, leaving the unappreciated spatial marker of a previous night's rehearsal. Other times, rooms were "so filled with furniture as to leave little space for an imaginary stage."[26] Residents thus instituted a new rule requiring all dramatic troupes to return furniture to its proper place after every rehearsal or production. Certainly the 1893 addition of the gymnasium offered more spatial resources to Hull-House thespians who placed folding chairs and a temporary stage in among the athletic equipment, using the interspatial convenience of the coffeehouse below for receptions after productions of *The Chimney Corner, A Scrap of Paper,* or *A Miracle Play.* However, since the gymnasium also served many functions—from calisthenics to dance parties to lectures—conflicts over its use were just as common.

> Rehearsals had to be held in a room, and scarcely even in the same room twice in succession. Not one of these rooms was large enough to properly teach voice inflection, and was unfitted in every way to give the young players a familiarity with the atmosphere of the stage. There was no Hull-House Playhouse then and it was only with difficulty that the cramped little stage of the gymnasium was secured even long enough for a dress rehearsal the night preceding the first performance.[27]

These difficulties suggest the particular negotiation that arose when the constraints of the theatrical performance process interspatially collided with the constraints of settlement activity. On the one hand, theater—like other performance forms—traveled, riding with the bodies of its performers to whatever empty corner it could find. On the other hand, theater was most recognizably practiced as "theater" in a space that allowed for a division between audience and spectator, that possessed good acoustics, and that had enough room for a range of movement onstage. The theatrical process thus differed from other reform practices and solicited different geographic accommodations. Other clubs did not demand the spatial continuity—the need to inhabit the same room in succession, to feel "the familiarity of the atmosphere of the stage," and to perform a dress rehearsal in the final performance space. The addition of the 1899 Hull-House Auditorium, along with a new first-floor coffeehouse, was thus a welcome relief.[28] "The stage will be much larger than the one in the gymnasium, and it is designed especially for the use of the Hull-House Dramatic Association and the Hull-House clubs, which have so carefully studied and presented plays during the last two winters."[29] The new Theatre Auditorium released the gymnasium of the theatrical burden while the relocation of the coffeehouse underneath the new second-floor stage reproduced familiar spatial practices.[30]

A recognition of the role of theater in forging collectivity underwrote many descriptions and accounts, and its historicization necessarily requires an analysis of theatrical rehearsal as much as of theatrical production. Settlers found that the process of producing a performance generated unique affective bonds among tentatively formed social groups. Thus, receptions that spawned weekly meetings and social clubs of immigrants and young people gained solidity and staying power when cautious ensembles turned into performance ensembles. The development of what Raymond Williams calls the "formations" of cultural production—those "forms of organization and self-organization" created by artists themselves—was in itself a pragmatic reform goal of Hull-House theater.[31] While other art forms require extra-artistic organization between fellow practitioners in the form of guilds and academies, some type of group formation is built into the execution of the theatrical artistic process itself. Therefore, it was ideally suited in Hull-House's formative years as a means of creating club camaraderie. As Edith de Nancrede would say of "dramatics" to a conference of reformers: "Certainly we at Hull House have found no other means so successful in holding a large group together from childhood, through adolescence and into maturity."[32] She argued that members could lose interest in other types of social activities while never allowing the sense of collectivity percolating around the practice of theater-making to diminish. "All of the clubs have a decidedly social side, and give numerous parties, cotillions, and picnics, until most of the members are thoroughly grown up and begin to marry and to settle down, when they become purely dramatic clubs."[33]

Individual accounts give a picture of how pragmatic sociality operated within the theatrical performance process at the highly local level of personal interaction. Madge Jenison, director of the Lincoln Club and of its 1901 performance of *The Merry Wives of Windsor*, recalled how the process of rehearsing the play together developed bonds among the club members and served a pedagogical function. She particularly focused on how the rehearsal process precipitated valued social interaction.

> Sometimes they came through blizzards. . . . [T]hey do not get away from work until six; it was nine when they came. We rehearsed until eleven o'clock, and then sometimes we sat and talked of the play until midnight. It was an endless delight to talk of it, especially of the costumes. . . . I never told them to read the notes and commissaries, but they did; there came this hunger to understand.³⁴

After a certain point, the play overtook the social life of the club. "It was splendid to see the play unfolding itself from month to month, and entering into their speech; conversation could only be conducted in terms of *The Merry Wives*."³⁵ At the same time, theatrical productions also could cause episodes of intraclub conflict. As an art form whose casting process occasionally necessitates exclusion, dramatics could also divide a group. Jenison reported that, though her club members "like a play better than 'running a dance' . . . a play is always opposed, because it injures the club within itself; those who are not in the cast lose that vital loyalty which makes the Lincoln Club what it is."³⁶ Fortunately for Jenison, *The Merry Wives of Windsor* had the opposite problem; it had to be cut to fit the club membership of fourteen. Given the unequal size of different roles, however, this still did not ensure harmony among the group.

> One boy became later a serious problem; he grew reproachful if two weeks passed without a rehearsal of his scenes;—something which often happened, as he had been cast for Shallow, a part much cut. He asked endless questions, and I think he meditated hugely on the part.³⁷

Other times individuals in the group suffered from an inadequate understanding of the demands of the theatrical process. While such incidents usually required the improvised intervention of club directors, more noteworthy were those moments when the young performers managed such crises among themselves. After a particularly arduous and disappointing rehearsal, Jenison recounted one such incident.

> One boy was tired, he wanted his supper, and he took his hat and overcoat to go home; I had seen him backed into a corner, with three irate Jewish boys shaking their fists in his face, and shrieking imprecations in his ear; in a few moments he came around, shamefaced and apologetic.[38]

Thus, in many cases, the performance process could combine with other contingencies of group dynamics—time constraints, power inequities, and personal differences—to bring embedded social difficulties to the surface. To the extent, however, that such conflicts were negotiated within the group, the resolution of moments of crisis exemplified the (often "shamefaced") use of peer interaction as an indirect method of socialization.[39]

Despite personal conflicts and logistical dilemmas, descriptions of the theatrical process confirm its enormous utility in building intraclub community. As an art form that required the cooperation of individuals in a group, as a creative endeavor whose success hinged upon mutual support among artists, theater was most productive in the service of a reform agenda. Edith de Nancrede romantically described the all-night technical rehearsals that, through shared trial, inevitably solidified the cast. Additionally, Jenison recalled the pleasures of group involvement.

> Best of all was the *esprit de corps* with which they came to line up about their play, this working for a common ideal which was without themselves. I take it that an office boy who feels that he is part of the firm is in step to become the firm itself.[40]

When the actual production of her club's *The Merry Wives of Windsor* took place, an already established sense of group affiliation was celebrated throughout, each member watching "without themselves" upon the creation of their cooperation. "At the end of each act they embraced each other and shook hands. During the scenes, they stood in silent, excited groups at the wings, listening." Accounts such as these illustrate the role of theater in achieving a highly local form of sociality, one that formed a provisional community along pragmatic lines and that incarnated a theatrical version of Jane Addams's theory of play. Facilitating the necessary "common mood" and state of "emotional expansiveness," theatrical activity enabled such ensemble sociality. "There is one thing I absolutely know," Nancrede wrote to Addams, "It is the 'art' side that holds them when they grow older. No matter how good a time I give them socially, they would drift apart after they are grown up but for the plays."[41] Through such aesthetic practices, the settlement actualized its social ideal of community, albeit in the otherwise unremarkable realm of a modest social club, led by less than famous female reformers, and receiving less than marginal status in the conventional history of the American theater.

Additionally, Hull-House theater provided a way for female reformers to participate in the active arena of socially conscious work while positioning themselves within the relatively unthreatening discourse of civic housekeeping. Borrowing evolution's conflicted ideology and methodology, women in the theater could argue for their extended domestic role in overseeing environmental reformation and in altering the materials of moral development. While not all Hull-House settlers and theater directors were female, women played most of the important roles in its creation and promotion. In addition to the general aid in recreational development received by the Woman's Club, women led a range of social-cum-dramatic clubs. When Laura Dainty Pelham left her post as president of the Hull-House Woman's Club to head up the Hull-House Players—the settlement theatrical troupe that would receive the widest attention and esteemed reputation—the two groups maintained a strong relationship of mutuality, the former financially and materially enabling theatrical productions, the latter performing at teas, talks, and gatherings sponsored by the former. The gendered authority underwriting Hull-House theater could even exist at the tacit level of spatial relations. When the settlement constructed a separate auditorium to house its theatrical productions, it was perhaps no coincidence that the Hull-House Woman's Club transferred the location of its meetings to this new space, storing cups and saucers for their weekly afternoon teas amid the props and costumes kept by the young people's clubs.[42] Furthermore, when the settlement later built Bowen Hall—a separate building to house the Hull-House Woman's Club—Edith de Nancrede again enacted the reciprocal relationship between female reform and theater by moving her productions to this new space.

The role of the theater in creating a context of affiliative collectivity existed not only at the level of intraclub interaction but also as a facilitator of *inter*club relations. Settlers made use of several aspects of the theater—in its status as a public event, its interdisciplinarity, and its paradoxical capacity to break up structural insularity among the clubs. First, the theatrical experience was inherently a collective event that extended to an audience beyond its club's performance ensemble. Madge Jenison acknowledged that a cub's decision to engage in dramatics served a function beyond intraclub cohesion for such "a public occasion . . . lends prestige to a club so small that it would otherwise remain obscure."[43] Thus, performance solidified the status and identity of a particular social club in the eyes of other ones. Furthermore, the public nature of theater encouraged communication and mutual support between clubs. Particularly illuminating is the fact that the first publication of the _Hull-House Bulletin_ coincided with the settlement's more active promotion of dramatics. The opening issue of the bulletin explicitly stated its goal as a means of encouraging communication among the various branches of the settlement. In articulating this hope, Jane Addams borrowed the language reformers generally used to theorize interactive play and ideal human communities in the city at large.

> During the past year there has been some difficulty in establishing communication among the members of the various societies, clubs, and classes meeting at Hull-House. Without this communication the advantage of coming to a social and education center such as Hull-House is largely lost. As a student in a large school becomes interested in studies and methods outside his own pursuits, so at a settlement each member should learn to know other characters, thoughts, and feelings. . . . It is hoped that these notices may prove suggestive and stimulate the clubs not only to a greater interest in each others' pursuits but toward a more generous cooperation.[44]

The rhetoric of the bulletin suggested that the settlement's efforts at creating intraclub community were almost too successful, that the social clubs promoted a kind of insularity that, if unchecked, ran counter to the ideals of Hull-House's mission. That Hull-House participants should "learn to know other characters, thoughts, and feelings" aligned with the metropolitan sensibility the settlement promoted. Influenced by the discursive sphere of Chicago School's "urban ecology" and its metaphors of "disorganization," settlement ethnographers often pointed to the increasing fragmentation and segregation of urban communities. Noting that different immigrant and laboring groups remained separately cloistered without a larger sense of the city's heterogeneity, they argued that such divisions made any cosmopolitan formation of community impossible. It was with these concerns and frameworks in mind that Hull-House residents made a temporally coincident decision to stage a series of Christmas plays and holiday contatas. "If the Christmas of 1896 should do

something toward breaking up the unconscious tendency of the clubs
and classes toward isolation and absorption in their own affairs, it
would prove a blessed Christmas indeed for Hull-House."[45] Thus, the
increase in dramatic activity in the middle of the last decade of the
nineteenth century strategically coincided with a shift in the structural orientation of the Hull-House Settlement in general. Since communication and cooperation across difference was an integral part of
the Hull-House agenda, the novelty and public nature of theatrical
performance could actualize this regenerative goal.

Later, Addams would note an additional attribute of theatrical
art. Not only was theater an expressly public art form, it was also an
essentially interdisciplinary one, often combining the skills of several
aesthetic forms—music, movement, speech, visual imagery—and
thus requiring the interaction of several resources of the settlement
for its execution. As Stuart Joel Hecht has argued, residents were
quick to note and appropriate theater's polyphonic nature.[46]

> Sometimes all the artistic resources of the House united in a
> Wagnerian combination; thus, the text of the "Troll's Holiday"
> was written by one resident, set to music by another, sung by the
> Music School, and placed upon the stage under the careful direc-
> tion and training of the dramatic committee; and the little brown
> trolls could never have bumbled about so gracefully in their gleam-
> ing caves unless they had been taught in the gymnasium.[47]

Thus, Hull-House residents capitalized upon particular aspects of the
theatrical medium—specifically its public nature and its interdisciplinarity—to promote a spirit of communication and cooperation. This use of dramatics does not only illuminate the means and
methods by which residents actualize a Progressive agenda in the
settlement locality. Their insights also foreground important characteristics of the theatrical event itself, particularly the extradramatic
aspects of its performance space, its ensemble of individuals, its process, its publics, and its integration of artistic forms.

Occasionally, Hull-House settlers made even more overt attempts
to use theater to break up the self-containment of the social clubs, a
complicated reformance that, at certain levels, violated pragmatic
sociality even as it relied on the collective and presumably democratic spirit of play. Such episodes trouble a naive celebration of
Hull-House settlers by showing their interventions in neighborhood
sociality, albeit with an informed knowledge of human nature and
human interaction. The most notable example involved the creation
of a new theater troupe composed of the "best" actors from different

clubs. Such an endeavor had been earlier proposed, but "the loyalty of these young people each to their own social organization, prevented carrying out any such idea. . . . [I]n spite of the envy and jealousy that was bound to occur, it was decided to try to form a Hull House Dramatic Association."[48] While the HHDA was ostensibly formed so that Hull-House could produce better plays, it is difficult to believe that Jane Addams would have agreed to this plan solely on the basis of aesthetic standards. In light of the settlement's larger attempt to discourage "clannishness" in community formation, however, the decision to form a new troupe suggests a decidedly social mission that could be couched in the language of artistic superiority. To the extent that a new formation would loosen club loyalties, it was worth risking "envy and jealousy" in order to achieve an ideologically justified structural shift. Negative feelings among individual club performers might have been necessary at an institution that sought to discourage social insularity and club autonomy.

Not surprisingly, the endeavor encountered many difficulties in its actualization. The idea of selecting from a pool of "some hundred and fifty to two hundred young people" immediately imposed an element of competition among a large group of performers who had been safely distanced from this common aspect of the theatrical process. Eventually, a production was staged followed by the temporary disbanding of the group and return of individual actors to their respective clubs, a development analogized by one chronicler to "the days of the feudal system, where to fight for the overlord was considered a greater honor than to fight for the king."[49] Later, however, the Dramatic Association regrouped and continued with another series of plays, eventually forming an entire theatrical season. Gradually, this "wobbly organization" became a more entrenched ensemble of its own, a development described by some in celebratory prose that echoed many a reformer's antiprovincialist ideals.

> Its members gradually became more loyal to it and sacrificed its interests less and less for their older affiliation. . . . From that time the permanency and success of the Hull House Dramatic Association was assured. The players became a unified body. Traditions formed and loyalty asserted itself. Enthusiasm took the place of doubt.[50]

Anticipating the metaphors of disorganization and reorganization formalized in urban ecology, the first stories of the Dramatic Association exemplify the role of dramatics in the creation and re-creation of Hull-House communities. In particular, it reflects Hull-House's

commitment to certain kinds of communities, ones that were out-
wardly directed as well as inwardly stable. It encouraged individuals
to be members of several communities rather than to remain solely
within a single group, to be a member of social club *and* a dramatics
club and so "to know other characters, thoughts, and feelings" besides those already familiar. While secondary historiography on
Hull-House theater has interpreted the formation of the HHDA as
a triumph of "aesthetic" concerns over "social" issues, another perspective that incorporates the complexity of the settlement's extratheatrical group relations demonstrates that the HHDA also served
particularly "social" ends.[51] It marked a theatrically achieved step
toward the ideal of progressive communities.

Cosmopolitan Theatricals

"Are you suggesting that there was some ill-will?" Dorothy Sigel
asked, looking at me from across a coffee table arranged with trin-
kets and a vase of tulips. Her question responded to my cumbersome
ones about her experience as a Jewish girl in a secularizing venue
such as Hull-House. My interest derived from multicultural and
pluralist critiques not only of Progressive Era reactions to immigrant
difference but also of Hull-House's assimilationist bent. Mrs. Sigel's
decision to answer the question with another question forces a more
careful consideration of exactly what principle gauges "good" or "ill"
in this complicated historical scenario, of what confirms "assimilationist" and what does not. In the Hull-House theater, the young
Dorothy acted in many different types of plays from Ibsen to Shakespeare to original plays of fellow Marionettes. During the Christmas
season—a period when Hull-House's reputed secularism revealed
its Christian underpinnings—Dorothy and her fellow Jewish friends
modified their participation, serving not as actors but as the technical crew in the backstage of Hull-House's annual Christmas tab-
leaux. "There was always respect for our religion," she said. "They
would never have had me dress up like the Virgin Mary, but this
way, I felt, the rest of us felt, like we could still participate."[52] Several
interpretations of such a statement present themselves to the contemporary cultural critic. Dorothy and Hull-House theater might be
placed on something like an assimilation continuum, with a Virgin
Mary costume on one end and nonparticipation on the other. Dorothy's modified participation might also be framed as an indirect—
and therefore insidiously effective—form of assimilation, one that
would make her assertion of settlers' "respect for our religion" a sign

The Hull-House Christmas tableau became a yearly tradition at
Hull-House. *(Photo courtesy of University of Illinois at Chicago,
the University Library, Jane Addams Memorial Collection, Wallace
Kirkland Papers.)*

of her false consciousness. Mrs. Sigel's story might also be a reminder
of the hidden hybridity underpinning (and, in this case, technically
supporting) arenas of apparent singularity or exclusion. In other
words, her narrative demonstrates that a production did not have to
be *about* cosmopolitan diversity to be—more or less unequally—a
cosmopolitan performance.

In her 1905 essay entitled "Recent Immigration—a Field Neglected by the Scholar," Jane Addams advocated a "cosmopolitan
standard" against American nativism and its "somewhat feeble attempt to boast of Anglo-Saxon achievement."[53] In the ensuing years,
Hull-House settler Grace Abbott would assume the directorship of
the Immigrant's Protective League to proclaim that "here in the
United States we have the opportunity of working out a democracy
founded on internationalism."[54] Many Hull-House affiliates and
their contemporaries shared this sensibility, though they variously
interpreted the sameness/difference axes of this international nation-

alism. Most employed some version of Grace Abbott's language of

"adjustment," an argument that weighed against immigrant "restriction" but promoted the partial refashioning of immigrant-American identity. Israel Zangwill's "melting pot" metaphor of 1908 also had ubiquitous discursive impact, even for its critics.[55] Such theories entered and reworked the perpetual paradox of American diversity, employing interdependent vocabularies of particularity and universality, preservation and assimilation, provincialism and cosmopolitanism, consent and descent, pluralism and conformism. John Dewey found himself arguing against both the prejudiced exclusiveness of American nativism and the "clannishness" of immigrant insularity in advocating an international form of American patriotism.

> No matter how loudly any one proclaims his Americanism if he assumes that any one racial strain, any one component culture, no matter how early settled it was in our territory, or how effective it has proven in its own land, is to furnish a pattern to which all other strains and cultures are to conform, he is a traitor to American nationalism.[56]

Perhaps the most famous particularist critic of Zangwill's melting and Dewey's interactionism was Horace Kallen. Kallen tried a musical metaphor to argue for a "federation of nationalities" and a pluralism of distinct ethnic groups.

> An orchestra is the free and well ordered cooperation of unique individualities toward the making of the common tune. . . . There is a true division of labor in the making of this tune, for although instruments are broadly interchangeable, there are limits set by the timbre to the adequacy and beauty of utterance.[57]

Condemning the "chameleon" or "spiritual mongrel" of hybrid American identities, Kallen argued that at base "an Irishman is always an Irishman, a Jew is always a Jew," resuscitating the descent-based arguments that nativist Americans also used to naturalize immigrant depravity. Even Kallen's pluralist paradigm on the "limits" of interchangeability, however, still incorporated an abstract reference to a "common tune."[58] As the United States entered World War I, Randolph Bourne's theories of a "Trans-National America" aligned with Kallen's concern over "a tasteless, colorless fluid of conformity" but also argued against the narrow provincialisms of group blocs: "America runs a very real danger of becoming not the modern cosmopolitan grouping that we desire, but a queer conglomeration of the prejudices of past generations."[59] Eventually adapting Darwin's hierarchical models with the latent Christian rhetoric of "universal regeneration," Hull-House settlers posited such interactive cosmopolitanism as "the next stage in the evolutionary progress of the human race," a mixed collectivity in which settled Americans and newer arrivals all underwent a process of regenerative adaptation and entered a more civilized plane of true internationalism.[60] As such debates about orchestras, melting pots, and colorless fluids waged, many could abstractly agree with Jane Addams that "the future of America must not depend so much upon conformity as upon respect for variety" without being entirely clear on where to locate sameness and difference or on what counted as a distinctive "timbre" and what a national "prejudice."[61]

Reworking the legacies of such Progressive Era theorists, a host of cultural critics have weighed the consequences and conundrums of fixing or unfixing ethnic locations and identifications. Such paradigms will suggest an intriguing connection to the range of identificatory positions within the event of theatrical performance. Extending Werner Sollors's historical "critique of pure pluralism" and, with it, a more recent multiculturalism, David Hollinger calls for a "postethnic" perspective that revisits cosmopolitanism. "Cosmopolitanism promotes multiple identities, emphasizes the dynamic and changing character of many groups, and is responsive to the potential for creating new cultural combinations."[62] Hollinger's postethnicity offers a poststructuralist continuation of the ethnic adjustment, using the language of "voluntarism" and "affiliation" over nonvoluntarist models of identity to "promote communities of consent. Affiliation is more performative while . . . the word *identity* implies fixity and givenness." Simultaneously acknowledging "today's greater sensitivity to roots," he and others nevertheless incorporate a "rooted cosmopolitanism," thus revisiting historic conundrums of how to distinguish among appropriate forms of ethnic rootedness and cosmopolitan expansiveness.[63] Additionally, it invites the question of how to figure voluntarism, and its implied intentionality, amid prevailing inequities of power. It is of course much harder to contend with the nonvoluntary "rootedness" of racialized poverty from which individual agents have a difficult time "disaffiliating."

When trying to analyze the role of Hull-House theater in negotiating immigrant difference, such theories of ethnicity combined with the range of specific productions inevitably challenge the definition of immigrant theater itself. This reorientation comes by integrating a complex undertanding of immigrant subjectivity with a complex understanding of theater as a polyphonic form. Indeed, the former's processes of subjectification interact with theater's many motile operations—the scripts, props, directors, costumes, gestures, back stages, front stages, emotions, sounds, actors, buildings, audiences, and locales that continually frustrate the attempt to decide where theater ends and its "context" begins. As such, theater also provides a technically useful arena with which to consider the performance of ethnicity in general. Theatrical simultaneity suggests that the question of ethnicity is ill conceived as a debate about where one draws a line between pluralist/assimilationist poles. Matching a performative concept of affiliation to the aesthetic event of theater reveals instead a field of operations, one whose coincident processes and overlapping realms bear little resemblance to a linear continuum. Within this formal hybridity, a variety of locations emerge—in casting and while spectating, on the stage and in the wings. At the same time, the power differentials between settler and neighbor—solidified in theater's hierarchical divisions of labor—show the constraints placed on an individual's field of affiliation. Theatrical performance thus enacts the opportunities and the limits of being a chameleon.

What was the dramaturgy of immigrant adjustment? On the one hand, it could appear in a play like *The Son of the Immigrant* that "depicted the insolent break between Americanized sons and old country Italians in the audience." Addams recalled its Hull-House production as a moment when fellow Italian-Americans "lost their sense of isolation." Using her distinctively indirect rhetoric, she represented the effect of its reception through the use of interrogative rather than declarative sentences. "Did the tears of each express relief in finding that others had had the same experience as himself, and did the knowledge free each one from a sense of isolation and an injured belief that his children were the worst of all?"[64] Here the issue of immigrant adjustment was itself the content of the drama, while the coterie of Italian-American spectators created an arena of identification, not only by recalling a shared immigrant past, but also by creating a new type of identification around the injuries of intergenerational change. It thus contained the dual qualities of "reminiscence" and "anticipation" that undergirded Addams's theories of play and public recreation, simultaneously providing a Hull-House "fable of rapport" for use in one of Addams's many ethnographic tales.[65] At the same time, such a representation of immigrant experience was of a particular variety, perhaps differing from the religious and ethnic programming offered at the nearby Catholic Madonna Center. Similarly, the Guardian Angel Mission or the Hebrew Institute—neighborhood ethnic institutions far more wary of Hull-House's intercultural mixing and the threat of assimilation—might not have indulged such tolerant tearfulness around the issue of intergenerational crisis. Subsequent attempts to respond to Jewish religious differences often ignored other cultural differences, especially when it came to valuing the styles, performances, storytelling, and speech of Yiddish culture. In one of the rare self-consciously "Jewish" episodes of immigrant theater at Hull-House, Edith de Nancrede staged performances of religious stories—*Joseph and His Brethren* and *Queen Esther*—but neighbors generally would have to go to the Metropolitan Hall on Jefferson Street to see Yiddish cultural performance.[66] Thus Hull-House theater's officially Jewish representation placed limits on which types of Jewish "past lives" would receive reminiscence.[67] Finally, the dramatic principle of "reminiscence" had other embedded exclusions. Such a mode was less easily embraced by African-Americans, the descendants of a decidedly nonvoluntary group of migrants. Paralleling other settlement social clubs, blacks rarely found their way onto Hull-House's West Side stage until after World War I; fleeting documentation of Celia Parker Wooley's 1906 rental of the stage for the Frederick Douglass Settlement's performance of a Lawrence Dunbar play seems to have been an exception.[68] Most significantly, the violent geographic and psychic displacement of slavery detached former Africans from the regenerative wellsprings of cultural memory so integral to Addams's theories of play and healthy cosmopolitanism. As such, they replicated the myopias of prevailing theories of ethnicity and American transnationalism, overlooking the basic disjuncture between the memorial rhetorics of "contributions" and the forced forgettings of African-American history.[69]

Adjustment looked somewhat different in two productions staged with Greek neighbors, *The Return of Odysseus* in 1901 and *Ajax of Sophocles* in 1904. Despite her sympathetic portrayal of Italian-Americans, Addams harbored her era's prejudices toward members of this "darker race." Hull-House residents often found it easier to develop alliances with Greek immigrants on different terms, particularly through their shared identification with Greece as the origin of Western civilization. Greeks, wrote Addams of Hull-House's dramaturgical experiments, "often feel that their history and classic background are completely ignored by Americans, and that they are easily confused with the more ignorant immigrants from other parts of southeastern Europe. [They thus] welcome an occasion to present Greek plays in the ancient text."[70] The fact that a history of Western civilization propped up both Greek and American nationalism was particularly convenient, for Addams and her colleauges could encourage Greek self-definition without severely testing the ethic of "international-mindedness." Rather than unsettling the conventions of American patriotism, declarations of Greek affiliation more often reinforced them. The performance of Greek plays also incarnated, without scandalizing, John Dewey's vaguely Arnoldian redefinition of cross-cultural exchange, a call for each group to maintain and to share "its distinctive literary and artistic traditions . . . to see to it that all get from one another the best that each strain has to offer from its own tradition and culture."[71] Educated Americans had already learned that such plays were "the best" of Greek culture. Hence, the notion that Greeks had "contributions" to offer American society was something of a Hellenic tautology, one that cast international mixing onto a cultural plane that felt comfortable and familiar.

Hull-House hired a visiting director named Mabel Barrows to stag the productions of *Odysseus* and *Ajax*. Barrows had previously organized several amateur productions of Greek tragedies, usually casting students from New England colleges. Hull-House embarked upon a much different experiment by casting Greek neighbors who performed the plays in their native tongue. The decision thus deepened and extended the breadth of this theater's touted cosmopolitanism; the plays were not only *about* Greek heritage but also incorporated Greek persons and linguistic forms into the apparatus of production. Performed for a diverse Hull-House audience of "university professors, devotees of the classics, men and women interested in the activities of Hull House," and neighboring Greek "merchants and vendors," the plays unevenly enacted the "reminiscent" function of ideal public recreation on two fronts, evoking an ideological past of Western civilization for some audience members and a nationalist enactment for those who had left their homeland.[72] To the extent that these two strains became blurred in the minds of some well-intentioned reviewers, the immediate lives of the latter became symbols of the past to the former.

Of all it may be said that the Greek syllables fell fluently from their lips and the blood of their ancestors beat in their hearts and spurred them to win credit for themselves and their land. The names of the entire cast, as given below, are extremely interesting as suggestive of an unforgotten past. It is a great pity that many of them have fallen victim to the modern habit of exchanging these sonorous and dignified names for "Jim" and "Bill" and "Pete."[73]

The temporal frame of "reminiscence" had a double edge with respect to immigrant difference, for positioning ethnic affiliation as an identity "recalled" simultaneously constructed ethnicity as something other than extant and contemporary. Naturalizing ancestral history with the blood "beat[ing] in their hearts," the spectator conflated "dignified names" with an "unforgotten past." She equated signals of cultural difference with symbols of temporal difference, nostalgically berating Americanization while simultaneously reiterating its modernity.

This doubled rhetoric continued in descriptions of the "peasant" men themselves. One reviewer, describing the "workingmen, clerks, bookkeepers, fruiters, and flower sellers" of the cast, also found noteworthy that there was "not a college graduate among them."[74] Another "Greek scholar" assured the audience that "there was no other people in the world where comparatively unlettered men could have played a Greek tragedy with so much fire and spirit."[75] At the same time, the historic legacies that ennobled these men also could be invoked to underscore their backwardness.

> The throwing up of parts for trivial reasons, the dropping out of members of the chorus after they had been trained to sing the difficult music, the drilling of men to sing who knew nothing of musical notation and with no conception of time, these are some of the things that called for infinite tact and good temper. Added to this was the fact that, with few exceptions, none of the twenty-five in the cast had command of English.[76]

A processual analysis of the theatrical apparatus exposes the ambivalence and complexity of cosmopolitian exchange around "the best" of each culture. The ensemble and rehearsal hybridized the representation of Greek "arts and literature," entailing cross-cultural socialities that settlers were less disposed to "preserve." Men who pounded with the ancestral blood of heroic Greece apparently adopted "trivial" priorities, were unused to "drilling," and "had no conception of time." As an artistic form, theater required logistical coordination, a contingency that unsettled illusionary boundaries between the "cultural" and the "social." The cumbersomeness of theatrical practice thus exposed reformers' difficulties in securing a separate cultural space of international indulgence, for theater necessarily confronted varieties of "rootedness" (sometimes language, sometimes "concepts of time") from which neither group was prepared to "disaffiliate." The productions nevertheless played to packed audiences of various backgrounds. The "nine men who had speaking parts frequently

earned applause with their fiery declamations," suggesting that some
audience members transgressed protocols of quiet spectatorship to
express their enthusiasm and perform their own nationalist alliances.[77]
Meanwhile, the rest of the audience members who did not speak
Greek watched from a different position as "the chorus . . . did their
duty of telling the audience—those that understood them—all about
what was happening with solumn unction."[78] Besides portraying
these legendary stories, the performance incorporated other forms.
The actors "executed a ghost dance with placid prancing which
evoked smiles"—perhaps eliciting a few more smiles from spectators
who felt that such bodily enactments deviated from the familiar
conventions of "the best" of Greek tragic form.[79] Doubling as performance space and reform space, these productions possessed different
resonances for its performers, directors, and varied audience members. Some expressed affiliation through smiles, others through applause, and others through declamations. While some spectators
might have felt hailed by the national dances, others conveniently
ignored the "prancing" to extol on the perfect "unity of classical
drama" instead. Reviewers most often repressed this heterogeneity,
ultimately crediting the director-reformer, Mabel Barrows, with re-
demptive power. Her "training developed sensitiveness to better
things. . . . The power to evoke the best in another is a noble endow-
ment of Miss Barrows."[80] As civic play-housekeeper, the sympathetic
skills of Mable Barrows positioned her as a virtuous domesticator of
international frictions and as the American instrument by which a
selective national "best" was gleaned.

Productions such as *The Son of the Immigrant, Joseph and His
Brethren,* or *Ajax of Sophocles* were, on some level, *about* Italian,
Jewish, or Greek national cultures. The "immigrant" status of other
Hull-House productions was differently mobile and tacitly intercultural, however, even when presumably "nonethnic" plays were being
produced. Occasionally, such plays also unsettled the confident adju-
dication of "the best." Madge Jenison's Lincoln Club, discussed
earlier, consisted of fourteen Jewish teenagers, and their production
of *Merry Wives of Windsor* was perhaps more hybrid than it may
appear superficially. While Shakespeare's "high" status as an art form
would suggest an assimilationist theatrical pedagogy, the investigation, debate, and production of this play also allowed this group
of young people to perform their pride in an aspect of Jewish
identity—specifically its much-touted intellectualism. Jenison noted
as much in the typifying language of a settlement ethnographer:
"Human affairs are what engage the mind of the Jew; sociology and
drama are his passions. These girls and boys read two newspapers a

day. . . . We discussed the New York and Chicago mayoralty elections endlessly. . . . I have grown to think that all Jews are debaters. . . . [T]hey read the notes, and asked questions as the day would quake to look on."⁸¹ More often, residents participated as directors, and therefore as leaders in Hull-House dramatics. Within this power differential, the intersubjective engagement of rehearsal still provided a space for her self-expansion. "I learned the meaning of 'kosher'; it is not kosher to eat milk within six hours of meat, and so no milk nor butter could go into our supper on the hearth. They used to tell me, too, of the Feast of Passover, of the Yiddish marriage rites, and of the customs of the synagogue."⁸² While these rehearsals still took place in the midst of prevailing social and cultural inequities, the Lincoln Club rehearsals managed a limited cosmopolitan exchange that occasionally decentered Jenison's cultural authority. In one self-reflexive statement, Jenison chronicled the experience of a well-intentioned reformer's personal unsettling. "You go to your work, fairly radiating culture, there is an enlarged halo of it enveloping you. It is not pride, you are not even stuck up. . . . [Y]ou are really full of tender thoughts. But you want to help some one, and you wear your rue with a difference."⁸³ In the day-to-day contact of settlement work, Jenison became more self-conscious about her "culture" and her longings, a recognition that transnational adjustment could and did unsettle all participants. At dancing classes, in rehearsal, in conversation, these encounters provoked a new attitude toward herself and her mission.

> Puff! something goes up in smoke; you shout to see the halo,—compounded of a few ancestors, a little travel, a few years at college, and a glimpse of the Parthenon and the British Museum,—to see the halo frizzling up. When the smoke clears away, it leaves you blinking, with a sobered mind and intent, new eyes upon yourself. . . . The first months are like beginning at one end of the social telescope which you have set up, and coming down again and again to the other—each time, be it said, with a less surprising jolt.⁸⁴

For her, club leadership meant reversing the ethnographic gaze, directing it inward and allowing settlement mimesis to expand in several directions.

> The leader of such a club gets into a way of pulling himself up before a meeting, taking himself in hand, trying to be more courteous, more sincere; it is a course in decorum and ethics with

fourteen professors. And who can say that the principle of give and take works only one way?[85]

In rhetorical moves reminiscent of Jane Addams's second- and third-person meditations on "the subjective necessity for settlement work," Jenison dramatized a reversal of the traditional relationship between club leader and club member. While the anxious, fractured moment-to-moment unfoldings of the performance process could lead Jenison to reify essentialized stereotypes about "the Jew," other times they caused her to "shout to see [her] halo . . . frizzling up."[86] Such jolting chronicles of personal displacement pushed within and against the conventions of the "fable of rapport," where settlers not only congratulated themselves on their work with the marginalized but also tread into other cosmopolitan territory where they found normalized hierarchies humblingly insecure.

One is hard-pressed to find such statements in the writings of Laura Dainty Pelham, the woman who took over as director of the HHDA, a reminder that residents varied in their willingness to unsettle themselves. Renamed the Hull-House Players in 1905, this theatrical group experienced intense critical success, attracting large Chicago audiences to the productions of Yeats, Synge, Shaw, Lady Gregory, and Galsworthy and eventually touring Ireland to collaborate with the Abbey Players. Conventionally regarded as an assimilationist vehicle separate from the melodramas and "vulgar" performances of immigrant and working-class culture, the cultivation of such an aesthetic repertoire often prompts historians to interpret the Hull-House Players as the most "Americanized" of the settlement's drama groups. What this critical lens represses, however, is the fact that most members of this troupe were Irish and that the performance of plays by such esteemed playwrights were simultaneously affiliative enactments of an Irish-American identity. Their connection to the Abbey Players in 1910 thus extended this national allegiance even as the less particularized language of artistic success and theatrical fame effectively denationalized their "Irishness" (and thus followed an early twentieth-century habit that deethnicized Irish difference more generally).

Upon returning from their tour of Ireland, the Hull-House Players faced a crisis over Pelham's artistic control that shows further how theatrical processes could incarnate asymmetrical variations on the "cosmopolitan standard." While the players objected generally to the maintenace of Pelham's authority over their repertoire and careers, they particularly argued against her decree in 1914 to "set aside the old rule limiting the company to fourteen and to bring in a number of the young people who had long been on our waiting list."[87] Pelham supported her decision to admit "new blood" by saying that "the members of the present company are not able to furnish altogether the right people for the parts. . . . This is the age of types."[88] Embittered by the decision and the fact that she had the power to make it, the players officially expressed their discontent to the Hull-House administration, comparing Pelham's typecasting to the nativist social theory and descent-based pluralism that they knew Hull-House reformers condemned.

> [I]t is an insult to the members of this organization. It implies that only some are mentally endowed to play the gentleman; that some have the intelligent earmarks of the crook or the rowdy; that only some can portray the lady of breeding and refinement, while the brains of others can understand only the feelings and actions of a school girl or parlor maid. . . . Your committee does not believe that this organization is ready to accept the mental theory of types. . . . Yet we have a variety—short and tall, fat and lean, blonde and brunette. . . . [E]ven here history gives us the lie; some great generals have been shrimps, some great athletes, midgets; some eight dollar clerks, Apollos. . . . [I]f the rowdy must always be the rowdy, the maid always the maid, the fine gentleman always the fine gentleman and no one capable of stepping out of himself, of what value the training?[89]

It was well-targeted argument for the occasion. Since Hull-House took as it starting point that individual behavior was not fixed and character not predetermined, the Hull-House Players adapted Progressive environmentalism to promote versatility in casting. The actor's chameleon-like potentiality was thus coextensive with the politics of consent-based collectivity. Instead of taking in new blood, they proposed a very different reorganization of the existing troupe, beginning with a reduction in Pelham's responsibility so that instead "the success of the organization was directly chargeable to the members." The clash underscored the complicated field and overlapping operations of theatrical cosmopolitanism. On the one hand, Pelham's push for a broadened cast membership could have been an index of expansiveness. On the other, internationalism could be located in the players' push for a broadened theory of acting, thereby testifying to their impulses to affiliate across difference. Conversely, whose cosmopolitanism had more limits? the group who wished to maintain its exclusivity? or the woman who wished to dictate the group's inclusivity on her own terms? The answer of the Hull-House administration tellingly illuminates the unevenness of settling and the retrenchment of power differentials. While members of the Hull-House Players had internalized many settlement values, the administration decided to uphold Pelham's control. When the decision was handed down, some players left the troupe, and others stayed, regrouping within a new ensemble after what Pelham would later euphemistically call the "natural changes" of theatrical selection.[90] The episode demonstrates how Hull-House residents placed prescriptions on patterns of rootedness and patterns of (dis)affiliation. Furthermore, some settlers were interested in generating new collectivities only if they were allowed to lead them.

When an earlier review recorded the fiery declamations of Greek actors, it also documented a particular type of spectatorial strategy, one continually aware that the dramaturgy of adjustment coincided with that of the lives of actors offstage. This kind of double seeing permeated reviews of Hull-House theater. In 1904, the settlement staged an adapted production of *The Three Gifts,* a labor play that dramatized the life of a striking bricklayer, his girlfriend's Irish family, and the dual effects of unemployment and immigration. Maintaining that "a play can tell certain things more potently and persuasively than can all the sociological pamphlets that ever fell from the groaning presses," the settlers recorded the intersubjective engagement of the audience with this ethnographic staging, hoping that "the intensely sympathetic interest with which it was followed might well suggest the effect of such an attitude on the public mind."[91] Especially important in generating such sympathetic introspection was the perception that the play mimicked the lives of the actors who performed it, producing portrayals that were "in some ways, more admirable, because a more actual, intimate and spontaneous interpretation than could have been professionally given."[92] Interestingly, then, audiences did not "suspend disbelief" while watching *The Three Gifts.* A slightly different kind of doubleness structured the reception of other Hull-House productions. After watching Louis Alter in Galsworthy's *Justice,* Maurice Brown celebrated the execution of a climactic scene where the protagonist undergoes a breakdown after solitary confinement.

> That scene left its audience with a memory of stricken and dry-eyed horror that will not easily be effaced. Nor can one forget that this great actor, in whose veins runs the blood of generations of oppressed ancestors, producing a temperament that can give unparalleled expression to such a part as Falder's—this great actor for twelve hours of everyday makes cigars—and Chicago lets him.[93]

Many Hull-House audiences were aware of such extratheatrical factors and fashioned relationships between them and their represented
fictions. Such cosmopolitan theatricals capitalized upon the double
consciousness of spectatorship. Sometimes it aligned character and
actor, art and apparatus, to highlight the continuity between circumstances staged and circumstances endured, disallowing the willing
suspension of disbelief, much as Hull-House neighbors could not
willingly suspend such social conditions. Other times, such dramaturgy foregrounded the disjunction between the expansiveness of the
actor onstage and the limitations of poor employment, reminding
audience members that the affiliative impulses of acting did not
allow the voluntary disaffiliation from a twelve hour-a-day job as a
cigar maker.

Corporeal Styles

In addition to the productive role theater played in the formation
and negotiation of cosmopolitan collectivity, the practice also served
another parallel brand of reform. Edith de Nancrede's dance class—
its orderly line, its bows and curtsies, it modes of address—illustrates
the settlement working within and against a discourse that assessed
the everyday performances of self enacted by heterogeneous city
inhabitants. In various types of urban writing at the turn of the
century, interpreters used tropes of difference in dress, grammar,
vocal volume, gaze, bodily comportment, spatial habits, and "habits
of thought" that often metonymically stood in for perceived social
problems that needed to be understood and in some way changed.[94]
As John Kasson has argued, reformers often focused on the realm of
manners as a means of re-creating human beings: "[T]he values of
these codes radiated both outward and inward. They provided standards by which to assess entire social classes, ethnic groups, and
cultures (often justifying their subordination), while at the same
time they extended deep into the individual personality."[95] Similarly,
to many reformers and Hull-House settlers, such material aspects of
personal identity engaged interactively with a person's mental life
and could lay the basis for the individual development of moral
character. This was felt to be especially true of young people, whose
adaptability made them more responsive to transformative repetition. Hull-House settlers often combined this effort with a Dewey-
ian model of the self, recognizing that learning happened pragmatically in the subtle give and take of daily interaction and, anticipating

Bourdieu's concept of habitus, in the habitual accumulation and adaptation of new encounters. Once again, female reformers found that this focus on young people's moral development easily supported the discourse of civic housekeeping and legitimated the domestic epistemology central to pragmatic reformation.

Meanwhile, as the arguments and enactments around theatrical collectivity reproduced Hull-House discourses of urban community, so those around the material and mental formation of young people advanced with the settlement's representation of juvenile development. During the same period, Hull-House's ethnographers and policy lobbyists developed discourses of juvenile health and delinquency that underwrote legislative reforms around child labor, the institution of separate juvenile justice systems, and the regulation of "stage children." Such sociological research both supported and complicated the efforts of the Hull-House theater. Forming the Juvenile Protective Association, Hull-House sent affiliates throughout the city to investigate urban sites reputed to breed juvenile corruption and criminality. In addition to billiard rooms, saloons, and dance halls, JPA researchers argued that local theaters were some of the worst offenders. The Tivoli Theatre was one of many where JPA officers found proprietors capitalizing upon the erotic presence of the child onstage. "At about eight o'clock, a prologue was given before the moving picture. A small boy, obviously under ten years old was seated on a fence in a rustic scene, fishing. He got down off the fence, came forward on the stage and sang 'O! By Jingo.' He danced and shimmied and made vulgar and suggestive gestures. . . . Officers went to the foyer of the theatre and tried to secure an interview with mother of the child."[96] Sometimes, however, the same probation officer wavered in her or his ability to assess moral uplift or degeneracy, and the same theater (the Tivoli) could elicit a perplexedly positive response. Describing a production called *Tulipland* that might well have appeared on the Hull-House stage, one probation officer's complimentary review tried to compensate for the violation notice she extended. "The dancing was very well done and suitable for children; the costumes were very attractive."[97] However, the fact that two of the tulips were portrayed by a nine-year-old and a ten-year-old violated new rules against the public exhibition of children. Given that Hull-House itself promoted theater for young people, settlers would walk a fine line when trying to distinguish their own practices from those they labeled corrupt. On the one hand, some sister sociologists (and Addams) spoke out against the theater as a vehicle of moral degeneracy. On the other, sister theater directors (and Addams) argued for theater as a vehicle of moral reformation, one that functioned as an appropriate substitute for highly inappropriate performances.

The uses of theater in the reformist cultivation of aesthetic and moral sensibility lay in the embodied, environmental, and enacted nature of the medium itself, one that uniquely facilitated the transformation in sensibility and behavior. Addams often commended the theater as a "means of training the young people of the neighborhood in manners and personal refinement and courtesy."[98] To the extent that theatrical performance required a certain amount of bodily discipline on the part of performers and to the extent that training in pesonal refinement also required a neighbor's bodily discipline, the former could be employed in service of the latter.

Theater club leaders, for instance, lamented young people's undisciplined comportment, using reformist language. One director described how a young boy "had that strolling tendency which seems to go nowhere and come nowhere, that moonlight-walk-by-daylight manner of exit and entrance which will make any scene lag." She thereby framed this aesthetic deficiency in language that echoed the discourse of juvenile delinquency, one that categorized the performed signs of juvenile "incorrigibility," "truancy," and "loitering."[99] Attention to theatrical blocking and movement encouraged young people to present their bodies differently. One young actor's initial efforts produced a disconcertingly disconnected series of motions.

> Miss Warsah was one of those conscientious people who will always sit down on the exact word at which it has been suggested that she should sit down. . . . She had a way too of backing about the stage . . . and of making preparations for her business— hanging out a sign. . . . She never walked across the stage; she edged over through twenty lines to be ready to drop into a chair on some inevitable word.[100]

The familiar rehearsal scene resonated with the discourse of a reform space that lamented the alienations and bodily disruptions of the modern city. Like an agrarian peasant "detached from his country experiences," Miss Warsah's body incarnated Addams's depiction of modernizing fracture, one that stalled "a perfectly simple and direct process between cause and effect, between the discharge of energy and its reward."[101] After much rehearsal, however, fellow performers celebrated the day when Miss Warsah, via the character of Mistress Page, achieved bodily coordination. "Mistress Page came dancing on . . . [in] a kind of rollicking pleasure. . . . From that night we saw no more of Miss Warsah at rehearsals. . . . [S]he was Mistress Page—an adventure—a new world. She has never been quite the same girl since then."[102] This theatrical success story was also an evolutionarily sound reform story. Reconnecting the discharges of energy and output, Miss Warsah's theatrical transformation fulfilled an extratheatrical adaptation.

To effect a transformation in the students' bodily comportment, Hull-House theater workers often solicited the aid of the dance studios, for, as Edith de Nancrede wrote, "[f]olk dancing and rhythmic dancing form a very important part in the training, and are invaluable in teaching expression through the use of the body."[103] Since the body was a sign system both on and offstage, its coordination and familiarity with new signals and motions also symbolized the success of Hull-House theater and of the Hull-House reform project more generally. On the day Dorothy Mittelman married Louis Sigel, Nancrede celebrated the grace with which Mittelman walked down the aisle, attributing the success of the "rhythm" classes in aestheticizing this performance of everyday life.[104] Thus, Nancrede enacted a classed cultivation of taste, Bourdieu's "distinction," in which agents learned not only "to take an aesthetic point of view on objects already constituted aesthetically . . . [but also] the even rarer capacity to constitute aesthetically objects [and I would add self-presentational styles] that are ordinary or even 'common,' " applying such principles to "the most everyday choices of everyday life."[105] Nancrede and other women colleagues tacitly invoked their own gendered authority as female theater workers, appealing to theater's reformative powers by highlighting its role in creating virtuous and healthy young people and thus placing theatrical practice on a gendered plane with other sanctioned efforts of women's civic housekeeping. The performed memory enacted by Dorothy Mittelman Sigel in my opening anecdote attests to the impact of such reformations on her embodied history, a restoration of behavior made possible by settlement play-housekeeping and its gendered space of memorial transmission.

Such cultivations in distinction and their reformation of neighbor habitus continued when settlers demonstrated that such bodily adjustments were intimately related to spatial habits—that body disciplines and the spatial configurations of rooms and furniture mutually reinforced each other. Since the assumption that changing an environment could change the character of its inhabitants underpinned positive environmentalism and public domesticity, the creation of and performance within alternative theatrical settings reinforced the environmental reforms sought during this period in

Chicago. By producing plays that took place in parlors and by inculcating the character behavior appropriate to such a space, some Hull-House productions indirectly initiated participants in the set of spatial styles also taught in the settlement's mother's clubs and model tenement exhibits across the street. Nancrede favorably underscored the intensity with which her theater troupes attended to the beauty of their sets—whether a bourgeois dining room or a more symbolic design—suggesting not only the development of an aesthetic sensibility per se but also the application of this sensibility to a surrounding environment. If young neighbors learned to inhabit and appreciate such settings onstage—sets whose furniture was of such "good taste," a costume wardrobe (gleaned mostly from the donations of wealthy Chicago philanthropists and Hull-House benefactors) of such "well-to-do heritage," and props sporting a china collection so lovely that, as one reviewer said, "many a woman envied the possessor"—they ideally became interested in re-creating such settings in their own homes.[106] When Addams asked Nancrede to help her argue to the Carnegie Foundation for the importance of the arts in settlement reform, Nancrede explicitly noted this valued relationship between aesthetic and everyday environments. "I am sure that it is impossible to judge of the results, only by those who make a profession of some form of art. . . . One has only to go to their homes to see the effects. You would be amazed at the charming apartments that girls like Anna Behr, Dorothy Mittleman, Chickie, and indeed most of the older young people have."[107] Noting that such "charming apartments" kept by dramatics club members were proof of the re-creative power of theater, Nancrede invoked theatrical practice once again as a means to inculcate the habitual behaviors and dispositions of a "better" habitus and more morally sound urban homes. The logic did not mean, of course, that individual agents could not find their own ways of incorporating the infectious example of settlement theater into a domestic imaginary. When an Italian-American girl named Carmella Gustaferre described "What Kind of a Home I would Like to Have," she properly confirmed that she wished for "a nice educated house" that included "a piano, a parlor, and room full of flowers." However, she also planned to secure an "empty room in my house so that I could fix it into a stage so that my friends and I could have acting." Gustaferre's ideals of living thus mimicked not only an onstage interior but also a theatrical version of Hull-House's internalized publicity, one where everyday spatiality included having a theater next to one's parlor. Additionally, she hoped for "a backyard with a swing in it and a sink."[108] Following the undoings and relocatings of settlement residence, its civic play-housekeeping could thus unsettle some conventions of domesticity in the same moment that it affirmed others.

Besides the embodied and environmental nature of the medium, theater's oral component proved useful in reforming the speech of its participating neighbors. Deviations from certain habits of speech signaled lack of refinement as obtrusively as did lapses in bodily discipline. Dramatics was thus particularly useful when teachers made "a great point of the use of the voice, of pronunciation and diction; and what could not possibly be taught in one play a year, can be inculcated in one play a year for ten years."[109] Sometimes such vocal reformation focused on developing grammatically "correct" habits of pronunciation in place of patterns endemic to a working-class performance of personal identity. Addams, for instance, noted that participation in the plays of the great dramatists necessarily required much work and "hours of labor that the 'th' may be restored to its proper place in English speech."[110] Sometimes the perceived need for training in pronunciation arose from the cultural diversity of Hull-House's immigrant neighborhood, a vocal reformation that facilitated immigrant assimilation. Thus, many would celebrate the fact that, despite the presence in one particular cast of "a Frenchman, a German, several Irish, and two Russian Jews who could not speak English when they landed in America . . . the elocution was almost without exception on a level of excellence unknown to the commercial stage."[111]

This microlevel reformance activity became even more personal and intimate when it channeled the emotional component of theatrical expression and hence the emotion management necessary for its execution. Associating a perceived excess of emotion with lack of refinement, settlers lauded Hull-House performers when they refrained from such affective indulgences. In the early production of *A Chimney Corner,* Addams noted that this "pretty domestic play . . . might easily be spoiled by ranting, but . . . because it was given with delicacy and real feeling, held the sympathy of the audience throughout."[112] Addams thus aligned delicacy, not with repressed emotion, but with "real" feeling. While, like all performance of the past, such enactments are "lost" to a performance historian, it is useful to speculate on the degree to which so-called realistic acting styles derived from the class and cultural sensibility of bourgeois residents and whether other performance styles that received the label "indelicate" or "theatrical" did so because they exceeded the constraints of delicacy and refinement of such "naturalized" behavioral styles. For instance, certain excessive performance styles were tolerated and even perceived as lifelike when used to portray certain characters. One theater

Child spectators watch attentively at the Hull-House theater. *(Photo courtesy of University of Illinois at Chicago, the University Library, Jane Addams Memorial Collection.)*

reviewer applauded a young Hull-House actor's depiction of a dishonest and immoral labor leader named Buck Foley in *The Walking Delegate,* saying his "brassy, magnetic, shrewd, and evil labor pirate is photographically conceived and colorfully executed." That a character could be "colorfully" performed and still be "photographically conceived" suggests that representations of working-class immorality easily turned to a broader performance style. The perception that this colorful portrayal was also "accurate" reflects the extent to which stereotypes of working-class emotionalism, vocal volume, and broadened gestural styles functioned as naturalized images and aural synecdoche in the Progressive Era's bourgeois imaginary. The text of the play further reinforced the stereotype by writing all of Buck Foley's lines in "improper English speech"—ungrammatical phrases whose words dropped their endings and their "th's." Unlike Buck Foley, Tom Keating—the honest working-class labor leader in *The Walking Delegate*—spoke in an accentlessly perfect grammar unaccompanied by "colorful" gestures and bodily comportment, performative styles that presumably symbolized honesty and morality.[113]

While much has been made of "realism" and "naturalism" as ideological dramatic literary strategies that work on their audiences, less has been made of the role of realism as an acting style in ideologically binding its embodied performers. At a settlement that argued more often for the reformative role of performance for its actors than for its audiences, the connection was more than peripheral. This question is also particularly interesting in light of the "naturalizing" rhetoric used finally to argue for performance-based settlement reformance. For Nancrede, its ultimate re-creative efficacy came from the fact that such performances felt natural to the actors themselves. Nancrede's theatrical rehearsals introduced new behaviors in a way that did not feel intrusive. Instead, habits were produced, restored, and altered gradually and in such a way that their enactment felt spontaneous, as if it emanated from "within" rather than being directed from without. As the twentieth century wore on, theater dirctors' expertise in sympathetic introspection developed alongside psychological models of social malaise, individuating paradigms that espoused therapeutic intervention into the mental life of reform.

> The drama is like Josephine Preston Peabody's "piper" always letting things out of cages. Sometimes, as I watch a young, self-conscious creature expanding and growing under the influence of the inspiring or poetic thoughts he is expressing, the drama appears to me like one of those Eastern magicians who puts seed into the earth and immediately before one's eyes it sends forth roots, branches, leaves, buds, and opens wide a flower.[114]

Nancrede's metaphors mingle connotations of release, self-expression, and personal growth while simultaneously suggesting intervention, constraint, and limitation. Borrowing the language of repression, the drama may let "things out of cages" but it always happens "under the influence of poetic thoughts," allowing soil to become fertile only when it encountered the seed a teacher had preselected. However, it was precisely the feeling of naturalness that allowed the reform mission to take root and blossom inside the bodies of Hull-House performers. "It is a drill that enables a child, through his lessons in dancing and rhythms, to move with grace and ease. He works only one hour a week, perhaps, but one hour a week for a number of years. . . . It is this drill over a period of years that we recommend."[115] Similar techniques were used in the music school, creating the effect in *A Troll's Holiday* that a refined performance emanated from the interior expression of the individual.

The chief merit of the performance lay in the spirit of the singing of the chorus. It is obvious that Miss Smith works "from within." Nothing so fresh and spontaneous and unspoiled could have been achieved by the methods of the ordinary automatic trainers.[116]

Consider one more description of Nancrede's method. "In two months—often in less time—they have mastered their lines without knowing it. They are never set to tasks of memorizing but naturally absorb the play. Hence the work is ever a pleasure. They creep into a perfect illusion and all is kept sweet, wonderful and spontaneous for them."[117] Thus, Nancrede's drills were not experienced as "drill-like" to the young performers, and her ability in this regard is the mark of her sensitivity as a theater director. Indeed, theater directors will recognize such an ideal of natural absorption as a sound means of creating good theater. In the settlement context, however, such an ability was also the mark of Nancrede's capacity as a productive reformer. The quality of spontaneity and pleasant absorption in these enactments obscured a tacit reformation. Rather than assuming the traits of absolute power, modernizing control, or hierarchized condescension of other Progressive Era reform projects, such theater matched the settlement's domestic ethic of neighborliness, subtlety, proximity, continuity, and quiet side-by-sideness. In a complicated incarnation of the Hull-House paradox, this device used pragmatic understanding even as its interventionist application sidestepped the ideal of reciprocity in a mimetic exchange. Successful at infiltrating the corporeal styles of the individual so deeply that their performance appeared and felt spontaneous, theater's feeling of unmediated sensation enabled the re-creation of the Progressive Nineteenth Ward bodies. As Dorothy Mittelman Sigel has repeatedly articulated to me in an effort to convey her experience of the settlement: "We never felt that we were being 'taught' anything. It's only when I look back now that I realize Miss Nancrede was teaching us our manners. But she didn't 'teach' it; it just happened naturally and by example."[118]

Edith de Nancrede's infectious example supremely exemplified the experiential ideal of settlement mimesis, pragmatic pedagogy, and civic play-housekeeping. It was such a realm of indirect influence that her fellow settlers and JPA investigators had in mind when they discoursed on the good and the bad of child theater. Both lady dancers and lady fact-collectors understood the susceptible affects and embodiments of theater and their capacity to elicit desires and identifications of all kinds. Even as the former concerned herself with its appropriate cultivation, the latter worried about whether they all could maintain a hold on this tenuous and volatile arena.

Critiquing the display of children in song-and-dance contests of local theaters, one JPA investigator waxed prophetic on the commercialization of such intimate emotions.

> By whatever name we call it, the truth appears to be that with the growth of vast commercial projects, the business of selling has become a science. The science deals with the knowledge of human reaction in relation to purchasable things. Each business has to work out for itself the method of persuading the greatest number of people to purchase the particular commodity it has for sale. . . . We have been accustomed to being sold the same shaped shoes, hats, dresses and suits for a generation. For the first time we have seen the amazing spectacle of excitement and entertainment in the form of a dance being publicly sold to a whole nation. Th[e] new element in this phase of production and consumption should startle us all awake.[119]

Settlers recognized the beginnings of a different type of consumer culture and the role that sentiment—formerly domesticity's epistemological domain—played in maintaining and extending it. Equipped with a "knowledge of human reaction," both social services and commercial interests tried to adjust the behavioral performances of targeted human beings. And settlers worried that commercialism was winning out. "While they are so richly entertained at their party; while they sing the popular sophisticated songs, dance, strut, and shimmy their own to applause and prizes . . . the settlement and neighborhood clubs where they used to play children's games, read good books, or learn carpentry, or sewing and cooking are deserted."[120]

Desertion was not nearly so absolute, of course, as long as club performers such as Dorothy Mittelman and her friends kept coming and indirectly learning new everyday performance. Nor, however, could settlement theater and consumer culture ever remain very neatly divided from each other. Mrs. Sigel now credits Nancrede's tacit lessons in manners with her own rise in economic mobility. Nancrede equipped her performers with valued cultural capital, even as Nancrede herself made life decisions that paradoxically distanced her from economic comforts. Dorothy Mittelman Sigel would take her reformed corporeal styles, iterating her speech and comportment to land a much-coveted position at Chicago's Merchandise Mart in her late teens.[121] She thus learned the self-presentational modes of commercialism. Now that she has iterated and reiterated such environmental practices in her exchange of "charming" Nineteenth

Ward apartments for larger ones farther north and finally to her charming Winnetka home, she frames Hull-House's impact as an extension, not a repression, of her own capacities, skills, and powers of expression. Meanwhile, as Mrs. Sigel embarked on a classic American story of economic and geographic mobility, Edith de Nancrede stayed put, living until her death at Hull-House, committing to a decision to abandon the burdens and entitlements of her gendered and classed familial upbringing. At one point, she asked Dorothy's husband Louis to hock a piece of Nancrede's family jewelry so that she could continue to pay her room and board at the settlement.

"Thank you, Miss Nancrede."

The expression of gratitude was simultaneously studied and heartfelt. To a former neighborhood child called to narrate the impact of Hull-House on her life, the memory dramatized symbolic moments in her personal re-formation, changes for which Mrs. Sigel is both grateful and proud. The bodily comportment, the gesture, the eye focus, and the spoken direct address—all pressed in as memory, circulating as both the content remembered and as the means of remembering. And so, within the performative exchange of our conversation, Dorothy Mittelman Sigel passed down a bit of history.

A wider interpretation of aesthetics and performance challenges some assumptions in the history of reform. It particularly troubles the interpretation that many have given to nineteenth- and turn-of-the-century women's associations and reform endeavors on the move from less significant cultural activities to the "more important" work in changing labor, immigration, urban, and welfare policy. Most significantly, investigation of Hull-House theater exposes the embeddedness of the social in the aesthetic, whether one sees in that sociality a possibility of interactive democracy or spies instead the forces of normalization. Indeed, I would suggest that you are pretty much guaranteed to find both. Cultural and social formations were the central methods by which Hull-House reformers worked to create neighborhood locality. At the same time, this production always occurred in an unequal encounter between settler and neighbor, one where mimetic exchanges did not happen symmetrically and where residents intervened in the reformation of communities and identities using a method that derived paradoxically from an antiinterventionist philosophy. Such philosophies and practices bear an intriguing relation to contemporary performance theory. They expose the gendered intellectual history behind the theorizing of affect and microperformance; they also highlight the evolutionary and indeed Lamarckian longings of acquired inheritance that cling to the restoration of behavior. Furthermore, Hull-House theater and reformance exemplify the significance of the experiential to the realm of the theoretical, a significance that means attending to non- verbal historiographical documents such as inventories and blue- prints and taking seriously the embodied aspects of an oral history interview.

Perhaps the enacted memories of Dorothy Mittelman Sigel are satisfying because they remind me that the archive is not the only place that performs the past or that the printed word was not the only medium that did the work of historical mediation. What was theorized verbally around discourses of evolution, womanhood, prag- matism, cosmopolitanism, community, and morality was also en- acted collectively and embodied viscerally in the motion of a civic housekeeper, the focused gaze of a theater director, the performed esprit de corps of a group of young people, and the extended arm of this first-generation Jewish imigrant girl. Finally, the work of settlers like Edith de Nancrede epitomized the intersection of performance and reform in all its conflicted productivity, a productivity that now circulates in the infinitely complicated, perpetually problematic, and always breathtaking moments when Dorothy Mittelman Sigel raises her arm, lowers her leg, and lifts her head to hold the eyes of an imaginary teacher whose eyes had once held hers.

Chapter 6

Professionalizing: "To Enlarge the Field of Activity"

Is there not a danger that everything that has so far protected the historian in his daily journey and accompanied him until nightfall (the destiny of rationality and the teleology of the sciences, the long, continuous labour of thought from period to period, the awakening and the progress of consciousness, its perpetual resumption of itself, the uncompleted, but uninterrupted movement of totalizations, the return to an ever-open source, and finally the historico-transcendental thematic) may disappear, leaving for analysis a blank, indifferent space, lacking both interiority and promise?
—Michel Foucault, *The Archaeology of Knowledge and the Discourse of Language*

We have to acknowledge that if in discourse the city serves as a totalizing and almost mythic landmark for socioeconomic and political strategies, urban life increasingly permits the re-emergence of the element that the urbanistic project excluded.
—Michel de Certeau, *The Practice of Everyday Life*

"Two Tenants May Delay U. of I. Campus," read the 1963 headline of a *Chicago Tribune* article, adding another in a series chronicling the conflicted process by which the City of Chicago eventually leveled Hull-House's thirteen buildings to make way for Mayor Richard M. Daley's University of Illinois. The two women were Jessie Binford, age eighty-six, and her younger friend Florence Scala, a forty-five-year-old proprietor of a local Italian restaurant and temporary Hull-House resident. The article ran a picture of Jessie Binford—seated, white-haired, eyes wide and angry—with Florence Scala standing protectively but resolutely behind her. Several decades earlier, Jessie Binford had been head of the Juvenile Protective Association; then, their positions might have been reversed. As principal leaders of the Harrison-Halsted Community Group (the descendent of the Nineteenth Ward Improvement Club), Scala and Binford led a suit in state and federal courts against Mayor Daley's administration and his Department of Urban Renewal. The suit also indirectly criticized the deal cut by the Hull-House Association, which, no longer attached to the settled bricks and mortar, agreed to sell the buildings for $875,000. "Mrs. Scala and I have decided to remain as tenants in Hull House until that decision is given. . . . If we were to turn our backs on the community and leave Hull House before the final court decision is made, we would be refuting this right in which we believe."[1] Officials at the University of Illinois were annoyed; underneath the building in which Scala and Binford resided lay "a large old brick sewer." "This building must come down first," said one official, "because the reconstruction of the sewer is one of the first underground projects that has to be done."[2] When the federal decision sided against them, Scala and Binford soberly walked from the settlement for the last time, meeting a coterie of neighbors and former residents who gathered along the edge of a fenced-in perimeter. Together they watched over Hull-House as the wrecking balls swung.

The 1963 destruction of the Hull-House Settlement marked a culminating moment in the history of social work even as it marked the beginning of the infamously misguided project of "urban renewal."[3] The "scaffolding" that Jane Addams could "scarcely recall" when she wrote *Twenty Years at Hull-House* also happened to be the architectural frame of an expanding apparatus of social welfare. The second generation of settlers—Jessie Binford among them—would embark upon a stream of new efforts. Recognizing the structural limits of an exclusive commitment to locality, they entered more powerful arenas to place the tasks of civic housekeeping under public administration, gradually altering the definition of the state and expanding the domestic reach of its policy umbrellas. Recognizing the limits of the settlement's volunteerism, they argued for the professionalization of social work, securing its intellectual legitimation through university departments and social scientific methods, creating a new niche of employment opportunities for women who accepted a gendered division of labor as applied sociologists and human welfare "experts." At each step, most of these developments felt like successes. Each success, however, occurred within an adjacent history, one that eclipsed the settlement's ethic of proximate urbanism and the local knowledges and neighborly humility that often went along with it. Each step supported the formation of what Hannah Arendt would call "the social" whose bureaucratic forces of normalization she and her critical descendants would condemn.[4] In the end, the settlement's effort to "enlarge the field of activity" ultimately participated in Jessie Binford's un-settling.

Stories of wrecking balls and lost proximity make me nostalgic for a thing I never knew—a local Hull-House milieu of care and memory whose destruction activates more longings. Not coincidentally, such nostalgia over a lost Hull-House milieu bears a formal resemblance to Jane Addams's earlier nostalgia for a lost agrarian milieu. In her meditations on the alienation of the modern city, Addams elegized a rural scene similar to the arena of integrated memory so fundamental to Pierre Nora.

> What happens to a man when he finds himself detached from his country experiences and permanently settled in a modern city? In the country he tilled his fields, harvested his crops and fed his children with the proceeds—a perfectly simple and direct process between cause and effect, between the discharge of energy and its reward.[5]

Decades later, Edith Abbott—social activist, University of Chicago professor, Hull-House settler—would quietly question the principles that undergirded Addams's longings. In a *New Republic* essay called "The Fallacy of Local Relief," she reminded readers that this presumably ideal peasant life was subject to feudal authority, a historical fact that qualified an exclusive belief on the ethics of locality.

> The principle of local relief belongs to the parochial England of the sixteenth century and not to modern America. It is the doctrine of a day and age when a man's parish was his world—not the accepted doctrine of any modern government. . . . It belongs to the day when national funds went to the king . . . when no one in London knew or cared about local highways or village destitution. The world has changed since that day.[6]

Abbott thus remembered that in lost agrarian spaces someone else took the "proceeds" of a country farmer's tilled fields, a king who did not always care about making "cause and effect" so neatly reciprocal. The reminder exposes the myopia of misdirected nostalgia—whether Jane Addams's or my own. At the very least, it asks for a complicated framing of Hull-House's competing attempts both to preserve the past and to enlarge its relation to a modern American government. It further suggests how the longings that drive the former can obscure as much as clarify the operations of the latter.

Currently, the Jane Addams' Hull-House Museum stands at the corner where an abbreviated Polk Street meets the expanded thoroughfare of Halsted. Before bringing in the wrecking crew, University of Illinois officials surveyed the early Hull mansion, measuring

The Jane Addams Hull-House Museum with buildings of the University of Illinois in the background. *(Photo courtesy of University of Illinois at Chicago, the University Library, Jane Addams Memorial Collection.)*

ceiling heights, doorways, and moldings to reconstruct the house before the new additions "submerged" it. From these speculations, they built a replica of the "original" mansion and a relocated Resident Dining Hall through which museum visitors could pass to learn settlement history. Labeled "UICC's Tribute to Jane Addams," the museum would function as Hull-House's *lieu de mémoire* on a site that could no longer be its *milieu de mémoire,* substituting the bicameral structure of museum display for the habitual, gestural, and ritual recallings of environmental historical performance. Behind the Hull-House Museum, the rest of the campus rises, "a misfit about to be expelled by the gross concrete structures that surround it."[7] Nearby these structures stand those of the Jane Addams College of Social Work, so named in 1961 when UIC decided to destroy its namesake's former neighborhood. In ways both official and unofficial, the museum and the school are thus memorial sites. They reverently, ironically, and sometimes unwittingly "remember" the last of the spatial networks I will analyze in this book—the Hull-House Labor Museum and the emergent schools of social science and social work linking the Hull-House Boys Club, the Mary Crane Nursery, and the Juvenile Protective Association. As such, they represent a struggle among competing types of memory as well as the unanticipated futurity of past historical performances. In the first two sections, the past Hull-House Labor Museum and the contemporary Hull-House Museum fed and feed similar types of nostalgia. In the last two sections, the College of Social Work participates in a Hull-House legacy of public welfare equally castigated by some as a force of social normalization and by others as a force of abnormal socialization. The juxtaposition of all these past and present sites brings to a conclusion my own unsettled engagement with Hull-House historiography.

Displaying Difference

In the replicated Resident Dining Hall, the museum's exhibit *Hull-House and the Neighborhood* attempts to represent in a single space the social complexity of a past immigrant milieu. The museum's representation of the neighborhood's diverse cultural identities draws from reformers' 1895 text, *The Hull-House Maps and Papers*. An enlargement of a color-coded map shows the ethnicity of the occupants of each neighborhood building—green for Irish, red for Russian, blue for Italian, yellow for Bohemian. The side walls of the contemporary museum are color-coded to spatialize the map into three dimensions. Newspaper excerpts, photos, and didactics on selected ethnic experiences such as Greek festivals or Italian parades hang on green, red, yellow, and blue walls. There is no black wall, reflecting the ambiguous location of African-Americans in a selective cosmopolitan history and the incapacity of the less-than-harmonious 1890s to accommodate the inclusive multiculturalist imaginings of the 1990s. Meanwhile, the walls of preserved documents begin and end with different colors, belying the tenuousness of each national border and the instability of the link between painted wall and ethnic referent.

> "This is an Irish lady spinnin', annyhow," Mrs. Sweeney explains, pointing with a soaked forefinger. "Shure, I'd know her, big or little, in all the worrld."[8]

In a 1904 article, a journalist named Marion Foster Washburne recounted his visit to the Hull-House Labor Museum, a display that attempted to represent in a single space the social complexity of another past immigrant milieu. At the Labor Museum, "actual" immigrant-Americans performed labor practices such as metallurgy, woodworking, and textile manufacture indigenous to their respective countries. Washburne recalled a particular moment when "Mrs. Sweeney, a neighborhood woman, employed in keeping the museum clean, rolls her bare arms in her little red shoulder shawl and examines the pictures with me." Together they looked at a display of "primitive" crafts—so designated by Jane Addams and the museum's curator Jessie Luther—and their contextualization within a teleological history of labor technology.

> Perhaps she overlooks a little the Kentucky spinner, whose picture hangs next, and disregards her blue and white quilt, which makes a background for the pictures; but, at least, she has seen the work of her own people under a new aspect: that is, with some historical perspective.[9]

True to a Progressive evolutionary mode, this particular exhibit on the practice of spinning placed performances and pictures in sequence, one national performer after another, to document a developmental history. Washburne's account referred to the Labor Museum's curatorial message, noting that Mrs. Sweeney "overlooks" and "disregards" the American Kentucky spinner who was placed *after* her own in this narrative of progress. While Washburne recuperated Mrs. Sweeney by saying that at least she has seen her own people "with some historical perspective," he may have documented a moment when the Labor Museum's historical narrative became somewhat vulnerable. Mrs. Sweeney conducted something like a resistant—or at least selective—reading of its textual and imagistic didactics. As a cultural receiver, her interest in this educational performance seems to have more to do with her national identification than with the museum's interpretation of technological progress. The moment suggests the double aspect of performance. On the one hand, the media of the museum—image, text, "actual" performers, absorbed spectators, walls, and referents—grounded a represented ideological history; on the other hand, these same elements made that representation vulnerable to lapses in its enactment, to alternative repetitions of its intended "historical perspective."

When the Hull-House coffeehouse moved to the new Theater Auditorium in 1899, it left the first floor of the Gymnasium Building empty. Around the same time, several residents had embarked on a variety of experiments that reconceptualized the settlement's relationship to aesthetics. Enella Benedict and her cohort began organizing exhibits of the work of their neighbors and children. After founding the Chicago Public School Art Society, Ellen Gates Starr searched for more ways to act upon the ideas of her essay "Art and Labor," eventually deciding to take an apprenticeship in bookbinding where she learned the skills of the craftsman.[10] Meanwhile, in Chicago's larger reform circles, various citizens gathered to promote the tenets of Arts and Crafts philosophies. Chicago reformer and Hull-House friend Oliver Triggs founded the Industrial Arts League to promote "a new industrialism" that would incorporate elements of the lost environment of the craftsman's studio into the sphere of modern labor. Hull-House resident George Twose was also president of the Chicago Arts and Craft Society, a parallel effort to the Industrial Arts League. At the same time, several Hull-House club leaders found great success in arranging industrial-arts experiments for groups of children and young people. George Twose in particular tried to ground the Arts and Crafts ideal by teaching woodworking classes, drawing from prevailing (gendered) theories of childhood that rationalized manual education and vocational training in healthful juvenile development.[11]

Around the same time, Hull-House became the recipient of several random donations—a collection of lithographs from the Field Museum that depicted varieties of women's textile manufacture and two pieces of "obsolete" machinery from a nearby factory. Amid Hull-House's network of aesthetic activities and unused resources, Jane Addams recalled a particular walk on Polk Street.

> I saw an old Italian woman, her distaff against her homesick face, patiently spinning a thread by the simple stick spindle so reminiscent of all southern Europe. I was walking down Polk Street, perturbed in spirit, because it seemed so difficult to come into genuine relations with the Italian women and because they themselves so often lost their hold upon their Americanized children.[12]

Perhaps this Italian woman looked very much like one of the women depicted in the Field Museum's lithographs, exemplifying the "simple stick" method of spinning in several types of women's textile manufacture. In any event, the Italian woman's labor recalled the preservationist discourses on handicraft and industry circulating in Chicago's reform circles at the end of the nineteenth century. As an immigrant woman, however, this neighbor possessed other levels of significance for Addams. She was also a symbol of Hull-House's repeated attempts to come into "genuine relations" with Italians and other immigrant populations. Gender difference compounded these difficulties as women more often remained within their relatively familiar spheres of tenement home life.

Innovating within a pool of industrial experiments and migrational dilemmas, the Labor Museum employed older immigrants of the neighborhood to perform and teach skills in craftsmanship. Hull-House provided supplies for metallurgy, woodworking, pottery, and textile manufacture and scheduled "classes" and lectures on the weekends. The initial outline of the program explicitly stated three goals: (1) to make industrial processes more picturesque (2) to give laborers a historical consciousness of the social value of their work, and (3) to give older people "the position in the community to which their previous life and training entitles them."[13] The Labor Museum thus joined other movements in manual education and the New Industrialism to reposition industrial labor as a valued activity. Motivated by an understanding of the monotonous, repetitive, alienated labor of average workers, settlers sought to instill a pride and interest in their "daily experiences."[14] While some workers may have taken little comfort in the Labor Museum's pedagogical history of technology (perhaps feeling that a redistribution in the means of production would have been a better way to unalienate their working lives), the experiment sought to raise the status accorded the practice of manual labor. Furthermore, Addams's reference to the "older people" who "lack certain superficial qualities" evoked the intergenerational predicament of immigrant families. The adults' inability to speak English, their styles of dress, and their "primitive" forms of labor "are considered uncouth and un-American; the children and more ambitious young people look down upon them and are too often ashamed of their parents."[15] Of course, while Hull-House residents rarely vocalized an assimilationist agenda, the acculturating curriculum of their classes, children's groups, and young people's clubs indirectly contributed to this intergenerational conflict. John Dewey reflected on what he conceived as the destructive aspects of such an overzealous assimilation. "The children are too rapidly, I will not say Americanized, but too rapidly de-nationalized. They lose the positive and conservative values of their own native traditions, their own native music, art, and literature."[16] Through the Immigrant's Protective League, Grace Abbott and other Hull-House settlers similarly would call for a more attenuated form of immigrant "adjustment" over full-scale "Americanization."[17] The Labor Museum was thus a somewhat self-conscious moment in this ongoing settlement process, inverting prevalent perceptions of who taught whom in the immigrant parent-child relationship while also delineating a circumscribed arena of "native music, art, and literature" in which to preserve national cultural heritages.

Pragmatist philosophy and settlement practice came together in another rationale behind the Labor Museum. Having noticed a drop in attendance at Hull-House, concerned that clubs were relying too heavily on the protocol of a traditional classroom, Addams also argued for the museum as alternative pedagogical space. "The residents of a settlement should be able to seize affections and memories which are not available in schools for children or immature youth."[18] She thus rearticulated the improvisational and sympathetic aspects of settlement work, strategies that should also identify and utilize the talents unique to a local community. Dewey would echo Addams's phrasing in his articulation of an educational space that required a change in form as well as content.

> It is a place where ideas and beliefs may be exchanged, not merely in the arena of formal discussion—for argument alone breeds misunderstanding and fixes prejudice—but in ways where the ideas are incarnated in human form and clothed with the winning grace of personal life. Classes for study may be numerous, but all are regarded as modes of bringing people together, of doing away with barriers of caste, or class, or race, or type of experiences that keep people from real communion with each other.[19]

Eschewing an exclusive focus on the direct encounters of public debate, Dewey's pedagogy valued the indirection of human forms and the charisma of personal life. Riding the liberal hope for a counterpublic sphere that bracketed power differentials, pragmatists and settlers hoped euphemistically that such affective representational arenas would "do away" with the barriers of class and discrimination.

While the former coffeehouse underwent a refurbishing process, the official Labor Museum began in 1900 in the smaller quarters of the Butler art exhibit room—next to the room allotted Starr's new bookbindery.[20] Growing from the image of the spinning Italian woman as well as from the material resources already in hand, the exhibit room initially housed only the "Textile Department." Open every Saturday evening, residents surrounded the space with "the raw materials from which textiles are made as well as the products of the textile art of all times and countries from the basket work, spinning, and weaving of the Indians to the thread and cloth of modern mills." Extending Starr's early arguments on the "re-creative" value of images and objects, they also made every attempt to see that "the picturesque and artistic side of industry should be portrayed."[21] Besides hanging the Field Museum's donated lithographs, they also commissioned Enella Benedict to paint thematic pictures. She responded with "North Carolina sketches of mountaineers shearing and spinning," an image that coalesced with urban settlers' nostalgic idealizations of the "natural" and "rural."[22] Residents also surrounded the walls with a series of "historic charts."[23]

Besides these visual and environmental elements, the *Hull-House Bulletin* announced the novel aspect of its performer-laborers and its strategies of display.[24] The settlers were aware that interest in a subject is created by framing it appropriately. "The word 'museum' is purposely used in preference to the word 'school,' . . . because the word museum still retains some of the fascinations of the 'show.' " The Labor Museum's pedagogy became "dramatic"—not only with these strategies of display—but with the incorporation of performed human activity.

> It may easily be observed that the spot which attracts most people at any exhibition or fair, is the one where something is being done, so trivial a thing as a girl cleaning gloves, or a man polishing metal will almost inevitably attract a crowd who look on with absorbed interest. The same thing is true of shop windows.[25]

Purposeful enactment—a copresent, temporally unfolding event performed by an embodied human agent deliberately to achieve an intended goal—immediately elicited a spectator-student's fascination. Thus, the graphic representation of spinning and weaving through "actual using" would similarly attract a crowd and cultivate their absorbed interest. Furthermore, these enactments grounded the historical lesson, using a material method to connect a student's "head" to the realm of the everyday and concrete, feeding "his thought as the present abstract and unconnected study utterly fails to do."[26] The museum employed other performance-based methodologies to create an integrated and multisensual curriculum. "Miss Eleanor Smith has set to music 'Das Machine' from Morris Rosenfelt's sweatshop songs. A collection is rapidly being made of folk-songs connected with all sorts of industrial occupations."[27] Such media quickly began to fulfill another mission—that of "seizing affections and memories."

> An unexpected addition to these was a song with which Mrs. Annunziata accompanied her spinning one evening in the textile room; and Miss Firstenberg has contributed a curious and very beautiful Russian folk song, portraying the joy of man digging a post-hole and discovering sand. The Labor Museum will be grateful for any songs connected with industry in any language which may be discovered in the neighborhood.[28]

jigs and Italian tarantellas, the Labor Museum elicited many unexpected performances. For Mrs. Annunziata, the space became a place of cautious reminiscence, an arena whose objects and activities allowed her temporarily to restore familiar behaviors of labor and song. Delighted by this gestural and sonic release of cultural memory, residents essayed to "discover" more, combining images, texts, bodies, songs, props, and actions in order to "make the teaching dramatic."[29]

The representational form of the living-history museum brought with it a complicated politics. By creating the feeling of the extraordinary from the stuff of the ordinary, the Labor Museum walked a double edge, producing the interest but also the discomfort of a manufactured spectacularity. The performance emerged alongside conversations around immigrant difference, internationalism, cosmopolitanism, and pluralism in the United States. During the same period, reactionary groups such as the Mount Vernon Ladies Association, the Sons of the American Revolution, and the Society for the Preservation of New England Antiquities restored the barns, mansions, and offices of the American Revolution, constructing a far more selective history than the one enacted at Hull-House. Anticipating early-twentieth-century debates over Israel Zangwill's "melting pot" and later Horace Kallen's "orchestra," settlers and immigrants still wondered whether to admit variation within and similarity between numerous national collectives.[30] Barbara Kirshenblatt-Gimblett's theorizing of the ethnographic museum suggests how such issues of identity fared within museological forms. "In-context approaches exert strong cognitive control over the objects, asserting the power of classification and arrangement to order large numbers of artifacts from diverse cultural and historical settings and to position them in relation to one another."[31] When it came time for Hull-House curators to channel their more international definition of American identity, they imported a national classification system drawn from *Hull-House Maps and Papers*. There, they distinguished immigrant "groups forming different elements in social and industrial life without confusing the mind by a separate recognition of the people of every country."[32] Exemplifying Eric Wolf's arguments about the political and economic basis of racial and ethnic categories, the American industrial order had created its own ethnic discriminations to fit its divisions of labor, and it was this system of categorization that Hull-House replicated.[33] From the population of a neighborhood roughly divided by cultural groups that did not always reflect distinct national identities,

Hull-House gleaned "representatives" nonetheless. The practices of individual agents were interpreted as metonoymic embodiments of larger national cultures drawn from unproblematized divisions of ethnicity. Thus, the spinning of a neighborhood woman named Mrs. Brosnahan came to stand for "Irish spinning." Mrs. Molinaro's labor stood for "Italian spinning" despite the fact that so-called Italians identified with their respective provinces. In the desire to frame these activities within a grand image of a "gallery of nations," the representation of ethnographic typicality anticipated Kallen's pluralist "federation of nations," but it did so by erasing any sense of individual creativity.[34] In myriad reports and articles used to publicize the museum, unnamed pictures of women dressed in "national costumes" were subtitled only by practice and national affiliation. Not only did a Neopolitan woman's labor stand in for "Italian," but the image of the Polish Hilda Satt—whose family emigrated to the United States to escape Russian invasions—was titled "Russian Spinning."

The selection and values implicit in the construction of this international "context" exerted even greater cognitive control, however, when the gallery of nations also underwent a hierarchical contextualization, one that drew, despite well-intentioned critiques of industrialism, on culturally situated interpretations of history, progress, and technology. Hence, the Labor Museum's "in-context" pedagogy charted the so-called evolution of machinery. Craft techniques from geographically disparate cultures were positioned along a single time line. Each marked a different point along a linear narrative that culminated in the machines of American industry. "Some of the old women still use the primitive form of the distaff. It will be possible to illustrate the history of textile manufacture, to reveal the long human effort which it represents, to put into sequence and historic order the skill which the Italian colony contains, but which is now lost or despised."[35] Welcoming the fact that some women "still" used certain "primitive" methods, this selective—if Progressive—hierarchical vision of American heterogeneity also found legitimation in Morris and Ruskin, linking the figure of the craftsman to the preindustrial parts of the world from which many immigrants came. Extant craft techniques drawn from a geographically diverse pool found themselves located in a temporal framework, the target of a well-intentioned chronopolitics.[36] The satisfying categorical and evolutionary connection further emphasized the benefits of only some "native traditions" and celebrated certain "immigrant contributions" in a way that dictated the terms of their inclusion. Unlike foreign languages, non-Christian religions, or unhygienic domestic practices that were being addressed much differently in other reform spaces, arts and crafts were

safe national gifts that spiced the American way of life without danger-
ously threatening the idealized dream of a clean, ordered, yet diverse
America. Immigrant difference thus provided a site on which reformers constructed divisions between "the cultural" and "the social,"
prompting them to delineate among practices worth preserving and
those in need of changing.

The Labor Museum also inadvertently inscribed a gender ideology.
Despite the fact that the Labor Museum represented four other crafts,
its thickest description remained in the realm of textile manufacture,
the labor practice gendered most female.[37] While occasional mention
was made of a silent male German potter and later of the men who
worked in metallurgy, most of the written and graphic representations
of the Labor Museum in publicity and reform journals focused on
women laborers.[38] Such indirect representation of the "craftswoman's
ideal" elided gender and nationalism. These women's culturally specific knowledge figured them "as participating centrally in the ideological reproduction of the collectivity and as the transmitters of its
culture" rather than as its subject. With their named agency more
easily eclipsed in favor of their relationality to others, these anonymous, traditionally costumed women functioned "as signifiers of
ethnic/national differences."[39] Not only were they interpreted as the
emblem of the bourgeoisie's romanticized past, immigrant women
thus became the idealized and constrained representation of cultural
stability and national tradition. Finally, the curatorship of the Hull-
House Labor Museum shows how the categories and discursive constructs of the living-history museum structured a well-intentioned
transnational exchange. Performance, furthermore, "realized" such
pluralist, evolutionary, and gendered constructs. As one reviewer
noted, one "needed scarcely to state that history looked at from the
industrial standpoint at once becomes cosmopolitan" so thorough
was the feeling of unmediated mediation.

In 1902, the settlement finished the reconstruction of the former
coffeehouse space and announced the transfer of the Labor Museum
to "new rooms on the first floor of the gymnasium building."[40]
Starr's bookbindery also moved from the Butler to the Gymnasium
Building, spatializing its distinctive status on the Labor Museum's
evolutionary hierarchy through a "higher" location on the second
floor.[41] Belying the gendered representations of the museum, several
male residents and neighborhood craftsmen worked there throughout the week.[42] Quietly enacting a modest version of the New
Industrialism advocated by Oliver Triggs, the arenas contained technology that allowed an integrated and connected labor process in the

midst of a collective social space. Furthermore, some laborers sold their products from the shops, and eventually Hull-House handicraft became a much desired souvenir. The status of the shops differed from the diachronic interspatiality of previous settlement practices in that their machinery required spatial permanence. What did change, however, was the influx of people. While shop managers remained most of the week, participants from the children's groups, young people's clubs, local guilds, and Chicago's curious population came and went with shifts in schedule and activity.[43] Consequently, the "shops" became the "Labor Museum" when spectators and practitioners differently framed the same space. Valued for producing artifacts on most days and for producing a cosmopolitan history of technology on the weekend, laborers thus navigated switches in performative modes. Sometimes a performer-laborer negotiated several modes at once—producer, spectacle, teacher, storyteller—depending upon the unanticipated influx of students, fellow workers, museum visitors, and "toters." Thus the dramaturgy of the Labor Museum's "show" became unstable, not only by virtue of its contextualizations and interspatial relations, but also when the identity of its audience members changed.

What the Visitor Cannot See

In the interior of the restored mansion, the Jane Addams Hull-House Museum displays pictures, props, and furniture of another era. One section displays some of the pottery made in the shops of the old Labor Museum. In another room, frayed children's books and preserved immigrant newspapers are strewn on an upholstered divan and coffee table as if spontaneously let by their readers. As I walk through the museum, the incontestable reality of such material objects provides a degree of comfort; history, they say to me, is still here. The effect of this sepia-toned vision of lived space is disrupted every once in a while by stark white pieces of paper whose typed black lettering contextualizes these remnants of the past. "Russian Newspaper, circa 1909." "Children met here for Jenny Dow's Kindergarten class, 1893." Across the hall, a writing desk holds a pen poised over a pile of papers inscribed in Jane Addams's indecipherable penmanship, a hand familiar to me after hours of squinting at microfiched copies of her letters. I respond to the documents with fetishistic fascination—Did she touch these? For a moment I imagine that I have come upon a piece of the past, a piece of Jane Addams, before realizing that—alas!—the papers are themselves microfiche copies. The fickle promise of authen-

ticity extends and retracts itself continually as I pass a fireplace, a
bulletin board, a photograph. The same strange feeling occurs when I
try to ignore the cash register and items for sale at the foot of the
staircase, or when I try to pretend that I am not standing on the
linoleum floor of an addition created to accommodate the administrative and lavatory needs of museum exhibition. Activated by the same
structure that defers its fulfillment, my nostalgia makes me want to
forget how extensively the original mansion was torn down before it
was "restored."

> Steadfast amidst the clash of industrial warfare, true to the En-
> glish tongue and the English better genius in the midst of a
> modern Babel, clean and wholesome on the edge of the Ghetto,
> serene among sweatshops and saloons, in the very center of toiling
> Chicago, stands Hull-House.[44]

The quotation was from the introduction to Marion Foster Washburne's 1904 essay, beginning in the ethnographic present before he
actually entered Hull-House to encounter Mrs. Sweeney. Washburne likened Hull-House to a lone diamond in a pile of rubble,
reproducing the image of the philanthropic institution as the single
representative of civilization in a barbaric, urban world. Before entering the museum, he noted "the lighted windows of the labor museum" and offered another description of the local color.

> [T]here a half-dozen street urchins were looking in. Swearing,
> twisting, pushing each other, using each other's backs and shoul-
> ders to obtain vantage-ground, clad in nondescript clothes, rough
> in manner, and of many nations, they looked in longingly from
> the cold alley where they lived upon these glorified workshops
> which promised pleasantness and peace.[45]

The passage dramatized the effect that the Labor Museum had on
children in the neighborhood, exemplifying Addams's earlier Aristo-
telean observation "that the spot which attracts most people at any
exhibition or fair is the one where something is being done."[46]
Similarly these boys were fascinated by the enactments behind the
labor museum's window. Of course, the boys might have been
looking at something else—perhaps teasing a friend for going in
rather than hoping for "pleasantness and peace."

But Washburne placed the behavior of these boys on display
within an interpretive frame that prevented alternative readings. This
passage more accurately documented a show other than the one at

Boys learning handicraft in the Hull-House Labor Museum. *(Photo courtesy of University of Illinois at Chicago, the University Library, Jane Addams Memorial Collection, Wallace Kirkland Papers.)*

which the boys are looking, for Washburne had taken up a spectatorial position already, one that interpreted the location of the Labor Museum itself, not simply the contents inside. Washburne's ethnographic gaze made a "show" of the subject on which it landed, evoking the behavior, dress, ethnicity, and environment of this group of boys in a way that signaled their "incorrigibility" to a reading audience of bourgeois reformers. When he entered the museum, he described a metal shop, "for a shop this room is in appearance, much more than a museum," noting the "grim picturesqueness" and "general tone of brown." His description of battered, bent, and heavy machinery "spitting blue and yellow flames" anthropomorphized unfamiliar technologies, creating a picture of a sentient industrial factory in miniature. When he exclaimed once again that he "still [did] not see what it is that makes this a Museum. What is it more than a series of manual training shops?" he concluded that the spectatorial structure was all that indicated its status. "True," he wrote, "the groups of onlookers mark a characteristic difference."[47]

Ushered through the side door and into the shops of wood, metal, and pottery, Washburne began gradually to sense that his gaze was

different from that of the neighborhood boys. "What does take
place," he suggested, "is what the visitor cannot see, although he
may afterwards experience it himself."[48] As the article continued,
Washburne's text figured a shaky authorial subjectivity trying to
move beyond the superficial encounter of "the casual observer."
Upon seeing a performer-laborer, his eye initially landed to assess
degrees of cleanliness and physical deformity.

> Standing at the table is a clean old German kneading clay, his
> squat, bowed legs far apart, his body leaning forward, his long
> and powerful arms beating upon the clay like piston rods. . . .
> [O]ne sees that he is bent and twisted by his trade, conformed to
> his wheel. Upon this he slaps his clay.[49]

To Washburne, the German potter was an emblem of the physical
laborer whose work and body are one, his joints and limbs likened to
the machinery around him. This individual became a living ethnographic object precisely because his audience member—one of the
"group of onlookers"—was disposed to turn him into one. As he
continued, Washburne seemed intent on defining the human being
beyond these observable characteristics, however, on sensing the
invisible through the visible:

> His hands open, his thumbs work in; one almost sees him think
> through his skillful thumbs and forefingers. Like some mystery of
> organic nature, the clay rises, bends, becomes a vase. . . . The old
> potter rises, lifts the vase in his mitten-like hands, and, bending,
> straddling sideways, his face unmoved, carries it tenderly to its
> place.[50]

To Washburne's eye, this worker seemed so intent on his manual
craft that his intelligence had a corporeal residence, epitomizing the
bourgeois projection of the nearly extinct craftsman and his labor's
reciprocal discharge of "cause and effect." At the same time, Washburne tried to "see" his thoughts, to locate an elusive sense of agency
nearly imperceptible in a "face unmoved."

Still curious about this quiet face and "tender" comportment,
Washburne responded to his frustrated search by beginning a new
paragraph, one that redirected its curious gaze from an external
focus on otherness to an internal focus on the self. For the first time,
Washburne used the first-person singular and shared an internal
monologue.

Looking at him, I wonder. My heart aches. My flower-pots at home made by such as he, gain a new significance. They are no longer mere receptacles for holding earth and guarding the roots of my plants. The rough, red surface of them is written all over with the records of human patience, human cooperation with nature, human hopes and fears.[51]

With his heart aching, Washburne interpreted the objects occupying his own life differently for having been introduced to the people and processes that created them. Not only were workers reconnected with their own labor processes but a member of the bourgeoisie was "unalienated" from his own material life. Other moments of modernist consciousness-raising used a romanticized anti-industrialist rhetoric; Washburne invoked Ruskin and Morris, who "recognize that the commercial custom of rating a laborer at what you can buy or rent him for is as low, as inadequate a measure of a human being as could well be devised."[52] The shift in writing style and increasing degree of self-consciousness dramatized what Kirshenblatt-Gimblett calls "the museum effect":

> Bleeding into the ubiquity of the common-sense world, the museum effect brings distinctions between the exotic and the familiar closer to home. Calibrations of difference become finer. The objects differentiated draw nearer. One becomes increasingly exotic to oneself, as one imagines how others might view that which we consider normal.[53]

The Labor Museum seized Washburne's affections, evoking memories of his own life whose normalcy was defamiliarized by the museum's differentiations. The image of the German potter juxtaposed with his own ceramic pots recalibrated his sense of self, ostensibly forcing him to see his own material life anew.

Washburne continued through the Labor Museum, each room offering a new exhibit that he received with more than a small dose of nostalgia. Here he described a space filled with images, texts, and objects to narrate the history of cooking:

> A low window seat to the right, and a big table before it, covered with a blue and white homespun cloth, make one wish that one could go back at once to the old colonial days, and make apple dowdy and mulled cider in this picture-booky place.[54]

Since the productivity of nostalgia lies in what it erases from memory as much as in what it retains, the idealized and selective vision of

"apple dowdy and mulled cider" substituted for the "colonial days,"
representing only that which induced longing in the visitor. Tan-
gible items such as the "blue and white homespun cloth" suggested
that the past was immediate and accessible. In the next moment,
however, the materialized reality of this "picture-booky place" dis-
solved as the gap between past and present, between referent and
representation, reasserted itself: "A dear little painted dresser stands
next to the window seat, set out with old blue and white china;
but an abrupt modern note is struck by the case of laboratory
samples which hangs beside it."[55] Washburne's rhapsodies about the
charms of the "old blue and white china"—a signal of the Arts and
Crafts aesthetic—were stalled by the abrupt reminder of modernity.
"Here is a fine old carved side-board with more blue and white china
on it—modern blue and white, alas! and not half so pretty as the old
kind."[56] The effectiveness of the Arts and Crafts representation was
proportionate with the degree to which it masked the act of preservation. An object signifying the past but created in the present was
(not unlike microfiched letters) a poor antidote for this peculiar
form of historical anxiety.

Washburne inadvertently documented more performative dislocations when he recounted his conversations both with Mrs. Sweeney
and another Irishwomen, Mrs. Brosnahan. While his quotations and
descriptions suggest a great deal about his use of these two women to
figure his own authorial subjectivity, they also indirectly point to the
Labor Museum's "hidden transcript."[57] Such encounters are thus
useful for theorizing a realm of performative agency for these
humans-turned-exhibit. As earlier noted, Washburne's ambivalent
tracking system structured his description of Mrs. Sweeney's "bare"
arms and "soaked" forefinger, underscoring the relentless embodiedness of a female manual laborer. At the same time, the text
showed Mrs. Sweeney deciding to conduct her own efforts at contextualization. Using the image of the "Irish lady spinnin' " as an object
of identification, Mrs. Sweeney asserted her own place in a national
community, countering the Labor Museum's evolutionary mode of
remembering.

The second woman with whom Washburne spoke at length was
another "Irish spinner." Mrs. Brosnahan functioned as the object of
the display for several years. By speaking, however, and participating
in her own self-contextualization, she was also the subject of display.
After using free indirect discourse to report that "she herself" knew
the entire process of linen making from sewing flax seed to dyeing
the fabric, Washburne quoted her directly, a displacement of his
own authorial voice that suggested the impact of the encounter.

"But, shure, dear," she exclaims, "it is not your chemical dyeing at all, but the home-dyeing, that I know. We made the dyes ourselves from log-wood, and barks, and stuff we took out of the bogs of old Ireland. But one thing I will say for it: it never faded as your high-toned dyes do."[58]

Mrs. Brosnahan vacillated between the first- and second-person pronoun to represent her labor processes, a discursive practice that delineated the boundaries of an Irish "we" and an American "you." Like Mrs. Sweeney, Mrs. Brosnahan placed herself within a circle of cultural affiliation to underscore the significance of past practices. In the process, the quotidian realities of daily life were held up again as emblems of a delineated national culture.

Jane Addams and fellow settlers counted on women's oral narratives to supplement this performance space; they were glad that "the whirl of the wheels recalls many a reminiscence and story of the old country, the telling of which makes a rural interlude in the busy town life."[59] Here Mrs. Brosnahan deployed this mode of personal narrative to distinguish her history. While a Progressive hereditary American might have nostalgically reinterpreted her statement as the loss of the craftsman's ideal, it also provided a space for a certain kind of self-definitional performance—one that was to become increasingly pointed and politicized.

> Presently she tells her story.
> "Yes, we all spun and wove in the old country . . ."
> "And how did you happen to come here?" I asked.
> Her serene face darkens. "Never will I forgive them that misled us to it!" she exclaims. "There in the old country we had our comforts, our own bit of land, my man making a dollar and a quarter the day, Irish money; a blissid union of ten children and never a shoe wanting to the foot of one of them. O, wirra the day that we left! I landed here with a baby in my arms—crippled—"
> "Crippled? how?" I cried.
> She passed the question. "Yes, crippled. She is a hump-back, dear, eleven by now, and none higher than my waist. The next to the baby had the spinal meningeetis soon after we landed[,] and his reason fled."[60]

Mrs. Brosnahan's story was far from the uncritical tale of a benevolent United States welcoming "the poor, the tired, and the hungry." In a move that was itself both nostalgic and resistant, she elegized lost national origins while defining herself against the idealizations of a progressive American ideology. As she continued, she told also of how her husband "took to the drink" in response to the sorry situation they faced. This story exceeded the conventions of the "rural interlude" Addams described picturesquely circulating among lithographs, glass casements, and textiles. Heightening the political economic realities of an immigrant-American, Mrs. Brosnahan used her capacity as performative signifier to push those narratives into the background. At the same time, she negotiated this new role on her own terms, evading the questions of a journalist now fascinated anew by her extra self-disclosure. Washburne would leave the museum troubled not to have known the cause of the crippled child's "mysterious" injury, another of the Labor Museum's invisible secrets. As her encounter with Washburne concluded, this Irish woman hinted at the disjuncture between her life experiences and her Labor Museum persona. It was to the latter that she eventually returned.

"And what did you do?" I asked.

"I begged on the streets, dear. Oh, I can smile and laugh with the best when I am at work here, but there's something else in my heart." She turned to a young lady pupil, whom she was teaching to spin, unreeled the broken thread, mended, and set it right with a skillful touch or two. "No I ain't discouraged," she told the young lady, in her soft, smooth voice, "for discouraging won't do for a pupil. You'll spin, dear, but it'll take a deal o' practice." A minute more and she and Mrs. Sweeney are speaking the Gaelic together, and laughing like two children. She dances a quiet shuffle under her decent skirts. "And can I dance? she asks. "It is a good old Irish break-down dancer I was in my young days. You should see me do a reel and a jig." Her hidden feet nimbly shuffle and whisper on the wooden floor.[61]

In this passage, Mrs. Brosnahan's movements, focus, and speech changed rapidly. At the moment that she came closest to sharing her deepest emotions—the "something else in my heart," she quickly switched performative modes by turning to her pupil instead. The combination of her role as instructor and the presence of stranger may have deterred too lengthy an indulgence. The next spoken words had the quality of double entendre. "No I ain't discouraged." Were they said to Washburne about life in the United States or to her student about her spinning prospects? "A minute more" and Mrs. Brosnahan engaged a third interlocutor, Mrs. Sweeney, in "the Gaelic." Washburne is charmed as "they laugh like two children," interpreting their conversation as another idyllically ethnic practice. Though he safely filtered them through a harmonizing ideological frame—as unthreatening "immigrant gifts" that spiced the American way of life and delighted the adventurer-journalist, his text also suggests the improvised creation of an oppositional linguistic space from which he was excluded. Their code switching to the Gaelic masked their conversation, and so, ultimately, the secret joke they shared. The laughter seems to have been fleeting, however. If non-English speaking had become too extensive and stories about the trials of immigrant life too long, the Labor Museum's idealized portrait might have been threatened. Fortunately, however, Mrs. Brosnahan concluded the visit by readdressing Washburne and offering an Irish jig—another "native tradition" that, like arts, literature, and crafts, could be celebrated as an unthreatening immigrant "contribution." Whether this dance too had a hidden transcript beneath its display on Hull-House's progressive public stage, whether Mrs. Brosnahan used an open admission of self-display to parody the ideology of cultural harmony that she was supposed to signify, also remained hidden from Washburne. And so now it remains hidden from his historian.

Finally, the Hull-House Labor Museum was a counterpublic sphere that responded to the increasing heterogeneity of the United States with different kinds of contradictions. To understand such a space is not simply to interpret its espoused ideology but also to understand the legitimating operations of its performative media. However, the analysis of the performative also means acknowledging the ways that such a space exceeds totalized understanding, that improvised ruptures in reception and enactment can destabilize the declared statements of museums, reformers, journalists, and historians. Within this local realm, cultural alignments have very different valences, and individuals affiliate and disaffiliate with various national identities in the space of an hour—sometimes with a turn in a story or the pointing of a finger, other times with a shuffle of the feet. However, as Mrs. Brosnahan's suggested in her chronicle of poverty and illness, nonvoluntary aspects of identity construction were "resisted" less easily. The performativity of cosmopolitanism was sometimes only fleetingly secured, often within a temporary space whose boundaries were prescribed. Finally, it is the acknowledgment of such a performative realm within the Labor Museum's incarnations—one to which I have, and do not have, access, thanks to and despite Washburne's authorial rendering—that continually leaves me wondering at what, or maybe it is "at whom," Mrs. Sweeney and Mrs. Brosnahan were laughing.

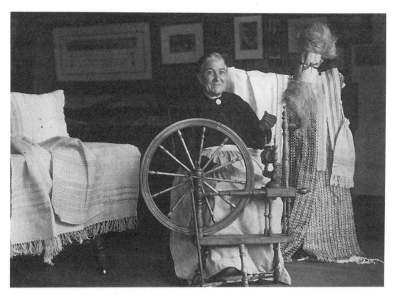

Irish immigrant Mrs. Brosnahan ready to greet visitors in the spinning room of the Hull-House Labor Museum. *(Photo courtesy of University of Illinois at Chicago, the University Library, Jane Addams Memorial Collection.)*

The Searchlight of Inquiry

The Jane Addams College of Social Work at the University of Illinois advertises the advantages of being part of an "urban university." For prospective social workers, "this means the opportunity for learning, for practice, and for research not only *about* the many facets of the urban society but also directly *in the midst* of them."

> The full sweep of private and public social welfare institutions, the presence of many national and regional agencies, and the activities of vigorous community organizations combine to provide the student with an exciting and living professional educational experience.[62]

Such an institution is one of many throughout the nation that educates students within a partially formalized curriculum on social work and within a partially formalized apparatus of social welfare. Thus descending from Hull-House, this "living professional educational experience" indirectly remembers the settlement through a range of agencies and activities. In the next two sections, I track the knotty and circuitous route of this descent, attending to collections of quantitative reports and urban writing and later to the administrative venues that they spawned. Buildings such as the Boys Club, the Mary Crane Nursery, and the Juvenile Protective Association follow the invention of social scientific study in the United States and, alongside it, the professionalization of social work. Second-generation settlers such as Edith Abbott and Sophonisba Breckinridge emerged as academic innovators within this history, while others such as Julia Lathrop and Florence Kelley became more involved in civic and federal administration. Most often remembered as a positivist strain of social analysis inimical to the qualitative methods of performance ethnography, the quantitative documents and formal apparatuses do not seem at first to have a place in a performance historiography of Hull-House. The numbers, categories, charts, and maps seem not to coincide with the contingent, ephemeral, affective, and narrative-based modes of knowing to which performers attend. At the same time, it is important to remember that Hull-House reform worked within several kinds of representation. While art classes, gymnastics, theater, and new rituals of everyday life took shape in various pockets of the settlement, Florence Kelley and other reformers believed that the new shapes of scientific study were also key to urban amelioration.

Fellow settlers greatly admired Kelley's skills and were hopeful about their anticipated efficacy. "She is going to Springfield in the fall to get a law passed that will give a blow to the sweating system. . . . [S]he's so amazingly clever . . . and she's got such a load of good black and white statistics."[63] To investigate the accumulation of "good black and white statistics" turns out to reveal a performance genealogy skirting between sociological categories and stalling the perspectives of urban cartography. It also highlights the embodiedness that supports all types of research, something that Kelley herself (and her swollen feet) made clear.

> You must suffer from the dirty streets, the universal ugliness, the lack of oxygen in the air you daily breathe, the endless struggle with soot and dust and insufficient water supply, the hanging from a strap of the overcrowded street car at the end of your day's work . . . if you are to speak as one having authority.[64]

Kelley's appeal anticipated James Clifford's analysis of ethnographic authority, basing itself on the "principal assumption that the experience of the researcher can serve as a unifying source of authority in the field. Experiential authority is based on a 'feel' for the foreign context, a kind of accumulated savvy and a sense of the style of a people or place."[65] When adapting the quantitative methods of the new social science, Kelley and her cohort invoked settling's epistemology of proximity, using the authenticity of continuous bodily participation—of being *in the midst*—as a legitimating foundation.

Kelley's skills in the creation of good black-and-white statistics laid the basis for the settlement's first forays into publicized scientific study, reaching a proud moment with the 1895 anthology *Hull-House Maps and Papers*. The text gathered several types of representation—maps, charts, and prose writing—into what residents affectionately named "the jumble book." Cartographical studies focused on roughly one-third square mile, recording immigrant residency in one map and residential incomes in another "wages map." Meanwhile, there were also essays from various Hull-House affiliates on different immigrant populations, on garment laboring conditions, on the corruption of the Cook County Charities, on art and labor, on the trades unions, and an appendix on Hull-House activities. One short-term resident, Agnes Sinclair Holbrook, took it upon herself to include a self-reflective statement on what she called "the painful nature" of this research, particularly the discomforting violations of privacy that accompanied the systematization of civic housekeeping.

> Insistent probing into the lives of the poor would come with bad grace even from government officials, were the statistics obtained so inconsiderable as to afford no working basis for further improvement. The determination to turn on the searchlight of inquiry must be steady and persistent to accomplish definite results and all spasmodic and sensational throbs of curious interest are ineffectual as well as unjustifiable. The painful nature of many of the questions asked, would be unendurable and unpardonable were it not for the conviction that the public conscience when roused must demand better surroundings for the most inert and long-suffering citizens of the commonwealth. Merely to state symptoms and go farther would be idle; but to state symptoms in order to ascertain the nature of disease, and apply, it may be, its cure, is not only scientific, but in the highest sense humanitarian.[66]

Calling such fieldwork "insistent probing" that verged on the "unpardonable," Holbrook's statement foreshadowed the scrutiny and shame that would accompany participation in "private and public social welfare institutions." Her quandary illustrated one of the many times when Hull-House residents found the impulse to care and the impulse to reform an uncomfortable mixture, one that became more unsettling and presumptuous when the "searchlight of inquiry" shone into the inside of a tenement, onto the unvaccinated arm of a tubercular laborer, or into the psyche of a baffling immigrant other. Hull-House settlers nevertheless produced maps and categories—supplemented by illustrative prose—that sought to convey the poverty, density, and mobility endured by Chicago's most "inert" citizens within a scene of "village destitution."

Settlers emulated the new brand of cartographical survey developed in Charles Booth's *Life and Labor of the People in London*.[67] Amid "endless struggle" and disorientation, a Boothian map offered a provisional degree of comfort. It reoriented a receiver's positionality from the ground of the street to the privileged site of the bird's-eye view. Reversing the logic of settling, competence in seeing came not with nearness but with distance. The truth of urban life would be derived by getting outside it, finding the figurative tower from which all could be surveyed. The map presented fixity where many experienced mobility and marked boundaries where there seemed to be none; it assured its spectators that the city was a knowable community despite its felt anonymity.[68] To effect the translation of their general impressions to the highly impressive graphic forms deployed in Charles Booth's volumes, settlers began the arduous process of data collection by first defining the terms and categories of the "facts" that they would map. The area was much smaller than that of Booth's studies, but Kelley and her team made up in depth what they lost in breadth, taking individuals, families, and buildings as the central units of analysis where Booth had used entire blocks and streets. Touting "the greater minuteness of this survey" (and thus civic housekeeping's insight into the minutia of daily experience), they hoped that this "photographic reproduction" would finally turn "the eyes of the world" upon a center of Chicago whose misery had been too long ignored.[69]

The creation of cartographical categories proved to be something other than an exercise in photographic realism, however. As earlier suggested, the immigrant map instantiated immigrant groupings even as it recorded them, conflating provincial identities under the label *Italian,* electing not to "confuse the mind by a separate recognition" of each country. The effort to map wages proved even more fitful, for settlers had difficulty coming up with a principle unit of analysis. Using questionnaires supplied by the department of labor, Florence Kelley, Agnes Holbrook, Alzina Stevens, and others attempted to track the "family wage" for each group, a task that often eluded their painstaking attempts to count.

It is not easy to say just what constitutes "family life" in this connection. It is not a common table—often enough there is, properly speaking, no table at all. It is not even a common cooking stove, for several families frequently use the same. The only constant factor in the lives of the members of such a circle, beyond the ties of kinship, is the more or less irregular occupancy of the same tenement, at least at night.[70]

Amid the spatial and economic survival strategies of the poor, there could be no easy interspatial alignments between the single family and the single family home. As Mrs. Brosnahan no doubt would have confirmed, "[T]he theory that 'every man supports his own family' is as idle in a district like this as the fiction that 'every one can get work if he wants it.' " Hull-House mappers nevertheless decided to plot within the functional analytic unit of the family wage.[71] They determined inclusion or exclusion within "a family" based on whether a circle member paid board. "Every boarder, and each member of the family who pays board, ranks as a self-supporting individual, and is therefore classed as a separate wage-earner."[72] As a means of troubling rather than capitulating to conventional elisions between the single space and the single family, this adjustment interpreted nonrelational boarding as a standard rather than anomalous housing strategy among the poor. At the same time, it ignored wage pooling and board paying as an income strategy *within* a kinship circle; such a familial group was represented as a series of separate "families" each of whom were "unable to get together $260 dollars a year."[73] The elision shows how the category of the "family wage" could shadow investigations, even those that acknowledged its "idle" fictionality. The ideal of a well-supported, single-income family would also permeate later reforms and redistribution models, distancing the figure of, for instance, a working mother from any vision of normal "family life."

"What is to go with the maps?" asked Agnes Sinclair Holbrook during a resident meeting.[74] She was worried about specific lacunae. Aware both of the precariousness of their mapping categories and of the partiality of cartography's bird's-eye view, Holbrook decided to write a prose introduction to convey those aspects of urban life that had gone unrepresented in the maps. In rendering this environment and these structures, she and fellow writers worked within the metaphors, adjectives, and typifications of their day. While this rhetoricity made their prose accessible to a middle-class and academic reading audience, it could also reinforce some of the stereotypes they were paradoxically trying to undo.

Rear tenements and alleys form the core of the district, and it is there that the densest crowds of the most wretched and destitute congregate. Little idea can be given of the filthy rotten tenements, the dingy courts and tumble-down sheds, the foul. stables and dilapidated outhouses, the broken sewer pipes, the piles of garbage fairly alive with diseased odors, and of the numbers of children filling every nook, working and playing in every room, eating and sleeping in every window-sill, pouring in and out of every door, and seeming literally to pave every scrap of "yard."[75]

In the attempt to support a Progressive environmentalism, Holbrook tried to demonstrate that urban inhabitants were the victims of an inhabitable urban space rather than innately responsible for their plight. She hence became linguistically productive, in many ways anticipating the organic metaphors that would become ubiquitous in the "urban ecology" of Chicago sociology.[76] In this passage, she dramatized the particularly offensive qualities of urban habitation—its density, its mobility, and its dirt. She attached these qualities to noteworthy objects of reform—the tenement, the street, the child. Living spaces were both dirty and broken. Holbrook turned to a series of present participles—*working, eating, pouring, seeming*—to convey the motion of the children. Holbrook's personification of the trash—"as piles of garbage fairly alive with diseased odors"—is tellingly provocative. Inspired by an increasing fascination with germ theory that would propel Alice Hamilton's career, the piles of refuse not only disturbed the superficial appearance of the street but were also experienced as something sentient, as an expanding and burgeoning organism. This "liveness" manifested itself most acutely as an "odor." Repeating a misguided if socially expedient miasmic theory of disease, the text evoked a noxious and contagious atmosphere that was materially invasive, threatening to engulf and contaminate with each inhalation.[77] Along the way, the text fixed the inhabitants of such urbanity anonymously in characterizations like "the destitute" or "the wretched." The deployment of all and more of these rhetorical techniques obliquely delineated differences of class, age, race, and gender, instantiating an ideological connection between materialism and morality. Even as Hull-House writers attempted to discuss the environmental nature of "social disease," their language slipped into metaphoric substitutions that threatened to naturalize that which they tried to socialize.[78] Sometimes their neighbors hardened into a layer of pavement.

"No clue to the density of the population is therefore given, except indirectly," apologized Holbrook.[79] The depravity of neighborhood life came not only from architectural deficiencies but also from the sheer number of inhabitants filling its narrow streets and unlit rooms. The "density" or "congestion" of humanity burst through urban spaces (and cartographical perspectives) ill equipped to contain it. The problem of quantifying congestion also ran into the difficulty of another frustrating factor—the neighborhood's mobility. "A morning walk impresses one with the density of the population," wrote *Hull-House Maps and Papers* contributor Charles Zeublin, "but an evening walk reveals a hive."[80] Tropes of motion thus persisted throughout all of these studies, often to document the political economic realities of employment and poverty.

> Families also move constantly, going from tenement to tenement, finding more comfortable apartments when they are able to pay for them, drifting into poorer quarters in times of illness, enforced idleness, or "bad luck." Tenants evicted for non-payment of rent form a floating population of some magnitude, and a kodak view of such a shifting scene must necessarily be blurred and imperfect here and there.[81]

Migrant families, "women adrift," and "teeming children" circulated in the alleys, backrooms, factories, sweatshops, and saloons of the neighborhood without ever resting long enough for a reformer to count. In the attempt to make a knowable community through maps and statistics, Hull-House writers were forced to recognize that the "facts" they produced were only provisional, that the motion of the neighborhood made a new "truth" every day.

Preoccupations with tenement conditions, congestion, and mobility underpinned another arena of Hull-House reform—the sweatshop. While the South Side of Chicago was most renowned for the meatpacking industry, the West Side was the industrial center of Chicago's garment manufacture. As companies such as Marshall Field's and Hart, Schaffner, and Marx tried to find ever-cheaper ways of producing clothing, they borrowed the methods of the sweating system by circulating partially completed clothing to be "finished" by home contractors and their hirelings.[82] Concerned to expose the financial and material hardship endured by sweatshop laborers, Kelley, Holbrook, and their crew made investigation of this system their central mission. "The back doors of large establishments give glimpses of the inwardness of factory life, and bent figures stitching at the basement windows proclaim that the sweater is abroad in the land."[83] The sweater represented the underbelly of well-to-do clothiers, the immoral individual who hid laboring bodies within depraved

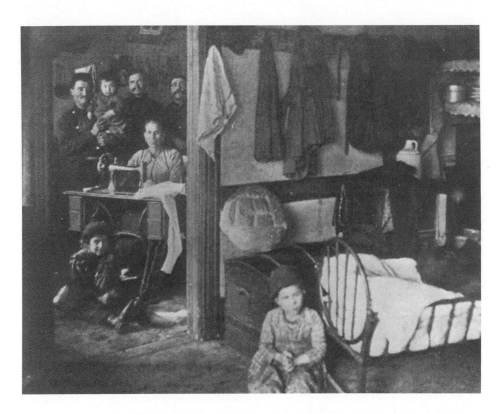

The mixture of living and working spatialized in the sweating system of a West-Side tenement. *(Photo courtesy of University of Illinois at Chicago, the University Library, Jane Addams Memorial Collection.)*

working conditions. Borrowing the prophetic style of the muckraker, Kelley's analysis of unregulated competition in the garment industry mixed macrostructural analysis with more minute examples or, what she would call in other writings, "the illustrative case."[84]

Thus, a recent night inspection of work given out from one of the largest cloak manufactories in the West resulted as follows: The garment maker was found in his tenement dwelling in the rear of a factory. With his family, a wife and four indescribably filthy children, he occupies a kitchen and two bedrooms. The father bedrooms could be entered only by passing through the other rooms. This farther bedroom, where the man was found at work, was 7 × 7 × 8 feet, and contained a bed, a machine, one chair, a reeking lamp, and two men. The bed seemed not to have been made up in weeks; and in the bed, in a heap, there lay two overcoats, two hats, a mass of bed-covers, and nine fine tan-color capes trimmed with ecru lace, a tenth cape being in the machine in process of stitching. The whole dwelling was found to be crawling with vermin, and the capes were not free from it.[85]

Kelley did not extrapolate from this case after she described it but switched to a new paragraph to condemn the large manufacturing companies for irresponsibility. The textual move demonstrates how little amplification the case seemed to need.

Several tropes in this passage recurred throughout her investigations, all of them playing on the threat of contact for their rhetorical force. First, Kelley represented the "sweater problem" as an interrelated aspect of the "tenement problem." A six-person family occupying three rooms suggested overcrowding, especially when one of those rooms was both a work space and smaller than that designated "habitable." It was not only the tenement structure that was the problem here but the daily performances that happened inside. Most telling was the interspatial mix of living and working. Kelley called the two nonkitchen rooms "bedrooms," reflecting a reformer's ambivalence in naming rooms whose usage did not conform to conventional practices of habitation. The nomination probably came from the fact that family members slept in both rooms. The practice prompted the name. In another tenement investigation whose agenda was slightly different, however, a reformer might have condemned the fact that family members (or boarders) slept in the "parlor." Then the practice defied the posited identity of the room. In both cases, the underlying assumption was that certain practices belonged in certain spaces and that their mixture was a danger.

> Under a clause of the law which prohibits the use of any bedroom or kitchen for the manufacture of garments by any person outside of the immediate family living therein, the inspectors are waging war upon contractors who employ help in a kitchen or bedroom, or in any room accessible only by going through the living-rooms of the family. . . . [P]rogress is slow towards an entire separation of shop and dwelling.[86]

In the attempt to delimit the definition of a work space, factory legislation and its enforcers precariously negotiated normalized assumptions about divisions between private and public. Sweatshop labor was, in Mary Douglas's memorable phrase, "matter out of place."[87] In prohibiting garment manufacture in any space that could be construed as a "living room," they tried to regulate motion and access between working and living. Thus, Kelley routinely noted whether "[t]he entrance is by a side door, used also in going to the living rooms."[88] The use of the label *bedroom* to describe the location of sweatshop labor in Florence Kelley's "illustrative case" was probably not arbitrary. Of all the rooms in the apartment, the bedroom was associated with the most privatized of activities—dressing, sleeping, copulation, and recovery from illness. To tell of commodity production in such a space was thus to rattle bourgeois sensibilities to the core. Kelley pushed these associations by noting, "The bed seemed not to have been made up in weeks" and, further, that these products made "actual" contact with its intimate world. Finally, the concluding sentence confirmed all the anxieties of a reader-consumer. Yes, this dwelling was filled with vermin; there was a legitimate reason to fear contagion. Like Holbrook's description of the garbage "fairly alive" with disease, infestation ran rampant around this dwelling, on its bed, and into these commodities. Such texts literally touched a reluctant reader, making the shudder of contact with the sweat of the sweatshop part of the experience of reading them.

The preoccupation with the laboring body evoked above did not always manifest itself through metaphors of contagion. Descriptions of physical deformity and the "bent" bodies of the sweating industry were equally ubiquitous.

> People are noticeably undersized and unhealthy, as well to the average observer as to the trained eye of the physician. Especially do the many workers in the tailoring-trades look dwarfed and ill-fed; they walk with a peculiar stooping gait, and their narrow chests and cramped hands are unmistakable evidence of their calling.[89]

Contact with machinery left its own peculiar kind of imprint, pressing onto laboring backs, swelling one side of the body more than the other. In describing the garment industry, writers often returned to the deformities of the hand. This most productive extremity endured debilitating bone and nerve damage, expending its supply of future labor power with every stitch. The few machines developed to increase productivity were seldom designed with attention to the safety of the body that operated it. Workers caught limbs in machinery with little union support to act against the employer. In her account of the plight of wage-earning children, Alzina Stevens offered a harrowing list of the dangers endured when body and industry met in the chaos of unregulated manufacture. The figure of the child in her text made these accounts all the more efficacious.

The tobacco trade, nicotine poisoning finding . . . many victims
among factory children . . . frame gilding, in which work a child's
fingers are stiffened and throat disease contracted; buttonholing,
machine-stitching, and hand-work in tailor or sweatshops, the
machine work producing spinal curvature, and for girls pelvic
disorders . . . bakeries where children slowly roast before the
ovens; binderies, paper-box and paint factories, where arsenical
paper, rotting past, and the poison of the paints are injurious;
boiler-plate works, cutlery works, and metal stamping, where the
dust produces lung disease; the handling of hot metal, accidents;
the hammer of plate, deafness.[90]

Employing a rhetorical technique often used by Karl Marx and
Friedrich Engels, Stevens juxtaposed lists of "particular made objects" with "an equally particular form of bodily extremity" such
that "the specific artifact and specific form of heightened embodiedness occur together."[91] All of these accounts highlighted the tremendous vulnerability of the body, its plastic deformation by un-
yielding machinery, the easy penetration and burning of its skin, the
openness of its susceptible pores, the access inside it through inhalation. No stereotypes of the strength, coarseness, and endurance capacity of the working-class body could deny the deleterious effects of
industrialization.

Could a bourgeois reader face these accounts without looking
anew at his picture frames, without pausing as he buttoned his
waistcoat, without feeling a wave of nausea as she contemplated her
morning bakery roll? With more intensity than the Labor Museum
could ever create, such accounts ripped the symbolic gloves of commodity fetishism from consumed objects. They forced potential
purchasers not only to confront a repressed contact in their "flower
pots at home" but also to consider consuming a little boy's lung
disease, a little girl's stiffened fingers. Upton Sinclair was perhaps the
most famous practitioner of this sentient punch, describing the
hands of meatpackers, which were "so criss-crossed with cuts, until
you could no longer pretend to count them or to trace them."[92]
When all was said and done, however, the appeal to the "health of
the employee" was less effective than the appeal to the "health of the
commodity" (and hence the purchaser who consumed it). In the
laborious effort to reconnect consumption to industrialized production, the threat of disease dubiously provided the most powerful
link. "The intimate connection," wrote Florence Kelley of sweatshop
literature's tactile alliance, "is too palpable to need comment."[93]

In her contribution to *Hull-House Maps and Papers,* Julia Lathrop analyzed the corruption and ineffectuality of county charities, offering descriptions of food lines along the way that conveyed what Francis Hackett called her "tragi-comic" sense of politics. "For one instant the visitor is hushed as he stands before the door, watching the straggling little procession of human wastage entering the dim apartment, and feels a thrill of thankfulness that these poor evidences of defeat and failure cherish a belief in some divine accounting more individual and generous than that of the sociologist and statistician."[94] There were more ironies surrounding the decidedly undivine accountings of settlers' sociological studies. For one thing, Hull-House residents themselves violated the categories and prescriptive spatializations they used in urban representation. If cartographers had tried to map Florence Kelley's residential arrangement—with several nonrelational friends watching her children at Hull-House, in a rented flat, or at the Lloyd's Winnetka "annex"—they would have had difficulty applying any spatial fixity to her "family life." Moreover, Hull-House itself was terminally guilty of mixing the practices of "living" and "working." If new home-work prohibitions had applied to the settlement, Edith de Nancrede would have had to store the "piecework" of theatrical costume-making in some place other than her bedroom. Nevertheless, as the next section makes clear, such principles of space, residence, family, occupation, and household structured many of their perspectives and later the policies and agencies they advocated.

Delicate Machinery

When the last group of settlers vacated Hull-House in 1963, Florence Scala's friend Frances Molinaro was among them. Molinaro had been employed for decades as both a household manager and receiver in the Hull-House entry. Molinaro's was the "first face visitors saw," recalled Scala, who also revered Molinaro because she came from the neighborhood rather than "the Hull-House aristocracy." Her mother, Carolina, was the "Mrs. Molinaro" of the Labor Museum whose spinning Frances remembered with affection, and the incorporation of the daughter Frances into the Hull-House entourage was a model case of intergenerational immigrant adjustment. As a stably fixed, paid "toter," however, Molinaro was also a symbol of the settlement's professionalization more generally.[95] Rather than crossing directly into the mansion's front entry, visitors encountered Molinaro after they walked through the corridor separating the mansion from the rest of the buildings. While the buildings were

linked by a network of "bridges," visitors and neighbors could often
be found coming and going through other building entrances, sometimes confining entry and exit to a single door without ever making
their way to other structures. This kind of segmented spatialization
both extended and countered settling's ethic of proximity. Settlement "enlargement" represented the expansion of the public mission
even as its everyday dramaturgy began to instantiate singular rather
than protean geographies.

The spatialization also existed in a recursive relationship with the
creation of American social welfare. The settlement's final buildings
housed the Boys Club, the Mary Crane Nursery, and the Juvenile
Protective Association—each structures that carried institutional
links to new scientific, educational, governmental, and professional
arenas. Such formations rode the paradox of the modern state, incorporating a belief in public responsibility for matters heretofore private while, at the same time, engaging in the discomforting activity
of codifying and regulating highly intimate realms. They thus inten-
sified the "searchlight of inquiry" radiating in the earlier *Hull-House
Maps and Papers,* looking prescriptively for similar signs of density,
mobility, household degeneration, and occupational violation. Combining the positivist methods of social science with the twentieth-
century invention of therapeutic interiority, these new institutions
illustrated Michel Foucault's critique of a modern apparatus and its
micro-operations of familial and sexual enforcement. As the early
twentieth century saw the rise of the "expert" in new fields of human
behavior, women reformers coincidentally saw an opportunity to
legitimate themselves and their vision of a new democracy.[96] This
section suggests some of the consequences of that historical coincidence, working to frame them as neither wholesale domination nor
pure alterity. When Allen Pond looked back at the architectural
history of Hull-House, he admitted that the environment hardly
embodied an ideal plan.

> Hull-House is plainly rather an aggregation of partially related
> units than a logical organism. It is, however, only fair that this
> rigor of judgement shall be somewhat abated for a building or
> group of buildings that have grown by a long series of wholly
> unforeseeable accretions to an original accidental unit.[97]

The aggregated institution emerged out of partial relations that
could not be foreseen. In asking evaluators to suspend judgment of
this accidental scaffolding, Pond might just as easily have been
referring to public welfare's series of accretions.

Even as the often unpalatable consequences of middle-class women's efforts elicit retroactive critique, the involvement of these reformers in state operations might prompt a feminist pause, calling for a complicated reminding of the social impulse to public responsibility embodied in the structures that Foucault's descendants now somewhat breezily reproach. "Anglo-American women's failure to overcome specific social hierarchies of race and class is not a symptom of capitulation to power in general," Lora Romero cautions. "Ideological dissemination works by inciting activity, not deadening it; however, the consequences of incitement produce unforeseen implementations, as they are integrated into discontinuous fields of power relations."[98] In hindsight, individuals such as Jane Addams, Edith Abbott, Sophonisba Breckinridge, Florence Kelly, Julia Lathrop, Louise Bowen, and Jessie Binford can be found engaging in several types of reform whose self-undermining contradictions come into high relief retroactively. "Jerry-built" operations, uneasy categories, and well-intentioned goals of prevention unleashed into a "discontinuous field of power relations" around family and sexuality to create the normalizing apparatus of the social. From the standpoint of feminist ethics, however, settlers can also be seen making urgent choices for immediate action whose consequences they did not anticipate. As contemporary analysts attempt to reconcile a critique of state normalization with the desire for state support, as they celebrate individual resistance while arguing for government-sponsored programming, a concluding look at both the historical embeddedness and unintended results of Hull-House expansion might provide richer insight, albeit a frustratingly complicated one, into the interdependent stakes of such ethical conundrums.

"Dear Mr. Garland," Jane Addams wrote the celebrated Chicago author in 1906, trying to arrange a visit. "I want so much to have you see the new Boys Club and our other enlargements. Would it be possible for you to bring your little girl to 'Alice in Wonderland' next Saturday afternoon."[99] Hoping to engineer a meeting around children's theatricals, Addams's invitation records a moment balanced between the excitement of enlargement and the poignancy of proximity. The new Boys Club was the settlement's interspatial response to a discourse on juvenile development. A year earlier, Hull-House ethnographers conducted a study of "newspaper boys" in Chicago, one of many documents that voiced concern over the proper spatialization of urban children. Though different in political persuasion, settlers joined law enforcement and bourgeois moralists who shared a similar language when it came to classifying truancy, loitering, and other violations of children's time-space appropriateness.

Boys gathered for different types of gaming in the courtyard of the Hull-House Boys Club. *(Photo courtesy of University of Illinois at Chicago, the University Library, Jane Addams Memorial Collection, Wallace Kirkland Papers.)*

Observers found it noteworthy to see children "playing . . . in a vacant house" or "in markets," or to find girls "skulking to the rear door of restaurants."[100] The "child in public" was an embodied reminder of the collapse of preindustrial spaces and traditions. As psychological discourses constituted the child as the origin of essential interiority, as capitalist binaries of work and leisure associated the child with the latter, children's appearances in alleys, streets, or abandoned lots felt psychically and materially transgressive in and of themselves. Newspaper boys, child laborers, stage children, and "street children" countered prevailing associations of the child as a symbol of privacy and nonutility and activated the nostalgia for order and cohesion as they raced across city streets.[101] After some initial disagreement with Helen Culver, Louise deKoven Bowen coordinated the funding and building of a Boys Club in which to house such juvenile mobility.[102] On the eve before its formal opening, Bowen wrote an unusually effusive letter to Jane Addams, using the doubled language of self-satisfaction and self-deferentiality peculiar to the civic housekeeper. "This is just a little note to tell you what I don't want to say in public tomorrow. What a Joy it has been to me to get the new building ready and to make it as good as I could, and how proud and happy I am that it has turned out so well and that it pleases you. . . . If this building helps to keep any boys from going wrong I shall be even more thankful."[103] Inside, the building welcomed boys from childhood to adolescence and of every cosmopolitan nationality represented in the neighborhood. Upon entering, they found spaces filled with the materials and activities recommended by G. Stanley Hall's gendered rhetoric of boyhood development—billiards, bikes, carpentry, metallurgy, wrestling, baseball. The building also contained two floors of dormitory rooms, housing to prevent the anticipated delinquency of "dependent" children.[104]

The construction of the Boys Club coincided with a related line of activity. In 1899, the same year that Hull-House began planning the Labor Museum, Lathrop and Addams had joined forces with Lucy Flowers, then president of the Chicago Women's Club, to found the Juvenile Court of Chicago. The figure of the child criminal underscored the philosophical difficulty of holding the individual accountable for the inequities of the modern city, offering the opportunity to reconceive public interest in systemic concerns. Playing in the midst of Chicago's "village devastation," the impressionable child—no longer conceived as a "pocket-sized adult"—could not be saddled with the intentionality of a "knowing" criminal. Before the establishment of the juvenile court, Julia Lathrop described the "demoralizing irresponsibility" of the justice and prison systems. "It was shown that children were arrested, kept in police stations, tried by police justices, and sentenced to fine or imprisonment."[105] Propelled by an interest in the healthful development of children and against the types of child labor that Alzina Stevens exposed, advocates of the Industrial Arts Leagues instituted vocational training for juvenile offenders, hoping that its palliative tactile pedagogies would distract wayward youth from other untoward occupations. "It was named the John Worthy School and its fine equipment and competent teachers at first gave hope that great good would result, and it was a long step in the right direction," Julia Lathrop recalled. "But because of the capricious and irregular commitments to this school, boys were found there living together in close association guilty of every variety of offense from snowballing and making bonfires to assault with deadly weapons and the

most skillful pocket picking."[106] Combining forces with Judges
Pickney, Mack, and other male reformers, settlers sought a separate
system of trial and punishment as well as the institution of a new,
less "capricious," detention center. The juvenile court legislation
passed, a domestication of politics that Julia Lathrop characterized
as "an illustration of the good Chicago fashion" of mixed-gender
coalition.[107] The effort marked a pivotal moment in Progressive
politics when the methods of social science, the desire for nonparti-
san coalition, and the civic goals of female reform cohered. Lathrop
chronicled the contribution of the Chicago Women's Club to this
effort. "They secured matrons in the police station and spent
nights in the station in order to get a basis of actual knowledge for
their appeal, using a method of first hand sympathetic dealing with
facts which gave an impetus to wise social effort far beyond the
club."[108] By rationalizing themselves as civic mothers, such women
channeled the affect of domesticity to conduct participatory fieldwork into juvenile justice.

During the same decade that the juvenile court and its offshoots
took hold, a second group of Hull-House reformers worked tire-
lessly to formalize social work as an academic field. Edith Abbott
and Sophonisba Breckinridge joined with Graham Taylor in the
founding of the Chicago School of Civics and Philanthropy.[109]
There the "elementary kindness classes" of George Twose's parodies
sought to integrate the settlement's proximate epistemologies with
the methods of social science increasingly valued by Chicago School
sociologists. Relegated initially to the University of Chicago's Department of Domestic Science, later forming a separate School of
Social Work, Abbott and Breckinridge legitimated the study of
human welfare through a scientifically informed civic housekeeping.
Particularly formative in the study of juvenile delinquency was Abbott and Breckinridge's *The Delinquent Child and the Home,* a text
that gave scientific substance to the juvenile court and Boys Club
activities. Opening with a quote from Addams's *Spirit of Youth and
the City Streets,* they called for a fuller understanding of the "wistful,
over-confident creature who walked through our city streets" and
hoped to "translate [his doings] into a solemn school for civic
righteousness."[110] Breckinridge and Abbott helped to codify a new
vocabulary for juvenile development. They used the word *dependent*
to refer to abandoned, poor, or neglected children, a substitute term
for the stigmatizing concept of the pauper.[111] At the same time,
Abbott and Breckinridge displayed an ironic sense of how the vagaries of urban childhood exceeded sociological categories. Their text
thus argued for the necessity of a new conceptual framework even

as they simultaneously recited its imperfection and provisionality. While organizing their investigation around "three classes" of juvenile court cases—dependency, truancy (school inattendance), and delinquency (violation of the law)—they pointed out that these categories leaked. "Some children will be brought in first as dependent or truant and afterwards as delinquent; others are at the same time both dependent and delinquent; or truant and delinquent, or truant and dependent."[112] Focusing on the difficulty of delineating between intentions and conditions and of formulating just retributions, Abbott and Breckinridge spent another portion of their time highlighting the internal variation within several judicial categories. *Stealing,* they reminded readers, could encompass "any sum" no matter how small as well as "finding something which can be sold as junk" after "a judicious hunt through alleys and garbage cans." The finer attributes of *disorderly conduct, vagrancy,* or *malicious mischief,* they argued further, were hardly clear in practicality. Meanwhile, *incorrigibility*—"a word coined of despair"—was a catchall term of circumspect referentiality, including anything from "using vulgar language" to "roaming the street late at night" to "going upon the roof of a building."[113] While a distinctive brand of settlement irony ran through their categorical constructions, their research would eventually enter a diagnostic realm with less interest in such qualification and healthy skepticism.

Similar paradoxes followed as the book sought to expose and thereby curtail the social conditions that produced juvenile delinquency. Spurred by their colleagues at the juvenile court, Abbott and Breckinridge tried to reorient public attention from a focus on punishment to one of prevention. *The Delinquent Child and the Home* tabulated the many hundreds of cases brought to the court, dividing them into several of the most ubiquitous factors. While two chapters focused on the absence of playgrounds and the role of public education, five focused on the problems of different types of homes. In the "The Child of the Immigrant: The Problem of Adjustment," Abbott and Breckinridge noted the disproportionate number of immigrant delinquents. In the "The Crowded Home: The Problem of Confusion," they discoursed on population density in poor neighborhoods. While the prose conveyed their awareness of such structural inequalities, the chapter headings offered a somewhat circumscribed rhetoric, inadvertently casting large-scale social issues as domestic maladjustment. In deprivatizing childhood, their text thus risked reprivatizing the family. Within the effort to contextualize the child criminal, this move was rhetorically expedient—"There is not one instance where the blame could not be clearly laid to some adult"—but it could also eclipse the material location of adults within immigration, poverty, disease, unemployment, and overcrowding.[114] Throughout the text, Abbott and Breckinridge offered qualifications. "In undertaking to supervise and to standardize the care of children within the family group . . . the court undertakes as difficult a task as has ever been attempted by the community through any agent," they cautioned. "Obviously such delicate and important machinery can be perfected only after a considerable effort; and not until experiments, perhaps marked by failure, have been tried again and again."[115] However, the effort of many juvenile advocates to expose the material conditions of childhood often ended up reindividuating parents. Though Abbott and Breckinridge were quick to say that the presence of certain factors did not "inevitably lead to delinquency," others would use their identification of "problem" factors to rationalize new prescriptions, to impute the inevitability back on to immigrants, or to blame an unemployed parent for having the gall to live in an overcrowded flat.[116]

Besides the Boys Club and the juvenile court, the preventive focus on the child's home as the breeding ground for unhealthful development prompted new reform spaces at Hull-House. Across Ewing Street, a group of settlers and affiliates opened a "Practical Housekeeping Center," advertising its training in appropriate domesticity for neighborhood mothers.[117] The publicity pamphlet opened with a 1907 quotation from Florence Kelley, then secretary of the Consumers' League, who fueled the concern with bad parenting.

> The bane of the tenement is the unskilled mother. She it is who feeds the baby foul milk, bananas, and beer. She drugs with sleeping draughts the crying victim of vermin she does not know how to banish. She exhausts him with excessive clothing which she washes so irregularly that he languishes for the want of simplest freshness. It often seems that of the baby's three enemies— milkman, landlord, and unskilled mother—the unskilled mother is the deadliest because her opportunities for doing him harm are continuous and her means of attack so varied.[118]

Here Kelley, her socialist consciousness well developed with respect to the deleterious social conditions of labor, displayed an equally vigorous tendency to privatize the demoralized condition of motherhood. The representation mimicked her earlier analyses of the sweating system in *Hull-House Maps and Papers*. Helping to arouse "public sentiment" for health education, working to expose the social conditions of childhood, Kelley and fellow reformers could end up vilifying poor mothers in naturalizing and individuating language, positing their intentionality as the "means of attack" of an enemy. With a board of directors that included Mrs. Edward (Maud) Yeomans, Norah Hamilton, and Jessie Binford, the model "four-room flat" displayed ideal housekeeping and furnishing practices that came "well within the means of the average tenement family." The furnishings included linen, china, kitchen utensils, and furniture. Its curators developed an interspatial method of reinforcement not only by offering instruction in "hygiene," "scrubbing," "food selection," and "coal economy" but by visiting "in their homes so that a friendly relation may be established between parents and teacher. In this way the children are encouraged to apply the principles learned at the Center and the practical results of the lessons are ascertained."[119] They thus euphemistically rationalized the intrusive aspects of such "ascertaining," reworking the legacy of "friendly visiting" for the goals of scientific motherhood. Simultaneously resisting and reifying patriarchal myopias, reformers took on the paradoxical responsibility of public health by mediating everyday performances of domesticity, promoting the ideal of the bounded private family through a method of enforcement that required that boundary's transgression.

"My dear Alice," Addams wrote semiapologetically for the delay in responding to her "natural sister," "I have had a busy and distracting summer with much building going on, the Cranes are putting up a building that will house all our children's work."[120] In the year following the erection of the Boys Club and coinciding with the creation of the Practical Housekeeping Center, Hull-House was in the midst of yet another enlargement—the addition of the Mary Crane Nursery. The nature of "children's work" altered and varied with new scientific vocabularies and affiliations. In addition to nurseries and kindergartens, it also housed the new "Child Problem Clinic," the Infant Welfare Society, a National Kindergarten College for prospective teachers, and the Open Air School begun by the Tuberculosis Institute and the board of education.[121] Besides "teacher training," the bulk of the curriculum at the Mary Crane Nursery was broken down into "Nursery School activities" and "Parental Education." The first included lessons in "Habit Formations" for "personal hygiene," "feeding," "sleep and relaxation." Each divided into "Sequences" for "washing face, hands, neck and ears," for "serving table," for "dressing and undressing."[122] The courses incorporated a pragmatic discourse on habits into the microdisciplinary performance of everyday life. Outlines for courses on "work and play" had as their guiding principles "respect for property and others' rights" with a sample mimicking of the child citizen's idealized interiority: "I can not paint now because it

is Betty's house." "I must put the beads away because I got them out."
As with Dewey's Lab School at the University of Chicago, the concept of play as the wellspring of human agency propelled some parts of
the curriculum, for "the child's choice of material directs the teacher
in education activities and method." Habit techniques became
routinized in Progressive education manuals. Some elaborated different types of habitual pedagogy, comparing more self-conscious modes
to less volitional and more literal modes of mimicry. They adapted a
spatiotemporal knowledge of human interaction and memorial association to ensure a child's everyday impulses of personal hygiene and,
in the following passage, self-ventilation.

> There are two kinds of cures or reminders—those of time and
> those of place. If we wish the bed aired, we will say, "_When you get
> up,_ throw the bed clothes over the foot of the bed," pressing
> deeply into the mind, the association of getting up and bed
> clothes. . . . Similarly, such reminders as follows may be applied:
> _When you put on your hat,_ look to see if your hands are clean";
> "_When you take off your stockings,_ hang them up;" "_When you
> crawl into bed,_ ask yourself, 'Have I opened the window?' " Fre-
> quently, the association acts tardily and there is left in the mind
> of the child, when he gets up or goes to bed, only a feeling that he
> was to do something but does not know what it is. If he makes an
> effort, he may remember.[123]

Filtered through theories of physical culture, domesticity, and scientific method, such sequential techniques inscribed restored behaviors
and encouraged an acute regulation of the tacit and the habitual.
The pedagogy of learning by doing further traveled to the Mary
Crane Nursery's parental classes, especially with immigrant mothers,
among whom reformers found that they did not always need "an
interpreter to get your meaning across." Instead, "we use a very
concrete method of giving the mothers something to do with their
hands. We have both sewing and cooking classes."[124] Meanwhile, the
Crane instructors' concrete method of gendered occupation produced their version of an ideal relationality between mother and
child. "Garments are chosen the making of which will be instructional and the correct method of dressing children. . . . Results of
the sewing class immediately began to appear: waists were made
for the children, side elastics appeared, and the children came more
cleanly in person and more daintily dressed."[125] The same went for
the cooking classes, where children learned to ask for the "chocolate
pudding" that mothers learned to make in an efficiently reciprocal

process of interdependent reform. Finally, reformers availed themselves of another "medium" by teaching mothers to sing children's songs. After a few weeks, the activities director reported that "the voices of the mothers have been noticeably softened."[126]

The Mary Crane Nursery thus addressed the immigrant parent-child relationship quite differently than did the Labor Museum, though they employed similar performance-based media of embodiment, occupation, display, and song. As one delineated a circumscribed arena in which to reaffiliate with national traditions, the other encouraged an immigrant mother's disaffiliation from other Old World practices. In the latter realm, "primitive" textile manufacture was not appreciated nearly as much as the sewing of "side elastics." The nursery's parental activities also most forcefully focused on maternal activities, a habit that anticipated the trajectory of social reform and that shows the persistence of normalizing as-

Mothers and children walking up the path to the Mary Crane Nursery. *(Photo courtesy of University of Illinois at Chicago, the University Library, Jane Addams Memorial Collection, Wallace Kirkland Papers.)*

sumptions of proper "family life." As all of these examples make
clear, Hull-House settlers had the easiest time arguing for public
responsibility when they highlighted its benefits to children. When
Julia Lathrop became the first director of a federally administered
Children's Bureau, her rise demonstrated the utility of the child as a
galvanizing figure in the formation of social welfare. The figure of
the child made clear the stakes of particular issues and, for good or
ill, rendered those issues undebatable. The Children's Bureau would
expand the maternal pedagogies of the Mary Crane Nursery, as
Molly Ladd-Taylor has shown, providing access to medicine and to
value-laden parenting classes that American mothers both embraced
and resisted. The unanticipated consequence of this type of formalization, however, was that it increasingly divorced the concerns of
children from the concerns of parents, especially mothers. Shadowed
by the (never viable) ideal of the "family wage" and its concomitant
nuclear family, the lives of poor and/or working mothers were not
theorized in consort with children but as the site for the production
of domestic behaviors that appropriately nurtured them. Eventually,
women's deferential relation to others would become "encoded in
state policy," hinging social support on the degree to which she
embodied an image of non-wage-earning maternalism.[127]

Prevention, the liberal alternative to child punishment, simultaneously legitimated the indelicate intervention into delicate matters.
This coincidence takes on another layer of resonance in the work of
a final Hull-House space—the Juvenile Protective Association. After juvenile court founder Lucy Flowers moved out of Illinois,
Louise deKoven Bowen took over as the "active, efficient, untiring,
unflinching leader" of its committee.[128] Arguing for an extension in
the umbrella of public welfare, they eventually succeeded in transfer-
ring the funding for officer salaries and the detention home to the
county civic service, redesigning themselves into a body that focused
instead on "preventive" measures. Naming themselves the Juvenile
Protective Association in 1907, they took office space at Hull-
House, looking out on the settlement courtyard and receiving affiliates and neighbor complaints at all hours of the day. President
Bowen along with a twenty-seven-member board initiated programs
along a tripartite mission: to investigate "individual cases" of child
welfare, to "repress the conditions which produce delinquency," and
to "arouse public sentiment for the establishment of parks, playgrounds, gymnasiums, free baths," and other arenas of wholesome
recreation. When Jessie Binford became president of the Juvenile
Protective Association in 1916, she continued these goals through
active publicity and legislative intervention. The case of the juvenile

court and the Juvenile Protective Association thus exemplified the successful, structural integration of public-mindedness within the powerful sites of civic policy and legislation. At the same time, the interaction of human welfare with the legacy of criminal punishment created a prime arena for the development of microdisciplinary operations. Former settlers began casting themselves as probation "officers" of the court who attended to the city children as "cases." Similarly, paid social workers increasingly borrowed the legitimating language of professionalism to figure such children as "clients." In social work's transformation from the sentimental to the scientific, the capillary streams of the former still structured the targets and classifications of the latter. This formalized expertise had increasingly less tolerance, however, for any kind of settlement irony.

The well-intentioned if temporally conflicted goal of "prevention" rationalized the JPA's indirect and anticipatory type of power apparatus. JPA officers researched various urban sites in order to locate and "repress" corrupting factors.[129] As noted in chapter 5, for example, they focused a great deal of energy on local theaters and the presence of "stage children." At such moments, the JPA occasionally had difficulty managing the relationship between correlation and cause, enforcing prohibitions against the exhibition of children that, they sometimes felt, were inadequate to the shaky task of assessing morality and degeneracy. Such juvenile investigations landed upon and emerged within another uneasy discourse—that of sexuality. The coincidence exemplifies a larger interdependence between the regulation of family and juvenile development and that of sexualized performance.

> The public dance halls filled with frivolous and vapid young people in a feverish search for pleasure are but a sorry substitute for the immemorial dances on the village green in which all of the older people of the village participated. Chaperonage was not a social duty, but natural and inevitable, and the whole courtship period was naturally guarded by the conventions and restraint which were taken as matter of course.[130]

Echoed in the *The Spirit of Youth and the City Streets* and *A New Conscience and an Ancient Evil,* Jane Addams's elegiac theories of public recreation thus framed immoral sexuality as an index of the modern city's alienation. The move coincided with a civic and national outcry over urban sexuality in the first decade of the twentieth century, one that preoccupied itself not only with children but also with the figure of the young single woman. The Chicago Vice

Commission reports of 1910 investigated so-called dens of iniquity, sometimes importing a racialized discourse of white slavery to "rescue" female victims from economic exploitation, sometimes naturalizing the waywardness of single women within the rhetoric of physical and moral contagion.[131] Such adolescent and postadolescent women became the focal point for anxieties over the criminalization of prostitution and the threat of women's increased public presence more generally. The language of sexuality and evolution also combined in a concern over women's reproduction. The impulses of familial and sexual normalization thus mixed once more, figuring the unmarried women's sexual degeneration as an obstacle to social regeneration.

Within this constrained discursive sphere, Hull-House's nostalgia for the "village green" was continuous with the formation of the Juvenile Protective Association. Substituting agrarian "chaperonage" with sympathetic surveillance, the JPA sent representatives to spaces deemed most immoral: billiard rooms, dance halls, ice cream parlors, five-cent theaters, vaudeville, and saloons. Hoping to offer an alternative to the unhelpfully scandalized rhetoric of federal vice commission reports, Bowen and her group drafted pamphlets to "arouse public sentiment" and "sympathetic understanding" for the concerns of young single woman. "Young girls all over the world require and want recreation," they wrote, "but the industrial life in which the majority of our young girls are engaged offers but little variety. . . . Pasting labels, dipping candy, wrapping soap, making eyelets in shoes is deadly monotonous and starves the imagination. Then comes the inevitable revolt."[132] Bowen's efforts to provide for wholesome urban recreation drew from Addams's writings on the need for "sympathetic" understanding of the youthful energy. Within a limited evolutionary vocabulary, JPA discourse significantly allowed the adolescent "youth" to be female, reminding readers that G. Stanley Hall's "savage boys" were not the only ones whose vigor and spirited energy needed release. At the same time, the titles of pamphlets like *The Straight Girl and the Crooked Path* or *The Road to Destruction Made Easy* borrowed the language of the muckraker to channel the morally outraged energy of civic sentimentality.

Hull-House's concern over "chaperonage" and appropriate heterosocial amusement had begun much earlier, of course, ever since the Hull-House Debating Club began "joining" the Hull-House Social Club, ever since the members of the Jane Club engaged in the scandalous task of "running their own evenings." JPA investigations of the "public dance halls of Chicago" illustrate the formalization and transformation of this early interest. In the dance halls, officers worried over an array of heterosexual rituals performed in the turn-of-the-century city. "There is an almost universal custom among the girls of keeping their powder puff in the top of their stockings, from which it is ostentatiously taken and used whenever a girl wishes to attract the attention of a young man."[133] With an emerging twentieth-century discourse of modern sexuality came new enactments of heterosexuality. While dismay over such ostentations translated into the vilification of female sexual disorder in a new urban imaginary, reformers often sought to redeem single women through the constrained discourse of white slavery. Many JPA investigations produced *Maggie* or *Sister Carrie*–like tales, representing the naïveté of young single women whose crooked paths were paved by morally corrupt males. "Our attention was drawn to a rather well dressed man who came in with a young girl. . . . The man was of the worldly type—disrespectful looking. The girl young, childish and very innocent. The girl seemed scared and unaccustomed to the place. . . . He ordered drinks. . . . The girl looked at it and shook her head, the man commenced to talk to her and persuade her. She tasted it, sipped a little of it and later drank it all. Her face became red as a beet and she looked happy and yet every few minutes she asked the man for the time."[134] In such moments, the justifications of JPA "prevention" became especially opaque. Did the possibility of sexual danger warrant intervention? Or did intervention translate into unwelcome sexual surveillance? The young woman's construction as the anticipated victim of white slavery saved her from culpability, but it also limited her agency. In a choice whose appropriateness would be decided retroactively, the JPA officers followed the couple as they walked out the door. Later, they and others like them would be celebrated and condemned for involving themselves in someone else's business.

Fueled by the charge of prevention, the Juvenile Protective Association worked to install civic prohibitions. They offered a list of proposed ordinances, asking for more active police involvement, more stringent regulation of the sale of liquor, and a general prohibition against "immoral dancing or familiarity." Unlike other reform institutions, they argued against the institution of a citywide closing hour, saying with a degree of class consciousness that "it does not seem best to limit the hours of pleasure for working people any more than for those who can afford to patronize the best hotels." Additionally, they did not seek to bar "the girl of sixteen" from dances altogether, staying consistent with their belief in the importance of recreation for an expressive female adolescence.[135] What they attempted to do instead was to separate dancing from the sale of liquor by enforcing a spatial separation between the dance hall and the saloon. Fixing the mobility of urban interaction, however, proved to be an elusive project. Subsequent JPA officers entered social spaces to evaluate the "Location of saloon in relation to dancing floor," offering warnings when the establishment's bar area was only "divided from [the] dance floor by a ladies cloak room and small hallway."[136] In a degenerate echo of the spatial dramaturgy of the Hull-House Auditorium and coffeehouse, the Vermont Gardens Dance Hall placed its saloon on the first floor, wine rooms and toilet on the second, and a dance hall on the third, thereby allowing access to the upper space of bodily recreation only by passing through the intermediary spaces of intemperate alimentation. "The dancers constantly circulated back and forth between the drinking room and the dance hall."[137] Dismayed by the rotating performance of suspect spatiality, the JPA began to recognize that repressive prohibitions against certain acts ended up producing new behaviors. A similar slipperiness shadowed the attempt to censor "immoral dancing." One officer reported the ineffectuality of politely direct measures. "The dancing was very bad in spite of the sign right on the wall saying 'No indecent dancing will be tolerated.' "[138] They struggled to generate a vocabulary for gauging indecency. Case forms asked for classification within a set of circumspect categories—"Kissing," "Embracing," "Fondling," "Soliciting," "Fights." Dancing warranted a more finely tuned set of principles. Forms noted whether its style was "Modern or old" and asked officers to identify and count instances of the "Close position," "Faces together," "Stationery wiggles," and "Arms around partners neck."[139]

Based upon their observations, the Juvenile Protective Association lobbied against the interdependence of "the saloon and vice interests." The indelicate delicacies of their moral justifications strain the ears of a contemporary analyst. "The women ordered highballs the men some beer and some highballs. . . . Close to 12 the company became well under the influence of liquor and each one related a dirty story."[140] At the same time, the evaluation of their evaluations might also require, even if it frustrates, a differently refined mode of discrimination. Within the undernuanced vocabularies of moral degeneracy, JPA officers also argued that alcohol sale facilitated men's unequal relations with women.[141] "Their first effort is to get the girl intoxicated. In one case the investigator saw a young girl held while four boys poured whiskey from a flask down her throat, she protesting half-laughingly all the time that she had never anything to drink before."[142] The parallel to what a present context might call sexual assault complicates a purely vilifying portrayal of the JPA's "policing" activities. "In one case where the girl screamed, the man choked her, and although her screams rang through the hall, those surrounding the couple only laughed and made no attempt at interference."[143] A feminist perspective foregrounds how the albeit constrained discourses of temperance and immoral sexuality simultaneously cleared a space for a critique of sexual violence. The coincidence stalls a purely dichotomous framing of sexual politics. Similarly, when Addams called for the "amelioration of economic conditions" contributing to prostitution's "traffic in women," her somewhat patronizing appropriation of the discourse of white slavery also created a feminist link between prostitutes and suffrage activists. "Women with political power would not brook that men should live upon the wages of captured victims. . . . If political rights were once given to women, if the situation were theirs to deal with as a matter of civic responsibility, one cannot imagine that the existence of the social evil would remain unchallenged in its semi-legal protection."[144]

While still maintaining class divisions regarding which women assumed this "civic responsibility," settlers developed an awareness of the gendered and economic politics of so-called immorality. The career of Hull-House resident Gertrude Howe Britton, for instance, shows a related interdependence between family and sexual politics. Once named a JPA superintendent, Britton prepared reports of her neighborhood activities that anticipated the overload of AFDC social workers. Beginning with forty-six "complaints received" between April and May 1907, the number would double to ninety and to ninety-seven over the next two two-month periods. In supplementary prose, she elaborated: "[T]he need which forces itself upon me in my work is the great necessity of protective work among very young girls." Out-of-wedlock pregnancies occupied much of her time, as she reported a "little girl of 14" whose "mother has to wash for a living and her absence from home made the opportunity for this most deplorable affair." The mother of another pregnant fifteen-year-old agreed to care for her daughter's child "as her own." Britton also arranged for charges to be brought up against a male boarder who had raped and impregnated the twelve-year-old daughter of his landlady.[145] It was within the conflicted space of welfare experimentation, one "marked by failure" and assuming the presumptuous capacity to name "deplorability," that Gertrude Howe Britton nevertheless came to a qualified feminist consciousness, eventually joining Hull-House settler Rachel Yarros as an active proponent of Chicago's birth control movement in the early twentieth century. Meanwhile, walking the course of her own unforeseen history, Britton kept writing up more case reports. In one of many, she admitted uncertainty about what action to take with regard to an abandoned,

pregnant sixteen-year-old. "I am still working on that," she wrote,
utopic energy as yet unexhausted.

A feminist and historically grounded understanding of sexuality and family might stall a facile critique of the social. The urge to denounce the presumptions of late-Victorian, white middle-class women is as seductive as is the impulse ahistorically to believe in their frigidity, busybody-ness, and sexual repression. And along with the embracing of such condemnations goes the capacity to notice the misogynist stereotypes they reify. The story of social welfare is not one of total female domination—the insidiously feminized infiltration of state power—any more than it is a story of absolute female heroism—the unproblematic celebration of marginal women reformers. It is neither and both. Middle-class women's contribution to an ethic of public responsibility also emerged within the discursive and mechanical administration of public bureaucracy. The unstigmatized use of the term *dependency* would become one of the worst of welfare's selectively stigmatizing inscriptions. The feminist undoing of public and private also could rationalize intimate regulation. Conversely, the discontinuous operations that produced a regulatory discourse on proper parenting also created a discourse against domestic violence. The same rationale behind the "policing" of single women's sexuality also could generate a critique of the unequal economic relations of prostitution. "Again and again," writes Lauren Berlant, "we see how hard it is to adjudicate the norms of a public world when it is also an intimate one."[146]

As the century wore on, however, modern discourses of sexual subjectivity would be less disposed to remember with complexity the attenuated feminism embodied in the early female reformer. This old New Woman served as a foil for a new New Woman, one cast by sexual revisionists as the independent and sexually expressive female of a modern era.[147] Younger members of a rising sexual culture would ultimately criticize their figurative mothers for speculating on their desires. They retroactively framed her interest in their sexual development as embarassingly misdirected, preferring instead to remember her as a suffocating force against sexual adventure. For the new young female "urban pioneer," hyperheterosexual "expression" as well as commercial consumption were testaments to her "freedom," though none of these experiments were reputed to undermine her ultimate goal of heterosexual marriage. "The sexual revisionists, in short, recognized improvements in women's status and power, yet encouraged women not to go too far, not to abandon men, and not to try to control them."[148] Furthermore, the reconstruction of the old New Woman as matriarchal antithesis conveniently embodied not only the traits of "repression" but also those—feminist, career-ist, lesbian, unmarried—that threatened the stability of a presum-ably more open form of sexual and capitalist patriarchy. Meanwhile, settlers and other female reformers would feel the sting of their own contribution to a discourse on degenerate sexuality from another direction. Through the twentieth century, these women's involve-ment in public welfare and in entities such as the Children's Bureau were disparaged as "unnatural."[149] As unmarried, "childless" women whose reforms paradoxically naturalized a concept of family life, they would later be vilified for not having one. The same discursive pull toward the identification of immoral sexuality undergirded the construction of the "lesbian"—a stigmatized category that would be pinned on many female reformers. The early bigendered image of the civic housekeeper—whose "masculine" analytic mind and "femi-nine" sympathetic powers had been easily embraced—now danger-ously coalesced with the lesbian's construction as a degenerately bigendered "invert." Finally, as the unwitting architect of the con-forming apparatus of "the social"—its public schools, prisons, hous-ing, health programs, and other bureaucracies—the maligned figure of the female reformer would propel many historical and rhetorical analyses of society and sexuality. Contemporary social critics con-tinue to neutralize the equivocal position of these nonnormative women in the history of social normalization.

When Jessie Binford left the Hull-House Settlement in 1963, her words to a local reporter suggested that she was mourning the loss of something other than bricks and mortar. "We didn't call them cases," she said, "they were our neighbors. And everything we did, we did because they were our friends. We did everything out of friendship, and respect, and because they were our neighbors." The papers of the Juvenile Protective Association of course show that Binford and her crew occasionally did use such juridical and profes-sional language, a vocabulary that, at the time, felt like an index of legitimation. In hindsight, the terminology appears to be an index of bureaucratization. In fact, the earlier genealogy of neighborliness had altered decades before 1963. "It is of course alright for you to live in Evanston," responded Jane Addams to a request from a teacher at the Mary Crane Nursery in 1933. Since neither Addams nor many other affiliates were maintaining the habit of proximate settling by that time, Hull-House's leader recognized the professional demand for a reduced form of spatial participation. "But I hope you will continue to use the sitting room upstairs as much as you care to."[150]

Richard M. Daley's administration was one of many in the 1960s

This *Chicago Sun-Times* cartoon appeared on March 25, 1962, next to an article entitled "Realizing Jane Addams' Dream" that celebrated West-Side urban renewal. (*Photo courtesy of University of Illinois at Chicago, the University Library, Jane Addams Memorial Collection, Hull-House Association Records,* Chicago Sun-Times.)

'Why, Dick—This Is Beyond My Wildest Dreams'

that aligned urban renewal with urban destruction, linking civic improvement with the "elimination of slums" (not recreational substitutes for the "village green") and the facilitation of suburban access (his method of tending to Edith Abbott's "local highways"). Along the way, the deployment of Jane Addams as a figure of legitimation illustrated the gendered surrogate's memorial flexibility and showed how easily urban forgetting undergirds public remembering. Throughout (and with the help of the *Chicago Sun-Times*), Daley invoked the ideal of Jane Addams despite a project that violated nearly every tenet of the settlement's spatial ethic.

The detached remnants of the Hull-House neighborhood now float along the edge of the UIC campus, divided by the Dan Ryan Expressway and separated from the rest of Chicago by the John F. Kennedy Expressway. (No, there is no Jane Addams Memorial Highway.) With a reduced tax-base and a stalled environmental practice, the remnants have become the subject of civic debate and helpless mourning. In articles such as "Goodbye Greektown" or "Maxwell Street Blues," these neighborhoods are emblems of a civic imperialist

The demolition of the Hull-House settlement in 1963. *(Photo courtesy of University of Illinois at Chicago, the University Library, Jane Addams Memorial Collection, Wallace Kirkland Papers.)*

nostalgia, their fracturing oft-lamented by the same persons who commute on the highways that run through them.[151] Of course, such nostalgia misremembers the discourse of dirt, chaos, contagion, and corruption that has always shadowed these sites, especially when Russian Jews, Italians, and Greeks were blamed for urban delapidation in much the same way that other racial and immigrant groups endure such accusation now.[152] I used to visit the old immigrant neighborhoods while I was growing up in the suburbs of Chicago. While Italian food was once the object of social reformation, it would later become a prime site of cross-cultural consumption— and my family's favorite Italian restaurants were on Taylor Street.[153] Later, when my friends and I had our drivers' licenses, we would drive on those highways to patronize Greektown's few remaining restaurants because we knew that they would serve us alcohol. (Fortunately, no one from the Juvenile Protective Association ever showed up.)

Now—with blue, yellow, red, and green walls obscuring the racial politics of a selective ethnic history—the Jane Addams Hull-House Museum functions as a symbol of civic relationality at a place where a city stalled the environmental conditions of extended affiliation. A block away from a UIC building, an aging man sets up an Italian ice stand. At the time of this writing, one passed by the time of your reading, children play on a highway overpass. I think that it is important to remember that these people are also inhabitants of a *milieu de mémoire*. Their behaviors and daily rituals are certainly "living memory," albeit of a discontinuous history that does not fulfill nostalgic fantasies for a time of authenticity and tradition. "The world has changed since that day," Edith Abbott might have said once more, while also calling "fallacious" our belief that such a time ever was.

Appendix

Hull-House Players

Cristin Hodgens and Shannon Jackson

Edith Abbott earned a Ph.D. from the University of Chicago in 1905, studied further at the London School of Economics, taught for a year at Wellesley College, and settled at Hull-House with her sister Grace in 1908. In 1910, she published *Women in Industry*, a landmark study of the labor conditions of women. Her first book was her most formidable, but her future works remain classics still studied by sociologists and historians. Along with Sophinisba Breckinridge, Edith Abbott wrote two volumes on delinquent children. In 1924, she became the dean of the University of Chicago's School of Social Service Administration.

Grace Abbott earned a master's degree in political science from the University of Chicago and became the director of the Immigrants' Protective League around 1910. Abbott authored *The Immigrant and the Community* in 1917. One of her particular concerns was the plight of young girls who arrived in Chicago by themselves. Extending her involvement in child labor reform, Abbott spent most of the 1920s in Washington D.C. as the head of the Children's Bureau. She returned to Chicago in 1934 to teach with her sister Edith at the University of Chicago School of Social Service Administration. Grace Abbott published her two volume study, *The Child and the State,* before her death in 1939.

Louise deKoven Bowen was one of the most active non-resident affiliates of Hull-House. Beginning in 1892, she served as the settlement's benefactor, later trustee and treasurer, donating funds for major buildings as well as the Bowen Country Club. Active in founding Chicago's juvenile court, she subsequently founded and directed the Juvenile Protective Association to educate the public about the social, sexual, industrial, and commercial conditions of Chicago's youth culture. She became president of the Hull-House Board of Trustees when Jane Addams died in 1935.

Sophonisba Breckinridge contributed greatly to the professionalization of social work after joining Hull-House and earning her doctorate in 1901. A lawyer, social worker, and later professor at the University of Chicago, she co-founded the Chicago School of Civics and Philanthropy. Often using Hull-House as place from which to gather data on urban conditions, she took particular interest in juvenile delinquency and feminist political economy, collaborating with Edith Abbott on several published studies in the first three decades of the twentieth-century.

James Britton and **Gertrude Howe Britton** were married at Hull-House and lived there for many years. Gertrude Howe reproduced many Hull-House lines of activity: she began as a kindergarten teacher, assembled sanitation surveys with Alice Hamilton, became a superintendent of the Juvenile Protective Association, served as director of Cook County Department of Public Welfare, and finally became the executive director of the Chicago Heart Association. Meanwhile, as the Hull-House physician, Dr. Britton worked with neighborhood tuberculosis patients and supervised boys' athletics.

Frederick Deknatel came to Hull-House as a widower in 1898. He first acted as caretaker to Mary Rozet Smith's aunt. Around 1900, the dependable Deknatel became Jane Addams's right-hand man; as her personal secretary, he scheduled her speaking engagements. Over the next thirty-three years, Deknatel supervised the financial affairs of the settlement and its leading residents. He spoke in Mexico and abroad for the benefit of Hull-House and served as Ellen Gates Starr's stockbroker. Deknatel married Wilfreda Brockway—another Hull-House resident—at the turn of the century. He and his new wife were particularly close with Rose Gyles and traveled with her to Europe on multiple occasions.

John Dewey was a leading Progressive educational philosopher in Chicago, later earning a national reputation after he left the city at the turn of the century. As a philosophy professor at the University of Michigan, the University of Chicago, and Columbia University, he authored hundreds of essays on ethics, experiential pedagogy, and pragmatism. His arrival at the University of Chicago marked a personal commitment to both education and Hull-House. He routinely spoke to the Chicago Kindergarten Conference and wrote numerous essays and books integrating the fields of education, psychology, and philosophy. In 1897, he was elected a Hull-House trustee and regularly visited the settlement. In "The School as Social

Center," Dewey praised Hull-House classes on Caesar and sewing alike, defining the institution as a leader in pragmatic educational reform.

Alex Elson grew up at Hull-House. Along with seven Russian-immigrant siblings, he participated in music, dancing, art classes, and, most of all, the Hull-House Theatre. **Elizabeth Elson** attended the Yale School of Drama, and became the first woman member of the school's faculty. **Charles Elson,** also a graduate of the Yale School, had an outstanding technical career on Broadway. Alex went on to practice law while remaining of service to Hull-House. During college and law school at the University of Chicago, he toted the front door to the settlement. Later in the century, Elson served as a member of the Hull-House Association's board of directors.

Charlotte Perkins Gilman lived at Hull-House for two years, beginning in 1895. Like Jane Addams, Gilman experienced nervous disorders in her early years. And like Florence Kelley, she divorced her husband and sent her daughter to live elsewhere while she worked and wrote. After living at Hull-House, Gilman wrote *Women and Economics.* Arguably the most important work of feminist theory in the emerging Progressive Era, the book argued for female economic independence and prescribed communal solutions to individual domestic predicaments. The work resonated with Hull-House women: according to one witness, the residents were "waiting in rows" to read it. Translated into seven languages, *Women and Economics* brought Gilman international acclaim and the economic security to found *Forerunner,* a largely self-funded magazine in which she featured her utopian *Herland.*

Rose Gyles was a graduate of Rockford College and also received a degree in physical education from Harvard's Hemenway Gymnasium. She came to Chicago in 1893; over the next forty-five years, Gyles ran the Hull-House physical education program. She taught women's and children's classes and implemented a diverse athletic program using dumbbells, wands, Indian clubs and free drills, fancy steps and figure marching, gymnastics, and games. Complimenting her bloomer-wearing woman's basketball team, the *Chicago Chronicle* remarked that "Hull-House is considered invincible." Gyles combined a zeal for physical activity with Progressive pragmatism: she taught "physical culture" classes at Hull-House when the Chicago Froebel Association made its headquarters there.

Alice Hamilton came to Hull-House in 1897, where she guided clubs and health clinics while teaching at the Women's Medical School at Northwestern. She did not leave until 1919, when she became the first female professor at Harvard Medical School. A pioneer in industrial toxicology, Hamilton became the director of the Illinois Occupational Disease Commission in 1910. The commission's crusades resulted in the passage of workmen's compensation and set the precedent for employee compensation.

Florence Kelley graduated from Cornell in 1882, graduated law school at Northwestern, 1894, studied further at the University of Zurich, and established a working friendship with Frederick Engels. In Europe, she married and bore three children. Following her divorce, Kelley re-assumed her maiden name and arrived at Hull-House on New Year's Day in 1892. The first woman to serve as chief factory inspector of Illinois, Kelley simultaneously earned her law degree in 1894 and implemented landmark protective legislation against sweatshops, child labor, and unprotected female labor. In 1899, she moved to Lillian Wald's New York settlement house to lead the National Consumer's League. Kelley was a founding member of both the NAACP and the Women's International League for Peace and Freedom.

Ethel and **Wallace Kirkland** moved into an apartment on the top floor of the Hull-House Boys' Club Building in the early twenties. Ethel worked as a Hull-House social worker. After her husband Wallace Kirkland graduated from the YMCA College in 1923, he became the director of the Boys and Men's Clubs. Wallace is best remembered for his photography, for he took over one thousand photographs of nearly every aspect of Hull-House life. His pictures range from men's typewriting classes, to bathing babies in the Mary Crane Nursery, to his son's junior boys gymnastics class. He went on to became a photographer for *Life* magazine in the late thirties.

Julia Lathrop graduated from Vassar College in 1880 and began her Hull-House work visiting Cook County families in 1892. Supplementing her dedication to Hull-House with a long-standing membership on the Illinois Board of Charities, Lathrop reformed the state's prisons, county farms, and almshouses. She actively participated in the founding of both the Immigrants Protective League and Chicago's juvenile court. Lathrop helped Edith Abbott and Sophonisba Breckinridge found the Chicago School of Civics and Philanthropy, later a part of the University of Chicago. When President Taft ap-

pointed her chief of the U.S. Children's Bureau in 1912, Lathrop left
Illinois for Washington, D.C. She later served on the Child Welfare
Committee of the League of Nations.

Henry Demarest Lloyd was a devoted friend to Hull-House residents. Florence Kelley placed her three children in his Winnetka
home when she came to Chicago in 1892. As the financial editor of
the *Chicago Tribune,* Lloyd first gained prominence as the nation's
premier antimonopoly journalist. His extensive writing included *A
Strike of Millionaires against Miners; or the Story of Spring Valley.*
Lloyd was actively involved with the Working People's Social Science Club at Hull-House and other arenas of civic activism.

Mary McDowell moved in to Hull-House in the mid-1890s to
become a kindergarten teacher, a Woman's Club president, and a
member of the Association of Neighborhood Workers Industrial
Committee. The Nineteenth Ward textile industry inspired her anti-
sweatshop crusades. When McDowell later directed the University
of Chicago's South Side settlement from 1894–1929, she agitated on
behalf of African Americans and became a member of the Committee on Interracial Relations for the National Federation of Settlements. She was known by many as "the garbage lady" for her efforts
to reform South Side stockyards. McDowell would eventually bring
her district's concerns to the worldwide stage as an active member of
the Women's International League for Peace and Freedom.

George Herbert Mead was a professor of philosophy at the University of Chicago, where his work complemented the pragmatism of
John Dewey. In the 1890s through World War I, he was a frequent
visitor and lecturer at Hull-House as well as a member of several
activist organizations in Chicago, including the Civic Federation.
Mead continually worked to integrate philosophical meditation with
the dynamics of civic politics and daily sociability, most significantly
developing his concept of "the social self." While Dewey remained
optimistic about the usefulness of philosophers in the reconstruction
of society, Mead grew to question the reconstructive potential of
applying philosophy to politics, especially in the postwar years.

Ernest Carroll Moore and **Dorothea Moore** came to Hull-House
as newlyweds in 1896. A young scholar working toward a Ph.D. at
the University of Chicago, Ernest Moore researched Nineteenth
Ward saloons and, in 1897, published "The Social Value of the
Saloon." Meanwhile, Dr. Dorothea Moore taught physiology at

Hull-House and served as Jane Addams' liaison with police stations. After Hull-House, Ernest taught at Harvard, Yale, and finally served as president of the University of California at Los Angeles.

Edith de Nancrede was a drama and dance teacher at Hull-House. She headed a six-club network of children's and young people's dramatic clubs for those ranging in age from three to twenty-one. Convinced that the arts were socially useful at all stages of her students' development, she once remarked that "instead of losing [her students'] interest, I can't get them to stop!" Except for occasional vacations—often with the Ponds, to whom she was related by marriage—Nancrede spent her entire adult life in residence at Hull-House.

Theodore Roosevelt—war hero, naturalist, American president— once told Jane Addams that although he "had such awful times with reformers of the hysterical and sensational stamp . . . I so thoroughly believe in reform, that I fairly revel in dealing with anyone like you." Roosevelt rallied behind the Vice Commission of Chicago's aim of the "extinction of [the] evil" of white slavery and was a proponent of women's suffrage. In 1912, Addams seconded Roosevelt's nomination for president at the Progressive Party's convention in Chicago. Reflecting on the event, he later told Addams that "it is idle now to argue whether women can play their part in politics, because in this convention we saw the accomplished fact."

Dorothy Mittlemen Sigel was a member of the Marionette club and the daughter of Jewish immigrants. In 1920, Wallace Kirkland photographed her as she performed in *Le Bourgeois Gentilhomme,* one of dozens of Hull-House productions in which she participated. Mittleman later married Louis Sigel, went on to raise a family, and became an active member of several civic organizations in Chicago and the North Shore.

Hilda Satt found work at the age of thirteen in a West Side knitting factory. But as a Nineteenth Ward child, she also found Hull-House and a liberal social education. When Satt was fired for union activities, Jane Addams helped her to find work writing articles for *Butterfly,* a Chicago magazine. In 1912, she married William Polacheck and moved to Wisconsin, where she organized a chapter of the Women's International League for Peace and Freedom and joined the National Women's Party. When her husband died, she moved back to Chicago, where she found employment in the Illinois Writer's Project during the New Deal. She wrote her autobiography, *I Came a Stranger: The Story of a Hull-House Girl*, in the fifties, although it was not published until 1989.

Eleanor Smith directed the Hull-House Music School from 1893 to 1935. Although it was designed to "give a thorough musical education to a limited number of children," the music school's scope was enormous. Under the guidance of Smith and her assistants, children mastered the violin, sang folk songs from their national heritage, and performed in countless recitals. Smith was on the faculty of the Chicago Kindergarten College and wrote a number of books on musical pedagogy, including the *Eleanor Smith Music Course*.

Mary Rozet Smith was a non-resident Hull-House volunteer, Jane Addams's longtime companion, and one of Hull-House's most significant financial benefactors. Hull-House records show that she provided unending monetary relief, endowing projects both large and small. Mary Rozet Smith served as Addams's traveling companion and devoted pen pal, later materializing their "healing domesticity" with the copurchase of a house near Bar Harbor, Maine, in 1904. Their relationship would last forty years.

Ellen Gates Starr met Jane Addams at Rockford College and celebrated September 11 as the anniversary of their first meeting. It was Starr who prodded Addams to leave her family, to come to Chicago, and to open a settlement. Starr began the Chicago Public School Art Society in 1895 and opened a bookbindery at Hull-House. She later became a labor activist and was arrested during a 1914 waitresses strike. Starr diverged from Addams and her secular Protestantism when she was later ordained a Catholic nun.

Alzina Stevens was born into a middle-class Maine family but became a wage earner at the age of thirteen when her father died. She lost her right index finger while working in a textile mill, which later inspired her to research child labor and occupational safety as a Hull-House resident. When she died prematurely in 1900, the Hull-House Woman's Club remembered their former president as "womanly and motherly," whose "life work has opened large possibilities to the club women of Chicago. The Vacation school, the Parental school, the Juvenile court, better industrial conditions for women and children—these she loved and these she worked for." The Woman's Club expressed their "appreciation of her life work" by hanging her picture over the living room mantel at Hull-House.

George Twose was a permanent fixture in the Hull-House Men's Club and in the Men's Club Building on South Halsted Street. He was particularly involved with artists' clubs at the Bowen Country Club, where he was dean of the Hull-House Summer School. In 1897, Twose founded the Chicago Arts and Crafts Society and became its first president. The Englishman also taught woodworking at the settlement, was active in Hull-House theater, and became involved in dozens of activist projects in the Nineteenth Ward.

Rachel Yarros was a physician and birth control activist who lived at Hull-House with her husband, Victor Yarros, from 1907 to 1927. She gave clinical instruction to medical students in Nineteenth Ward homes. A professor of obstetrics and lecturer on sex hygiene at the University of Illinois Medical College, Yarros was executive officer of the Illinois Society for Birth Control, secretary of the Illinois Social Hygiene League, and author of *The Modern Woman and Sex*. She also delivered over three thousand settlement children. **Victor Yarros** worked as Clarence Darrow's law partner as an editorial writer for the *Chicago Daily News*. He often acted as a political liaison between Hull-House workers and city officials.

Manuscript Collections Consulted

Edith and Grace Abbott Papers, University of Chicago

Jane Addams Memorial Collection (Microfilm Edition), University of Illinois at Chicago

Jane Addams Papers, Swarthmore College Peace Collection, Swarthmore College

Jane Addams School of Social Work Papers, UIC

Louise deKoven Bowen Papers, Chicago Historical Society

Helen Culver Papers, University of Illinois at Chicago

Dewey Family Papers, Southern Illinois University

Richard T. Ely Papers, State Historical Society of Wisconsin

Alice Hamilton Papers, Arthur and Elizabeth Schlesinger Library, Radcliffe College

Hamilton Family Papers, Arthur and Elizabeth Schlesinger Library, Radcliffe College

Hutchinson Papers, Newberry Library, Chicago

Italians in Chicago Project, Oral Histories of Chicago's Italian-Americans, Special Collections, University of Illinois at Chicago

Florence Kelley Papers, Columbia University

Nicholas Kelley Papers, New York Public Library

The Schlesinger Library on the History of Women in America, Radcliffe College

Julia Lathrop Papers, Rockford College Archives

Juvenile Protective Association Papers, University of Illinois, Chicago

Oral History Archives of Chicago Polonia, Chicago Historical Society

Henry Demarest Lloyd Papers, State Historical Society of Wisconsin

George Herbert Mead Papers, University of Chicago

Social Welfare History Archives, University of Minnesota

Ellen Gates Starr Papers, Sophia Smith Collection, Smith College

Madeleine Wallin Sikes Papers, Chicago Historical Society

Graham Taylor Papers, Newberry Library, Chicago

Notes

CHAPTER 1

1. Ellen Gates Starr to Mary Blaisdell, July 25, 1892, Ellen Gates Starr Papers, Sophia Smith Collection, Smith College (hereafter cited as EGS Papers).

2. Starr to Blaisdell, July 25, 1892.

3. Walter Benjamin, *Illuminations: Essays and Reflections,* ed. Hannah Arendt, trans. Harry Zohn (New York: Schocken, 1968), 255.

4. Antonio Gramsci, *Prison Notebooks,* trans. Quintin Hoare and Geoffrey Nowell Smith (London: Lawrence and Wishart, 1971) 276.

5. The Social Welfare History Archives at the University of Minnesota are devoted to tracking this process. See Clarke Chambers, "Toward a Redefinition of Welfare History," *Journal of American History* 73 (1986): 407–33, and *Seedtime of Reform: American Social Service and Social Action, 1918–1933* (Minneapolis: U of Minnesota P, 1963). For recent feminist histories of welfare, see Linda Gordon ed., *Women, the State, and Welfare* (Madison: U of Wisconsin P, 1990), and *Pitied but Not Entitled: Single Mothers and the History of Welfare, 1890–1935* (Cambridge: Harvard UP, 1994); Molly Ladd-Taylor, *Mother-Work: Women, Child Welfare, and the State, 1890–1930* (Urbana: U of Illinois P, 1994); Sonya Michel and Seth Koven, eds., *Mothers of a New World: Maternalist Politics and the Origins of Welfare States* (New York: Routledge, 1993); Judith Trolander, *Professionalism and Social Change: From the Settlement House Movement to Neighborhood Centers, 1886 to the Present* (New York: Columbia UP, 1987); Robyn Muncy, *Creating a Female Dominion in American Reform, 1890–1935* (New York: Oxford UP, 1991).

6. See, for example, Mary Jo Deegan, *Jane Addams and the Men of the Chicago School, 1892–1918* (New Brunswick: Transaction, 1988); and Andrew Feffer, *The Chicago Pragmatists and American Progressivism* (Ithaca: Cornell UP, 1993).

7. Kathryn Kish Sklar, "Coming to Terms with a Colossus: Tales of a Reluctant Biographer," in *Writing Women's Lives: The Challenge of Feminist Biography,* ed. Joyce Antler, Elizabeth Perry and Sara Alpern (Urbana: U of Illinois P, 1992).

8. Hannah Arendt, *The Human Condition* (Chicago: U of Chicago P, 1958); Jacques Donzelot, *The Policing of Families,* trans. Robert Hurley (New York: Pantheon, 1976). Some argue that this interpretation derives from undernuanced readings of Michel Foucault's *Discipline and Punish: The Birth of the Prison,* trans. Alan Sheridan (New York: Vintage, 1979) and *History of Sexuality: An Introduction,* trans. Robert Hurley (New York Vintage, 1980). See

critiques of these readings in history, philosophy, and literary studies respectively: Linda Gordon, "Family Violence, Feminism, and Social Control," in *Women, State, and Welfare,* 178–98; Nancy Fraser, "Foucault on Modern Power: Empirical Insights and Normative Confusions," in *Unruly Practices: Power, Discourse, and Gender in Contemporary Social Theory* (Minneapolis: U of Minnesota P, 1989); and Lora Romero, *Home Fronts: Domesticity and Its Critics in the Antebellum United States* (Durham: Duke UP, 1997), 19, 25, 50.

9. Clifford Geertz, *Local Knowledge: Further Essays in Interpretive Anthropology* (New York: Basic Books, 1983), 167. See also James Scott on *metis* in *Domination and the Arts of Resistance: The Hidden Transcript* (New Haven: Yale UP, 1989) and *Seeing Like a State: How Certain Schemes to Improve the Human Condition Have Failed* (New Haven: Yale UP, 1998).

10. Background historical literature on the settlement includes Allen Davis, *Spearheads for Reform: The Social Settlements and the Progressive Movement, 1890–1914* (1967; New Brunswick: Rutgers UP, 1984), and with Mary Lynn McKree Bryan, eds., *One Hundred Years at Hull-House* (1969; Bloomington: Indiana UP, 1990); Rivka Shpak Lissak, *Pluralism and Progressives: Hull House and the New Immigrant, 1890–1919* (Chicago: U of Chicago P, 1989); Mina Carson, *Settlement Folk* (Chicago: U of Chicago P, 1990). Kathryn Kish Sklar, *Florence Kelley and the Nation's Work: The Rise of Women's Political Culture, 1830–1900* (New Haven: Yale UP, 1995), "Hull-House in the 1890s: A Community of Women Reformers," *Signs* 10 (1985): 658–77, and "Who Funded Hull-House?" in *Lady Bountiful Revisited,* ed. Kathleen McCarthy (New Brunswick: Rutgers UP, 1990), 94–115; Elisabeth Lasch-Quinn, *Black Neighbors: Race and the Limits of Reform in the American Settlement Movement, 1890–1945* (Chapel Hill: U of North Carolina P, 1993); Helen Lefkowitz Horowitz, "Hull-House as Woman's Space," *Chicago History* (winter 1983): 40–55; Jill Conway, "Women Reformers and American Culture," *Journal of Social History* 5 (winter 1971–72): 164–77; John Rousmaniere, "Cultural Hybrid in the Slums," *American Quarterly* 22 (1970): 45–66. Hull-House figures prominently in a variety of other works of American history such as Eileen Boris, *Art and Labor; Ruskin, Morris, and the Craftsman Ideal in America* (Philadelphia: Temple UP, 1986), and her *Home to Work: Motherhood and the Politics of Industrial Homework in the United States* (Cambridge: Cambridge UP, 1994); Muncy, *Creating a Female Dominion;* Trolander, *Professionalism and Social Change;* Dolores Hayden, *The Grand Domestic Revolution* (Cambridge: Harvard UP, 1982); Lillian Faderman, *Odd Girls and Twilight Lovers: A History of Lesbian Life in Twentieth-Century America* (New York: Penguin, 1991); Helen Lefkowitz Horowitz, *Culture and the City* (1976; Chicago: U of Chicago P, 1989); Anna Firor Scott, *Natural Allies: Women's Associations in American History* (Urbana: U of Illinois P, 1992). See Allen F. Davis's biography, *American Heroine: The Life and Legend of Jane Addams* (Oxford: Oxford UP, 1973). Several more biographies of Addams are in process, including ones from Louise Wilby Knight, Gioia Dilberto, Barbara Garland Polikoff, and Jean Bethke Elshtain; see also Barbara Sicherman, *Alice Hamilton: A Life in Letters* (Cambridge: Harvard UP, 1984).

11. See for example, Thomas Haskell, *The Emergence of Social Science* (Ur-

bana: U of Illinois P, 1977); George Stocking, *Race, Culture, and Evolution* (Chicago: U of Chicago P, 1982); Paul Boyer, *Urban Masses and Moral Order in America* (Cambridge: Harvard UP, 1978); Dorothy Ross, *The Origins of American Social Science* (Cambridge: Cambridge UP, 1991). For related literary analyses of Progressive Era rhetorics, see Alan Trachtenberg, *The Incorporation of America: Culture and Society in the Gilded Age* (New York: Hill and Wang, 1982); Philip Fisher, "Appearing and Disappearing in Public: Social Space in Late Nineteenth-Century Literature and Culture," in *Reconstructing American Literary History*, ed. Sacvan Bercovitch (Cambridge: Harvard UP, 1986), and *Hard Facts: Setting and Form in the American Novel* (New York: Oxford UP, 1985); Amy Kaplan, *The Social Construction of American Realism* (Chicago: U of Chicago P, 1988).

12. Jane Addams, *Twenty Years at Hull-House* (New York: Macmillan, 1910), 104.

13. On "high modernism," see Scott, *Thinking Like a State;* Robert Wiebe, *The Search for Order* (New York: Hill and Wang, 1967); Jacob Karger, *The Sentinels of Order: A Study of Social Control and the Minneapolis Settlement House Movement, 1915–1950* (Lanham, MD: University Press of America, 1987); Lissak, *Pluralism and Progressives,* 25.

14. See for example, Kenneth Burke, *A Grammar of Motives* (Berkeley and Los Angeles: U of California P, 1945); J. L. Austin, *How to Do Things with Words* (Cambridge: Harvard UP, 1962); Victor Turner, *The Ritual Process* (Chicago: Aldine, 1969), *Dramas, Fields, and Metaphors* (Ithaca: Cornell UP, 1974), and *The Anthropology of Performance* (New York: Performing Arts Journal P, 1986); Erving Goffman, *Presentation of Self in Everyday Life* (Garden City, NY: Doubleday, 1959), and *Frame Analysis* (New York: Harper and Row, 1974); see also John MacAloon, ed., *Rite, Drama, Festival, Spectacle: Rehearsals toward a Theory of Cultural Performance* (Philadelphia: Institute for the Study of Human Issues, 1984); Gregory Bateson, *Naven* (Stanford: Stanford UP, 1977); Richard Bauman and Joel Sherzer, *Explorations in the Ethnography of Speaking* (New York: Cambridge UP, 1974); Clifford Geertz's review of "Blurred Genres," *American Scholar* 49.2 (1986): 165–82; and Marvin Carlson's *Performance: A Critical Introduction* (New York: Routledge, 1996).

15. Richard Schechner, *Between Theatre and Anthropology* (Philadelphia: U of Pennsylvania P, 1985); see also Schechner's *Essays in Performance Theory* (New York: Drama Book Specialists, 1977), and *The End of Humanism: Writings on Performance* (New York: Performing Arts Journal, 1982).

16. See Margaret Thompson Drewal's *Yoruba Ritual: Performers, Play, Agency* (Bloomington: Indiana UP, 1992), and "The State of Research on Performance in Africa," *African Studies Review* 34.3 (1991): 1–64. For instance, Drewal's theory of performance as "repetition with critical difference" reworks Schechner's "restoration of behavior" and incorporates social and literary theory from Pierre Bourdieu, *Outline of a Theory of Practice,* trans. Richard Nice (Cambridge: Cambridge UP, 1977), and *The Logic of Practice,* trans. Richard Nice (Stanford: Stanford UP, 1990); Anthony Giddens, *The Constitution of Society* (Berkeley and Los Angeles: U of California P, 1982); Michel de

Certeau, *The Practice of Everyday Life,* trans. Steven Rendall (Berkeley and Los Angeles: U of California P, 1984); Henry Louis Gates, *The Signifying Monkey* (New York: Oxford UP, 1988); and Linda Hutcheon, *A Theory of Parody: The Teaching of Twentieth Century Art Forms* (New York: Methuen, 1985), and *A Poetics of Postmodernism: History, Theory, Fiction* (New York: Routledge, 1988). While differently situated, similar epistemological debates appear in the work of other scholars. See Eve Kosofsky Sedgwick and Andrew Parker, eds., *Performance and Performativity* (New York: Routledge, 1995); Judith Butler, *Gender Trouble: Feminism and the Subversion of Identity* (Routledge: New York, 1990), *Bodies That Matter: On the Discursive Limits of "Sex"* (New York: Routledge, 1993), and *Excitable Speech: The Politics of the Performative* (New York: Routledge, 1997); Kimberley Bentson, "Being There: Performance as Mise-en-Scene, Abscene, Obscene, and Other Scene," *PMLA* 107.3 (1992): 434–49; Dwight Conquergood, "Poetics, Play, Process, and Power: The Performative Turn in Anthropology," *Text and Performance Quarterly* 1 (winter 1989): 82–95; Henry Sayre, *The Object of Performance* (Chicago: U of Chicago P, 1989); Peggy Phelan, *Unmarked: The Politics of Performance* (New York: Routledge, 1993); Homi K. Bhabha, "Signs Taken for Wonders," *Critical Inquiry* 12 (1985): 144–65, and "DissemiNation: Time, Narrative, and the Margins of the Modern Nation," in *Nation as Narration,* ed. Homi K. Bhabha (New York: Routledge, 1990), 291–322; Josette Féral, "Performance and Theatricality: The Subject Demystified," trans. Terese Lyons, *Modern Drama* 25 (1982): 170–81; Sue-Ellen Case, *The Domain Matrix: Performing Lesbian at the End of Print Culture* (Bloomington: Indiana UP, 1996); Sue-Ellen Case, Philip Brett, and Susan Leigh Foster eds., *Cruising the Performative: Interventions into the Representation of Ethnicity, Nationality, and Sexuality* (Bloomington: Indiana UP, 1995), Janelle Reinelt and Joseph Roach, eds., *Critical Theory and Performance* (Ann Arbor: U of Michigan P, 1992); Elin Diamond, introduction to *Performance and Cultural Politics* (New York: Routledge, 1997).

17. Addams, *Twenty Years,* 96.

18. Mary H. Porter, "A Home on Halsted Street," *Advance,* July 11, 1889.

19. Richard Bauman places George Herbert Mead in the history of performance theory, locating Mead's idea of the "social self" as predecessor to the theories surveyed above, as well as to other work: Richard Bauman, "Performance," *International Encyclopedia of Communications,* vol. 3 (New York: Oxford UP, 1989), 266, and *Verbal Art as Performance* (Rowley, MA: Newbury House, 1977); and Dell Hymes, *Foundations in Sociolinguistics* (Philadelphia: U of Pennsylvania P, 1977). Richard Rorty is especially credited with the reinvigoration of pragmatism in the later twentieth century. See *Philosophy and the Mirror of Nature* (Princeton: Princeton UP, 1979), and Rorty, ed., *Consequences of Pragmatism* (Minneapolis: U of Minnesota P, 1982). For more philosophical and historical explorations of pragmatism, see R. W. Sleeper, *The Necessity of Pragmatism* (New Haven: Yale UP, 1986); Feffer, *Chicago Pragmatists;* Thomas Alexander, *John Dewey's Theory of Art, Experience, and Nature: The Horizons of Feeling* (New York: SUNY P, 1987); J. David Lewis and Richard L. Smith, *American Sociology and Pragmatism* (Chicago: U of Chicago P, 1980); Cornel

20. George Herbert Mead, "The Working Hypothesis in Social Reform," *American Journal of Sociology* 5 (1899): 370.

21. George Herbert Mead, "The Social Settlement: Its Basis and Function," *University of Chicago Record* 12 (1907–8): 110. See also, Feffer, *Chicago Pragmatists,* 149.

22. Charlene Haddock Seigfried, *Feminism and Pragmatism: Reweaving the Social Fabric* (Chicago: U of Chicago P, 1996). See Richard Rorty, "Feminism and Pragmatism," *Michigan Quarterly Review* 30 (1991): 231–58; and the responses of Nancy Fraser, "From Irony to Prophecy to Politics: A Response to Richard Rorty," *Michigan Quarterly Review* 30.2 (1991): 259–66; and Sabina Lovibond, "Feminism and Pragmatism: A Reply to Richard Rorty," *New Left Review* 193 (May–June 1992): 56–74. See also Lisa Heldke, "John Dewey and Evelyn Fox Keller: A Shared Epistemological Tradition," *Hypatia* 2.3 (1987): 129–40; and Susan Laird, "Women and Gender in John Dewey's Philosophy of Education," *Educational Theory* 38.1 (1988): 111–29; Gregory Fernando Pappas, "Dewey and Feminism: The Affective and Relationship in Dewey's Ethics," *Hypatia* 8.2 (1993): 78–95.

23. Seyla Benhabib, *Situating the Self* (New York: Routledge, 1991); Donna Haraway, "Situated Knowledges: The Science Question in Feminism and the Privilege of Partial Perspective," *Feminist Studies* 14 (1988): 575–99; Seyla Benahabib, Judith Butler, Drucilla Cornell, and Nancy Fraser, *Feminist Contentions: A Philosophical Exchange* (New York: Routledge, 1994); Iris Marion Young, *Intersecting Voices: Dilemmas of Gender, Political, Philosophical, and Policy* (Princeton: Princeton UP, 1997); Nancy Fraser, "Structuralism or Pragmatics," in *Justice Interruptus: Critical Reflections on the "Postsocialist" Condition* (New York: Routledge, 1997), and *Unruly Practices;* Alison Jaggar, ed., *Living with Contradictions: Controversies in Feminist Social Ethics* (Boulder: Westview, 1994).

24. Romero, *Home Fronts.*

25. John Dewey to A. Dewey, Oct. 9 and 10, 1894, Dewey Family Papers, Southern Illinois University (hereafter cited as DF Papers).

26. Feffer, *Chicago Pragmatists,* 122. See John Dewey, "School as Social Center," *Proceedings of the National Education Association* (1902): 374–83, where he uses the settlement as an example of the ideal educational environment. Many have contributed to a renewal of theoretical interest in pragmatism and pedagogy: Paolo Friere, *Pedagogy of the Oppressed,* trans. Myra Bergman Ramos (New York: Continuum, 1982); Henry A. Giroux and Peter McLaren, *Between Borders: Pedagogy and the Politics of Cultural Studies* (New York: Routledge, 1994); Peter McLaren, *Schooling as a Ritual Performance: Towards a Political Economy of Educational Symbols and Gestures* (Boston: Routledge and Kegan Paul, 1986); Henri A. Giroux, *Schooling and the Struggle for Public Life:*

Critical Pedagogy in the Modern Age (Minneapolis: U of Minnesota P, 1988); Peter McLaren and Peter Leonard, eds., *Paulo Freire: A Critical Encounter* (New York: Routledge, 1993).

27. Lawrence Grossberg's introduction to *Cultural Studies,* ed. Lawrence Grossberg, Paula Treichler, and Cary Nelson (New York: Routledge, 1992) gives an overview. The volume's bibliography demonstrates the impact of critics such as Raymond Williams, *Culture and Society* (Harmondsworth: Penguin, 1963), and *The Sociology of Culture* (New York: Schocken, 1982); Stuart Hall, *Media, Language, Culture* (London: Hutchinson, 1981); and Pierre Bourdieu, *Distinction: A Social Critique of the Judgement of Taste,* trans. Richard Nice (Cambridge: Harvard UP, 1984). Ian Hunter's "Aesthetics and Cultural Studies," (in *Cultural Studies,* 347–66) in turn critiques what he sees as the overdetermined quality of subsequent analyses in the field.

28. For the utility of this approach in the study of contemporary art forms, see the essays collected by W. J. T. Mitchell in *Art and the Public Sphere* (Chicago: U of Chicago P, 1990).

29. Turner on "liminality" in *The Ritual Process* and *Dramas, Fields, and Metaphors;* Laurence Senelick, ed., *Gender in Performance: The Presentation of Difference in the Performing Arts* (Hanover: U of New England P, 1992), introduction; this approach interacts with what historians Sara Evans and Harry Boyte define as "free spaces" or Nancy Fraser defines as "alternative counter-public spheres." See *Free Spaces: The Sources of Democratic Change in America* (New York: Harper and Row, 1986), and "Rethinking the Public Sphere," in *Habermas and the Public Sphere,* ed. Craig Calhoun (Cambridge: MIT Press, 1990), 109–42.

30. Jane Addams, *The Long Road of Woman's Memory* (New York: Macmillan, 1916); Alexander, *John Dewey's Theory.*

31. Boris, *Art and Labor;* David Whisnant, *All That Is Native and Fine: The Politics of Culture in an American Region* (Chapel Hill: U of North Carolina P, 1983).

32. Dorothea Moore, "A Day at Hull-House," *American Journal of Sociology* (1897): 629–32, 634–36, 638–40.

33. *Lines of Activity* roughly follows the spatial arc charted in figure 5; chapter 2 primarily focuses on the Original Mansion (1889) and anticipates the Smith Building (1895); Chapter 3 focuses on the Butler Building (1891), the Gymnasium with first Coffeehouse below (1893), and the Jane Club (1898); chapter 4 focuses on the Mansion and third story additions added to it and to the Butler (1896), the Apartments (1902), the Dining Hall (1905), and the new Front Door (1905); chapter 5 focuses on the Auditorium with new Coffeehouse and Theater (1899) and Bowen Hall (1904), anticipating the Music School; chapter 6 focuses on the Boys Club (1906) and Mary Crane Nursery (1907), anticipating the Immigrant's Protective League (I.P.L.) and the Juvenile Protective Association (J.P.A.).

34. Henri Lefebvre, *The Production of Space,* trans. Donald Nicholson-Smith (Oxford: Basil Blackwell, 1991), 110.

35. Lefebvre, *The Production of Space,* 137.

36. For differently framed reviews, see H. Aram Veeser, ed., *The New*

Historicism (New York: Routledge, 1989); and Lynn Hunt, ed., *The New Cultural History* (Berkeley and Los Angeles: U of California, 1989); Martin Jay, "The Textual Approach to Intellectual History," in *Fact and Fiction: German History and Literature, 1848–1924* (Berlin: Frandke Verlag, 1990), 77–86; Rhys Isaac, "On Explanation, Text, and Terrifying Power in Ethnographic History," *Yale Journal of Criticism* 6.1 (1993): 217–35; Robert Berkhofer Jr., "The Challenge of Poetics to (Normal) Historical Practice," in *The Rhetoric of Interpretation and the Interpretation of Rhetoric,* ed. Paul Hernadi (Durham: Duke UP, 1989), and "A New Context for a New American Studies," *American Quarterly* 41 (1989): 588–600; Peter de Bolla, "Disfiguring History," *Diacritics* (winter 1986): 49–57. On metahistorical theory in particular, see Dominick La Capra, *History and Criticism* (Ithaca: Cornell UP, 1985); Hayden White, *Tropics of Discourse* (Baltimore: Johns Hopkins UP, 1978), and *The Content of the Form* (Baltimore: Johns Hopkins UP, 1987); Michel de Certeau, *The Writing of History,* trans. Tom Conley (New York: Columbia UP, 1988); and the *Critical Inquiry* essays collected by James Chandler, Arnold Davidson, Harry Harootunian in *Questions of Evidence: Proof, Practice, and Persuasion across the Disciplines* (Chicago: U of Chicago P, 1991).

37. Scott, *Gender and the Politics of History* (New York: Columbia UP, 1988) 38; Joan Wallach Scott, "The Evidence of Experience," *Critical Inquiry* 17 (1991): 793.

38. John E. Toews, "Intellectual History after the Linguistic Turn: The Autonomy of Meaning and the Irreducibility of Experience" *American Historical Review* 92 (1987): 881–907; Christine Stansell, "A Response to Joan Scott," *International Labor and Working-Class History* 31 (spring 1987): 28. See also Bryan Palmer and Anson Rabinach's responses in the same issue of *ILWCH;* Louise Tilly, "Gender, Women's History, and Social History," *Social Science History* 13.4 (winter 1989): 439–61; Louise Newman, "Critical Theory and the History of Women," *Journal of Women's History* 2.3 (1991): 59–68.

39. Linda Gordon, "Review of Joan Scott," *Signs* (1990): 854.

40. Scott, "The Evidence of Experience," 786. She quotes Stansell, "Response to Joan Scott," 28.

41. Judith Butler and Joan Wallach Scott, introduction to *Feminists Theorize the Political* (New York: Routledge, 1992), xv.

42. Scott's use of Karen Swann's rereading of Delany actually lays the basis for a connection between the language question and theatrical mediation. Scott and Swann notice that Delany's epiphanic moment in *The Motion of Light and Water* is not unfettered *experience* but structured by the refractions and spill of a "dim blue light." The insight that lighting mediates experience is, to a theater designer, axiomatic.

43. Judith Lowder Newton, "Feminism and the 'New Historicism,' " in Veeser, *The New Historicism,* 165.

44. Della Pollock, "Making History Go," in *Exceptional Spaces: Essays in Performance and History* (Chapel Hill: U of North Carolina P, 1998), 27.

45. Moore 635.

46. Edward Soja, *Postmodern Geographies* (London: Verso, 1989); David Harvey, *The Condition of Postmodernity* (Oxford: Basil Blackwell, 1989), and his

earlier *Social Justice and the City* (London: Edward Arnold, 1973); Allan Pred, "Structuration, Biography Formation, and Knowledge," *Environment and Planning* 2 (1984): 251–75, *Lost Words and Lost Worlds* (Cambridge: Cambridge UP, 1990), and *Making Histories and Constructing Human Geographies* (Boulder: Westview P, 1990).

47. Lefebvre, *The Production of Space,* 7.

48. Giddens, *The Constitution of Society,* 49. His extended definition of practical consciousness (375) resonates with the classical notion of *metis* (Scott, *Thinking Like a State*). "All human beings are knowledgeable agents. That is to say, all social actors know a great deal about the conditions and consequences of what they do in their day-to-day lives. Such knowledge is not wholly propositional in character, nor is it incidental to their activities. Knowledgeability embedded in practical consciousness exhibits an extraordinary complexity—a complexity that often remains completely unexplored in orthodox sociological approaches, especially those associated with objectivism. Actors are also ordinarily able discursively to describe what they do and their reasons for doing it. However, for the most part these faculties are geared to the flow of day-to-day conduct. The rationalization of conduct becomes the discursive offering of reasons only if individuals are asked by others why they acted as they did."

49. Pierre Bourdieu and Loïc J. D. Wacquant, *An Invitation to Reflexive Sociology* (Chicago: U of Chicago P, 1992), 127; the connection between Bourdieu and Dewey is suggested in this book. See also de Certeau, *Practice of Everyday Life,* 91–130. John Fiske makes a plea for such an orientation in cultural studies by way of Bourdieu: "Cultural Studies and the Culture of Everyday Life" in Grossberg, Treichler, and Nelson, *Cultural Studies,* 154–65.

50. Bourdieu, *Distinction,* 77.

51. Jane Addams, *Democracy and Social Ethics* (New York: Macmillan, 1902), 14.

52. Addams, *Twenty Years,* xviii.

53. Joseph Roach, *Cities of the Dead: Circum-Atlantic Performance* (New York: Columbia UP, 1996), 26–27.

54. Paul Connerton, *How Societies Remember* (Cambridge: Cambridge UP, 1989), 72.

55. Pierre Nora, "Between Memory and History: *Les Lieux de Mémoire,*" *Representations* 26 (spring 1989): 7–25; see Michael Kammen's study of American memorial spaces, *Mystic Cords of Memory: The Transformation of Tradition in American Culture* (New York: Alfred A. Knopf, 1991); and Jacquelyn Dowd Hall's reflections on Nora, " 'You Must Remember This': Autobiography as Social Critique," *Journal of American History* 85 (1998): 439–65.

56. See important essays such as Gayle Rubin, "The Traffic in Women: Notes on the 'Political Economy' of Sex," in *Toward an Anthropology of Women,* ed. Rayna Reiter (New York: Monthly Review P, 1975); and Micaela di Leonardo, "The Female World of Cards and Holidays," *Signs* 12 (1987): 246–61. See Romero's *Home Fronts* and Lynn Wardley's forthcoming book *The Angel at the Grave* on the gendering of cultural transmission. Feminist geography specifically interprets the spatial politics of such gendered spheres. See Gillian Rose, *Feminism and Geography* (Minneapolis: U of Minnesota P,

1993); Daphne Spain, *Gender Spaces* (Chapel Hill: U of North Carolina P, 1992): Gill Valentine, ed., *Mapping Desire: Geographies of Sexualities* (London: Routledge, 1995); Nancy Duncan, ed., *Bodyspace* (London: Routledge, 1996). Judith Butler expands upon Rubin's insight into the interdependent inscriptions of heterosexuality and kinship in *Gender Trouble*, 35–78. Chapter 4 of this book will interpret Hull-House as a partial and unannounced loosening of this matrix.

57. Gordon, *Pitied but Not Entitled*, 1.

58. Roach, *Cities of the Dead*, 2–3; René Girard, *Violence and the Sacred*, trans. Patrick Gregory (Baltimore: Johns Hopkins UP, 1981); Michael Taussig, *Mimesis and Alterity: A Particular History of the Senses* (New York: Routledge, 1993), and *The Nervous System* (New York: Routledge, 1992).

59. Nancy Fraser and Linda Gordon, "A Genealogy of 'Dependency': Tracing a Keyword of the U.S. Welfare State," *Signs* 19 (1994): 309–36; Molly Ladd-Taylor and Lauri Umansky, eds., *"Bad" Mothers: The Politics of Blame in Twentieth-Century America* (New York: New York University P, 1998).

60. The title of a formative collection in the American women's history: Lois Banner and Mary Hartman, eds., *Clio's Consciousness Raised* (New York: Harper and Row, 1974).

61. Jacques Derrida, *Archive Fever*, trans. Eric Prenowitz (Chicago: U of Chicago P, 1996), 43. For further investigation, see the special issue "Women and Memory," ed. Margaret A. Lourie, Donna C. Stanton, and Martha Vicinus, *Michigan Quarterly Review* 26 (1987).

62. Derrida, *Archive Fever*, 2, 36, 67.

63. Elin Diamond, *Unmaking Mimesis: Essays on Feminism and Theater* (New York: Routledge, 1997), 142.

64. Diamond, *Unmaking Mimesis*, 146–47. See also Taussig on the dialectical image as "montage" in *The Nervous System*, 44–45, as well as his *Mimesis and Alterity*. See also Rebecca Schneider's connections between Walter Benjamin and performance in *The Explicit Body in Performance* (New York: Routledge, 1997). For an earlier montage experiment, see Shannon Jackson, "Hull-House in Performance: Museum, Micro-fiche, and Historiography," in Pollock, *Exceptional Spaces*.

65. Addams, *Twenty Years*, xviii.

66. Phelan, *Unmarked*, 146.

67. Peggy Phelan, *Mourning Sex: Performing Public Memories* (London: Routledge, 1997), 3.

68. Pollock, *Exceptional Spaces*, 1–45; see also Jacquelyn Dowd Hall, "Open Secrets: Memory, Imagination, and the Refashioning of Southern Identity," *American Quarterly* 50 (1998): 109–23.

69. Phelan, *Mourning Sex*, 3.

CHAPTER 2

1. "Oprah's Closet Cache," *Chicago Sun-Times*, June 19, 1994, People Plus, p. 2.

2. "Oprah Winfrey Commits $6 Million for CHA Families," *Chicago Tribune,* Sept. 14, 1994, N3.

3. Gordon, *Pitied but Not Entitled,* 1.

4. Linda Gordon, "The New Feminist Scholarship on the Welfare State," in *Women, State, and Welfare,* 23.

5. Foucault, *History of Sexuality.* See Christina Simmons, "Modern Sexuality and the Myth of Victorian Repression," in *Passion and Power: Sexuality in History,* ed. Kathy Peiss and Christina Simmons (Philadelphia: Temple UP, 1989), 157–77; and Judith Butler's comparison of *The History of Sexuality* to the earlier *Discipline and Punish* in *The Psychic Life of Power: Theories in Subjection* (Stanford: Stanford UP, 1997), 83–105. In *Home Fronts,* Lora Romero critiques the persistence of this unexamined tendency in works such as Ann Douglas, *The Feminization of American Culture* (New York: Avon, 1977); D. A. Miller, *The Novel and the Police* (Berkeley and Los Angeles: U of California P, 1988); and Nancy Armstrong, *Desire and Domestic Fiction* (New York: Oxford UP, 1987).

6. Addams, "The Subjective Necessity," in *Twenty Years,* 13.

7. Addams, "Filial Relations," in *Democracy and Social Ethics,* 95–96. For an analysis of this metaphor see Louise Wilby Knight, "Biography's Window on Social Change: Benevolence and Justice in Jane Addams's 'A Modern Lear,'" *Journal of Women's History* 9.1 (spring 1997): 111–38. The significance of such a familial experience in the lives of other Hull-House women is discussed in Virginia Kemp Fish, "The Hull House Circle: Women's Friendships and Achievements," in *Gender, Ideology, and Action,* ed. Janet Sharistanian (New York: Greenwood, 1986), 185–227; and in Rebecca L. Sherrick, "Private Visions, Public Lives: The Hull-House Women in the Progressive Era," Ph.D. diss., Northwestern University, 1980.

8. Such father-daughter conflicts became a recognizable trope in the discourse of female reform, fictional and otherwise. See Elia Peattie's reprinted 1914 novel, *The Precipice,* intro. Sidney H. Bremer (Urbana: University of Illinois P, 1989), 20.

9. Judith Butler developed the notion of citational performance in *Gender Trouble,* in *Bodies That Matter,* and in several essays and book chapters.

10. Jean Bethke Elshtain, "A Return to Hull House: Reflections on Jane Addams," *Cross Currents* 38.3 (1988): 260.

11. Mary Simkovitch, "Settlements' Relation to Religion," *Annals of the American Academy of Political and Social Science* 30.3 (1907): 62.

12. Martin Marty, *Modern American Religion: The Irony of It All, 1893–1919* (Chicago: U of Chicago P, 1986), 76. See also, Susan Curtis, *A Consuming Faith: The Social Gospel and Modern American Culture* (Baltimore: Johns Hopkins UP, 1991); Richard Ely, *Social Aspects of Christianity and Other Essays* (New York: Thomas Y. Crowell and Co., 1889); and Ralph Luker, *The Social Gospel in Black and White: American Racial Reform, 1885–1912* (Chapel Hill: U of North Carolina P, 1991). For an elaboration on the settlement's connection to such ideas, see Carson, *Settlement Folk,* 10–26.

13. Charles Sheldon, *In His Steps* (Chicago: Advance Publishing Co., 1897).

14. Addams, "The Social Situation: Religious Education and Contemporary Social Conditions," *Religious Education* 6 (June 1911): 146. See also Jane Addams, "The Reaction of Modern Life upon Religious Education," *Religious Education* 4 (April 1909): 23–39, and "Social Settlements in Illinois," *Transactions of the Illinois State Historical Society* (1906): 162–71. On the religious backgrounds of Hull-House reformers, see Eleanor Joyce Stebner, "The Women of Hull-House: A Study in Spirituality, Vocation, and Friendship," Ph.D. diss., Northwestern University, 1994.

15. Simkovitch, "Settlements' Relation to Religion," 64.

16. Ellen Gates Starr to Mary Blaisdell, Feb. 23, 1889; EGS Papers. For a history of mission-based social reform, see Vivia H. Divers, *The "Black Hole" or The Missionary Experience of a Girl in the Slums, 1891–2* (Chicago: private publisher, 1893); Timothy Smith, *Revivalism and Social Reform in Mid–Nineteenth Century America* (New York: Abingdon, 1957); Norris Magnuson, *Salvation in the Slums: Evangelical Social Work, 1865–1920* (Metuchen, NJ: Scarecrow P, 1977); Robert Crunden, *Ministers of Reform* (Urbana: U of Illinois P, 1982).

17. Starr to Blaisdell, Feb. 23, 1889.

18. Addams, *Twenty Years,* 98.

19. In *The Chicago Pragmatists and American Progressivism,* Andrew Feffer's analysis of Protestantism's conceptual role in the development of pragmatist philosophy suggest that such links are more than coincidental.

20. Carson, *Settlement Folk,* especially chapters 2 and 3; Christopher Lasch, ed., *The Social Thought of Jane Addams* (Indianapolis: Bobbs-Merrill, 1965), and Christopher Lasch, *The New Radicalism in America, 1889–1963* (New York: Alfred A. Knopf, 1965).

21. Davis, *Spearheads for Reform,* 6.

22. Samuel Barnett, "Ways of 'Settlements' and of 'Missions,' " *Nineteenth Century* 42 (Dec. 1897): 975.

23. Addams, *Twenty Years,* 74.

24. See T. Jackson Lears, *No Place of Grace* (Chicago: U of Chicago P, 1994); Tom Lutz, *American Nervousness, 1904* (Ithaca: Cornell UP). Classic studies of Progressive Era reform emphasize this structure of feeling; see especially Richard Hofstadter, *The Age of Reform* (New York: Alfred A. Knopf, 1955); and Lasch, *New Radicalism in America.* Thorsten Veblen advanced the critique of privilege in *The Theory of the Leisure Class* (1899; New York: August M. Kelley, 1965).

25. See Helen Lefkowitz Horowitz, *Alma Mater: Design and Experience in the Women's Colleges from Their 19th-Century Beginnings to the 1930s* (New York: Alfred A. Knopf, 1984); and Barbara Miller Soloman, *In the Company of Educated Women: A History of Women in Higher Education in America* (New Haven: Yale UP, 1985).

26. Starr to Blaisdell, Feb. 23, 1889.

27. Martha Banta, *Imaging American Women: Idea and Ideals in Cultural History* (New York: Columbia UP, 1987); Carroll Smith-Rosenberg, "Bourgeois Discourse and the Progressive Era," and "New Woman as Androgyne," in

Disorderly Conduct: Visions of Gender in Victorian America (New York: Alfred A. Knopf, 1985), 177–81, 245–96.

28. Starr to Blaisdell, Feb. 23, 1889.

29. Elaine Showalter, *The Female Malady: Women, Madness, and Culture in England, 1830–1980* (New York: Pantheon, 1985), 138; and Conway, "Women Reformers," 165. See also selections from Rosalind Rosenberg, *Beyond Separate Spheres: Intellectual Roots of Modern Feminism* (New Haven: Yale UP, 1982); Judith Walzer Leavitt's edited collection, *Women and Health in America: A Historical Reader* (Madison: U of Wisconsin P, 1984); and Nancy Cott, *The Grounding of Modern Feminism* (New Haven: Yale UP, 1987).

30. "To Meet on Common Ground," *Chicago Tribune*, March 8, 1889. On women's relationship to spiritual service see Rosemary Skinner Keller, ed., *Spirituality and Social Responsibility: Vocational Vision of Women in the United Methodist Tradition* (Nashville: Abingdon P, 1993); Carol Ochs, *Women and Spirituality* (Totowa, NJ: Rowman and Allanheld, 1983); and Amanda Porterfield, *Feminine Spirituality in America: From Sarah Edwards to Martha Graham* (Philadelphia: Temple UP, 1980).

31. Many feminist histories track the movement from separate-spheres ideology to a limited sanctioning of women's public role. See Barbara Welter, "The Cult of True Womanhood, 1820–1860," *American Quarterly* 18 (1966): 151–74; Nancy Cott, *The Bonds of Womanhood: "Women's Sphere" in New England, 1780–1835* (New Haven: Yale UP, 1977); Mary P. Ryan, *Cradle of the Middle-Class: Family and Community in Oneida County, New York, 1780–1865* (Cambridge: Cambridge UP, 1981), and *Women in Public: Between Banners and Ballots, 1825–1880* (Baltimore: Johns Hopkins UP, 1990); Linda Kerber, "Separate Spheres, Female Worlds, Women's Place: The Rhetoric of Women's History," *Journal of American History* 75 (1988): 9–39; Paula Baker, "The Domestication of Politics," in *Unequal Sisters*, ed. Carol DuBois and Vicki Ruiz (New York: Routledge, 1990), 66–91; Nancy Cott, "Equality versus Difference," in *A Heritage of Her Own*, ed. Nancy Cott and Elizabeth Pleck (New York: Simon and Schuster, 1979); Joan Landes, "Women and the Public Sphere: A Modern Perspective," *Social Analysis* 15 (Aug. 1984): 20–31; Berkshire Conference on the History of Women, *Gendered Domains: Rethinking Public and Private in Women's History* (Ithaca: Cornell UP, 1992). Jean Bethke Elshtain speculates on Addams's relationship to this binary in *Democracy on Trial* (New York: Basic Books, 1995), 128–29.

32. Starr to Blaisdell, Feb. 23, 1889.

33. Addams, *Twenty Years*, 78. Having refused an offer of marriage from her stepbrother, Addams joined with Starr in a commitment to each other as they ventured upon the Hull-House scheme. While chapter 4 more explicitly considers the contemporary speculation into the nature of noncontemporary sexuality—and discusses Addams's eventual relationship with longtime companion Mary Rozet Smith—it is worth noting that this mixture of romantic and domestic discourse could rationalize an endeavor that ultimately challenged privatized and heteronormative conceptions of marriage and family.

34. Starr to Blaisdell, Feb. 23, 1889.

35. Starr to Blaisdell, Feb. 23, 1889.

36. Starr to Blaisdell, Feb. 23, 1889.

37. Kelley, *The Autobiography of Florence Kelley: Notes of Sixty Years,* ed. Kathryn Kish Sklar (Chicago: Charles H. Kerr, 1986), 78.

38. Dorothy Mittelman Sigel, interviews by the author, October 1994, May 1995. See depiction of such scenarios in Peattie, *The Precipice,* 24. References to different financial arrangements occur throughout the ensuing chapters and in the appendix.

39. Muncy, *Creating a Female Dominion,* 47.

40. Expenses soon far exceeded the resources of Addams, who, by 1893, had contributed a total of $14,684 to its operations. Bowen and Smith tapped the coffers of their family wealth time and again over the next forty years— writing checks for roof repairs and band uniforms, new furnaces and new buildings. See Sklar, "Who Funded Hull-House?" 96.

41. See in the context of Chicago history in this period, Louise Bessie Pierce, *A History of Chicago: The Rise of the Modern City, 1871–1892,* vol. 3 (Chicago: U of Chicago P, 1957); William Cronon, *Nature's Metropolis: Chicago and the Great West* (New York: W. W. Norton, 1991); Henry Binford, *The First Suburbs: Residential Communities on the Boston Periphery* (Chicago: U of Chicago P, 1984); and Donald Miller, *City of the Century: The Epic of Chicago and the Making of America* (New York: Simon and Schuster, 1996).

42. Starr to Blaisdell, Feb. 23, 1889.

43. Ellen Gates Starr to Starr family, Nov. 3, 1889, EGS Papers.

44. Mary Argenzio, interview, July 2, 1980, Italians in Chicago Project, Special Collections, University of Illinois, Chicago.

45. Theodore Dreiser, *Sister Carrie* (1900: New York: American Library, 1964).

46. William Stead, *If Christ Came to Chicago* (1894; New York: Hill and Wang, 1957); Lincoln Steffens, "Chicago: Half Free and Fighting On," in *The Shame of the Cities* (1904; New York: Hill and Wang, 1957), 162–94.

47. Carl Degler, *In Search of Human Nature: The Decline and Revival of Darwinism in American Social Thought* (New York: Oxford UP, 1991); Gillian Beer, *Darwin's Plots: Evolutionary Narrative in Darwin* (London: Routledge and Kegan Paul, 1983); Stocking, *Race, Culture, and Evolution;* Eric Wolf, *Europe and the People without History* (Berkeley and Los Angeles: U of California P, 1982); Gwendolyn Mink, *Old Labor and New Immigrants in American Political Development: Union, Party, and State, 1875–1920* (Ithaca: Cornell UP, 1986); John Higham, *Strangers in the Land: Patterns of American Nativism, 1860–1925,* 2nd ed. (New Brunswick, NJ: Rutgers UP, 1988). See also Lynn Wardley's forthcoming book *The Angel at the Grave* on the persistence of evolutionary paradigms in American literature and culture.

48. Charles French, ed., *Biographical History of the American Irish in Chicago* (Chicago, 1897); Steven P. Erie, *Rainbow's End: Irish-Americans and the Dilemmas of the Urban Machine Politics, 1840–1985* (Berkeley and Los Angeles: U of California P, 1988); Hasia Diner, *Erin's Daughters: Irish Immigrant Women in the Nineteenth Century* (Baltimore: Johns Hopkins UP, 1983).

49. On late-nineteenth-century U.S. constructions of whiteness, see Noel Ignatiev, *How the Irish Became White* (London: Routledge, 1995); David Roeddiger, *The Wages of Whiteness: Race and the Making of the American Working Class* (London: Verso, 1991), and *Towards the Abolition of Whiteness: Essays on Race, Politics, and Working Class History* (London: Verso, 1994).

50. Teresa De Falco, interview, Apr. 28, 1980, Italians in Chicago Project, University of Illinois, Chicago.

51. Dominic Candeloro, "Chicago's Italians: A Survey of the Ethnic Factor, 1850–1990," in *Ethnic Chicago: A Multicultural Portrait,* ed. Melvin G. Holli and Peter d'A. Jones (Grand Rapids: William Eerdmans, 1995); Humbert Nelli, *The Italians in Chicago: A Study in Ethnic Mobility* (New York: Oxford UP, 1970).

52. deFalco, interview.

53. S. D. Soter, "Jane Addams, The Hull House & The Early Greek Immigrant," *Greek Press,* November 25, 1964; Henry Pratt Fairchild, *Greek Immigration to the United States* (New Haven: Yale UP, 1911); Theodore Saloutos, *The Greeks in the United States* (Cambridge: Harvard UP, 1964); Andrew T. Kopan, "Greek Survival in Chicago," in Holli and Jones, *Ethnic Chicago,* 260–302.

54. Bruce Nelson, *Beyond the Martyrs: A Social History of Chicago's Anarchists, 1870–1900* (New Brunswick: Rutgers UP, 1988); Leslie Tischauser, *The Burden of Ethnicity: The German Question in Chicago, 1914–1941* (New York: Garland, 1990); Hyman Meites, ed., *A History of Jews in Chicago* (Chicago: U of Chicago P, 1924); Seymour Pomrenze, "Aspects of Chicago Russian-Jewish Life, 1893–1915," in *The Chicago Pinkas,* ed. Simon Rawidowicz (Chicago: U of Chicago P, 1952); Melvin Holli, "German American Ethnic and Cultural Identity from 1890 Onward," and Irving Cutler, "The Jews of Chicago: From Shtetl to Suburb," in Holli and Jones, *Ethnic Chicago,* 93–99, 122–72.

55. Hilda Satt Polacheck, *I Came a Stranger: The Story of a Hull-House Girl,* ed. Dena Polacheck Epstein (Urbana: U of Illinois P, 1989), 21.

56. St. Clair Drake and Horace Clayton, *Black Metropolis: A Study of Negro Life in a Northern City* (New York, 1945); Neil Fligstein, *Going North: Migration of Blacks and Whites from the South, 1900–1950* (New York: Academic Press, 1981); James Grossman, *Land of Hope: Chicago, Black Southerners, and the Great Migration* (Chicago: U of Chicago P, 1989); Emmett J. Scott, *Negro Migration during the War* (New York: Oxford UP, 1920); Franklin Frazier, *The Negro Family in Chicago* (Chicago: U of Chicago P, 1932).

57. Louise deKoven Bowen, "The Colored People of Chicago," Juvenile Protective Association (1913), 1–26. See also Elisabeth Lasch-Quinn and the relationship between African-Americans and the settlement movement in *Black Neighbors.* Jane Addams later became a cofounder of the NAACP and colleague of W. E. B. DuBois, who critiqued her decision to join Roosevelt's Progressive Party despite its stance on race relations. See Mary White Ovington, "How the National Association for the Advancement of Colored People Began," *NAACP* (1914): 1–5; see Davis's analysis of the Progressive Party in *American Heroine.* For one exceptional and very temporary case of a northern black female Hull-

House settler, see Lucy Knight, "Harriet Rice," in *The Encyclopedia of Chicago Women's History* (Indiana UP, forthcoming).

58. Starr to Blaisdell, Feb. 23, 1889.

59. Mary Richmond, *Friendly Visiting among the Poor: A Handbook for Charity Workers* (New York: Macmillan, 1899).

60. Starr to Starrs, Nov. 15, 1889, EGS Papers. On gendered space and immigrant experience in New York, see Elizabeth Ewen, *Immigrant Women in the Land of the Dollars: Life and Culture on the Lower East Side, 1890–1925* (New York: Monthly Review Press, 1985).

61. Starr to Starrs, Nov. 15, 1889.

62. Starr to Starrs, Nov. 15, 1889.

63. Nora Marks, "Two Women's Work," *Chicago Tribune,* May 19, 1890, n.p.

64. Ellen Gates Starr to Mary Blaisdell, May 18, 1890, EGS Papers.

65. Marks, "Two Women's Work."

66. Marks, "Two Women's Work."

67. Marks, "Two Women's Work."

68. Marks, "Two Women's Work."

69. Starr to Blaisdell, May 18, 1890.

70. Marks, "Two Women's Work."

71. Starr to Blaisdell, May 18, 1890.

72. Lissak's *Pluralism and Progressives* critiques Hull-House with an interpretation influenced by Horace Kallen's concept of pluralism. The writings of Jane Addams, Grace Abbott, and John Dewey suggest more of an emerging kinship with Randolph Bourne's notion of "transnational America." Lissak's perspective also affects her methodology when, for instance, she determines the number of official "ethnic" clubs by their declared names. This principle would not count the Lincoln Club or the Hull-House Players as "ethnic," despite their respectively Jewish and Irish membership.

73. Kopan, "Greek Survival in Chicago"; Lissak, *Pluralism and Progressives,* 104–7.

74. Cutler, "The Jews of Chicago" 143; Edward Kantowicz, "The Ethnic Church," in Holli and Jones, *Ethnic Chicago,* 574–603; Michael Funchion, "Irish Chicago," in *Ethnic Chicago,* 57–92; Candeloro, "Chicago's Italians," in *Ethnic Chicago,* 229–59; Lissak, *Pluralism and Progressives,* 80–103.

75. Addams, "Recreation as a Public Function in Urban Communities," *American Journal of Sociology* 17 (1912): 615–19. See also Israel Zangwill, *The Melting Pot* (1909; New York: Macmillan, 1910); John Dewey, "Nationalizing Education," *Addresses and Proceedings of the Fifty-Fourth Annual Meeting of the National Education Association* (1916), 183–89; Horace Kallen, *Culture and Democracy* (New York: Boni and Liveright, 1924), "The Ethics of Zionism," *Maccabean* 11.2 (1906): 61–71, and "Democracy versus the Melting Pot," in *Immigration,* ed. Benjamin Ziegler (Boston: D.C. Heath, 1953), 25–35; Randolph Bourne, "Transnational America," in *The Radical Will: Selected Writings, 1911–1918,* ed. Olaf Hansen (Berkeley and Los Angeles: U of California P, 1977), 248–64, and "The Jew and Transnational America," in *War and Intellec-*

tuals: *Essays by Randolph Bourne, 1915–1919,* ed. Carl Resek (New York: Harper and Row, 1964), 124–33.

76. Grace Abbott, *The Immigrant and the Community* (New York: Century, 1917), 277; Addams, "Recent Immigration: A Field Neglected by the Scholar," *Education Review* 29 (Mar. 1905): 245–263, and her "Americanization," *American Sociological Society Publication* 14 (1919): 206–14.

77. Frances Hackett, "As an Alien Feels," *New Republic* 3 (July 1915): 303–5. For secondary literature on theories of American ethnicity, see Werner Sollors, *Beyond Ethnicity: Consent and Descent in American Culture* (New York: Oxford UP, 1986); Micaela di Leonardo, *The Varieties of Ethnic Experience* (Ithaca: Cornell UP, 1984); Mitchel Cohen, "Rooted Cosmopolitanism," *Dissent* (fall 1992): 483–87; Bruce Ackerman, "Rooted Cosmopolitanism," *Ethics* 104 (1994): 516–35; David Hollinger, *Postethnic America: Beyond Multiculturalism* (New York: Basic Books, 1995).

78. Starr to Starrs, Nov. 3, 1889.

79. Addams, *Twenty Years,* 127.

80. Carolyn Steedman, *Strange Dislocations: Childhood and the Idea of Human Interiority, 1780–1930* (Cambridge: Harvard UP, 1995). See also James Kincaid, *Child-Loving: The Erotic Child and Victorian Culture* (New York: Routledge, 1992) with whom Steedman differs to some degree.

81. Steedman, *Strange Dislocations,* 97.

82. "Hull-House Program, Lectures, Clubs, Classes, Etc.," Mar. 1, 1892, Jane Addams Memorial Collection, microfilm edition, University of Illinois at Chicago (hereafter cited as JAMC).

83. Kelley, *Autobiography,* 77.

84. Dominick Cavallo, *Muscles and Morals: Organized Playgrounds and Urban Reform, 1880–1920* (Philadelphia: U of Pennsylvania P, 1981), and "From Perfection to Habit: Moral Training in the American Kindergarten, 1860–1920," *History of Education Quarterly* 16 (1976): 147–61. A related, but by no means exhaustive, list of relevant historical and contemporary scholarship on the rhetoric of childhood includes Joseph Hawes, *Children in Urban Society* (New York: Oxford UP, 1971); Bernard Wishy, *The Child and the Republic* (Philadelphia: U of Pennsylvania P, 1968); Philippe Ariès, *Centuries of Childhood,* trans. Robert Baldick (London: Verso, 1962); Allison James and Alan Prout, eds., *Constructing and Reconstructing Childhood* (London: Falmer, 1990); Robert Coles, *The Political Life of Children* (Boston: Atlantic Monthly P, 1986); F. S. Kessel and A. W. Siegel, *The Child and Other Cultural Inventions* (New York: Praegaer, 1983); Sharon Stephens, ed., *Children and the Politics of Culture* (Princeton: Princeton UP, 1995); Bill Brown, "American Childhood and Stephen Crane's Toys," in *The Material Unconscious: American Amusement, Stephen Crane, and the Economies of Play* (Cambridge: Harvard UP, 1996), 167–98; Lauren Berlant, "The Theory of Infantile Citizenship," in *The Queen of America Goes to Washington City* (Durham: Duke UP, 1997).

85. Anne Kuhn, *The Mother's Role in Childhood Education: New England Concepts, 1830–1860* (New Haven: Yale UP, 1947); Michael Moon, "The Gentle Boy and the Dangerous Classes," *Representations* 19 (summer 1987): 87–110.

86. G. Stanley Hall, "Corporal Punishments," *New York Education* 3 (Nov. 1899): 163, quoted in Gail Bederman, *Manliness and Civilization: A Cultural History of Gender and Race in the United States, 1880–1917* (Chicago: U of Chicago P, 1995), 78. See also G. Stanley Hall, *Adolescence: Its Psychology and Its Relations to Physiology, Anthropology, Sociology, Sex, Crime, Religion, and Education*, 2 vols. (New York: Appleton, 1904), and *Life and Confessions of a Psychologist* (New York: Appleton, 1923); Dorothy Ross, *G. Stanley Hall: The Psychologist as Prophet* (Chicago: U of Chicago P, 1972); Cavallo, *Muscles and Morals*, 88–106; Benjamin Rader, "The Recapitulation Theory of Play: Motor Behaviour, Moral Reflexes, and Manly Attitudes in Urban American, 1880–1920," in *Manliness and Morality: Middle Class Masculinity in Britain and America, 1800–1940* (Manchester: Manchester UP, 1987), 123–34.

87. "Dr. Hall's Ultra Views," *Chicago Evening Post*, Apr. 4, 1899, 163, quoted in Bederman, *Manliness and Civilization*, 78.

88. Jane Addams, *The Excellent Becomes the Permanent* (New York: Macmillan, 1932), 17–22.

89. Addams, *Excellent Becomes Permanent*, 51; Kelley, *Autobiography*, 78; Addams, *Twenty Years*, 83. The kindergarten of thirty-five children was transferred to Mary McDowell's leadership in 1892, and a hierarchy of assistants was established that provided schooling in kindergarten teaching as well as nursery care. By 1895, the Froebel Kindergarten Society used Hull-House for its weekly meetings and instructor teaching.

90. Starr to Blaisdell, May 18, 1890.

91. Allen Pond, "The Settlement House III" *Brickbuilder* 11 (Sept. 1902): 178–83.

92. This description derived from "Weekly Programme of Lectures, Clubs, Classes, Etc.," Jan. 1891, JAMC: 763–68; "Hull-House Program, Lectures, Clubs, Classes, Etc.," Mar. 1, 1892, JAMC: 783–88; Moore, "Day at Hull-House," 638.

93. Giddens, *The Constitution of Society*, 118. Such an analysis of the performance of everyday life builds on Dolores Hayden's insights into domestic space and material culture in *The Grand Domestic Revolution*. Feminist geography's theorizing of microperformance provides paradigms for understanding the incarnation of domesticity: Catharine Beecher, *Treatise on Domestic Economy* (1841; New York: Schocken, 1977); Kathryn Kish Sklar, *Catharine Beecher: A Study in American Domesticity* (New York: W. W. Norton, 1973); L. McDowell, "Space, Place, and Gender Relations, Part II: Identity, Difference, Feminist Geometries and Geographies," *Progress in Human Geography* 17 (1993): 305–18; Doreen Massey, "Power Geometry and a Progressive Sense of Place," in John Bird, ed., *Mapping the Futures: Local Cultures, Global Changes* (London: Routledge, 1993), "The Political Place of Locality Studies," *Environment and Planning* 23 (1991): 267–81, and "Flexible Sexism," *Environment and Planning D* 3 (1991): 31–57; Rose, *Feminism and Geography*. Compare and contrast Hull-House's mobility to Lora Romero's reading of "bio-power" in Catharine Beecher's formative theories of domesticity ("Bio-Political Resistance," *Home Fronts*, 70–88).

94. Marks, "Two Women's Work."

95. Marks, "Two Women's Work."

96. Ellen Gates Starr to Mary Blaisdell, Dec. 21, 1890, EGS Papers.

97. James Weber Linn, *Jane Addams: A Biography* (New York: Appleton-Century, 1935) 119; George Twose, "Settlement Reflections or Why he left for Egypt: A Comedietta," Dec. 1901, JAMC.

98. Dewey to A. Dewey, Oct. 9 and 10, 1894. See Dewey's related writings: "Results of Child-Study Applied to Education," *Transactions of the Illinois Society for Child Study* (Jan. 1895), "Interest in Relation to Training of the Will," *Second Supplement to the Herbart Yearbook for 1895* (Bloomington, IL: National Herbart Society, 1896), "The Reflex-Arc Concept in Psychology," *Psychological Review III* (July 1896: 357–70), "Pedagogy as a University Discipline," *University Record,* Sept. 1896, "Ethical Principles Underlying Education," in *Third Yearbook* (Chicago: U of Chicago P, 1897), and "Froebel's Educational Principles," *Elementary School Record,* June 1900. See also Alice Dewey, "The Place of the Kindergarten," *Elementary School Teacher,* Jan. 1902); and John Dewey, *The Child and the Curriculum* (Chicago: U of Chicago P, 1902). For a history of Dewey's Lab School at the University of Chicago, see Katherine Camp Mayhew and Anna Camp Edwards, *The Dewey School* (New York: Atherton, 1966).

99. Giddens, *The Constitution of Society,* 72.

100. "Weekly Programme of Lectures, Clubs, Classes, Etc.," Jan. 1891; "Hull-House Program, Lectures, Clubs, Classes, Etc.," Mar. 1, 1892; Marks, "Two Women's Work."

101. "Hull-House Program, Lectures, Clubs, Classes, Etc.," Mar. 1, 1892.

102. More analysis of such sites appears in chapters 3, 5, and 6.

103. For a review of the racialization of Italian-Americans, see David R. Roediger, "Whiteness and Ethnicity in the History of 'White Ethnics' in the United States," in *Towards Abolition of Whiteness,* 181–98; and Micaela di Leonardo's *Varieties of Ethnic Experience.*

104. Marks, "Two Women's Work."

105. Starr to Starrs, Nov. 15, 1889.

106. Addams, *Twenty Years,* 85–86.

107. The adjustment followed an increase in attendance. Twelve Hull-House teachers taught 120 Italian girls by 1892. In 1895, they added three more teachers to the initial twelve in order to maximize the attention these 120 Italian girls received. "Hull-House Lectures, Clubs, Classes, Etc.," Mar. 1, 1892; Hull-House schedule (draft) winter–spring 1894, JAMC; "Afternoon Clubs and Classes," Jan. 15, 1895, JAMC; "Afternoons," Apr. 1895, JAMC.

108. Ellen Gates Starr to Mary Blaisdell, (Dec. 21, 1889 or 1890), EGS Papers.

109. Starr to Blaisdell, Dec. 21 [1889 or 1890].

110. Starr to Blaisdell, Dec. 21 [1889 or 1890]. See Irwin St. John Tucker's recall of Starr's friendships with Italian immigrants, "Personal Recollections of Hull-House," Sept. 1969, passim, EGS Papers.

111. Resident meeting, Oct. 5, 1896, JAMC.

112. Club members were offered possible topics and speakers for their lecture evenings from a list of settlement volunteers: "What to do in Emergencies," Dr. Moore; "Travel Talks," Miss Barnum; "Historic Talks," Mrs. Hill; "Civics," Mr. Hill; "Labor Movements," Mrs. Stevens; "Birds," Miss Pitkin; "The Conquest of India," "South African Wars," Mr. Bruce; "Pueblo Indians Life on the Plains," Dr. Moore; "Russia," Miss Thomas; "Three Heroes," Miss Addams. *Hull-House Bulletin,* Dec. 1, 1897, JAMC.

113. Molly Ladd-Taylor, "Hull-House Goes to Washington: Women and the Children's Bureau," *Gender, Class, Race, and Reform in the Progressive Era* (Lexington: U of Kentucky P, 1991), 110–26 and her *Mother-Work.* See also Kathryn Kish Sklar, "Historical Foundations of Women's Power," in Michel and Koven, *Mothers of New World;* and Gordon, *Pitied but Not Entitled,* 99–108.

114. Fraser, "Rethinking the Public Sphere," 115. On settlement philosophy, pragmatism, and labor, see Davis, *Spearheads for Reform;* Michael Rogin, "Voluntarism: The Political Functions of an Antipolitical Doctrine," *Industrial Labor Relations Review* 15.4 (1962): 521–35; Herbert Gutman, "Protestantism and the American Labor Movement: The Christian Spirit in the Gilded Age," *American Historical Review* LXXII 1 (1966): 74–101; Carson, *Settlement Folk,* 68–84; Feffer, *Chicago Pragmatists,* 91–116, 212–35.

115. Social Science Club announcements, Apr. 7, 1890, JAMC. For related histories of the labor movement and its relation to socialism: Ira Katznelson and Aristotle Zolberg, eds., *Working Class Formation* (Princeton: Princeton UP, 1986); Amy Bridges, *The City in the Republic: Antebellum New York and the Origins of Machine Politics* (New York: Cambridge UP, 1984); Oakley C. Johnson, *Marxism in United States History before the Russian Revolution, 1876–1917* (New York: Humanities, 1974); Christopher Tomlins, *The State and the Unions: Labor Relations, Law, and the Organized Labor Movement in America, 1880–1960* (Cambridge: Cambridge UP, 1985); Louis Reed, *The Labor Philosophy of Samuel Gompers* (New York: Columbia UP, 1930); Leon Fink, *Workingmen's Democracy: The Knights of Labor and American Politics* (Urbana: U of Illinois P, 1983); Michael Frisch and Daniel Walkowitz, eds., *Working Class American: Essays on Labor, Community, and Society* (Urbana: U of Illinois P, 1983); Daniel T. Rodgers, *The Work Ethic in Industrial America 1850–1920* (Chicago: U of Chicago P, 1974); Roy Rosenzweig, *Eight Hours for What We Will: Workers and Leisure in an Industrial City, 1870–1920* (Cambridge: Cambridge UP, 1983); Herbert Gutman, *Power and Culture: Essays on the American Working Class* (New York: Pantheon, 1987).

116. Non-Hull-House clubs ranged widely: Ladies Bookbinders Union, the Froebel Club, the Textile Workers Association, the Anti-Cigarette Club, the Federation of Social Justice, and dozens more. See *Hull-House Bulletins* and *Yearbooks* (1894–1910).

117. Carl Smith, *Urban Disorder and the Shape of Belief: The Great Chicago Fire, the Haymarket Bomb, and the Model Town of Pullman* (Chicago: U of Chicago P, 1995), 7. See Irving Werstein, *Strangled Voices: The Story of the Haymarket Affair* (New York: Macmillan, 1970); Henry David, *The History of*

the Haymarket Affair: A Study of American Social-Revolutionary and Labor Movements (New York: Farrar and Rinehart, 1936).

118. Julia Lathrop, "What the Settlement Stands For," *National Conference
of Charities and Correction Proceedings*, 1896, 106–10, Julia Lathrop Papers,
Rockford College.

119. "Hull-House Lectures, Clubs, Classes, Etc.," Mar. 1, 1892, Blanc, *Condition of Women, 78*.

120. For instance, an 1891 lecture series included Chicago reformer and
longtime Hull-House friend Henry Demarest Lloyd on "Conservative Views of
the Radical Movement," Jane Addams herself on Toynbee Hall, and Ellen
Henrotin—lead organizer of the Woman's Building at the Colombian Exposition—on "Woman of the Twentieth Century." Other topics included "Municipal Government" and several religious themes such as "Christian Socialism" or
"The Divine Law of Service." ("Hull-House Lectures, Clubs, Classes, Etc."
Jan. 1891).

121. Mme. Blanc, *The Condition of Woman in the United States, A Traveler's
Notes,* trans. Abby Langdon Alger (Boston: Roberts Bros., 1895), 74.

122. James Gilbert, *Perfect Cities: Chicago's Utopias of 1893* (Chicago: U of
Chicago P, 1991), 215; Jeanne Madelein Weimann, *The Fair Women: The Story
of the Woman' Building, World Columbian Exposition, Chicago, 1893* (Chicago:
Academy Chicago, 1981).

123. Blanc, *Condition of Woman,* 78.

124. Blanc, *Condition of Woman,* 79.

125. Blanc, *Condition of Woman,* 79–80.

126. Blanc, *Condition of Woman,* 81.

127. Addams, *Twenty Years,* 140.

128. Blanc, *Condition of Woman,* 86.

129. Addams, *Twenty Years,* 140. For historical support of this assertion,
Richard Ely, *Recent American Socialism* (Baltimore: Johns Hopkins UP, 1884),
and *The Labor Movement in America* (New York: Thomas Y. Crowell, 1886);
Morris Hillquit, *History of Socialism in the United States* (New York: Funk and
Wagnalls, 1910); Werner Sombart, *Why Is There No Socialism in the United
States?* trans. Hocking and Husbands (1906; New York: Macmillan, 1976); John
A. De Brizzi, *Ideology and the Rise of Labor Theory in America* (Westport, CT:
Greenwood, 1983).

130. Addams, *Twenty Years,* 140.

131. Andrea Lunsford, ed., *Reclaiming Rhetorica: Women in the Rhetorical
Tradition* (Pittsburgh: U of Pittsburgh P, 1995), especially Joanne Wagner's
essay in that volume, " 'Intelligent Members or Restless Disturbers': Women's
Rhetorical Styles, 1880–1920," 185–202; Nan Johnson, *Nineteenth-Century
Rhetoric in North America* (Carbondale: Southern Illinois UP, 1991); Lynn
Gordon, *Gender and Higher Education in the Progressive Era* (New Haven: Yale
UP, 1990); Catherine Hobbs Peaden, "Jane Addams and the Social Rhetoric of
Democracy," in *Oratical Culture in Nineteenth Century America: Transforma-
tions in the Theory and Practice of Rhetoric,* ed. Gregory Clark and S Michael
Halloran (Carbondale: Southern Illinois UP, 1993); James Farrell, *Democratic*

Eloquence: The Fight over Popular Speech in Nineteenth-Century America (New York: William Morrow, 1990); Robert Harriman, *Political Style: The Artistry of Power* (Chicago: U of Chicago P, 1995); Thomas Benson, ed., *Rhetoric and Political Culture in Nineteenth-Century America* (East Lansing: Michigan State UP, 1997); Michael Leff's comparisons of Lincoln and Jane Addams in Benson's volume, "Lincoln amongst the Nineteenth-Century Orators," 131–56.

132. Blanc, *Condition of Woman*, 82.

133. Ellen Gates Starr to Mary Allen, Dec. 24 [1890s], EGS Papers; Scrapbook, Apr.–May 1892, JAMC.

134. Blanc, *Condition of Woman*, 82.

135. *Hull-House Bulletin*, Jan. 1897.

136. Blanc, *Condition of Woman*, 87.

137. Addams, *Twenty Years*, 133.

138. Resident meeting, Sept. 24, 1893, JAMC; Jane Addams, appendix, *Hull-House Maps and Papers: A Presentation of Nationalities and Wages in a Congested District of Chicago*, ed. Residents of Hull-House (New York: Thomas Y. Crowell & Co, 1895) 220.

139. Resident meeting, Nov. 12, 1893, JAMC. See also Isabel Eaton, "Hull-House and Some of Its Distinctive Features," *Smith College Monthly*, Apr. 1894, 1–10.

140. Resident meeting, Dec. 2, 1893, JAMC.

141. Almont Lindsey, *The Pullman Strike: The Story of a Unique Experiment and of a Great Labor Upheaval* (Chicago: U of Chicago P, 1942), 38–89. See also Colston E. Warne, ed., *The Pullman Boycott of 1894: The Problem of Federal Intervention* (Boston: D. C. Heath, 1955); William H. Carwardine, *The Pullman Strike* (Chicago: Charles H. Kerr and Co., 1894); "Pullman Investigations," *Chicago Tribune*, Sept. 21, 1888, 9.

142. Addams, "A Modern Lear," *Survey*, Nov. 2, 1912, 134–35.

143. Addams, "A Modern Lear," 137.

144. Kelley, "The Need of Theoretical Preparation for Philanthropic Work" (1887), reprinted in *Autobiography*, 94, 104. For a thorough account of Florence Kelley's impact on Hull-House, see Sklar, *Florence Kelley*, especially parts 2 and 3. For different angles on the relationship between women and the labor movement (a subject that will return in chapters 3 and 6), see Nancy Schrom Dye, *As Equals and as Sisters: Feminism, the Labor Movement, and the Women's Trade League of New York* (Columbia: U of Missouri P, 1980); Mary Jo Buhle, *Women and American Socialism, 1870–1920* (Urbana: U of Illinois P, 1981); Harris, *Out to Work;* Susan Levine, *Labor's True Woman: Carpet Weavers, Industrialization, and Labor Reform in the Gilded Age* (Philadelphia: Temple UP, 1984).

145. Though usually against any system that replicated a structure of charity, residents of the house decided the 1893–94 post-Exposition depression was an emergency. Resident meeting, Sept. 24, 1893, and Oct. 29, 1893, JAMC.

146. Resident meeting, Dec. 10, 1893, JAMC.

147. Bridges, *City in Republic;* Blaine A. Brownell and Warren E. Stickle, *Bosses and Reformers* (Boston: Houghton Mifflin, 1973); John M. Allswang,

Bosses, Machines, and Urban Voters (Baltimore: John Hopkins UP, 1986); Paul Green and Melvin Holli, *The Mayors: The Chicago Political Tradition* (Carbondale: Southern Illinois P, 1995).

148. Resident meeting, Dec. 10, 1893.

149. Resident meeting, Dec. 10, 1893.

150. In response to Paula Baker's "Domestication of Politics," see Sklar on cross-gender coalitions in "Historical Foundations."

151. Quoted in John Patrick Walsh, "The Catholic Church in Chicago and Problems of Urban Society, 1893–1915," Ph.D. diss., University of Chicago, 1948.

152. Addams, "Political Reform," in *Democracy and Social Ethics,* 273.

153. Addams, "A Modern Lear."

154. Howard E. Wilson, *Mary McDowell, Neighbor* (Chicago: U of Chicago P, 1928).

155. Alpha Fuller, "An Acrostic," Dec. 6, 1893, JAMC.

156. Jane Cunningham Croly, *History of the Woman's Club Movement* (New York: Henry Allen, 1898); Karen Blair, *Clubwoman as Feminist: True Womanhood Redefined, 1868–1914* (New York: Holmes and Meier, 1980); Scott, *Natural Allies.* On the politics of women's volunteerism, Kathleen McCarthy, *Noblesse Oblige: Charity and Cultural Philanthropy in Chicago, 1849–1929* (Chicago: U of Chicago P, 1982), and her edited *Lady Bountiful Revisited;* Lori Ginzberg, *Women and the Work of Benevolence: Morality, Politics, and Class in the Nineteenth Century United States* (New Haven: Yale UP, 1990); Peggy Pascoe, *Relations of Rescue: The Search for Female Moral Authority, 1874–1939* (Oxford: Oxford UP, 1990); Sara Deutsch, "Learning to Talk More Like a Man: Boston Women's Class-Bridging Organizations, 1870–1940," *American Historical Review* 97 (1992): 379–404.

157. Marks, "Two Women's Work."

158. Henriette Greenebaum Frank and Amalie Hofer Jerome, *Annals of the Chicago Women's Club, 1876–1916* (Chicago: Chicago Woman's Club, 1916), 13.

159. "What the CWC Has Done for Chicago," *Woman's Home Companion,* Mar. 1907.

160. Jane Addams, "Cultural Approach to Civic Problems through Early Women's Clubs," in *The Second Twenty Years at Hull-House* (New York: Macmillan, 1930), 97.

161. The first published list shows that only a few members went by the title *Miss.*

162. Polacheck, *I Came a Stranger,* 101.

163. Fuller, "An Acrostic."

164. See "Nationalities Map," *Hull-House Maps and Papers,* 15.

165. Addams, "Cultural Approach to Problems," 97.

166. Blair, *Clubwoman as Feminist;* Scott, *Natural Allies.*

167. Hull-House Woman's Club circular, JAMC.

168. Addams, "Cultural Approach to Problems," 96.

169. Frank and Jerome, *Annals,* 15.

170. Frank and Jerome, *Annals,* 15; Ruth Bordin, *Women and Temperance:*

The Quest for Liberty and Power 1873–1900 (Philadelphia: Temple UP: 1981); Cott, "Equality versus Difference"; Carol DuBois, *Feminism and Suffrage: The Emergence of an Independent Women's Movement in America, 1848–1969* (Ithaca: Cornell UP, 1978); Barbara Epstein, *The Politics of Domesticity: Women, Evangelism, and Temperance in Nineteenth-Century America* (Middletown, CT: Wesleyan UP, 1981).

171. Jane Addams, "Why Women Should Vote," *Ladies Home Journal,* Jan. 1910.

172. Alzina Stevens's brief Woman's Club presidency before her untimely death facilitated this conversation. *Hull-House Bulletin,* autumn–midwinter 1900.

173. Mary McDowell, "Friendly Visiting," *NCCC, Proceedings* (1896); 254; quoted in Boyer, *Urban Masses,* 155–56.

174. Addams, "Cultural Approach to Problems," 97.

175. Alpha Fuller, "Our Club Names," Feb. 8, 1896, JAMC.

176. Hull-House inventory, 1903, JAMC addendum 10.

177. Starr, "Settlements and the Church's Duty," *The Church Social Union* 23, (Aug. 15, 1896): 8.

178. *Neighbors* 4.3 (1997): 1; *Neighbors* 2.3 (1995): 1.

179. "Because of you . . ." *Hull-House Association Annual Report* (1996), 18–19.

180. On the divorce between labor and welfare in the United States see Gordon, *Pitied but Not Entitled,* 287–306; Gwendolyn Mink, "The Lady and the Tramp," and Barbara Nelson, "The Origins of the Two-Channeled Welfare State: Workmen's Compensation and Mother's Aid," in Gordon, *Women, State, and Welfare,* 92–122; Sklar, "Historical Foundations."

181. Louise Kiernan, "Oprah's Poverty Program Stalls," *Chicago Tribune,* Aug. 27, 1996, N1.

182. *Neighbors* 3.2 (1996): 2.

183. Kiernan, "Oprah's Poverty Program Stalls," N1.

CHAPTER 3

1. Miriam Gusevitch, unpublished statement in possession by the author. Preliminary articles on the park include Adrienne Drell, "Addams Memorial Gets OK," *Chicago Sun-Times,* Oct. 12, 1994, 28; Pater Baniak, "Navy Pier Memorial to Hail Jane Addams," *Chicago Tribune,* Nov. 4, 1994, N1; Charles Storch, "When Do We See Addams Tribute?" *Chicago Tribune,* June 19, 1994, C1; Adrienne Dell, "Finally, a Fit Tribute to Addams," *Chicago Sun-Times,* Mar. 24, 1995.

2. Barbara Johnson, *The Wake of Deconstruction* (Oxford: Blackwell, 1994), 60.

3. Addams, *Twenty Years,* 61.

4. Marianne DeKoven, " 'Excellent Not a Hull-House,' Gertrude Stein, Jane Addams, and Feminist Modernist Political Culture," in *Rereading Modern-*

ism: New Directions in Feminist Criticism, ed. Lisa Rado (New York: Garland, 1994), 336.

5. Addams, *Twenty Years,* 113–14.

6. Ellen Gates Starr, "Art and Labor," in *Hull-House Maps and Papers,* 165.

7. Addams, appendix, *Hull-House Maps and Papers,* 211.

8. Addams, appendix, *Hull-House Maps and Papers,* 225.

9. Addams, *Twenty Years,* 113–14.

10. Addams, *Twenty Years,* 113–14; Hull-House account books, Oct. 1891, JAMC; Sklar, "Who Funded Hull-House?" 100.

11. Guy Szuberla, "Irving Kane Pond: A Michigan Architect in Chicago," *Old Northwest* 5.2 (1979): 109–39, and "Three Chicago Settlements: Their Architectural Form and Meaning," *Illinois State Historical Society* 52.2 (1977): 114–29; Horowitz, "Hull-House as Woman's Space," 40–42; Pond, "The Settlement House," 178.

12. Charles L. Hutchinson, "Art: Its Influence and Excellence in Modern Times," *Saturday Evening Herald,* Mar. 31, 1888, Hutchinson Papers, Newberry Library.

13. Horowitz, *Culture and the City,* 79, 129.

14. John D. Rosenberg, *The Darkening Glass: A Portrait of Ruskin's Genius* (New York: Columbia UP, 1961); E. P. Thompson, *William Morris: Romantic to Revolutionary* (New York: Pantheon, 1977); Boris, *Art and Labor.*

15. "Hull-House Lectures, Clubs, Classes, Etc.," Mar. 1, 1891, 13, JAMC.

16. Neil Harris, "Museums, Merchandizing, and Popular Taste: The Struggle for Influence," in *Cultural Excursions* (1974; Chicago: U of Chicago P, 1990), 56.

17. Starr, "Art and Labor," 165.

18. Addams, appendix, *Hull-House Maps and Papers,* 211.

19. Addams, appendix, *Hull-House Maps and Papers,* 211. They continued, "Frequently recurring exhibitions of a few very choice pictures might do more toward educating the public taste of the locality in which they occur than many times the number less severely chosen and less often seen."

20. Ellen Gates Starr and Mrs. Henry W. Mager, "Chicago Public School Art Society," undated newsletter JAMC. See Bourdieu, *Distinction.*

21. Starr, "Art and Labor," 166.

22. Starr, "Art and Labor," 167.

23. Starr, "Art and Labor, 167.

24. Starr, "Art and Labor, 169.

25. Starr, "Art and Labor," 168.

26. George Herbert Mead to H. N. Castle, George Herbert Mead Papers, University of Chicago.

27. For primary and historical contextualization, see William James, *Principles of Psychology* (1890; Cambridge: Harvard UP, 1981); Gerald Myers, *William James: His Life and Thought* (New Haven: Yale UP, 1986); Feffer, *Chicago Pragmatists,* 179–83; Mead, "Industrial Education, the Working Man, and the School," *Elementary School Teacher* 2 (1900–1901): 370–75; David Miller, *George Herbert Mead: Self, Language, and the World* (Austin: U of Texas P,

1973); Dewey, "Reflex-Arc Concept," 96; Dewey, "Place of Manual Training," in *The Early Works of John Dewey,* 5 vols. (Carbondale: Southern Illinois UP, 1967–72); 96, "Interest in Relation to Training of the Will," 220–24, and "Froebel's Educational Principles," 219–25; A. W. Richards, "The Thought Side of Manual Training," *Manual Training Magazine* 3 (1902–3): 65–66; Lewis Flint Anderson, *History of Manual and Industrial School Education* (New York: D. Appleton and Co., 1926).

28. Michael Newbury, "Healthful Employment: Hawthorne, Thoreau, and Middle-Class Fitness," *American Quarterly* 47 (1995): 683. This essay complicates Nicholas Bromell's important book, *By the Sweat of the Brow: Literature and Labor in Antebellum America* (Chicago: U of Chicago P, 1993).

29. "Hull-House Lectures, Clubs, and Classes, Etc.," Jan. 1891, JAMC.

30. Hackett, "Hull House—a Souvenir," *Survey,* June 1, 1925, 276.

31. Jane Addams to Esther Linn, July 16, 1901, JAMC; Richard T. Ely to Jane Addams, July 5, 1902, Richard T. Ely Papers, State Historical Society of Wisconsin.

32. Starr, "Art and Labor," 166.

33. Addams, appendix, *Hull-House Maps and Papers,* 211.

34. "Hull-House Lectures, Clubs and Classes, Etc.," Jan. 1891; Kelley, *Autobiography,* 79.

35. Daniel Bluestone, *Constructing Chicago* (New Haven: Yale UP, 1991), 169–70.

36. "Hull-House Lectures, Clubs, Classes, Etc.," Mar. 1, 1891, 13.

37. Addams, appendix, *Hull-House Maps and Papers,* 210.

38. "Afternoon Clubs and Classes," Jan. 15, 1895.

39. Bourdieu, *Distinction,* 54.

40. Enella Benedict to Jane Addams, Aug. 19, 1931, JAMC.

41. Addams, *Twenty Years,* 114.

42. John Camaroff and Jean Camaroff, *Ethnography and the Historical Imagination* (Boulder, CO: Westview, 1992), 70, 72. Recreation and physical reform thus exemplify Foucauldian critiques of power and embodiment found in texts such as *Discipline and Punish* and *The History of Sexuality.*

43. R. T. Trall, *Family Gymnasium* (New York: Fowler and Wells, 1857), x. On the YMCA and related movements, see Nina Mjagkij and Margaret Spratt, eds., *Men and Women Adrift: The YMCA and YWCA in the City* (New York: NYU Press, 1997); David Macleod, *Building Character in the American Boy: The Boy Scouts, YMCA, and Their Forerunners, 1870–1920* (Madison: U of Wisconsin P, 1986); Nina Mjagkij, *Light in the Darkness: African-Americans and the YMCA, 1852–1946* (Lexington: U of Kentucky P, 1994); James Whorton, *Crusaders for Fitness: The History of American Health Reformers* (Princeton: Princeton UP, 1982); Peter Levine, "The Promise of Sport in Antebellum American," *Journal of American Culture* 2 (winter 1980); Martha Verbrugge, *Able-Bodied Womanhood: Personal Health and Social Change in Nineteenth-Century Boston* (New York: Oxford UP, 1988); Frances Cogan, *All-American Girl: The Ideal of Real Womanhood in Mid–Nineteenth Century America* (Athens: U of Georgia P, 1989); Melvin Adelman, *A Sporting Time: New York City and the Rise of Modern*

Athletics, 1820–1870 (Urbana: U of Illinois P, 1986); Steven Riess, _City Games: The Evolution of American Society and the Rise of Sports_ (Urbana: U of Illinois P, 1989). For rhetorical studies of the concept of play in American culture, see Michael Oriard, _Sporting with the Gods: The Rhetoric of Play and Game in American Culture_ (Cambridge: Cambridge UP, 1991); and Brown, _The Material Unconscious._

44. F. G. Welch, _Moral, Intellectual, and Physical Culture or, The Philosophy of True Living_ (New York: Wood and Holbrook, 1869); J. Madison Watson, _Elocution, Calisthenics and Gymnastics_ (New York: Steiger and Co, 1889).

45. Theodore Roosevelt, _Harper's Weekly_ (1893), quoted in Bederman, _Manliness and Civilization,_ 186. See also Rader, "Recapitulation Theory of Play"; Mark C. Carnes and Clyde Griffen, eds., _Meanings for Manhood: Constructions of Masculinity in Victorian America_ (Chicago: U of Chicago P, 1990). On Addams's ongoing relationship with Roosevelt (through and beyond her seconding of his nomination for the Progressive Party), see Davis, _American Heroine,_ 148–49, 184–97.

46. Bederman, _Manliness and Civilization,_ 184.

47. George Eliot Flint, _Power and Health through Progressive Exercise_ (New York: Bake and Taylor, 1905), 197.

48. Flint, _Power and Health,_ 139–40.

49. Charles Zueblin, "The City Child at Play," paper presented at the Chicago Child Welfare Exhibit, School of Civics and Philanthropy, in _The Child in the City_ (Chicago: Hallister Press, 1912), 443–50; Henry Stoddard Curtis, _The Play Movement and Its Significance_ (New York: Macmillan, 1917); Clarence Elmer Rainwater, _The Play Movement in the United States: A Study of Community Recreation_ (Chicago: U of Chicago P, 1922); Horace Leland Friess, _Felix Adler and Ethical Culture: Memories and Studies,_ ed. Fannia Weingartner (New York: Columbia UP, 1981).

50. Jane Addams, _The Spirit of Youth and the City Streets_ (New York: Macmillan, 1909); G. Stanley Hall's _Adolescence_ was published five years earlier, in 1904.

51. "Hull-House Lectures, Clubs, Classes, Etc.," Mar. 1, 1892, 5, 8.

52. Verbrugge, _Able-Bodied Womanhood;_ Whorton, _Crusaders for Fitness;_ Cavallo, _Muscles and Morals._

53. Jessie Bancroft, _School Gymnastics_ (New York: E. L. Kellogg and Co., 1896), 9; see also William Blaikie, _Sound Bodies for Our Boys and Girls_ (New York: Harper and Brothers, 1889).

54. "College Extension Schedule," 1893, JAMC; Jane Addams to Rose Gyles, Jan. 11, 1894, JAMC.

55. Polacheck, _I Came a Stranger,_ 77.

56. Announcement, JAMC reel 50: 1686.

57. Foucault, _History of Sexuality,_ 135–59; Verbrugge, _Able-Bodied Womanhood,_ 81–161.

58. Ward Crampton, _The Pedagogy of Physical Training_ (New York: Macmillan, 1922), 60.

59. Bancroft, _School Gymnastics,_ 34.

60. Crampton, *Pedagogy of Physical Training,* 174–75.

61. Victor von Borosini, "Our Recreation Facilities and the Immigrant," *Annals of the American Academy,* Mar. 1910, 141–51.

62. Addams, "Recreation as Public Function," 618. See also Addams, "Public Recreation and Social Morality," in *Charities and Commons* (1907), 21–24, "What the Theatre at Hull-House Has Done for the Neighborhood People," *Charities,* Mar. 29, 1902, 284–86, and *Spirit of Youth.*

63. For a more detailed analysis of dance at Hull-House, see a discussion of visiting dance teacher Mary Wood Hinman in Linda Johnston Tomko, "Women, Artistic Dance Practices, and Social Change in the United States, 1890–1920," Ph.D. diss., U of California, Los Angeles, 1991, 141–213.

64. *Hull-House Bulletin,* June 1897; by 1901, there were numerous athletics courses for women (*Hull-House Bulletin,* Jan.–May 1901, midwinter 1902–3).

65. *Chicago Chronicle,* May 25, 1902; also in Davis and Bryan, *One Hundred Years,* 73–74.

66. *Chicago Chronicle,* May 25, 1902.

67. Galen Cranz, "Women in Urban Parks," *Signs* 5.3 (spring 1980) S79–S95.

68. Bluestone, *Constructing Chicago,* 37–61, 198.

69. See Horowitz, *Culture and the City,* 140; Elizabeth Halsey, *The Development of Public Recreation in Metropolitan Chicago* (Chicago: Chicago Recreation Commission, 1940), 17.

70. Addams, appendix, *Hull-House Maps and Papers,* 224.

71. Addams, appendix, *Hull-House Maps and Papers,* 224; the same language appears in the *Hull-House Bulletin*'s announcement of more "Greek national dances so spontaneously and spiritedly given" (Jan.–May 1901).

72. Resident meeting, Feb. 18, 1894, JAMC.

73. For renditions of this story, see Linn, *Jane Addams,* 127; Polacheck, *I Came a Stranger,* 74; and Addams, appendix, *Hull-House Maps and Papers,* 224.

74. Resident meeting, July 23, 1893, JAMC.

75. Resident meeting, July 30, 1893, JAMC.

76. Resident meeting, Jan. 14, 1894, JAMC; *Hull-House Bulletin,* autumn 1900, 7.

77. Polacheck, *I Came a Stranger,* 73; see Marilyn T. Williams, *Washing the Great Unwashed* (Columbus: Ohio State UP, c. 1991).

78. Starr to Blaisdell, July 25, 1892.

79. "Hull-House Lectures, Clubs, and Classes, Etc.," Jan. 1891; "Hull-House Lectures, Clubs, and Classes, Etc.," Mar. 1, 1892; resident meeting, July 16 and July 23, 1893, JAMC.

80. Starr to Blaisdell, July 25, 1892.

81. Addams, appendix, *Hull-House Maps and Papers,* 219; See their discussion over shower lockers and scheduling of male and female showers in the gymnasium, resident meeting, July 23, 1893, and resident meeting, July 16, 1893, JAMC.

82. Addams, appendix, *Hull-House Maps and Papers,* 225.

83. Addams to Gyles, Jan. 11, 1894, JAMC.

84. Resident meeting, Nov. 25, 1893, JAMC.

85. *Hull-House Bulletin,* Jan. 1897.

86. Addams, *Twenty Years,* 102–3.

87. Carolyn Hunt, *The Italians of Chicago: A Social and Economic Study,* Ninth Special Report of the Commissioner of Labor (Washington, D.C., 1897), 46.

88. Addams, *Twenty Years,* 103.

89. Nelli, *The Italians in Chicago,* 46.

90. Led by Frances Willard, the Woman's Christian Temperance Union built female coalitions and a discourse against domestic violence even as it also reproduced racist and classist visions of the degraded saloon and an ideal nation (Bordin, *Women and Temperance*).

91. Perry R. Duis, *The Saloon: Public Drinking in Chicago and Boston, 1880–1920* (Urbana & Chicago: U of Illinois P, 1983), 5.

92. Addams, appendix, *Hull-House Maps and Papers,* 227.

93. Hayden, *The Grand Domestic Revolution,* especially chapt. 4.

94. "Hull-House Program, Diet Kitchen" 1891, JAMC. Already offering cooking classes by this time, Hull-House extended its reach by starting a "Diet Kitchen" in a nearby rented cottage at 221 Ewing specifically for classes in nutrition and "food preparation for the sick." The Woman's Club raised funds to support Edith Nason, who served as Hull-House's visiting nurse in the mornings and as a cooking instructor in the afternoons. Thus, in the years leading up to the 1893 founding of the public kitchen, Hull-House's affiliated women—both its residents and Woman's Club members—had already incorporated food preparation and a local effort in public health into their repertoire of civic housekeeping.

95. Addams, *Twenty Years,* 102–3; See also Hayden, *The Grand Domestic Revolution;* Harvey A. Levenstein, *The Revolution at the Table: The Transformation of the American Diet* (New York: Oxford UP, 1988); Robert Clarke, *Ellen Swallow: The Woman Who Founded Ecology* (Chicago: U of Chicago, 1973); Ruth Schwarz, *More Work for Mother: The Ironies of Household Technology* (New York: Basic Books, 1983). Innovations in scientific domesticity built upon the ideas of Catharine Beecher and nineteenth-century health reform: Catharine Beecher, *Treatise on Domestic Economy* and *Letters to the People on Health and Happiness* (New York, 1856); Stephen Nussbaum, *Sex, Diet, and Debility in Jacksonian America: Sylvester Graham and Health Reform* (Westport, CO: Greenwood, 1980); Joan Burbick, *Healing the Republic: The Language of Health and the Culture of Nationalism in Nineteenth-Century America* (Cambridge: Cambridge UP, 1994).

96. Notes on prospective candidates, JAMC.

97. Addams, appendix, *Hull-House Maps and Papers,* 227; Alice Hamilton, *Exploring the Dangerous Trades,* (Boston: Little, Brown & Co, 1943) 68.

98. Boris, *Art and Labor,* 131–34.

99. Hull-House lunch room and kitchen menu, Julia Lathrop Papers, Rockford College Archives, and JAMC.

100. Moore, "Day at Hull-House," 636.

101. Addams, *My Friend Julia Lathrop* (New York: Macmillan, 1935), 65.

102. Resident meeting, Nov. 18, 1893, JAMC; Addams, *Twenty Years,* 102–3.

103. Addams, *Twenty Years,* 102–3.

104. Duis, *The Saloon,* 18–19.

105. Ernest C. Moore, "The Social Value of the Saloon," *American Journal of Sociology* (1897): 6.

106. Moore, "Social Value of Saloon," 7.

107. Addams, *Twenty Years,* 102–3; quoted in Hayden, *The Grand Domestic Revolution,* 159.

108. Levenstein, *Revolution at the Table,* 53.

109. Polacheck, *I Came a Stranger,* 66.

110. Resident meeting, Jan. 7, 1895, JAMC.

111. Moore, "Day at Hull-House," 634.

112. Resident meeting, Dec. 2, 1893, JAMC.

113. Resident meetings, Dec. 2, 1893 to Apr. 6, 1895, JAMC.

114. Resident meeting, Jan. 7, 1895.

115. Resident meeting, Mar. 18, 1894, JAMC.

116. Resident meeting, Jan. 7, 1895.

117. Addams, *Twenty Years,* 103.

118. Moore, "Day at Hull-House," 636.

119. Moore, "Day at Hull-House," 636.

120. Resident meeting, Nov. 25, 1893; resident meeting, Dec. 2, 1893; Addams, appendix, *Hull-House Maps and Papers,* 227–28.

121. Resident meeting, Nov. 12, 1893, JAMC.

122. Addams, "Appendix," 227–28.

123. Resident meeting, Dec. 2, 1893.

124. Addams, *Twenty Years,* 103; *Hull-House Bulletin,* midwinter 1902–3, and numerous stories of social and theatrical events.

125. Addams, appendix, *Hull-House Maps and Papers,* 225–26.

126. Resident meeting, July 30, 1893, JAMC.

127. Resident meeting, Mar. 5, 1894, JAMC.

128. Established inductively by analyzing schedules and bulletins where, unlike all other/non-bedroom spaces, this room is not listed as an option for other gatherings.

129. Resident meeting, July 30, 1893; see Men's Club heading in the *Hull-House Bulletin,* Jan. 1897, Feb. 1897, June 1897, Mar. 1898.

130. Theodore Dreiser, *Sister Carrie* (1904; New York: W. W. Norton, 1970), 8.

131. Mary Kenney O'Sullivan, unpublished autobiography, Schlesinger Library, Radcliffe College.

132. Joanne Meyerowitz, *Women Adrift: Independent Wage-Earners in Chicago, 1880–1930* (Chicago: U of Chicago P, 1988), 32–33. See also Elizabeth Wilson, *The Sphinx in the City: Urban Life, the Control of Disorder, and Women* (Berkeley and Los Angeles: U of California P, 1991); and Kathy Peiss, "Charity Girls and City Pleasures: Historical Notes on Working-Class Sexuality," in

Powers of Desire: The Politics of Sexuality, eds. Ann Snitow, Christine Stansell, and Sharon Thompson (New York: Monthly Review P, 1983), and *Cheap Amusements: Working Women and Leisure in Turn-of-the-Century New York* (Philadelphia: Temple UP, 1986).

133. For a literary analysis of this figure, see Laura Hapke, *Tales of the Working Girl: Wage-Earning Women in American Literature, 1890–1925* (New York: Twayne, 1992), and "The American Working Girl and the New York Tenement Tale of the 1890s," *Journal of American Culture* 15 (summer 1992): 43–50. Related historical analyses include Alice Kessler Harris, *Out to Work: A History of Wage-Earning Women in the United States* (New York: Oxford UP, 1982); Levine, *Labor's True Woman;* Ardis Cameron, *Radicals of the Worst Sort: Laboring Women in Lawrence, Massachusetts, 1860–1912* (Urbana: U of Illinois P, 1993); Carole Turbin, *Working Women of Collar City: Gender, Class, and Community in Troy, 1864–86* (Urbana: U of Illinois P, 1987); Dorothy Sue Cobble, *Dishing It Out: Waitresses and the Unions in the Twentieth Century* (Urbana: U of Illinois P, 1991); Susan Porter Benson, *Counter Cultures: Saleswomen, Managers, and Customers in American Department Stores, 1890–1940* (Urbana: U of Illinois P, 1986); Ava Baron, ed., *Work Engendered: Toward a New History of Labor* (Ithaca: Cornell UP, 1991). For contemporaneous studies, see Katherine Jones, "Working Girls of Chicago: Their Wages, Their Homes, and Their Summer Outings," *Review of Reviews*, Sept. 1891, 168–72; Louis Albert Banks, *White Slaves or the Oppression of the Worthy Poor* (Boston: Lew and Shepard, 1893); and later, Edith Abbott, *Women in Industry: A Study in American Economic History* (New York and London: D. Appleton and Co., 1910).

134. O'Sullivan, autobiography.

135. O'Sullivan, autobiography.

136. O'Sullivan, autobiography.

137. Mary Kenney, cloakmakers circular, Mar. 1892, JAMC.

138. Kenney, cloakmakers circular.

139. See Martha Vicinus for a parallel analysis of this figure in England, *Independent Women: Work and Community for Single Women, 1850–1920* (London: Virago, 1985).

140. Addams, *Twenty Years*, 105.

141. The Jane Club constitution reveals similar debates in these meetings over the payment of food (they agreed to deduct fifteen cents for each meal not eaten) and household chores (they pledged to do an hour of "general domestic work" or be fined twenty-five cents) (Jane Club constitution, 1893; newsclipping, 1894; and scrapbook, JAMC addendum 10).

142. Hayden, *The Grand Domestic Revolution*, 168; Meyerowitz, *Women Adrift*, 47. For more on the YWCA, see Mary S. Sims, *The Natural History of an Institution—the Young Women's Christian Association* (New York: Woman's Press, 1936); Anna V. Rice, *A History of the World's Young Women's Christian Association* (New York: Woman's Press, 1947); Mjagkij and Spratt, *Men and Women Adrift*, especially Sarah Heath, "Negotiating White Womanhood," 86–110; Lasch-Quinn, *Black Neighbors*, especially chapter 4.

143. Mary Packneham, "Guest of Honor, 88, Aids Hull House Drive," *Chicago Tribune,* Oct. 2, 1963, 2:7.

144. Newsclipping, 1894, and scrapbook, JAMC addendum 10.

145. JAMC clippings. I thank Lucy Knight for sharing her interpretation of these events. More on this incident appears in chapter 4.

146. Peiss, *Cheap Amusements;* Meyerowitz, *Women Adrift;* Depuis, *The Saloon.*

147. Kenney, autobiography.

148. Valentine's party invitation, 1895, JAMC; invitation to Jane Club dance, Dec. 14, 1893, JAMC; resident meeting, Oct. 5, 1896, JAMC; resident meeting, Jan. 28, 1895, JAMC.

149. *Hull-House Bulletin,* June 1897, JAMC.

150. Addams, *Twenty Years,* 105–6.

151. *Hull-House Bulletin,* June 1897, JAMC.

152. Jane Club blueprints, JAMC addendum 10; Pond, "Settlement House III."

153. *Hull-House Bulletin,* semiannual 1902.

154. *Hull-House Bulletin,* semiannual 1902.

155. *Hull-House Bulletin,* semiannual 1902.

156. Gordon, *Pitied but Not Entitled,* 67–110, 287–303; Meyerowitz, *Women Adrift,* 54–55. On this development generally, see Theda Skocpol, *Protecting Soldiers and Mothers: The Political Origins of Social Policy in the United States* (Cambridge: Harvard UP, 1992); Sonya Michel, "The Limits of Maternalism: Policies toward Wage-Earning Mothers during the Progressive Era," in Michel and Koven, *Mothers of a New World;* Muncy, *Creating a Female Dominion;* Ladd-Taylor, *Mother-Work;* Nelson, "Two-Channeled Welfare State"; Harris, *Out to Work;* Baron, *Work Engendered;* Nancy Fraser, "After the Family Wage: A Postindustrial Thought Experiment," in *Justice Interruptus,* 41–68.

157. Addams, *Twenty Years,* 114.

158. Twose, "Settlement Reflections."

159. Louise Kiernan, "Hidden in Plain Sight," *Chicago Tribune,* Sept. 28, 1997, 4:2.

160. Barbara Brotman, "Must Memorials to Heroic Females Hit Rock Bottom?" *Chicago Tribune,* Nov. 20, 1994, 6:1, 8.

161. Kiernan, "Hidden in Plain Sight," 1.

CHAPTER 4

1. Ella Waite, Jessie Luther, and Rose Gyles, "Edith Nancrede: Her Birthday Party," Dec. 14, 1901, JAMC.

2. The Men's Club was also rehoused in the Butler along with the male residents. On their activities and this move, see *Hull-House Bulletin,* autumn 1900, Jan.–May 1901, semiannual 1902, midwinter 1903–4.

3. Debates about the utility of the private/public opposition have of course long preoccupied feminist theorists. See Jean Bethke Elshtain, *Private*

Man, Public Woman (Princeton: Princeton UP, 1981); Carol Pateman, *The Sexual Contract* (Stanford: Stanford UP, 1988), and *The Disorder of Women* (Cambridge: Polity, 1989); Teresa de Lauretis, ed., *Feminist Studies/Critical Studies* (Bloomington: Indiana UP, 1986); Linda Nicholson, *Gender and History: The Limits of Social Theory in the Age of the Family* (New York: Columbia UP, 1986), and her edited *Feminism/Postmodernism* (New York: Routledge, 1990); Landes, *Women and Public Sphere;* Susan Reverby and Dorothy Helley, *Gendered Domains: Rethinking the Public and Private in Women's History* (Ithaca: Cornell UP, 1992); Seyla Benhabib and Drucilla Cornell, *Feminism as Critique* (Minneapolis: U of Minnesota P, 1987). I see Hull-House space as akin to Eve Sedgwick's rendering of queer space in Melville; she helpfully adapts the theatrical analogy of "the boards," where "the space for those acts whose performative efficacy depended on their being defined as either private or public had to be delineated and categorized anew for each. A model for this definition might be the rhetorical art of the actor, whose (for instance) relaxation of tone in the focal muscles of the eye can organize a sudden soliloquial space by which every other body on the stage is at once rendered invisible and *deaf.*" *Epistemology of the Closet* (Berkeley and Los Angeles: U of California P, 1990), 110.

4. Addams, *Twenty Years,* 88.

5. Bourdieu and Wacquant, *Invitation to Reflexive Sociology,* 127.

6. Addams, *Twenty Years,* 77.

7. Addams, *Twenty Years,* 77; Marks, "Two Women's Work."

8. Sicherman, *Alice Hamilton,* 118; Hamilton, *Exploring the Dangerous Trades,* 120. See also Eaton, "Hull-House Distinctive Features," 1; and Horowitz, "Hull-House as Women's Space," 40, 45.

9. Moore, "Day at Hull-House," 629.

10. Hackett, "Hull House—a Souvenir," 275.

11. Addams, *Twenty Years,* 78.

12. Quoted in Davis, *American Heroine,* 71.

13. Dorothy Mittelman Sigel, interview by the author, March 1994.

14. "Settlement Head Daughter of North Illinois," 1929, JAMC.

15. Kelley, *Autobiography,* 23.

16. Alice Hamilton to Agnes Hamilton, July 3, 1898, Hamilton Family Papers, Schlesinger Library, Radcliffe College (hereafter cited as HF Papers).

17. Addams, *Twenty Years,* 75.

18. Kelley, *Autobiography,* 78–79.

19. Jane Addams informally instituted what she called "fellowships" that matched a wealthy sponsor to a settler with valuable talents. Other times, Hull-House residents tried to find other financial umbrellas with which to fund a new position. Graduate students Edward and Dorothea Moore were funded by the University of Chicago while they conducted research in the neighborhood. Carolyn Hunt, a "slum investigator" under Carroll Wright, resided at Hull-House while analyzing the nutritional habits of the immigrant poor (Muncy, *Creating a Female Dominion,* 20; resident meeting, Apr. 6, 1895).

20. Starr to Blaisdell, July 25, 1892.

21. Starr to Blaisdell, Feb. 23, 1889.

22. Addams, "Filial Relations," 78, 82–83.

23. Addams, "Filial Relations," 78.

24. Davis, *American Heroine,* 6, 28; Anna Addams to John Addams, Jan. 11, 1869, Jane Addams Papers, Swarthmore College Peace Collection, Swarthmore College (hereafter cited as JA Papers).

25. Addams, "Filial Relations," 73–74.

26. Jane Addams to Alice Addams, Aug. 12, 1891, JAMC, reel 2.

27. Alice A. Haldeman to Jane Addams, Feb. 16, 17, 1896, JAMC.

28. Jane Addams to Alice Addams, Sept. 23, 1900; Davis, *American Heroine,* 84.

29. Jane Addams to Mary Smith, Aug. 14, 1899, JAMC.

30. Alice Hamilton to Florence Kelley, May 31, 1899, Hull-House, and June 2, 1899 Fort Wayne, HF Papers.

31. Alice Hamilton to Agnes Hamilton, Apr. 30, 1900, HF Papers.

32. Alice Hamilton to Agnes Hamilton, Aug. 8, 1900, HF Papers.

33. Hackett, "Hull House—a Souvenir," 276; Sicherman, *Alice Hamilton,* 141.

34. For more on Florence Kelley's early life, see Sklar, *Florence Kelley,* 3–170.

35. Florence Kelley to Caroline Kelley, Feb. 24, 1892, Nicholas Kelley Papers, New York Public Library; see also Caro Lloyd, *Henry Demarest Lloyd, 1847–1903: A Biography,* 2 vols. (New York: G. P. Putnam's Sons, 1912).

36. Florence Kelley to Henry Demarest Lloyd, Nov. 28, 1892, Henry Demarest Lloyd Papers, State Historical Society of Wisconsin; Chester M. Destler, *Henry Demarest Lloyd and the Empire of Reform* (Philadelphia: U of Pennsylvania P, 1963).

37. Jane Addams to Florence Kelley, Sept. 7, 1901, JAMC.

38. Hamilton to Kelley, May 31 and June 2, 1899.

39. Waite, Luther, and Gyles, "Edith Nancrede."

40. Hamilton to Kelley, May 31 and June 2, 1899. For an analysis of the social hopes of this fictive parenting in female social reform, see Dorothy Berkson, " 'So We All Become Mothers': Harriet Beecher Stowe, Charlotte Perkins Gilman, and the New World of Women's Culture," in *Feminism, Utopia, and Narrative,* ed. Libby Falk and Sarah Webster Goodwin (Knoxville: U of Tennessee P, 1990), 101. For a contemporary analyses see Kathy Weston, *Families We Choose: Lesbians, Gays, Kinship* (New York: Columbia UP, 1991); Nicholson, *Gender and History;* Sheila Rothman, "Other People's Children," *Public Interest* 30 (1973).

41. Gordon, *Pitied but Not Entitled,* 291; Fraser, "After the Family Wage," 41–68; Nelson, "Two-Channeled Welfare State"; Michel, "The Limits of Maternalism."

42. Lauren Berlant, "Intimacy," *Critical Inquiry* 24.2 (1998): 286. On the relationship between sexuality and social reorganization, see Gayle Rubin, "Thinking Sex: Notes for a Radical Theory of the Politics of Sexuality," in *Pleasure and Danger: Exploring Female Sexuality,* ed. Carol S. Vance (Boston:

Routledge and Kegan Paul, 1984), 267–318; Butler, _Gender Trouble_, 35–78; Michael Warner, ed., _Fear of a Queer Planet: Queer Politics and Social Theory_ (Minneapolis: U of Minnesota P, 1993), especially his introduction, vii–xxxi; Warner, "Something Queer about the Nation State," in _After Political Correctness: The Humanities and Society in the 1990s,_ ed. Christopher Newfield and Ronald Strickland (Boulder, CO: Westview, 1995), 361–71, which is also in conversation with Jürgen Habermas, "The New Obscurity: The Crisis of the Welfare State and the Exhaustion of Utopian Energies," in _The New Conservatism: Cultural Criticism and the Historians' Debate,_ trans. Shierry Weber Nicholesen (Cambridge: MIT P, 1989), 48–70.

43. An example of this kind of accusation appears in James Johnson, "The Role of Women in the Founding of the United States Children's Bureau," in _"Remembering the Ladies": New Perspectives on Women in American History_ (Syracuse: Syracuse UP, 1975), 191.

44. Lauren Berlant and Michael Warner, "Sex in Public," _Critical Inquiry_ 24.2 (1998): 558. For more contemporary analyses of the interaction between queer theory and cultural geography, see Gordon Brent Ingram, Anne Marie Bouthillette, and Yolanda Retter, eds., _Queers in Space: Communities, Public Spaces, Sites of Resistance,_ (Seattle: Bay Press, 1997); Gill Valentine, "(Hetero)-sexing Space: Lesbian Perceptions and Experiences of Everyday Spaces," _Environment and Planning D_ 11 (1993): 395–413; D. Bell and Gill Valentine, eds., _Mapping Desire: Geographies of Sexualities_ (London: Routledge, 1995).

45. Sicherman, _Alice Hamilton,_ 133.

46. Dorothy Mittelman Sigel, interview by the author, May 1994, May 1995.

47. Sicherman, _Alice Hamilton,_ 121–22.

48. Hackett, recalling 1906, in "Hull-House—a Souvenir," 275.

49. See Davis, _American Heroine,_ 12; Kelley, _Autobiography,_ 49; Helen Lefkowitz Horowitz, _Alma Mater_ and _Campus Life: Undergraduate Culture from the End of the Eighteenth Century to the Present_ (Chicago: U of Chicago P, 1987); Soloman, _Company of Educated Women._

50. Starr to Blaisdell, Feb. 23, 1889.

51. Davis, _American Heroine,_ 11.

52. Spain, _Gendered Spaces,_ 141–68.

53. "Main House, Inventory," 1901, JAMC, addendum 10.

54. "Main House, Inventory," 1901.

55. Quoted in Davis, _American Heroine,_ 13.

56. Sicherman, _Alice Hamilton,_ 116.

57. Carol Smith Rosenberg, "The Female World of Love and Ritual" (1975), in _Disorderly Conduct,_ 53–76.

58. Ellen Gates Starr to Jane Addams, n.d., JAMC; JA to EGS, Apr. 23, 1883, EGS Papers.

59. See for instance, Faderman, _Odd Girls,_ 11–36.

60. Martha Vicinus, introduction, to _Lesbian Subjects: A Feminist Studies Reader,_ ed. Martha Vicinus (Indianapolis: Indiana UP, 1996), 2. See related work on this debate in several fields: John d'Emilio and Estelle B. Freedman,

Intimate Matters: A History of Sexuality in America (New York: Harper and Row, 1988); Sheila Jeffreys, "Does It Matter If They Did It?" in *Not a Passing Phase: Reclaiming Lesbians in History, 1840–1985,* ed. Lesbian History Group (London: Woman's Press, 1989), 19–28; Blanche Weisen Cook, "Women Alone Stir My Imagination: Lesbianism and the Cultural Tradition," *Signs* 4 (summer 1979): 716–27; Martin Duberman, Martha Vicinus, and George Chauncey Jr., eds., *Hidden from History: Reclaiming the Gay and Lesbian Past* (New York: New American Library, 1989); Terry Castle, *The Apparitional Lesbian: Female Homosexuality and Modern Culture* (New York: Columbia UP, 1993); Biddy Martin, "Lesbian Identity and Autobiographical Difference(s)," in *The Lesbian and Gay Studies Reader,* ed. Henry Abelove, Michèle Aina Barale, and David Halperin (New York: Routledge, 1993); Martha Vicinus, " 'They Wonder to Which Sex I Belong' " (1989), reprinted in *Lesbian Subjects,* 233–59; Sue-Ellen Case, introduction, to *Performing Feminisms* (Baltimore: Johns Hopkins UP, 1989), and *The Domain Matrix,* 17–23; Diana Fuss, *Essentially Speaking: Feminism, Nature, and Difference* (New York: Routledge, Chapman, and Hall, 1989), 99, and introduction to *Inside/Out* (New York: Routledge, 1991).

61. On the relationship between female activism and same-sex attachment, see Blanche Weisen Cook, "The Historical Denial of Lesbianism," *Radical History Review* 20 (spring–summer 1979): 60–65, and "Female Support Networks and Political Activism: Lillian Wald, Crystal Eastman, Emma Goldman," in Cott and Pleck, *Heritage of Her Own,* 412–44; Micaela di Leonardo, "Warrior Virgins and Boston Marriages: Spinsterhood in History and Culture," *Feminist Studies* 5 (1985): 47–68; Estelle Freedman, "Separatism as Strategy: Female Institution Building and American Feminism, 1870–1930," *Feminist Studies* 5 (1979): 512–29, and *Maternal Justice: Miriam Van Waters and the Female Reform Tradition* (Chicago: U of Chicago P, 1996); Gordon, *Pitied but Not Entitled,* 78; Christine Simmons, "Compassionate Marriage and the Lesbian Threat," in *Women and Power in American History,* ed. Kathryn Kish Sklar and Thomas Dublin (Englewood Cliffs, NJ: Prentice-Hall, 1991), 183–94; Lillian Faderman, *Surpassing the Love of Men: Romantic Friendship and Love Between Women from Renaissance to the Present* (New York: Morrow, 1981) 204–31.

62. Jane Addams to Mary Rozet Smith, May 26, 1902; Jane Addams to Mary Rozet Smith, Mar. 22, 1904, JAMC; Davis, *American Heroine,* 85–91.

63. Jane Addams to Mary Rozet Smith, Aug. 14, 1904; Addams to Smith, July 21, 1892; Addams to Smith, July 22, 1897; Addams to Sarah Alice Addams Haldeman, Dec. 4, 1896; Addams to Smith, Aug. 4, 1904, JAMC. At the behest of doctors, Addams kept a weight diary from 1922 until her death in 1935 (JAMC).

64. Linn, *Jane Addams,* 289–90.

65. Jane Addams to Mary Rozet Smith, Mar. 2, 1897; Addams to Smith, July 29, 1895; Addams to Smith, Aug. 9, 1904; Addams to Smith, Apr. 8, 1902, JAMC.

66. Jane Addams to Mary Rozet Smith, Jan. 15, 1895.

67. Addams to Smith, July 29, 1895.

68. Ann Ferguson, "Patriarchy, Sexual Identity, and the Sexual Revolution," *Signs* 7 (autumn 1981): 158–72. See "Records of Mary Rozet Smith's contributions to Hull House," JAMC.

69. JA to MRS, Apr. 1, 1898; Addams to Smith, Mar. 2, 1897; JA to MRS [n.d., around 1894]; JA to MRS, June 18, 1896, JAMC.

70. Mary Rozet Smith to Jane Addams, Dec. 1896, JAMC.

71. Addams to Smith, July 29, 1895.

72. Addams to Smith, Apr. 1, 1898.

73. Addams to Smith, Mar. 2, 1897.

74. Addams to Smith, Mar. 2, 1897.

75. Indeed, a contemporary perspective might not only emphasize Hull-House's figurative relation to many nonbiological children and neighbors, but also interpret the number of "Jane" namesakes (new babies, in the Jane Club) as an instance of non-bio-reproductive queer cloning.

76. Sicherman, *Alice Hamilton,* 130.

77. Clara Paige to Jane Addams, Mar. 14, 1922, JAMC.

78. Hamilton, "Exploring the Dangerous Trades," 122.

79. Waite, Luther, and Gyles, "Edith Nancrede."

80. Sklar, "Hull-House in 1890s," 659.

81. Rosenberg, *Beyond Separate Spheres,* 127.

82. Kelley, *Autobiography,* 49.

83. Davis, *American Heroine,* 12.

84. Beatrice Webb, *American Diary, 1898,* ed. David A. Shannon (Madison, WI: U of Wisconsin P, 1963), 108; quoted in Davis and Bryan, *One Hundred Years,* 61.

85. Alice Hamilton to Agnes Hamilton, May 18, 1897, HF Papers.

86. Hamilton, "Exploring the Dangerous Trades," 120.

87. Starr to Blaisdell, July 25, 1892.

88. Quoted in Horowitz, "Hull-House as Women's Space," 52.

89. Madeline Wallin to unknown, Sept. 22, 1896, Madeleine Wallin Sikes Papers, Chicago Historical Society (hereafter cited as MWS Papers).

90. Ellen Gates Starr to unknown [1890s], EGS Papers.

91. Quoted in Carson, *Settlement Folk,* 82.

92. AH to Agnes Hamilton, Jan. 28, 1904, box 29, subseries B, HF Papers.

93. Ellen Gates Starr to Jane Addams, Apr. 12, 1935, EGS Papers.

94. Ellen Gates Starr to Caleb Starr, Dec. 9, 1910, EGS Papers.

95. Florence Kelley to Mary Smith, Feb. 14, 1899, Florence Kelley Papers, Columbia University.

96. Resident meeting, Mar. 6, 1894, JAMC.

97. Addams to Smith, Jan. 15, 1895.

98. Hackett, "Hull-House—a Souvenir," 275.

99. Sicherman, *Alice Hamilton,* 115–17.

100. Sicherman, *Alice Hamilton,* 133.

101. Addams to Gyles, Jan. 11, 1894; JA to Eleanor Smith, Aug. 6, 1901, JAMC.

102. Jane Addams to Mary Rozet Smith, Feb. 23, 1897, JAMC.

103. Addams to Smith, July 29, 1895.

104. Sicherman, *Alice Hamilton,* 134.

105. Sicherman, *Alice Hamilton,* 131.

106. Sicherman, *Alice Hamilton,* 116.

107. Leila J. Rupp, " 'Imagine My Surprise': Women's Relationships in Historical Perspective," in Leavitt, *Women and Health,* 92; Faderman, *Surpassing Love of Men,* 190–230; Martha Vicinus, " 'One Life to Stand Beside Me': Emotional Conflicts in First Generation College Women in England," *Feminist Studies* 8 (1982): 610.

108. For a theorizing of identification and desire, see Diana Fuss, *Identification Papers* (New York: Routledge, 1995), and "Freud's Fallen Women: Identification, Desire, and 'A Case of Homosexuality in a Woman'," in Warner, *Fear of Queer Planet,* 69–81.

109. Madeleine Wallin to Father, Oct. 27, 1896, MWS Papers.

110. Max Weber, *On Charisma and Institution Building,* ed. and trans. S. N. Eisenstadt (Chicago: U of Chicago P, 1968); Hackett, "Hull-House—a Souvenir," 277.

111. For a comparative analysis of Addams's leadership styles, see Louise Wilby Knight, "Jane Addams and Hull-House: Historical Lessons on Nonprofit Leadership," *Nonprofit Management and Leadership* 2.2 (1991): 125–41.

112. Hamilton, "Exploring the Dangerous Trades," 120.

113. AH to Margaret Hamilton, June 22, 1915, series I, folder 3, Alice Hamilton Papers, Schlesinger Library, Radcliffe College (hereafter cited as AH Papers).

114. Wallin to Father, Oct. 27, 1896. See also "Genius of Hull House Is 'First Citizen of Chicago,' " 1910, clippings, JAMC; Walter Lippmann, "Today and Tomorrow," *Los Angeles Times,* May 23, 1935; Graham Taylor, "Of the Places That Knew Her," *Chicago Tribune,* May 23, 1935, clippings, JAMC.

115. Hackett, "Hull-House—a Souvenir," 275, 277.

116. Alice Hamilton to Agnes Hamilton, April 3, 1898, HF Papers.

117. Webb, *American Diary,* 108.

118. Hackett, "Hull-House—a Souvenir," 275.

119. Eve Sedgwick, *Between Men: English Literature and Male Homosocial Desire* (New York: Columbia UP, 1992).

120. Sedgwick, *Epistemology of the Closet,* 193.

121. Hackett, "Hull House—a Souvenir," 276.

122. Hackett, "Hull House—a Souvenir," 276.

123. Alice Hamilton to Agnes Hamilton, Oct. 13, 1897, HF Papers: "Civic Leader Deknatel [Jr.] Rites Monday," *Chicago Sun-Times,* clippings, JAMC.

124. Francis Hackett to Alice Hamilton, Apr. 16, 1925, series I, folder 6, AH Papers, 276.

125. Waite, Luther, and Gyles, "Edith Nancrede."

126. Hackett, "Hull-House—a Souvenir," 276–77.

127. Waite, Luther, and Gyles, "Edith Nancrede."

128. Hackett, "Hull-House—a Souvenir," 276–77.

129. Ellen Gates Starr to Mary Blaisdell, Dec. 19 [1889 or 1890], EGS Papers.

130. Moore, "Day at Hull-House," 635.

131. AH to Agnes Hamilton, July 3, 1898. Hamilton further distinguished Miss Brockway from other female settlers. "Aren't things badly mixed in this world? Here is a girl who hates independence and longs to be shielded and protected and managed and has no cravings after latch-keys and money for her own earning, while hundreds of much-fathered and mothered girls would gladly change places with her."

132. See Paul Boyer's passing reference to this brand of irony in Mary McDowell in *Urban Masses,* 155.

133. Upton Sinclair, *The Jungle,* (1906; Urbana: U of Illinois P, 1988), 198.

134. Hackett, "Hull House—a Souvenir," 276.

135. Hackett, "Hull-House—a Souvenir," 276.

136. Twose, "Settlement Reflections."

137. Kelley, *Autobiography,* 94–95.

138. Addams, "The Subtle Problems of Charity," in *Democracy and Social Ethics,* 16.

139. George Twose, "The Song of the Noble Soul," JAMC reel 50: 431.

140. Twose, "Song of Noble Soul."

141. Alice Hamilton to Agnes Hamilton, Aug. 8, 1900.

142. Resident meeting, May 18, 1896, JAMC.

143. Waite, Luther, and Gyles, "Edith Nancrede."

144. Waite, Luther, and Gyles, "Edith Nancrede."

145. Hackett, "Hull House—a Souvenir," 276.

146. Lela B. Costin, *Two Sisters for Social Justice: The Biography of Grace and Edith Abbott* (Chicago: U of Illinois P, 1983), 36.

147. Hackett, "Hull House—a Souvenir," 277.

148. Addams, *Twenty Years.*

149. For an analysis of Hull-House's place in what Dolores Hayden calls a materialist feminist movement in cooperative living, see *The Grand Domestic Revolution.* Other work on cooperative housing experiments are Carl J. Guarneri, *The Utopian Alternative: Fourierism in Nineteenth Century America* (Ithaca: Cornell UP, 1991); Michael Fellman, *The Unbounded Frame: Freedom and Community in Nineteenth-Century American Utopianism* (Westport, CO: Greenwood, 1973); Edith Roelker Curtis, *A Season in Utopia: The Story of Brook Farm* (New York: Nelson, 1961); Mark Holloway, *Heavens on Earth: Utopian Communities in America, 1680–1880* (New York: Dover Publications, 1966). Some experiments adapted cooperative living strategies in the face of Charlotte Perkins Gilman's critique in *Women and Economics* (1898; rpt. New York: Harper and Row, 1966).

150. Kelley, *Autobiography,* 78.

151. Resident meeting, Nov. 4, 1894, JAMC; *Hull-House Bulletin,* Jan. 1897.

152. Addams, *Democracy and Social Ethics*, 102. See Judith Rollins, *Between Women: Domestics and Their Employers* (Philadelphia: Temple UP, 1985).

153. Addams, *Democracy and Social Ethics*, 102–3.

154. Resident meeting, June 9, 1896, JAMC.

155. Resident meeting, Feb. 16, 1895, JAMC.

156. Resident meeting, Mar. 20, 1895, JAMC.

157. *Hull-House Bulletin,* Jan. 1897.

158. Linn, *Jane Addams,* 119.

159. Twose, "Settlement Reflections."

160. Waite, Luther, and Gyles, "Edith Nancrede."

161. Waite, Luther, and Gyles, "Edith Nancrede."

162. Waite, Luther, and Gyles, "Edith Nancrede."

163. Webb, *American Diary,* 107.

164. John Dewey to Alice Dewey, Oct. 7 and 19 [1894] DF Papers.

165. Alice Hamilton to Agnes Hamilton, June 23, 1899, HF Papers.

166. Resident meetings, Aug. 8, 1893 to Apr. 6, 1895, JAMC. For an analysis of the resident meeting as itself a weekly social performance, see Shannon Jackson, "Lines of Activity: Performance, Space, and Pedagogy at Hull-House," Ph.D. diss., Northwestern University, 1995, 294–306.

167. Resident meeting, Dec. 10, 1893.

168. Hackett, "Hull House—a Souvenir," 275–76. See Hilda Satt Polacheck's description of toting as mode of class effacement for the residents and later a mode of employment for herself in *I Came a Stranger,* 75.

169. Resident meeting, May 11, 1896, JAMC.

170. Sicherman, *Alice Hamilton,* 122.

171. Hackett, "Hull House—a Souvenir," 277.

172. Review of "Fanchon the Cricket," Hull-House Theatre, JAMC.

173. Review of "Fanchon the Cricket."

174. Linn, *Jane Addams,* 119.

175. Louise deKoven Bowen, *Growing Up with a City* (New York: Macmillan, 1926), 86. Alex Elson, former neighborhood child, later paid toter, noted that non-Hull-House groups who met at the settlement did not appreciate toting (Alex Elson to JA, May 16, 1927, JAMC).

176. Alice Hamilton to Agnes Hamilton, Jan. 28, 1904.

177. Moore, "Day at Hull-House," 645.

178. Fraser, "Rethinking the Public Sphere," 137.

179. Resident meeting, Oct. 8, 1893; resident meeting, Sept. 17, 1893, JAMC.

180. Resident meeting, Oct. 15, 1893, JAMC.

181. Resident meeting, Sept. 28, 1894, JAMC.

182. Resident meeting, Oct. 8, 1893.

183. Moore, "Day at Hull-House," 635.

184. Resident meeting, July 24, 1896, JAMC.

185. Waite, Luther, and Gyles, "Edith Nancrede."

186. Waite, Luther, and Gyles, "Edith Nancrede."

187. *Hull-House Bulletin,* midwinter 1903–4.

188. Resident meeting, Oct. 8, 1893.

189. *Hull-House Bulletin,* 1905–6.

190. *Hull-House Bulletin,* 1905–6.

CHAPTER 5

1. Stephen Greenblatt, "Towards a Poetics of Culture," in Veeser, *The New Historicism,* 12. For more meditations on the relationship between theater and historiographic method, see the historicism section in Reinelt and Roach, *Critical Theory and Performance;* Bruce McConachie and Thomas Postlewait, eds., *Interpreting the Theatrical Past: Essays in the Historiography of Performance* (Iowa City: U of Iowa P, 1989); Sue-Ellen Case and Janelle Reinelt, eds., *The Performance of Power: Theatrical Discourse and Politics* (Iowa City: University of Iowa P, 1991); Pollock, *Exceptional Spaces;* Roach, *Cities of the Dead,* especially 1–32, 179–201, and *The Player's Passion: Studies in the Science of Acting* (Ann Arbor: U of Michigan P, 1985).

2. "Rites for Miss Nancrede, Famed Hull House Worker," newspaper clipping, JAMC Small Manuscripts Collection; Josephine de Nancrede Henry, grand-niece of Edith de Nancrede, interview by the author, 1998.

3. Edith de Nancrede, "Creative Possibilities of Art for Children," Midwest Conference on the Emotional Life of the Child, Mar. 7, 1930, JAMC Small Manuscripts Collection.

4. Alex Elson, "Edith de Nancrede 1887–1936: Funeral Program," JAMC Small Manuscripts Collection.

5. Miriam Almond Elson, "Edith de Nancrede: A Poem" (1936), JAMC Small Manuscripts Collection.

6. More discussion on this research and writing appears in chapter 6. See also chapter 5 of Jackson, "Lines of Activity," 329–406; Boyer, *Urban Masses;* Haskell, *Emergence of Social Science;* Stocking, *Race, Culture, and Evolution.* On the relationship between Hull-House and the Chicago School, see Deegan, *Jane Addams;* and Ulf Hannerz's second chapter in *Exploring the City: Inquiries toward Urban Ethnography* (New York: Columbia UP, 1980); brief mention is made in Stow Persons, *Ethnic Studies at Chicago* (Urbana: U of Illinois P, 1984). Other significant histories of Chicago School sociology: Robert Faris Thompson, *Chicago Sociology* (1967; Chicago: U of Chicago P, 1979); and Martin Bulmer, *The Chicago School of Sociology* (Chicago: U of Chicago P, 1984). For differently situated discussions of Chicago's discursive context, see Carla Cappetti, *Writing Chicago: Modernism, Ethnography, and the Novel* (New York: Columbia UP, 1993); and Carl Smith, *Chicago and the American Literary Imagination* (Chicago: U of Chicago P, 1984), and his *Urban Disorder and the Shape of Belief.*

7. Eaton, "Hull-House Distinctive Features," 9.

8. Addams, *Twenty Years,* 98.

9. James Clifford, *The Predicament of Culture: Twentieth Century Ethnography, Literature, and Art* (Cambridge: Harvard UP, 1988), 34.

10. Addams, *Spirit of Youth*, 8.

11. Talal Asad discusses "reading the implicit" as a "theological exercise" in "The Concept of Cultural Translation in British Social Anthropology," in *Writing Culture: The Poetics and Politics of Ethnography*, eds. James Clifford and George Marcus (Berkeley: U of California P, 1986) 141–65. On the gendering of Addams's epistemology, see Deegan, *Jane Addams;* Seigfried, *Pragmatism and Feminism;* and Dorothy Ross's forthcoming work, "Gender Social Knowledge: Domestic Discourse, Jane Addams, and the Possibilities of Social Science."

12. Mead, "Working Hypothesis," 370. See also "The Social Settlement," 110; Dewey, "School as Social Center"; Feffer, *Chicago Pragmatists*, 91–116, 159–78.

13. Porter, "Home on Halsted Street."

14. Addams, *Twenty Years*, 92–93.

15. Addams, *Democracy and Social Ethics*, 16.

16. Jane Addams to Eleanor Smith, Aug. 6, 1901.

17. Addams, "Public Recreation," 21.

18. Hull-House Shakespeare Society, 1895, 1896, JAMC reel 59: 177.

19. Addams, *Twenty Years*, 253.

20. Addams, *Twenty Years*, 254.

21. Jürgen Habermas, *The Structural Transformation of the Public Sphere*, trans. T. Burger and F. Lawrence (Cambridge: Harvard UP, 1989).

22. Mead, "Working Hypothesis," 370.

23. Addams, "Public Recreation," 24.

24. Addams, *Democracy and Social Ethics*, 57.

25. *Hull-House Bulletin*, Dec. 1896, June 1897, Dec. 1, 1897; Albert D. Phelps, "How the Hull House Players Fought Their Way to Success," *Theatre Magazine*, Nov. 1914, 230.

26. Phelps, "Hull House Players," 230.

27. Phelps, "Hull House Players," 229.

28. *Hull-House Bulletin*, Apr. and May 1898.

29. *Hull-House Bulletin*, Oct. 1898.

30. *Hull-House Bulletin*, Oct. 1898.

31. Williams, *The Sociology of Culture*, 57.

32. Edith de Nancrede, "Dramatic Work at Hull-House," *Playground*, Aug. 1928, 371, JAMC, and "Creative Possibilities."

33. Nancrede, "Dramatic Work," 278.

34. Madge Jenison, "A Hull-House Play," *Atlantic Monthly* (1906), 86.

35. Jenison, "A Hull-House Play," 88.

36. Jenison, "A Hull-House Play," 84–85.

37. Jenison, "A Hull-House Play, 85.

38. Jenison, "A Hull-House Play," 88.

39. Cavallo, *Muscles and Morals*, 103, 118.

40. Jenison, "A Hull-House Play," 90.

41. Edith de Nancrede to Jane Addams, Aug. 13, 1931, JAMC Small Manuscripts Collection.

42. Hull-House inventories, 1901 and 1903.

43. Jenison, "A Hull-House Play," 85.

44. *Hull-House Bulletin*, 1896.

45. *Hull-House Bulletin*, Dec. 1896.

46. Stuart Joel Hecht, "Hull-House Theatre: An Analytical and Evaluative History," Ph.D. diss. Northwestern U, 1983, and "Social and Artistic Integration: The Emergence of Hull-House Theatre," *Theatre Journal* 34.2 (1982): 172–82.

47. Addams, *Twenty Years*, 273.

48. Phelps, "Hull House Players," 230.

49. Phelps, "Hull House Players," 231.

50. Phelps, "Hull House Players," 231–32.

51. Stuart Joel Hecht uses the social-versus-aesthetic paradigm to evaluate Hull-House theater in "Hull-House Theatre" and "Social and Artistic Integration."

52. Dorothy Mittleman Sigel, interview by the author, Aug. 1994. See Hilda Satt Polacheck on Christmas at Hull-House, *I Came a Stranger*, 51–52, 103.

53. Addams, "Recent Immigration," 253–54.

54. Abbott, *Immigrant and Community*, 277.

55. For an analysis of the varied interpretations of the "melting pot" see Sollors, *Beyond Ethnicity*, 66–70.

56. Dewey, "Nationalizing Education," 184–85.

57. Kallen, *Culture and Democracy*, 180–81.

58. Kallen, "The Ethics of Zionism," 71.

59. Bourne, *The Radical Will*, 254, and *War and Intellectuals*, 131.

60. Lissak, *Pluralism and Progressives*, 142.

61. Addams, "Recreation as Public Function," 616–17.

62. Hollinger, *Postethnic America*, 3–4.

63. Hollinger, *Postethnic America*, 7; Cohen, "Rooted Cosmopolitanism"; Ackerman, "Rooted Cosmopolitanism."

64. Addams, *Twenty Years*, 269.

65. Clifford, *Predicament of Cultures*, 86.

66. Charles Zeublin, "The Chicago Ghetto," *Hull-House Maps and Papers*, 91–114.

67. Lissak, *Pluralism and Progressives*, 79–107.

68. *Hull-House Yearbook*, 1906–7, JAMC.

69. For a critique of the return of such a tendency, see Eric Lott's "The New Cosmopolitanism," *Transition* 72 (fall 1997): 108–35.

70. Addams, *Twenty Years*, 268.

71. Dewey, "Nationalizing Education," 185, 187.

72. "Greeks in Old Play," Dec. 1903, JAMC.

73. Elizabeth C. Barrows, "The Greek Play at Hull-House," *The Commons* (Jan. 1904).

74. "Greeks in Old Play"; Barrows, "Greek Play at Hull-House," 8–9.

75. Barrows, "Greek Play at Hull-House," 9.

76. Barrows, "Greek Play at Hull-House," 8.

77. "Greeks in Old Play."

78. "Greeks in Old Play."

79. Barrows, "Greek Play at Hull-House," 6; "Greeks in Old Play."

80. Barrows, "Greek Play at Hull-House," 10.

81. Jenison, "A Hull-House Play," 83, 84, 88.

82. Jenison, "A Hull-House Play," 86.

83. Jenison, "A Hull-House Play," 91.

84. Jenison, "A Hull-House Play," 91.

85. Jenison, "A Hull-House Play," 92.

86. Jenison, "A Hull-House Play," 91.

87. Laura Dainty Pelham, "The Story of the Hull-House Players," *Drama Magazine* (May 1916): 260.

88. Hull-House Players, "Report of Special Committee on Constitutional Revision and Policy," JAMC.

89. Hull-House Players, "Report."

90. Pelham, "Story of the Hull-House Players," 260.

91. *Hull-House Bulletin,* 1905–6; " 'The Three Gifts—A Labor Play," JAMC, 846.

92. "The Three Gifts," 846.

93. Brown, "The Hull House Players in 'Justice,' " *Theatre Magazine* (Sept. 1911): 90.

94. Boyer, *Urban Masses;* Wiebe, *The Search for Order;* see also John Kasson's differently conceived project in *Rudeness and Civility: Manners in Nineteenth-Century Urban America* (New York: Hill and Wang, 1990).

95. Kasson, *Rudeness and Civility,* 7.

96. "Tivoli Theatre: J.P.A. Investigation," Apr. 8, 1921. The Juvenile Protective Association will be discussed further in chapter 6. More documents illustrate perspectives on stage, children, including *Illinois Senate Record,* typed transcript, Capitol Shorthand Service, Jan. 8, 1910, JAMC; Jane Addams, "Stage Children," *Survey,* Dec. 3, 1910, 342–43 and "The Reaction of Moral Instruction upon Social Reform," *Survey,* Apr. 3, 1909, 19. J.P.A. Investigation, "Local Song Contests in Neighborhood Theatres," n.d.; Zeta Youmans, "Modern Commercialism and Childhood," n.d. [after 1916], 23–24; Jessie Binford and Zeta Youmans to Margaret Ritscher, Industrial Commission of Wisconsin, Oct. 27, 1922, Juvenile Protective Association Papers (hereafter cited as JPA Papers).

97. "Tivoli Theatre: J.P.A. Investigation," Dec. 5, 1922, JPA Papers. Studies of sexual and moral scandal in American theater include Abe Laufe, *The Wicked Stage: A History of Theater Censorship and Harassment in the United States* (New York: Ungar, 1978); Robert Allen, *Horrible Prettiness: Burlesque and American Culture* (Chapel Hill: U of North Carolina P, 1991); Lawrence W. Levine, *Highbrow/Lowbrow: The Emergence of Cultural Hierarchy in America* (Cambridge: Harvard UP, 1988); Ronald Wainscott, *The Emergence of the Modern American Theater, 1914–1929* (New Haven: Yale UP, 1997).

98. Addams, *Spirit of Youth,* 76.

99. Jenison, "A Hull-House Play," 86. See Kasson, *Rudeness and Civility,* 112–14. As an example of Hull-House residents' theories of the relationship between child development and environment, see Sophonisba Breckinridge and

Edith Abbott, *The Delinquent Child and the Home* (New York: Charities Publication Committee, 1912).

100. Jenison, "A Hull-House Play," 87.

101. Addams, "Public Recreation," 21–22.

102. Jenison, "A Hull-House Play," 88.

103. Nancrede, "Dramatic Work," 277.

104. Sigel, interview, May 1994.

105. Bourdieu, *Distinction,* 40.

106. "Hull-House Theatre," June 1902, JAMC.

107. Nancrede to Addams, Aug. 13, 1931.

108. Carmella Gustaferre, "What Kind of a Home I Would Like to Have," first printed in "Ideals of Life and Living," *Survey,* July 18, 1914, 420 and also excerpted in Bryan and Davis, *One Hundred Years,* 132–33.

109. Nancrede, "Dramatic Work," 277.

110. Addams, *Spirit of Youth,* 89.

111. Brown, "Hull-House Players," 90.

112. *Hull-House Bulletin,* Jan. and Feb. 1898.

113. *The Walking Delegate,* adapted by Hilda Satt, JAMC.

114. Nancrede, "Creative Possibilities," 8.

115. Nancrede, "Dramatic Work," 277.

116. *Hull-House Bulletin,* 1905–6.

117. James O'Donnell Bennett, "Music and the Drama," *Chicago Record-Herald,* Mar. 6, 1906, 8; Joseph Roach explores ambivalent definitions of "naturalness" and "spontaneity" in earlier acting styles in *The Player's Passion.*

118. Dorothy Mittelman Sigel, interview by the author, May 1994 and April 1995.

119. Youmans, "Modern Commercialism and Childhood," 24. On consumption in the twentieth-century United States, see Trachtenberg, *The Incorporation of America;* Stuart Ewen, *Captains of Consciousness: Advertising and the Social Roots of the Consumer Culture* (New York: McGraw-Hill, 1976); Richard Wightman Fox and T. J. Jackson Lears, eds., *The Culture of Consumption: Critical Essays in American History, 1880–1980* (New York: Pantheon, 1983); Benson, *Counter Cultures;* Lizabeth Cohen, "Embellishing a Life of Labor: An Interpretation of Material Culture of American Working-Class Homes, 1885–1915," *Journal of American Culture* 3 (winter 1980): 752–75, and "The Class Experience of Mass Consumption," in Fox and Lears, *The Power of Culture,* 135–62; and Joan Shelley Rubin, "Between Culture and Consumption," also in Fox and Lears, *The Power of Culture,* 163–94.

120. Youmans, "Modern Commercialism and Childhood," 20.

121. See Benson on the performance of "middle class" in the new service industries, *Counter Cultures,* 240–65.

CHAPTER 6

1. Thomas Buck, "Two Tenants Delay Campus," *Chicago Tribune,* Apr. 19, 1963, 1, 4.

2. Buck, "Two Tenants Delay Campus," 4.

3. See Harvey, *Social Justice and City, The Condition of Postmodernity,* and numerous other works; R. Beauregard, *Voices of Decline: The Postward Fate of US Cities* (New York: Basil Blackwell, 1993); R. Walker, "A Theory of Suburbanization," in *Urbanization and Planning in Capitalist Society,* ed. Michael J. Dear and Allen John Scott (London: Methuen, 1981); Neil Smith, *The New Urban Frontier: Gentrification and the Revanchist City* (New York: Routledge, 1996). See earlier critiques and anticipations of Chicago urban renewal and gentrification: Harvey Zorbaugh, *The Gold Coast and the Slum* (Chicago: U of Chicago P, 1929); H. Hoyt, *One Hundred Years of Land Values in Chicago* (Chicago: U of Chicago P, 1933).

4. Arendt, *The Human Condition.* Such valuable analyses include Warner, *Fear of Queer Planet,* xxvii; B. Honig, "Toward an Agonistic Feminism: Hannah Arendt and the Politics of Identity," in Butler and Scott *Feminists Theorize the Political,* 215–38; Wendy Brown, *States of Injury: Power and Freedom in Late Modernity* (Princeton: Princeton UP, 1995).

5. Addams, "Public Recreation," 21–22.

6. Edith Abbott, "The Fallacy of Local Relief," *New Republic,* Nov. 9, 1932, 349–50.

7. Christine Ziomek, "Hull House: UICC's Tribute to Jane Addams," *Chicago Illini,* Sept. 1, 1966, 13.

8. Marion Foster Washburne, "A Labor Museum," *Craftsman,* Sept. 1904, 576. An abridged form of this essay is reprinted in Bryan and Davis, *One Hundred Years,* 74–81.

9. Washburne, "A Labor Museum," 578.

10. Ellen Gates Starr, "A Note of Explanation," EGS Papers; also published in *Hull-House Bulletin* (May 1900) and *The Commons* (June 1900); Ellen Gates Starr, "Bookbinding," *Industrial Arts Magazine,* Mar. 1916.

11. Boris, *Art and Labor,* 48–51, 93; Oscar Lovell Triggs, *Chapters in the History of the Arts and Crafts Movement* (Chicago: Bohemian Guild of Arts and Crafts, 1902); *Hull-House Bulletin,* Oct. to Dec. 1897, June 1897, Apr. and May 1898, autumn 1900; George Herbert Mead, "The Relation of Play to Education," *University of Chicago Record I* (1896) Mead Papers; Jane Addams, "The Humanizing Tendency of Industrial Education," *Chautauquan* 39 (May 1904): 266–72; Frank Lloyd Wright gave a lecture, "The Use of Machinery," *Hull-House Bulletin,* Nov. 1897.

12. Addams, *Twenty Years,* 172.

13. Addams, "First Outline for the Labor Museum," JAMC.

14. Addams, "First Outline," 8.

15. Addams, "First Outline," 3.

16. Dewey, "School as Social Center," 379. See also his later "Nationalizing Education," 183–89.

17. Later published in Abbott, *Immigrant and Community,* 10–20, 222, 236; Abbott, "True Americanization," *Americanization Bulletin* 1 (Nov. 1918): 4.

18. Addams, "First Outline," 1.

19. Dewey, "School as Social Center," 107.

20. For a lengthier analysis of the goals and limits of this bindery, see

Shannon Jackson, "Lines of Activity," 509–13 and "Museum, Microfiche, and Historiography: Performance at Hull-House," in Pollock, *Exceptional Spaces,* 261–93.

21. *Hull-House Bulletin,* autumn 1900.

22. *Hull-House Bulletin,* autumn 1900.

23. *Hull-House Bulletin,* Jan. to May 1901.

24. *Hull-House Bulletin,* autumn 1900, Jan. to May 1901.

25. Addams, "First Outline," 5.

26. Addams, "First Outline," 5.

27. *Hull-House Bulletin,* autumn 1900.

28. *Hull-House Bulletin,* autumn 1900.

29. Addams, "First Outline," 4.

30. Michael Wallace, "Visiting the Past: Historical Museums in the United States," in *Presenting the Past: Essays on History and the Public,* ed. Susan Porter Benson, Stephen Brier, and Roy Rosenzweig (Philadelphia: Temple UP, 1986), 138; David Glassberg, *American Pageantry: The Uses of Tradition in the Early Twentieth Century* (Chapel Hill: U of North Carolina P, 1990), 48, 126, 131, 133; Bruce McConachie and Darryl Friedman, eds., *Theatre for Working-Class Audiences, 1830–1980* (Westport, CT: Greenwood, 1984). See Werner Sollors on Henry Ford's version of the melting pot as a straw man in pluralist debates, *Beyond Ethnicity,* 94–101.

31. Kirshenblatt-Gimblett, "Objects of Ethnography," *Exhibiting Cultures: The Poetics and Politics of Museum Display,* ed. Ivan Karp and Steven D. Lavine (Washington, DC: Smithsonian Institution P, 1991), 390. See Karp's "Culture and Representation" and related essays in the same volume. See also Michael Bowman, "Performing Southern History for the Tourist's Gaze," and Elizabeth Gray Buck, "Museum Author-ity and Performance," in Pollock, *Exceptional Spaces,* 142–60, 294–318.

32. Holbrook, introduction to *Hull-House Maps and Papers,* 15.

33. Wolf, *Europe.*

34. Sally Price, *Primitive Art in Civilized Places* (Chicago: U of Chicago P, 1989), 59.

35. Addams, "First Outline," 3.

36. Johannes Fabian, *Time and the Other: How Anthropology Makes Its Object* (New York: Columbia UP, 1983), 23; see Whisnant's analysis of a parallel reform effort, *All That Is Native.*

37. Inventory, 1903, JAMC addendum 10.

38. *Hull-House Bulletin,* autumn 1904.

39. Floya Anthias and Nira Yuval-Davis, *Woman-Nation-State* (New York: Macmillan, 1989), 7.

40. *Hull-House Bulletin,* semiannual 1902.

41. "As the need of books came into man's life later than the necessity for means of feeding, clothing and housing himself, this department of the labor museum naturally follows those of the grains, textiles, wood, and metals" (*Hull-House Bulletin,* semiannual 1902).

42. "Mr. Klindera" in carpentry, "Mr. Milliard" in a new "printing outfit,"

"Mr. Will La Favor" in clay modeling, "Mr. Caruso" in wood inlaid and metal, and "Mr. Alex Colarossi," "Mr. Fogliati," and "Mr. Friedman" in metal and enamel (*Hull-House Bulletin,* semiannual 1902, autumn 1904).

43. Kirshenblatt-Gimblett, "Objects of Ethnography," 434.

44. Washburne, "A Labor Museum," 570.

45. Washburne, "A Labor Museum," 570.

46. Addams, "First Outline," 18.

47. Washburne, "A Labor Museum," 572.

48. Washburne, "A Labor Museum," 571. See Polacheck's memory of the Labor Museum in *I Came a Stranger,* 65.

49. Washburne, "A Labor Museum," 574.

50. Washburne, "A Labor Museum," 574.

51. Washburne, "A Labor Museum," 574.

52. Washburne, "A Labor Museum," 574.

53. Kirshenblatt-Gimblett, "Objects of Ethnography," 410.

54. Washburne, "A Labor Museum," 575.

55. Washburne, "A Labor Museum," 575.

56. Washburne, "A Labor Museum," 575.

57. Scott, *Domination.*

58. Washburne, "A Labor Museum," 578.

59. Addams, *Twenty Years,* 172.

60. Washburne, "A Labor Museum," 579.

61. Washburne, "A Labor Museum," 579.

62. "Report to Commission on Accreditation," Council on Social Work Education, 1976, Jane Addams School of Social Work Papers, Special Collections, University of Illinois at Chicago.

63. Starr to Blaisdell, July 25, 1892.

64. Florence Kelley, "Hull House," *New England Magazine,* July 1898, 550.

65. Clifford, *Predicament of Culture,* 35.

66. Holbrook, introduction, *Hull-House Maps and Papers,* 13–14.

67. Settlers were encouraged to use these techniques by Mr. and Mrs. Canon Barnett when they came to visit the United States. See Kathryn Kish Sklar, "Hull-House Maps and Papers: Social Science as Women's Work in the 1890s," in *The Social Survey in Historical Perspective, 1880–1940,* ed. Martin Blumer, Kevin Bales, and Kathryn Kish Sklar (Cambridge: Cambridge UP, 1991) and essays on Booth in this collection.

68. On mapping and visuality, see Jonathon Crary, *Techniques of the Observer: On Vision and Modernity,* (Cambridge: MIT P, 1990); Hal Foster, ed., *Vision and Visuality* (Seattle: Bay Press, 1988); Martin Jay, *Downcast Eyes: The Denigration of Vision in Twentieth-Century French Thought* (Berkeley and Los Angeles: U of California P, 1993); Benedict Anderson analyzes the similar role of the map in nation building in *Imagined Communities* (1983; London: Verso, 1991).

69. Holbrook, introduction, *Hull-House Maps and Papers,* 11.

70. Holbrook, introduction, *Hull-House Maps and Papers,* 20.

71. Holbrook, introduction, *Hull-House Maps and Papers,* 21.

72. Holbrook, introduction, *Hull-House Maps and Papers,* 20.

73. Holbrook, introduction, *Hull-House Maps and Papers,* 35.

74. Resident meeting, Aug. 27, 1893, JAMC.

75. Holbrook, introduction, *Hull-House Maps and Papers,* 5.

76. On Hull-House, the Chicago School, Chicago and the Progressive discursive context, see Deegan, *Jane Addams,* and Hannerz's second chapter in *Exploring the City;* Persons, *Ethnic Studies at Chicago;* Thompson, *Chicago Sociology;* Bulmer, *Chicago School of Sociology;* Cappetti, *Writing Chicago;* Smith, *Chicago and Literary Imagination* and *Urban Disorder;* Trachtenberg, *The Incorporation of America;* Fisher, "Appearing and Disappearing" and *Hard Facts;* Kaplan, *Social Construction.*

77. Carson, *Settlement Folk,* 70; George Rosen, *A History of Public Health* (New York: MD Publications, 1958); Stephen Smith, "The History of Public Health, 1871–1921," *A Half Century of Public Health: Jubilee Historical Volume of the American Public Health Association,* ed. Mazyck P. Ravenel (New York: American Public Health Association, 1921) 1–21.

78. Peter Stallybrass and Allon White make a similar point about the paradoxes in the language of Dickens and Engels where "the representation of filth which traverses their work is unstable, sliding between social, moral, and psychic domains" in *The Politics and Poetics of Transgression* (Ithaca and New York: Cornell UP, 1986) 130.

79. Holbrook, introduction, *Hull-House Maps and Papers,* 8.

80. Zeublin, "The Ghetto," in *Hull-House Maps and Papers,* 95.

81. Holbrook, introduction, *Hull-House Maps and Papers,* 13, also 5–6.

82. Boris, *Home to Work.*

83. Holbrook, introduction, *Hull-House Maps and Papers,* 4.

84. Florence Kelley, "Second Annual Report, Factory Inspectors of Illinois for Year Ending December 15, 1894," (Springfield, IL: State Printers, 1895), 28–30, 52–55, 57–59; Davis and Bryan, *One Hundred Years,* 29.

85. Florence Kelley, "The Sweating System," in *Hull-House Maps and Papers,* 30. For an analysis of Kelley's role in the larger movement against home manufacture, see Boris, *Home to Work,* 49–80; and Sklar, *Florence Kelley and the Nation's Work,* 207–68.

86. Kelley, "The Sweating System," 35.

87. Mary Douglas, *Purity and Danger* (1966; New York: ARK, 1989).

88. Kelley, "Second Annual Report"; Davis and Bryan, *One Hundred Years,* 33.

89. Holbrook, introduction, *Hull-House Maps and Papers,* 6.

90. Alzina Stevens, "Wage Earning Children," in *Hull-House Maps and Papers,* 58.

91. Elaine Scarry, *The Body in Pain: The Making and Unmaking of the World* (Oxford: Oxford UP, 1985), 267.

92. Sinclair, *The Jungle.*

93. Kelley, "The Sweating System," 41.

94. Lathrop, "The Cook Country Charities," in *Hull-House Maps and Papers,* 147.

95. On paid toting as an index of Hull-House institutionalization, see Polacheck, *I Came a Stranger*, 75; Elson to JA, May 16, 1927; and Jackson, "Lines of Activity," 313–16.

96. Muncy, *Creating a Female Dominion;* Gordon, *Pitied but Not Entitled;* Sklar, *Florence Kelley;* Smith-Rosenberg, "Bourgeois Discourse," draws heavily from Robert Wiebe's *Search for Order.*

97. Pond, "The Settlement House III," 182. Another reflective remark sets up a link between Linda Gordon's discussion of a "jerry-built" welfare apparatus and Hull-House space: "It was 12 big, dark buildings, all patched up with different kinds of brick and gerry-repaired wood here and a staircase propped up there. This was right, of course, because it was a working building, and working buildings don't wear white gloves!" (Georgie Anne Geyer, *Chicago Daily News,* Sept. 26, 1965, 2)

98. Romero, *Home Fronts,* 112.

99. Jane Addams to Hamlin Garland, Apr. 29, 1907, JAMC.

100. Superintendent's Report, "Analysis of Work on Individual Families," Nov. 1, 1916, 17, JPA Papers.

101. Zueblin, "City Child at Play," 443, 447.

102. Louise deKoven Bowen to Jane Addams, Nov. 24, 1905, Louise deKoven Bowen Papers, Chicago Historical Society; Helen Culver to Louise deKoven Bowen, Nov. 23, 1905; Allen Pond to Helen Culver, Apr. 18, 1906; Helen Culver to Jane Addams, May 3, 1906; Helen Culver, speech on Opening of Boys' Club, n.d., Helen Culver Papers, University of Illinois at Chicago.

103. Louise deKoven Bowen to Jane Addams, June 11, 1907; Bowen to Addams, Oct. 4, 1906; Bowen to Addams, May 6, 1906; Bowen to Addams, May 7, 1906, Louise deKoven Bowen Papers.

104. Hull-House blueprints; Hull-House Boys Club lists, Jan. 1907, JAMC; Lissak cites these lists repeatedly and uses them as the basis for tables charting Hull-House ethnicity in *Pluralism and Progressives,* 113–21.

105. Julia Lathrop, memorandum, May 3, 1917, 2; see also Henry Goddard, "The Responsibility of the Juvenile Court," *Journal of American Institute of Criminal Law and Criminology* 3.3 (1912): 1–13, footnote on juvenile court.

106. Lathrop, memorandum, May 3, 1917, 3.

107. Lathrop, memorandum, May 3, 1917, 6.

108. Lathrop, memorandum, May 3, 1917, 6.

109. Ellen Fitzpatrick, *Endless Crusade: Women Social Scientists and Progressive Reform* (New York: Oxford UP, 1990), 173–76. See also, Graham Taylor, *Pioneering on Social Frontiers* (Chicago: U of Chicago P, 1930); and Costin, *Two Sisters.*

110. Breckinridge and Abbott, *Delinquent Child and Home,* v.

111. Linda Gordon and Nancy Fraser, "A Genealogy of Dependency," reprinted in Fraser, *Justice Interruptus,* 121–50.

112. Abbott and Breckinridge, *Delinquent Child and Home,* 11.

113. Abbott and Breckinridge, *Delinquent Child and Home,* 29–30.

114. Superintendent's Report, "Analysis of Work," 16.

115. Abbott and Breckinridge, *Delinquent Child and Home,* 19, 20.

116. Donzelot, *The Policing of Families;* Anthony Platt, *The Child Savers: The Invention of Delinquency* (Chicago: U of Chicago P, 1969); John Ehrenriech, *The Altruistic Imagination: A History of Social Work and Social Policy in the United States* (Ithaca: Cornell UP, 1985); Thomas Pegram, *Partisans and Progressives: Private Interest and Public Policy in Illinois, 1870–1922* (Urbana: U of Illinois P, 1992); Irene Diamond, ed., *Families, Politics, and Public Policy* (New York: Longman, 1983); James T. Kloppenberg, *Uncertain Victory: Social Democracy and Progressivism in European and American Thought, 1870–1920* (New York: Oxford UP, 1986).

117. For background on similar movements, see Barbara Ehrenreich and Deirdre English, *For Her Own Good: One Hundred and Fifty Years of the Expert's Advice to Women* (Garden City, NY: Anchor/Doubleday, 1978); Gwendolyn Wright, *Moralism and the Modern Home: Domestic Architecture and Cultural Conflict in Chicago, 1873–1913* (Chicago: U of Chicago P, 1980); Cohen, "Embellishing a Life"; Ewen, *Immigrant Women.*

118. "Practical Housekeeping Center," n.d., 1, JAMC; quotation from *Century Magazine,* Feb. 1907. This extended earlier domestic science classes, often sponsored by the Hull-House Woman's Club, that taught child care and hygiene for "principles underlying an intelligent care of the body" (*Hull-House Bulletin,* autumn 1900).

119. "Practical Housekeeping Center," 3.

120. Jane Addams to Alice Addams Haldeman, Aug. 27, 1907.

121. Jane Addams to Anita McCormick Blaine, Dec. 31, 1925, JAMC; Leonard P. Ayres, *Open-Air Schools* (New York: Doubleday, Page, & Co., 1910), 68.

122. Mary Crane Nursery, "Activities of the Project," n.d., 7–9, JAMC.

123. Crampton, *Pedagogy of Physical Training,* 181–82.

124. Mary Crane Nursery, "Activities of the Project," 13.

125. Mary Crane Nursery, "Activities of the Project," 14.

126. Mary Crane Nursery, "Activities of the Project," 15.

127. Molly Ladd-Taylor, *Raising a Baby the Government Way: Mothers' Letters to the Children's Bureau, 1915–1932* (New Brunswick, NJ: Rutgers UP, 1986); Gwendolyn Mink, "Lady and the Tramp," 107; Gordon, *Pitied but Not Entitled,* 291.

128. Lathrop, memorandum, May 3, 1917, 6. Hull-House's first officer of the juvenile court, Alzina Stevens, advertised Saturday discussions for "parents who find their children are incorrigible, or are exhibiting tendencies which cause anxiety" (*Hull-House Bulletin,* autumn 1900).

129. "The Juvenile Court Committee, Incorporated," Mar. 26, 1904, 1, JPA Papers.

130. Addams, "Public Recreation," 24.

131. The Vice Commission of Chicago, *The Social Evil in Chicago: A Study of Existing Conditions* (Chicago: Gunthrop Warren, 1911); Steffens, *Shame of the Cities;* Ernest Bell, *Fighting the Traffic in Our Girls* (1909; New York: Gordon P, 1975). For an analysis of female reformers' relationship to female criminalization, see Ruth Rosen, *The Lost Sisterhood: Prostitution in American, 1900–*

1918 (Baltimore: Johns Hopkins UP, 1982); Estelle Freedman, *Their Sisters' Keepers: Women's Prison Reform in America, 1830–1930* (Ann Arbor: U of Michigan P, 1981), and *Maternal Justice*. For those who lament the apparent contradiction of homosocial attachment among women who participate in state normalization, a redirected line of questioning foregrounds the albeit ambivalent impulse to public-mindedness embodied in both state welfare work and nonnormative kinship. For a discursive and historical analysis of urban sexuality in the English context, see Judith Walkowitz, *City of Dreadful Delight: Narratives of Sexual Danger in Late-Victorian London* (Chicago: U of Chicago P, 1992).

132. Louise DeKoven Bowen, *The Public Dance Halls of Chicago,* Juvenile Protective Association, 1911, 1, JPA Papers. Edited and reprinted in 1916. See also *Our Most Popular Recreation Controlled by Liquor Interests: A Study of Public Dance Halls* (1911), *Five and Tent Cent Theatres* (1909 and 1911), *The Girl Employed in Hotels and Restaurants* (1912), *The Department Store Girl: Based upon Interviews with 200 Girls* (1911) as well *The Straight Girl and the Crooked Path* (1916) and *The Road to Destruction Made Easy* (1916), JPA Papers.

133. Bowen, "Public Dance Halls," 7.

134. Juvenile Protective Association investigation, Fountain Inn, Dec. 1, 1917, JPA Papers.

135. Bowen, "Public Dance Halls," 9–10.

136. Juvenile Protective Association investigation sample form, Bohemian Ladies Association, Dec. 1, 1917, JPA Papers.

137. Juvenile Protective Association investigation, Vermont Gardens Dance Hall, Dec. 8, 1917, JPA Papers.

138. Juvenile Protective Association investigation, Fountain Inn, Dec. 1, 1917.

139. Juvenile Protective Association investigation sample form, Bohemian Ladies Association, Dec. 1, 1917; Juvenile Protective Association investigation, Vermont Gardens Dance Hall, Dec. 8, 1917.

140. Juvenile Protective Association investigation, Fountain Inn, Dec. 1, 1917.

141. Bowen, "Public Dance Halls," 2.

142. Bowen, "Public Dance Halls," 6.

143. Bowen, "Public Dance Halls," 9.

144. Addams, *A New Conscience and an Ancient Evil* (New York: Macmillan, 1912), 192.

145. Gertrude Howe Britton to Emily Washburn Dean, secretary of the Juvenile Court Committee, July 13, 1907, 23; secretary's minutes, Oct. 26, 1907; Juvenile Court Committee, Gertrude Howe Britton's reports enclosed, 28, 29, JPA Papers.

146. Berlant, "Intimacy," 282.

147. Carroll Smith-Rosenberg, "Discourses of Sexuality and Subjectivity: The New Woman, 1870–1936," in Duberman, Vicinus, and Chauncey, *Hidden from History,* 264–80; Simmons, "Modern Sexuality."

148. Simmons, "Modern Sexuality," 169.

149. Johnson, "Role of Women," 191.

150. Jane Addams to Nina Kenagy, Oct. 17, 1933, JAMC.

151. "Market Was Chicago's 'Little Bit of Europe,' " *Chicago Sun-Times,* Oct. 23, 1987, 87–91; "Maxwell Street," *The Reader: Chicago's Free Weekly,* July 27, 1990, 1, 12–27; Constantine D. Orphan, "Goodbye Greektown," JAMC supplement 20–24; Alf Sewers, "Maxwell Street Blues," *Chicago Sun-Times,* Dec. 24, 1989, 4–5.

152. Thomas L. Philpott, *The Slum and the Ghetto: Neighborhood Deterioration and Middle-Class Reform, Chicago, 1880–1930* (New York: Oxford UP, 1978).

153. On the University of Illinois at Chicago and the Taylor Street neighborhood, see Candeloro, "Chicago's Italians," 244.

Index